THE
JANUS
REPORT

THE
JANUS
REPORT
ON
SEXUAL
BEHAVIOR

Samuel S. Janus, Ph.D.
Cynthia L. Janus, M.D.

John Wiley & Sons, Inc.
New York • Chichester • Brisbane • Toronto • Singapore

Copyright © 1993 by Samuel S. Janus and Cynthia L. Janus
Published by John Wiley & Sons, Inc.

Library of Congress Cataloging-in-Publication Data

Janus, Sam, 1930–
    The Janus report on sexual behavior / by Samuel S. Janus and Cynthia L. Janus.
        p.   cm.
    Includes bibliographical references and index.
    ISBN 0-471-52540-5 (cloth : alk. paper)
    1. Sex customs—United States.   2. Sexual behavior surveys—United States.   I. Janus, Cynthia L.   II. Title.
HQ18.U5J36   1993
306.7'0973—dc20   92-33572

Printed in the United States of America

10 9 8 7 6 5 4 3 2 1

To SAUL KARLEN, M.D.,

for his brilliant insights, guidance, and gentle prodding.
He showed us that the world is there for living.

To SIMEON FEIGIN, M.D.,

who stayed the course with us and helped to iron out the
curves of life. He displayed his professionalism and generosity
of character many times.

To OUR SON LAZAR,

the sweetest part of our lives, who constantly shows us the
experience of joy. His world is a wonderland and playhouse.
He reflects, even at age two, an awareness that he is loved,
treasured, and adored, and he responds with his own
interpretation of love straight from the heart. As we made this
book a reality, he helped by sleeping through many all-night
word-processing sessions.

Preface

How would you define sexual deviance today, when practices that were considered kinky a few years ago now seem to be everyday fare? What has allowed women to become so sexually aggressive?

We heard these two questions asked repeatedly when we discussed this book with friends and colleagues. The answers are not complicated or obscure. There has been a redistribution of values in our society. In the area of sexuality, the redistribution has involved everyone, but particularly women, the postmature age group, and children. What we call the First Sexual Revolution occurred during the 1960s and 1970s; for many, it was characterized by the development of "the pill." It was, for the most part, a revolution about sex and the communication of information. For the first time in our history, people were able to ask questions and get information publicly, discuss their own behavior, and compare it to their friends' and neighbors'.

Most importantly, during that time, Americans celebrated sexual love— both in and outside of marriage—as a joyful and legitimate end in itself. Sexual partners had a new power to experiment and to alter their sexual behavior, based on what they perceived their friends and neighbors—and even strangers—were ready to engage in or were already doing. True, there was a large increase in the number of divorces, and more young people were living together without being married, but these decisions did not necessarily reflect changes in sexual behavior. Rather, they were modifications of the context within which sexual behavior occurred.

A Second Sexual Revolution has now taken place. As reported in our study, it is also rooted in a redistribution of power. However, it is not based on what referent groups are doing but, instead, represents the individual's freedom to choose to engage in behavior that may even go *against* what others are believed to be doing. Two major findings characterize this Second Sexual Revolution: a willingness to engage in a variety of sexual practices, some of which may once have been deemed deviant or at least unacceptable to one's social status, and a regeneration of sexual interest and behavior among the postmature population.

Do these two findings represent recent changes or are we just discovering trends that have been growing for some time? We may never know

vii

the answer. Very little research in these areas of sexual functioning has been published during the past several years because of the unavailability of governmental research grants for this purpose. Several agencies of the federal government have decried the dearth of information about contemporary sexual practices, yet Congress and the Bush Administration have withheld funding for any large-scale study of American sexual behavior.

Early in February 1989, an expert panel of the National Academy of Science's National Research Council, investigating AIDS prevention, urged federal authorities to sponsor more research on sexual behavior.[1] Later that month, in response to the mushrooming incidence of sexually transmitted diseases, teen pregnancies, and child sex abuse, a branch of the U.S. Department of Health and Human Services (HHS) was scheduled to pretest a National Survey of Health and Sexual Behavior. The White House Office of Management and Budget (OMB) effectively blocked the research. OMB Director Richard Darman returned the project to HHS Secretary Louis Sullivan and stated in the accompanying letter: "I have a great deal of difficulty understanding how many of the questions are related to essential public interests."[2] Although there have been periodic attempts by relevant scientific groups to reactivate the project,[3] the survey has not been heard from since.

The Janus Report on Sexual Behavior is intended to fill in the gaps in our knowledge about sexual behavior and attitudes. Research on a national scale, reflecting a wide spectrum of ages, incomes, educational attainments, and religious beliefs, has been scant since the major studies of Kinsey and Masters and Johnson. No single study can be the definitive work on recent revolutionary changes in sexual attitudes and behavior; much more ongoing research needs to be done. If our report generates the interest and discussion needed to continue and expand the task we have begun, and if our readers are helped to think about their own sexuality with far less anxiety, our work will have achieved its major goals.

SAMUEL S. JANUS
CYNTHIA L. JANUS

Vineland, New Jersey
December 1992

Panel of Experts

The panel of experts assembled to assist in the preparation of this study represents the fields of psychiatry, sociology, psychology, medicine, anthropology, law enforcement, and history. The authors acknowledge their contributions toward publication of *The Janus Report on Sexual Behavior*.

Abraham Cohen, M.D. Associate Attending Gynecologist, Lenox Hill Hospital, New York. Former Instructor in Gynecology, New York Medical College, Valhalla, New York.

Elliot L. Cohen, M.D. Assistant Professor and Attending Urologist, Mt. Sinai Hospital and Medical Center, New York City.

Joseph Dorinson, Professor and Chairman, Department of History, Long Island University.

Simeon Feigin, M.D. Assistant Clinical Professor of Psychiatry, New York University, and Associate Attending Psychiatrist, Lenox Hill Hospital, New York.

Louis Lieberman, Ph.D. Associate Professor, Department of Sociology, and Chairman, Committee on Family Life, John Jay College of Criminal Justice, City University of New York.

William McCarthy, Ph.D. Associate Director of the Criminal Justice Center, John Jay College of Criminal Justice, City University of New York. Former Lieutenant and Chief of the Vice Squad, New York Police Department.

Diane Rothenberg, Ph.D. Anthropologist and Research Director, Planned Parenthood, San Diego, California.

Richard Sethre, Ph.D. Private Clinical Psychology Practice, Minneapolis.

Mark Sullivan, M.D. Chief of Surgery and Urology, Mission Community Hospital, Mission Viego, California.

Halina Wiczyk, M.D., Assistant Professor Obstetrics-Gynecology, Chief of the Division of Reproductive Endocrinology, and Director, Bay State In-Vitro-Fertilization Clinic of the Bay State Medical Center, Boston.

Michael Yapko, Ph.D. Psychologist and Director of the Milton Erickson Institute, San Diego, California.

Acknowledgments

We would like to express our deep gratitude to our super-editor, Herb Reich, for his care, humanity, and support. His professional expertise and guidance were of vital significance in the development of this book. His patience, acerbic wit, and breadth of knowledge helped this study to come alive. Through the countless hours consumed in organizing an incredible number of details, Herb never lost patience. Few authors can claim that their editors made their book a cause célèbre; we can, and we are profoundly indebted to Herb for his talent and caring.

We would like to express our appreciation, for encouragement, assistance, and support, to the University of Virginia and specifically our respective, distinguished chairmen: Dr. Wilford Spradlin, Professor and Chair, Department of Human Behavior and Psychiatry; Dr. Theodore Keats, Professor and Chair, Radiology; and Dr. Paul Underwood, Professor and Chair, Department of Obstetrics and Gynecology.

We are most grateful to our "gang of 200," who helped to make this project a reality. We offer our particular thanks to two of the original "gang": Michael Yapko, Ph.D., a psychologist in practice in San Diego, California, and author of *When Living Hurts,* for his unstinting help and insight; and Richard Sethre, Ph.D., a psychologist in St. Paul, Minnesota, who added the magic touch of unity in rounding out the regional picture.

We owe appreciation to Mark Sullivan, M.D., chief of surgery and urology at Mission Community Hospital, Mission Viego, California, for sharing with us his pioneering work in urology and in new medical sexual developments, including penile pumps for impotent men. He has been described as a stand-up comic who wasn't sure whether to be a comedian or a physician, so he decided to do both.

For his insights on sex and vice, we are deeply obliged to William McCarthy, Ph.D., former chief of the vice squad of the New York Police Department, a special human being who cares about people and who has reached out to others in many life roles he has played—academician, nurse, police officer, and teacher.

Many thanks to Diane Rothenberg, Ph.D., anthropologist in San Diego, California, for her talented contributions, awareness, and unstinting devotion to this study; and to Stanley Keyles, Psy.D., a respected psychologist from New Jersey, whose sense of humor kept our spirits up when problems seemed overwhelming.

Professor Louis Lieberman, sociologist at John Jay College of Criminal Justice, City University of New York, co-author of *Sex and Morality* and *Dr. Ruth's Guide to Erotic and Sensual Pleasures*, and a respected sex authority, was a brilliant bulwark from the early stages to the conclusion of the study. He graciously shared with us his wealth of knowledge, understanding of social issues, and sex expertise.

Mary Cuadrado, Ph.D., made her talented programming available to us; Professor Donald Schneller, Department of Sociology, and Professor Jeanette Heritage, Department of Psychology, Middle States University, Murfreesboro, Tennessee, contributed their insight into the ethos of the South.

Sgt. John Johnstone, of the New York State Police, retired, and Mary Lou Johnstone, of Accamac, Virginia, helped with data gathering on special populations. Our thanks also go to Abraham Cohen, M.D., Park Avenue, New York; Bruce Lieberman, M.D., of the Payne-Whitney Clinic; and Barbara Bess, M.D., Professor of Clinical Psychiatry at New York Medical College, a noted sex researcher. Richard Cancilla was our electronics maven, responsible for communication with the outside world. Thanks also to Ed Buhrer of Piedmont Community College in Virginia and Professor Patricia Keats, Ed.D., Sex, Marriage, and Family Counseling.

Among university faculty and professionals, our appreciation goes to Professor George Asteriadis, Chair, Biological Sciences and Chemistry Section, Purdue University; Professor Billy Gunter, College of Social and Behavioral Sciences, University of South Florida; Professor Joseph Dorinson, Chairman, and Professor Gerald Atlas, both of the Department of History, Long Island University; Professor Robert Taylor, Jr., Department of History, Middle States University, Murfreesboro, Tennessee; Professor Peter Petschauer, a noted historian, Appalachian State University, Boone, North Carolina; Professor Mel Goldstein, University of Hartford; Robert Zussman, Ph.D., a psychologist in practice in New Mexico; and Professor Kenneth Adams, sociologist, Jacksonville State College, Alabama.

For her insight on women, we thank Alice Eicholz, Associate Professor of Psychology in Liberal Studies, Vermont College, Norwich University; and Gary Cowan, M.D., a psychiatrist in practice in Duluth, Minnesota. Many thanks to Professor Howard Stein, a cultural anthropologist, University of Oklahoma. Our appreciation to James Masters, Ph.D., Professor of Education, Rocky Mountain College, Billings, Montana, and to Ardyce Masters.

There were many others who assisted in a plethora of ways and to whom we owe a debt of gratitude. Maryann Milstein, Ph.D., consultant in nursing and gerontology, helped enormously in the subject area of mature and postmature Americans. Thanks to Michael Peltz and Andrew Martin of Virginia Computers, Inc. In the nonacademic area, we had assistance from many people in a variety of industrial, commercial, retail, and glamour industries. We particularly thank Bernard Friedel, businessman; Rhett Sheslow, of the American and New York Stock Exchanges; and Dolores Veneziano, for sharing with us her experiences with young people. Jean Power, who has done pioneering counseling work with prostitutes and abused women, lent us insight into this area of life; Joanne Ferro contributed information about sex surrogacy. We thank Vivian Eskin, M.S.W., for her social work insights, and Natalie Alfandre, Ph.D., and Leah Schaeffer, Ph.D., both nationally prominent figures in sexology. Many thanks to Don Sloane, M.D., Associate Professor of Obstetrics-Gynecology at New York Medical College and attending gynecologist at Lenox Hill Hospital, New York.

We were fortunate in having the resources of Publications Development Company of Texas assigned to the production of our book, especially Maryan Malone's thoroughly professional editing. Maryan's good judgment, exemplary care, and attention to detail made a valuable contribution to the book's readability.

Finally, we must acknowledge our thanks to countless others, too numerous to list here, particularly each of our respondents, who took the emotional time and energy to thoughtfully and sincerely complete their questionnaires, and ultimately made this study possible. To others who preferred anonymity, and to anyone we may have overlooked, our heartfelt thanks for helping us to present an accurate portrait of American sexuality.

S.S.J.
C.L.J.

Contents

Introduction   **1**

1   Sex in the Twentieth Century   **7**

2   Sexual Passages: From Late Adolescence to Postmaturity   **19**

3   Men and Women: A Study in Contrasts   **53**

4   Sexual Deviance   **103**

5   The Singles' Scene   **135**

6   Marriage and Divorce   **169**

7   Children: To Have or Have Not   **203**

8   Religion and Sex   **227**

9   Politics and Sex   **263**

10   Education and Sex   **295**

11   Money, Power, and Sex   **323**

12   Region and Sex   **351**

13   Looking Forward from the Past   **375**

Appendix A: Comparison of Janus Report Sample with National Census Data   **401**

Appendix B: The Janus Report Questionnaire   **405**

Index of Tabulated Results by Questionnaire Item   **414**

Notes   **417**

Index   **423**

THE
JANUS
REPORT

Introduction

The idea for this study emerged from years of research and professional practice, as well as from our numerous seminars, courses, and lectures on human sexuality. We were often asked to document the frequency of various sexual practices and attitudes in the United States, but the data to answer these questions adequately were not available. During the 1980s, we noted with interest the conflicting media reports that traditional sexual behaviors and attitudes were past history, and, conversely, that people were drastically curtailing their sexual interactions because of fear of contracting herpes and, later, AIDS. Although almost nothing about sex in America is easily definable or lacking in controversy, we doubted that its demise was imminent or that traditional values had changed very significantly.

During the years from 1983 to 1985, it did appear reasonable to conclude, based on media reporting, that sexually active people across the country were consumed with anxiety about herpes. A new abbreviation appeared routinely in the popular press: STD, for sexually transmitted diseases. Occurrences of AIDS had begun to be reported with increasing frequency, and it was starting to be clear that heterosexuals as well as homosexuals were at risk. We began to suspect, although we could not yet document it, that America was about to undergo some major changes in sexual attitude and behavior. In line with our academic interests, we decided to observe these new developments and, if our findings warranted it, follow up with a major research study.

THE PILOT STUDIES

Between 1983 and 1985, we developed a series of pilot studies to answer some key questions. Working with fellow professors and our graduate-student research associates, we formulated the areas to be researched. These students were primarily doctoral candidates, in several areas of psychology and sociology. Although they totaled 210, we took to calling

1

them "the gang of 200." ("The gang of 210" just didn't sound right.) Most were experienced researchers; some were already practicing professionals in various areas of mental health and social psychology. Because this was a large group, we organized a core of 14 persons who eventually acted as directors of the various areas of the project. Our "gang of 200" ranged in age from 26 to 55 years, but most were between ages 26 and 39. We had an almost equal number of men and women. The gang very quickly became a cohesive group and a productive thinktank.

Our first concern was to identify what a relevant research project should cover. Our interests went beyond the mechanics of sex—"What do you do and how often do you do it?"—which had been the subject of a few limited-scope surveys in the 1970s and 1980s. We decided to examine sexual behavior along a broad spectrum of issues relating to sexuality, and to do so within the basic context of American daily life. We aimed to reach people who represented the various stages of the life cycle, in order to study patterns of both sexes at all adult ages. We set about gathering information about the variety of singles' life-styles, sex within marriage, sex among the postmature group, and the relationship of sexuality to family roles and divorce. We planned to evaluate the influences of several variables—income, religion, education, politics, and geographic region—on sexual behaviors.

In preparation for developing a questionnaire for our pilot study, we did a great deal of archival research, examining how earlier research had dealt with particular issues and analyzing the results of those earlier studies for their appropriateness to our study. The next step was to develop a survey instrument. We narrowed our efforts down to two versions of a questionnaire that served as the basis of the pilot studies. When 200 responses had been gathered (100 for each questionnaire version), we compared the results and selected the wording of each question that had elicited from respondents the more clearly focused answers.

The process was ultimately repeated five times, as we revised and refined the most pertinent questions. The new and better questionnaire that evolved was then tested with a group of 300 new respondents. Before we were satisfied that we had a final version, we spent two years developing and revising three preliminary versions of the questionnaire and testing them in pilot studies. Each new version was pretested on several hundred respondents. From the first to the final version, we pretested a total of 4,510 persons. Some of the data derived in our preliminary studies are analogous to the data collected from 1988 to 1992, in our large national survey. Comparisons are presented in Chapter 13.

At an early stage, word about our study spread in the academic and professional communities, mostly through our graduate-student researchers' mention of the study to their colleagues. We began getting queries and offers of cooperation from sociologists, mental health professionals, historians, and sex researchers around the country. Some were helpful in reaching potential respondent groups; others were mainly interested in following the results of the research itself.

THE CROSS-SECTIONAL NATIONAL SURVEY

After more preliminary trials, we launched our cross-sectional national survey in 1988. Most of the original "gang of 200" had by then received their advanced degrees, and many had gone into rewarding professional positions in academia, industry, the armed forces, and social agencies. Although they were dispersed about the country, we were still in touch with them. Working with this network, we assembled a professional advisory panel of psychological, medical, sociological, and other experts, to represent a variety of appropriate disciplines. This group helped us to place in proper context the data we subsequently collected.

We designed our sample to represent every region of the contiguous 48 states. This design was facilitated by our graduate-student researchers, now located in states in every region of the country, who were able to provide the contacts and resources that allowed us to interview respondents in every part of the United States. Because of the complexity of different states' regulations governing the interviewing of children and adolescents concerning sexual behavior, we limited our sample to individuals 18 years of age and older.

In considering the research design, we realized that it would not be sufficient to merely conduct a standard questionnaire survey, although that would be necessary in order to determine the frequency distribution of the various sexual behaviors and attitudes throughout the country. We would also have to carry out a large number of in-depth interviews, in order to understand the subtleties and complexities implicit in respondents' questionnaire answers.

DATA GATHERING

All data were gathered under the direction of the authors. For our national sample, a group of professors of sociology, psychology, psychiatry, history, biology, and political science were trained in the specific requirements of the sexual data and their acquisition; they in turn supervised the graduate students, who were experienced researchers in these fields. Questionnaires were distributed to subjects at a wide variety of sites. The sample design was planned to conform to the population distribution of the United States, as reported by the U.S. Bureau of the Census, in the areas of sex, age, region, income, education, and marital status. The final sample population for the Janus Report, defined by age, marital status, education, and region is shown in Table I.1. If, despite our best efforts, we have not

TABLE I.1

FINAL SAMPLE POPULATION BY AGE, REGION, EDUCATION, AND MARITAL STATUS			
		Number	Percent
Age:	18 to 26	532	19%
	27 to 38	741	27
	39 to 50	587	21
	51 to 64	464	17
	65+	441	16
	Total N*	2,765	100%
Marital Status:	Married†	1,576	57%
	Divorced	249	9
	Single	820	30
	Widowed	107	4
	Unidentified	13	—
	Total N*	2,765	100%
Education:	Jr. high school	45	2%
	High school	1,335	48
	Some college	666	24
	College graduate	412	15
	Postgraduate	302	11
	Unidentified	5	—
	Total N*	2,765	100%
Region:	Northeast	561	20%
	Midwest	672	24
	South	936	34
	West	580	21
	Unidentified	16	1
	Total N*	2,765	100%

* *Men* = 1,347. *Women* = 1,418.

† Each year, 20% of men and women remarry. Some of these "Married" persons had been divorced and some had been widowed. Eleven percent of our sample had been married twice, and 3% had been married three or more times.

met the most stringent requirements of scientific sampling, our demographics are sufficiently representative of the characteristics of the national population of the United States that our findings are likely generalizable for the country as a whole. A comparison of our sample with the national census data is presented in Appendix A.

For our national survey, we distributed 4,550 questionnaires. The returned questionnaires totaled 3,260, of which 495 were immediately discarded because of major omissions or improperly completed material. Satisfactorily completed questionnaires (no more than 8 omitted answers) totaled 2,765: 1,347 men and 1,418 women. The number of respondents for each survey item varies because of omitted answers. Each table, throughout the book, indicates the exact sample used in each category that is reported.

To supplement the questionnaires, we conducted 125 in-depth interviews; this subsample was interviewed between 1988 and 1992.

All respondents were assured anonymity. Where actual interviews are quoted in the book, only general descriptions of the speakers are given. To secure maximum candor, all respondents were offered the opportunity to personally mail—or hand-deliver—the questionnaires in pre-addressed envelopes that would ensure their return directly to the authors.

The initial computer programming and the processing of the questionnaires were carried out at the John Jay College of Criminal Justice of the City University of New York; subsequently, the data were checked and processed at New York University's Courant Institute of Mathematical Sciences and at the University of Virginia Computer Center in Charlottesville. The final examination and processing of data were completed at John Jay College, CUNY.

A NOTE TO OUR READERS

This book is the result of a nine-year investigation of sexuality in the United States. Our research, conducted between 1983 and 1992, was done primarily in two stages. In our pilot or feasibility study, undertaken between 1983 and 1986, we developed our instruments and learned how well people would respond to questions in this area. Our large scale, cross-sectional survey, which comprises the bulk of the Janus Report, was conducted between 1988 and 1992.

It is important to understand that our statements in the book have the following origins:

- The 280 statistical tables, in which we have sorted the data gathered in our national survey according to respondents' age, sex, marital status, religious and political self-descriptions, education, income, and region. In each of the tables, the seminal item from our questionnaire is indicated just above the results.
- In-depth interviews of 125 random respondents who had completed our questionnaire. The recurring feature "In Their Own Words" offers the directness and poignancy of some of their narratives.
- Our years of professional practice in the specialty of aiding individuals to understand their sexual nature and to enjoy satisfying sexual experiences, and in the study of sexual behavior as an influence in couples, families, and our society in general.

- Other research, both in printed media and in the dialogue of seminars and courses we have conducted and attended.

As our research progressed, we became aware of numerous new or related issues unearthed by our probing. These issues appear in the book as open questions. They can be answered only by future, detailed study, using methods similar to those we have employed.

We have investigated the realities of sexual activity in America and have included how people think about and plan for sex as well as how they engage in sexual behavior. The main purposes of our study were to bring into clear focus sexual behavior *as lived by* Americans in the 1980s and early 1990s, and to examine how Americans engage in sex, what they believe about their sexuality, and the most relevant related social issues.

To make the study a more personally meaningful experience, readers can complete the questionnaire in Appendix B, and are encouraged to compare their responses to those of other Americans, given in the tables throughout the book.

CHAPTER ONE

Sex in the Twentieth Century

THE VOICES OF THE 1990s

When I have sex, and they all want that, I am the observer. I watch them. Most seem to enjoy my body a lot. I can participate only up to a point, and then something inside me clicks off, and I am no longer a participant.

—A single professional woman, age 27

✦ ✦ ✦

A few days after we saw a movie about wife-swapping, my husband told me that one of our close friends and his wife were swingers. I was really shocked. Then he began telling me about other people we knew who were swingers, and finally suggested we should try it. By then we had been married seven years and had two small children. I naively thought that I was happy. I'll admit I wasn't very sophisticated when we married, and I was a virgin, but I learned fast. It was quite a blow to realize that my husband was bored with our sex life.

—A married professional woman, age 43

✦ ✦ ✦

It was very difficult for us to decide to use contraceptives, but we felt that it was the only ethical and responsible way we could adequately care for the four children we have and not destroy the quality of life of my wife. As a minister, I counsel my congregants in the same way that I live my life. I don't see any conflict between my love of the Lord and the love and care of my family.

—A married Baptist minister, age 39

✦ ✦ ✦

You have to take things in context. My goodness, just because you sleep with someone doesn't mean that you're in love. You may be in lust, but that is not the same thing. My mother used to tell me the most horrendous stories of men promising to marry women and offering these women the world, just to get them into bed. But afterward, the men would run off because now

7

they didn't need the women. She told me to get engaged, at least have a ring on my finger to show the world, before I even think of going to bed with a man. She was somewhat ahead of her times, really.

—A single professional woman, age 28

✦ ✦ ✦

It was very hard for me to get into the dating scene again. I had married very young. Honestly, there is no one to match my late wife. I don't know if I am still responding to the wonderful life I had in my marriage, or have just lost all interest in romance. I meet quite a few young women and can see that they are attractive, and to someone else may be desirable, but I hardly give it a blink.

—A widowed professional man, age 49

✦ ✦ ✦

Did you know that all women are fortune-tellers? I'll prove it to you! When a guy goes out on a date, does he know whether he will have sex that night? No! But the girl does. So *she* is a fortune-teller. Personally, I have no trouble finding sex partners.

—A divorced professional man, age 34

✦ ✦ ✦

I can't begin to tell you how happy I am. I am married to a wonderful woman who loves me as much as I love her. My children gave me a hard time of it at first, especially because she is a bit younger than me, but they finally accepted the relationship and came to our wedding. In fact, they gave me away at the ceremony. That's a switch, isn't it? I put some humor into this situation when my oldest son, who is in the business with me, objected. He was telling me that marrying again and trying to have a lot of sex—imagine that, saying to me *trying* to have sex—could be dangerous to the marriage. So, I said to him with a straight face, "Do you think she'll survive it?" He was so shocked, he laughed.

—A 73-year-old retiree

AMERICANS AND SEX

Across the length and breadth of America live many different people with many distinct ways of life stemming from their varied religious, social, and sexual beliefs. Just as Americans take pride in the political independence and individual freedoms given to them by the founders of this country, so too do they take pride in acting on these freedoms to find their own unique style in every aspect of their lives. Especially in regard to sexuality, our most personal and private sphere, each of us likes to believe that our experiences are unique and are an integral part of our personalities.

Ultimately, however, we're not as unique as we like to think. As human beings living at a particular time in American society, we share deep as well as superficial characteristics. In sex, as in most areas of our lives, we agree, disagree, and sometimes even agree to disagree. In a variety of ways, we express our sexuality and merge it with the rest of our lives.

WHAT IS SEX?

We think about it a lot, talk about it endlessly, and spend a great deal of time engaging in it, but just what is sex anyway? No matter how they vary or have changed over the years, most definitions agree on a few basics: sex is concerned with activities involving genital and other body parts; these activities generally produce feelings of physical pleasure, and certain sexual acts may, if engaged in by a potent male and a fertile female, result in reproduction. The term "sex" is also used to refer to the reproductive capabilities of males and females, who are considered to be the "two sexes." Members of each sex refer to members of the "other" or the "opposite" sex. ("Opposite" is somewhat awkward, but it has been used in this way for generations.) A preferred term for this duality of male and female is "gender."

"Sex" should not be confused with "gender"—although it usually is. The division of most living species into males and females is, properly speaking, a gender distinction. Gender refers to the femaleness or maleness of an individual. Behavior that is generally expected of females or of males, because it is considered characteristic of one or the other sex, constitutes gender roles.

Identification as belonging to one sex or the other is essentially the same for all human beings. Males everywhere have essentially the same physiological equipment; females everywhere have the same sexual organs, which, when functioning normally during a certain span of years, are capable of reproduction. However, the way people behave in regard to their sexuality differs dramatically by place, culture, time, personal age, and numerous other factors. Gender roles also vary according to these factors.

The goal of our study was to identify, track, and clarify Americans' sexual practices, attitudes toward sex, and patterns of sexual behavior.

SEX RESEARCH: A CHECKERED PAST

When we chose an extensive, nationwide survey as the means of our research, we knew we would be standing on the shoulders of those who had surveyed sexual behavior and attitudes earlier in the century. Amazingly, the open discussion and study of sexuality dates back only about a century, to the work of Sigmund Freud. As his patients in psychoanalysis persistently recalled sexual encounters of their earlier lives, and reported current sexual problems, Freud could not avoid concluding that the sex drive, or sexuality, was a basic aspect of human existence. Indeed, Freud believed that sexuality was innate, present in humans at birth, and perhaps even during fetal life. This was a new and shocking notion. Freud lived at a time when sexuality was considered unsavory, or, at best, was an aspect of life that was necessary to produce progeny but was to be avoided in all polite conversation or social interaction. (Of sex, Freud's older contemporary, Queen Victoria, was quoted as giving this advice to her daughter, "Close your eyes and think of England.")

Freud was a theorist; he used in-depth data from a limited selection of patients to arrive at his views. From his theories, he intuitively developed a system for helping those patients bring hidden recollections of forbidden sexual activities to conscious awareness during psychoanalytic therapy. Freud found evidence, in his patients' recollections, that improper sexual events of childhood had been repressed, causing various adjustment difficulties later in life. Such events might involve hearing parents' sexual intercourse or experiencing direct sexual abuse. Freud opened the door to sex research, but he never engaged in the kinds of investigation that have resulted in so much of our present knowledge.

Among the first of the large-scale modern studies were surveys conducted by Alfred C. Kinsey and his colleagues: *Sexual Behavior in the Human Male* (1948)[1] and . . . *Female* (1953).[2] One earlier study, in 1929, had investigated the sexual factors in the lives of young women.[3]

Kinsey, a zoologist by training and a professor at a midwestern state university, began by surveying his students about their sexual lives in order to get up-to-date material for a course on marriage. At the time (the late 1930s), statistical surveys were being used in market research and were just beginning to be adopted for political polling purposes. Thus, Kinsey drew on *accepted,* though sometimes faulty, research techniques, but he applied them to a dramatically new subject. By the time his second study was published in 1953, Kinsey and his colleagues had acquired detailed data on the sex lives of some 17,000 people.

The next pace-setting sex research was applied to the physiological aspects of sexual responsiveness. Gynecologist William Masters and his research assistant, Virginia Johnson, developed specialized laboratory techniques for determining exactly what happens physiologically when people become sexually aroused and experience orgasm. This work resulted in the 1966 publication of *Human Sexual Response,*[4] whose descriptions, especially of women's physiological responses, were both shocking to the public and vastly liberating to millions of women. At last these women could understand the most profound experiences of their own bodies. Masters and Johnson next began to apply what they had learned to people whose sexual responses were dysfunctional,[5] and the techniques they developed became the basis of the sexual therapies practiced widely today. The usefulness of sex research had been not only proved but had become accepted. This was, in itself, a startling shift, occurring less than a quarter-century after the first Kinsey report, and barely three-quarters of a century after Freud's pioneer work.

HISTORICAL PERSPECTIVE

Freud's breakthrough thinking affected social practices as well as therapeutic ones. It began a liberating trend that, after a slow start, has led us to where we are today. In Freud's own era, the moral fog that had enshrouded sexuality for most of the nineteenth century did not begin to lift until after the First World War. Hollywood, new and increasingly influential, spread the new enlightenment and displayed the gods and goddesses who openly practiced it. "It," spoken with quiet emphasis, became the buzzword for sex appeal, as in "She really has 'It.'" Women's hemlines rose. Brassieres and female sanitary supplies became commercially available in the 1920s, and contraceptive devices for both women and men were widely distributed. The women's suffrage movement succeeded in giving women nationwide the right to vote, although most states already had passed women's voting laws. Women were expected to enter the labor force—if they were young, unmarried, and not wealthy. For a while, it seemed as though sexual liberation was at hand.

The 1929 stock market crash and the Great Depression of the 1930s curtailed the tentative sexual loosening that had begun in the Roaring Twenties. During the Second World War, sex was sublimated to The War Effort as a generation regressed into enforced repression. An entire nation was, to some extent, restraining its sexual urges until the war was over and the men returned.

Finally, the war ended in 1945, but the sexual revolution kindled in the 1920s would continue to be anticipated for some time to come. The idealized view of business and sex as usual returned. Women, who had been the aggressive mainstays of factories and businesses all over the country while men were serving on military duty, now returned to homemaking and husband-pleasing, baby-making and child-rearing. Marriage and birth rates soared. So did the economy, as millions of young couples set up housekeeping, started families, and spent money on a grand scale. Buried under all the statistics was an infant phenomenon, alliteratively nicknamed the Baby Boom, that would, years later, change American sexual mores more dramatically than any previous force.

In the late 1940s and early 1950s, after Alfred Kinsey and his colleagues published their studies of the sexual behavior of several thousand white American males and females, Americans had to face some shocking new sexual facts. "Seven out of ten farm boys did what?" Titillation mixed with incredulity as people across the country pondered—

most of them, for the first time—the practice of bestiality and other acts of sexual experimentation. Kinsey's statistics on more familiar sexual behavior were equally unnerving: 83% of his male respondents said that they had had sexual intercourse before marriage; half of the married men had had extramarital sexual relationships; almost all men surveyed had masturbated until they reached orgasm; and more than a third had had at least one homosexual experience after puberty—generally, during their adolescent years. Kinsey's findings also confirmed the existence and demonstrated the extent of female sexuality: half of the women had had premarital sexual experience, and one-fourth of married females had had extramarital relationships. Kinsey's studies were widely reviewed and commented on by everyone from social scientists to stand-up comedians. It was clear that Americans were not practicing what they preached: their sexual activities did not conform to their moral standards. Actual sexual behavior was already more liberated than public attitudes. American morality was a myth.

BETWEEN SEXUAL REVOLUTIONS

In some ways, the late 1950s through the 1980s were heady, exciting times. Change of every sort was in the air in the tumultuous 1960s. The Beat Generation of the late 1950s had set the stage; having gone "on the road" as part of their rebellion, they sought ultimate truths without hobbling ties. In the 1960s, a goal-oriented generation, the first wave of the Baby Boomers, was coming of age. Born to parents who had been deprived through the Depression and war years, these wanted children grew in tandem with their parents' and the nation's postwar prosperity. Neither parents nor nation, it seemed, could deny its youth any material goods they might desire. The United States involvement in Vietnam and the Cold War's specter of mutual East–West nuclear destruction only emphasized the merits of living to the max—now!

People of this "Now Generation" of the 1960s were followed by the "Me Generation" of the 1970s, who believed that everything should be coming to them. They too were goal-oriented, out to "make it" in every way. Growth in productivity and population, in mass mobility and mass prosperity, had been dramatic. A civil rights revolution had taken place and was followed by a remarkable social consensus. In an age of political peace and unprecedented prosperity, all citizens were offered access to a Great Society. Health care for the needy and elderly became subsidized under Medicare and Medicaid; disadvantaged toddlers could get a Head Start on their schooling. The best of all possible worlds was truly upon us, and its perceived benefits were applied to sexual as well as political civil rights.

New phrases started to appear in the American vocabulary—performance anxiety, open marriage, sex surrogates, swinging, couples' clubs.

Sexy publications were sold openly on corner newsstands; some traditional groups protested, but to little avail. "Midnight Blue" and other sex-oriented television shows offered wet T-shirt contests, male and female models in the flimsiest of underwear, bumps and grinds more extreme than any performed by the legendary striptease artists of the past, excerpts from pornographic films, and advertisements for sexual devices previously unknown to many of the viewers who incredulously paused in their dial-twirling.

In the new climate of open sexuality and hedonism, love often seemed to be an endangered anachronism. Long a uniquely prized institution, a reflection of freedom, and the ultimate demonstration of individuality, love gave way to sex for sex's sake. People had sex because it felt good or seemed the thing to do. Sexual activity became an evening's recreation, replacing "dinner and a show." One-night stands and disposable sex, once considered a degrading demonstration of lust, became not only commonplace but commercial. Entrepreneurs began to market "one-night-stand kits" in variety stores. A few dollars bought the necessaries: a toothbrush, mouthwash, condoms, cologne, and either a disposable razor (for men) or an extra pair of panties (for women).

A generation entered adulthood without seeking the permanent affectional attachments that had always been the goal of young adults. Suddenly, lack of commitment was prized, and some cynics even claimed that to spend an entire night with another person was too much of a commitment. Young people confronted their new sexuality in a climate of disposable products and relationships. Nothing was meant to last forever, and that included intimate relationships. The new sexual climate flourished as another wave of "Boomers" came along in the 1970s. Building on the foundation laid by their older sisters and brothers, the "Me Generation" took as its motto the popular phrase, "We want it all!" The First Sexual Revolution was in full bloom.

In the mid-1960s, as sexual experimentation began to come out in the open and the seeds of a sexual revolution were being planted, another revolution was also underway. The women's liberation movement was encouraging women to assert their rights to equality in the workplace, the political arena, the home, and the bedroom. Books and magazines gave instruction and support for an assault on traditional sexist attitudes that had kept women "barefoot and pregnant" home-loving homemakers with time on their hands. In the 1970s, the First Sexual Revolution began to claim older partisans as well, particularly following publication of the book *Open Marriage*,[6] by George and Nena O'Neill, in 1972. The O'Neills held that, as long as both spouses knew about each other's sexual adventuring, anything was acceptable. Divorce rates soared, partly because of insistence on personal rights after years of putting up with unsatisfying relationships. Suddenly, thousands of mature adults, newly single, looked to younger ones as sexual role models.

Perhaps after envying the unattached and open sexual activities of the young folks, the formerly married (along with many still-married) joined them. Sexual experimentation was in vogue, and multiple partners spread the joy around.

The momentum had begun with Betty Friedan's 1963 book, *The Feminine Mystique*,[7] which took a long look at at-home postwar women. Friedan perceived that these women had been "bludgeoned into the belief that they can find happiness only by confining themselves to their 'feminine' role as wives and mothers." Her call for emancipation was picked up in the 1960s mostly by educated younger women, still unmarried, who refused to accept a subsidiary role in any aspect of their lives. Meeting informally in "women's groups" in neighborhoods or during office lunch hours, women of all ages exchanged experiences, raised each others' consciousness, and supported one another's efforts in taking control of their lives. They focused both on philosophical aspects of gender equality and on practical aspects of employment and legal equality. Within a few years, the National Organization for Women (NOW) was formed, Gloria Steinem launched *Ms.* magazine, and women throughout the United States were putting pressure on friends, spouses, employers, and governments in their efforts to achieve true equality, personally and professionally, in banks and bedrooms, in commerce and community, in finance and family.

In the 1970s, although gross inequalities still remained, women's skills in the workplace could no longer be ignored. Even after becoming parents, many women refused to give up their workplace identities. Inflation was rampant, and all but the most macho of husbands were coming to rely on that second paycheck. At all ages, in every marital or nonmarital status, women were going to work and staying there.

Having tasted the sweetness of equal opportunity in the workplace, women were ready to bring their hard-earned rights to their personal lives as well. The timing couldn't have been better: reports by Masters and Johnson on the precise nature of women's sexual responsiveness had given women new courage in the bedroom. The O'Neills, in *Open Marriage*, gave them courage to enter new bedrooms.

Almost without our realizing it, attitudes about marriage and the relationship between husband and wife were changing. Only a decade or so earlier, a new and easy-to-use contraceptive device, "the pill," had made it possible for women to be prepared well in advance of a sexual encounter. This allowed for—and, some said, encouraged—sexual spontaneity with minimal risk of unwanted pregnancy. In *Roe v. Wade* (1973), the U.S. Supreme Court ruled that the Fourteenth Amendment right of privacy was broad enough to protect a woman's decision to have an abortion. It was no longer necessary to resort to a high-risk kitchen-table operation, if an unwanted pregnancy occurred. New laws and subsequent rulings applied the right of privacy to a variety of sexual situations. Women's magazines especially brought all these new developments to their millions of readers; television did the rest. No woman who could hear or read was unaware of the new sexual rules.

Few adults could remain uninvolved in the vast social and sexual changes that were taking place. The 1970s were a time of consolidation. People had to adjust to the new social and sexual standards, the new ways of marriage, the increasing willingness of independent-minded women to chuck husbands whose behavior was out-of-date. At the same time, countergroups made a strong effort to return American customs to the morality of an earlier era. Their yearning for the earlier, restrictive tradition, vocally and politically expressed, succeeded in thwarting the Equal Rights Amendment, and contributed to the election and reelection of conservative candidates who proclaimed themselves "pro-family."

THE NEW SEXUAL ERA

By the early 1980s, which were the twilight years of the First Sexual Revolution, liberty in sexual matters was stretching into license. Limits that had long been seen as restrictive were being replaced, often with more open definitions and sometimes with no definition at all. A visible few showed the way, and a vocal few shouted in opposition; the vast majority were confused about what they could and/or should be doing sexually. Anxiety began to creep into the sexual lives of average, middle-income people. Afraid that their sex partners would find their efforts and achievements tame, people bought the new how-to books, which gave instructions for every imaginable possibility. Step-by-step details were often illustrated with explicit photographs or harshly graphic drawings. The promise of achieving perfect sex performance brought wealth to a few ambitious authors, and hope, and then disillusionment, to countless readers. Some people, trying to cope with more distressing problems, went to sex therapists.

From the 1960s to the 1980s, changes in the ways Americans behaved sexually were so vast that many older adults, at first, found little to relate to in the life-styles of younger ones. The new social and sexual roles had been unheard of only a generation earlier. Many mature and postmature adults, who once looked on in envy, or perhaps in horror, at the living-together arrangements and the easy coming and going of sexual partners and marriage partners, now, in considerable numbers, joined the crowd. Because of their ages and situations, some differences continue in how older adults use the new sexual freedom. For example, men and women of the postmature generation, living together in Florida and other popular retirement areas, often do not marry for fear of losing widows' social security benefits and/or their children's approval. Single parenthood among unmarried career women is accepted. Women and mature adults have taken the lead in establishing new moral norms. Women no longer have to prove they are liberated by agreeing to go to bed with a man.

Adults of both sexes and all ages are now acting in their new age-appropriate sex roles. A period of greater sexual caution is underway. The one-night stand is seen by many as far too risky. Casual sex, while still practiced by both sexes, is not favored as much as commitment. When the herpes crisis hit 25 million to 30 million people nationwide, many herpes victims panicked. When AIDS surfaced as a national problem in the mid-1980s, the sexually active momentarily panicked again. The enormous tensions and backlash generated by these devastating sexually transmitted diseases made the practice of casual sex pause; from this hesitation, and reaction to it, came the beginning of the Second Sexual Revolution. Sexual liberation in the mid-1980s was too uneasy to be called freedom.

The new social and sexual changes in life-styles have been adopted by many other participants. Divorced or separated men and women, newly single, are dating again and searching for sex partners and new love. Parents in their 40s, 50s, and 60s are enjoying a new sexual style at the same time their teenage or young adult children are also experimenting with sex and seeking loving relationships. There are few guidelines now, except for cautions about sexually transmitted diseases. The old rules governing sex no longer apply, and many individuals and couples now ad lib moral and life-style decisions, or make them within the morality of their own small, peer-reference groups. The broader society, with its variety and factionalism, has become too chaotic to even offer a norm.

Other issues relating to sexuality have also made headlines over the past two decades. Divorce rates leaped in the 1970s; absent or self-involved parents and permissive child-rearing practices were blamed for creating misbehaving, out-of-control youngsters; the family as an institution was believed to be in deep trouble. Very young adults were living together without benefit of marriage.

Meanwhile, youngsters were experimenting with their own sexuality at earlier and earlier ages. Barely out of their own childhood, teenagers were producing babies at ever-growing rates. By the 1980s, nearly a million mothers under 18 were giving birth every year. Of these young women, 70% were unmarried, up from 30% only a decade earlier.[8]

Some estimates indicate that as many as 10,000 extremely young women, age 12 or even younger, become pregnant every year. The younger these children are when they have their first child, the more likely they are to have at least one more child before their teen years end. These children-who-have-children are particularly at risk of dropping out of school and becoming social throwaways who face a bleak future and are wanted only on the streets. Later, unable to get and hold jobs, they will drop out of the labor market as well, creating or perpetuating cycles of deep, depressing, unrelenting poverty as their children and grandchildren in turn become teenage, single, unemployable parents.

THE AIDS IMPACT

An explosion of news stories in the past decade or so has focused public attention on a new truth in our society: We share our sex lives with a dread disease. Sexually transmitted diseases are perhaps as ancient as humanity, but the affliction of AIDS is more devastating than any that has come before. AIDS has made pale, by comparison, the concern over herpes that was newly rampant only a few years earlier.

By 1984, news of AIDS had begun to shock the nation. At first, little was known about this disease, other than the broadest profile of those whom it afflicted. Speculation of all sorts was rife, and so was fear. Media reports, reflecting more speculation than science, were often contradictory. However, all agreed that gay men were at risk.

Homosexuals, especially gay men, experienced devastating changes in their social world in just a few years. Only recently, in the 1960s, had many of them begun to "come out of the closet" and follow their sexual proclivity openly. In the early 1980s, AIDS struck at this population first, cutting down thousands of young men in their most productive years, and bringing upon the survivors not only the devastation and depression of personal loss of loved ones, but also renewed calumny from the religious right and other social conservatives who saw the plague of the 1980s as punishment for sexual deviance. By March 1992, AIDS had caused 139,269 adults' and adolescents' deaths, and 1,954 children's deaths in the United States.[9] Gay men rallied to provide support to the afflicted and bereaved in their midst. They became political activists, pressuring governments for increased funding for research and services. They organized to spread information about safe sex practices throughout the gay community. By the end of the 1980s, the spread of AIDS among gay men had slowed significantly, although the disease itself continued to afflict those who had been infected earlier.

It soon became obvious that gay men and their sex partners were no longer the only target of AIDS. The disease went on to bring even greater devastation to drug addicts. Among drug abusers, AIDS was spread first by contaminated intravenous needles and next through unprotected sex. Drug abusers, however, too oblivious to reality to recognize their risk or understand how to control it, continued to spread infection widely through reused hypodermic needles and unprotected sexual exchanges.

There were no safe havens, not even for innocent children. Reports of children who were discriminated against because they had received contaminated blood transfusions shocked caring people everywhere. By the

1990s, the risk of AIDS clearly enveloped heterosexual men and women and their children as well.

Yet, although the changes in how Americans interact sexually have been dramatic, overall sexual activity has not diminished in mainstream America; in fact, we found in our study that, in the past several years, overall sexual activity has increased. Most people we surveyed expressed great anxiety about sexual diseases, but they also admitted that sex was so important in their lives that not even the threat of AIDS would get them to cautiously adopt a more limited sex life. Most have, however, made some changes in their actual practices.

This background of social and sexual change led us to seek valid, up-to-date information on sexual behavior in the United States. This book is the result of that search.

CHAPTER TWO

Sexual Passages: From Late Adolescence to Postmaturity

SOME SIGNIFICANT FINDINGS ABOUT SEXUAL PASSAGES

✦ 14% of men 65 and over reported daily sexual activity, compared to only 1% of women in that age group.

✦ 19% of men, but only 7.5% of women, reported they had had full sexual relations by age 14.

✦ When asked whether they had ever experienced orgasm during lovemaking, 13% of women ages 18 to 26, 3% of women ages 51 to 64, and 9% of women over age 65 said No.

✦ In all age groups questioned, more men than women reported they had become more cautious about sex in the past 3 years.

✦ The younger the woman responding to our questionnaire, the younger the age at which she had her first full sexual experience.

QUESTIONNAIRE SUBJECTS TABULATED IN THIS CHAPTER	

	Table
Frequency of Sexual Activity	2.1
Orgasm During Lovemaking	2.2
Masturbation Frequency	2.3
Recently Increased Caution About Sex	2.4
Comparative Sexual Activity, Three Years Ago Versus Now	2.5
Age at First Full Sexual Relations	2.6
Traditional Sex Roles in Modern Society	2.7
A Double Sexual Standard	2.8
Male Premarital Sexual Experience	2.9
Female Premarital Sexual Experience	2.10
The Family as a Social Institution: Current Views	2.11
Unequal Spousal Earnings Levels	2.12

F ew people anywhere in the world are as concerned with appearance, youthfulness, health, and aging as we Americans are. We spend billions of dollars each year to look and feel young. Appearing sexy and youthful has external significance, but our more important reason is that diminution of sexual ability and activity because of age is a frightening specter for most Americans. Merely appearing energized in later years is not enough for those who identify sexual vigor with the thirst for life itself and who seek the joys of Eros throughout their lives.

THE OLD AND THE YOUNG

Time brings changes in how much and how fast individuals interact sexually, but the effects are not necessarily negative. Men who cling to the idea of "the 60-second man" have distorted notions of the lovemaking process: Rapid ejaculation is important to them; it makes them feel powerful. Mark Sullivan, M.D., a urologist, gave this perspective to the issue of exaggerated potency versus slower ejaculation with aging:

> If the goal is 60-second intercourse, then this may be viewed with dismay, but if the goal is mutually satisfactory intercourse, then, I think, this delayed response will be rather greeted with some enthusiasm.[1]

Our culture exerts pressure to conform behavior to particular age-related patterns. As Dr. Jack Weinberg wrote in 1969, in *The American*

Journal of Psychiatry, "Culturally, the two poles of the human cycle, the very young and the old, are especially singled out for inhibition of their basic sexual expression—the young because they 'should not' and the old because they 'ought to know better.'"[2]

Variations in sexual needs and abilities during different life phases fulfill functions that are appropriate to the individual's development in each phase. In most traditional settings, these variations are interpreted as being cautionary to older people—a notice that they should pull in their horns, not expect too much from their dwindling sexual function, and not make themselves and their families look foolish by trying to be overtly sexy. Our research data have proved the opposite to be true. At *no* age below 90 (we cite 90 because that was the age of the oldest person in our sample) did we find older people *not* having sex when they were interested and had a sex partner.

Today, medicine and psychology advise that people *should* keep on having loving sex as long as they wish. Postmature men and women—people in their 70s, 80s, and 90s—who are, and have been, experiencing sex continuously, report that it is at least as gratifying as ever. Some found sex more gratifying than in earlier years because they had no worry about pregnancy, and, when enjoyed with the same partner they had lived with for 50 or more years, there was little fear of contracting AIDS. Their lovemaking may occur only once a week now, instead of three or four times weekly as it did in their younger years, but their desire and ability to have satisfying sex remain an important element of their life together.

Our research findings indicated that, among respondents over age 65, 93% of the men and 50% of the women often or always have orgasms when they have sex. For those over 50 who are parents, their progeny, not their biology, may exert a depressing influence on their sexual activity. For example, adult children of a widowed parent, fearing the loss of their inheritance, may discourage their parent from having another sexual or marital partner. Or, because the adult children may not wish to face the competition represented by their parents' sexuality, they actively maintain the myth that "acting your age," when one is a senior citizen, means having no interest in sex.

YOUTH AND SEX

We live in a sexual world, but Americans have been slow to fully acknowledge its enormous impact. Among those we interviewed who were 18 to 26 years old, 21% of the men and 15% of the women had had sexual intercourse by age 14; a small percentage of them had had their first intercourse before age 10. (See Table 2.6.) In the South, the leading region in precocious sexuality, by age 19, 82% of the young people had had full sexual relations. (See Table 12.19.) New sexual practices are in vogue.

Sexuality becomes adapted to the context of the sexual experience, at all ages. While early adolescents are experimenting with full sexual activities of diverse varieties and young couples are seeking sex for reproduction, older couples are enjoying the comfort and excitement of sex without reproductive pressures. A new, vital, and active sexuality has been identified among mature and postmature Americans. While society frets about preteens' frolicking and college students' antics on Spring break in Florida, the graying segment of Americans may be leading the way in superior sexual experience.

Parents, counselors, and educators have become increasingly concerned about young people's early intensity and obsession with sex as a performance game. When we searched for scientific data on the possible repercussions, in later years, of early sexual activity, we found a 1972 article by Dr. Eric Pfeiffer and Glenn C. Davis that declared the early-intensity/early-loss-of-capacity assumption a "popular myth." Instead, these researchers found "a significant positive correlation" between high levels of sexual activity in youth and greater sexual activity in later years. They advised:

> [T]he data support another, more scientific notion, that is, the continuity of life style. Persons to whom sex was of great importance early in life are more likely to continue being sexually active late in life. Persons to whom sex was of little importance early in life will be more likely to reach an early terminus to their sexual activity late in life.[3]

David Rubin gave a similar "Use it or lose it!" injunction in his book, *Everything You Always Wanted To Know About Sex, But Were Afraid To Ask.*[4] Our data, too, support the idea of a continuity in sexual activity from youth to old age, without any necessary decline occurring in the postmature. Life-span studies of many individuals is certainly an area for further research.

Sexual practices are not always determined by oneself. Lovers, husbands, and wives have input, and society and peers influence a person's choice of sexual activities, partners, and sexual attitudes. One old tradition, believed to have originated in Europe, has become a popular myth of sexual initiation. Among some ethnic groups, it was said to be acceptable and desirable for a father to take a young son to the local house of prostitution for the boy's first sexual experience. No data were gathered on the number of boys for whom this was actually their first sexual experience, or on the whereabouts of the father when the boy was elsewhere on the brothel's premises.

Several cultures have maintained sexual rites of passage, but in the United States there is no formalized sexual initiation for young men or women. To some extent, ritual initiation legitimizes the family's role in the control of a child's sexual activity. Today, most American parents are too embarrassed or too sexually illiterate to discuss sex with their children, and have only the vaguest awareness of their children's sexual knowledge and experience. Among our respondents, only 25% of the men and 40% of the women reported having learned about sex at home. (See Table 3.41.) Siblings, as well as parents, were possible sources of instruction. For many women, sex instruction at home was primarily concerned with menstruation. Conflicting cultural pressures may confuse and bewilder some youngsters, but they are not a barrier to sexual interest and experimentation. The cross-currents of economic, political, religious, and peer pressures are often in conflict, and children and young adults are not the only ones who are confused.

SEX AMONG MATURE AND POSTMATURE PERSONS

Of all the issues concerning sexuality, one that has received little attention in the past has been sex among the mature and the postmature. As a youth-oriented society, we traditionally assigned sex-as-passion to the young and consigned sex-as-handholding to their elders, ignoring the passionate responses of the no-longer-young. Sex for pleasure must be understood in a new perspective; a balanced approach must take into account the problems and functions of sex for reproduction as well as for pleasure. At present, over 50% of married women are working outside the home, and this percentage is steadily rising. Many couples are delaying starting a family until they achieve a goal of financial security or until the woman's progress in her career can absorb a maternity leave and subsequent flexible hours. Unfortunately, many married and cohabiting unmarried couples who have pursued careers and now, in their mid- to late 30s, want children, are having difficulty in becoming parents. Their fertility problems have brought a business boom to in-vitro fertilization clinics and fertility experts. For these mature persons, the desire to have sex has not been lost, but "finding oneself" before becoming a parent, although socially and psychologically acceptable, may run counter to their personal biological clocks. Some couples whom we interviewed felt betrayed—their dreams and careful planning had been shattered. They were trying to speed up their production of a family, to catch up with the years of expenditure on their careers and their life-style.

In the following narrative, the first of several that appear throughout the book, expressed by various individuals *in their own words*, life events are described that we have found repeated among countless other women.

Well, here we are. We thought we were living the American Dream. We are both successful, sensitive, and sophisticated. We thought we had the answers. In a way, we did, for most of life; but I didn't have the same priorities I have now. I am fairly obsessive, and I plan and plan. I was sure I had everything. I have no one to blame. I always had the awareness that I would like to have a child someday—maybe even two—if it were economically possible.

My parents took pride in my achievements, although my grandmother used to constantly tell me I was wasting my life chasing around in the business world. Her message was simple: Get married and have children. That's what a woman is meant for. I would gently try to tell my grandmother that times had changed, and women no longer served only in the kitchen and the bedroom. She was never satisfied with my answers. All of my friends agreed with me, as did my professors in school. I had taken women's studies and was convinced that there was a whole new world for women out there, and there *was*. But—and this sounds as if I am an idiot—I didn't plan for a baby. That would take care of itself, whenever I wanted it to happen.

Well, it's now been over 3 years and it hasn't happened. I am on my second fertility expert, and getting worked up. My husband and I have had all the tests and, medically, there is no reason why I can't get pregnant. One of these days I'm going to punch my grandmother. She not only tells me "I told you so," but says that I should relax. That's all I need to get pregnant now.

It is strange when I meet other young women waiting in the doctor's reception area and we get to talking. They all look bright and successful, and everyone has a story that's not too unlike mine.

—A 40-year-old female retail executive

The increasing number of couples who are putting off the start of families until their 30s, and even their 40s, has sparked new interest in the relationship of sex and age. All the tables in this chapter present responses to our questionnaire in age-related groupings, using the same five adult age groups throughout the chapter. From their answers on each of a series of key developmental issues, the age groups can be profiled individually across all the issues and compared with each of the other age groups. Although the factors of age and aging have been traditionally linked to stereotyped sexual responses, the data gathered do not support age as having a determining role sexually. To what degree have medicine, changes in psychological views, and social acceptance influenced and, in some areas, negated the traditional connection between age and the appropriate priority of sex? The tables reveal some startling modifications of long-held beliefs. For example, although hypersexuality has traditionally been ascribed to the young, the youngest group surveyed (those 18 to 26 years) have no more active sex lives than their parents and even their grandparents, when Active is defined to mean a few times weekly, or daily. (See Table 2.1.)

Another striking aspect of the data in Table 2.1 is that the responses of men and women were roughly similar—within 10 percentage points—at a majority of the age levels. These results were supported by the responses we received elsewhere in the questionnaire. For example, the women surveyed generally reported less daily sexual activity than the men. Only in the 18- to 26-year-old group did we find that women's frequency of daily sex was nearly the same as men's. When we combined lines a and b (daily, and a few times weekly) to form the Active category, we found that, for all age groups, men reported having sex more frequently than women. The highest frequency was among men 51 to 64 years old. The combined frequency for women declined from ages 27 to 64, but there was an upswing after the age of 65. These responses tend to indicate that women, as well as men, have a vigorous and active sex life as they enter and go beyond middle age.

Despite the "slippage" between the start and the end of the three middle-years categories surveyed, a most interesting finding was the increased number of women who rarely have sex. The low of 12% in the 27- to 38-year-old group spiked to 27% for the 51- to 64-year-olds. We could not ascertain a specific reason for our data, but increasing rates of widowhood among older women, and women's reluctance to enter into sexual relationships soon after a divorce, are possible causes. Our interviews supported these assumptions. We also observed that women ages 51 to 64 reported that, after they became widowed or divorced, they did not know how to find a sex partner when they wanted one.

TABLE 2.1   **Survey Item G.6.**

FREQUENCY OF ALL SEXUAL ACTIVITY IS:									
	Ages (Years)*								
	18 to 26		27 to 38		39 to 50		51 to 64		65+	
	M	F	M	F	M	F	M	F	M	F
N =	254	268	353	380	282	295	227	230	212	221
a. Daily	15%	13%	16%	8%	15%	10%	12%	4%	14%	1%
b. A few times weekly	38	33	44	41	39	29	51	28	39	40
c. Weekly	19	22	23	27	29	29	18	33	16	33
d. Monthly	15	15	8	12	9	11	11	8	20	4
e. Rarely	13	17	9	12	8	21	8	27	11	22
Active = lines a + b	53%	46%	60%	49%	54%	39%	63%	32%	53%	41%
At Least Weekly = lines a through c	72%	68%	83%	76%	83%	68%	81%	65%	69%	74%

*Data tabulated throughout this chapter are presented uniformly for these five age groups.

Our findings on male sexual activity are in sharp contrast to the type of findings reported as late as 1974 in an article in *The Journal of Sex Research,* in which W. H. James stated that "couples' coital rates halve between ages 20 and 40."[5] The apparent contradiction dissolves when we acknowledge that many men do not limit their sexual activity to their marital bed and many men masturbate. (We do recommend for further research a detailed study of the range of types of sexual activities among the different age groups, but it is clear from our findings that, overall, male sexual activity does not decline with age.)

The 65+ age group responses were especially interesting because this group has traditionally been considered asexual, especially in literature and the mass media, where they are often represented as only remembering earlier-in-life sexual experiences. The reality, reflected in our findings, is quite different. The percentage of Active men (lines a and b combined, in Table 2.1) dropped from 63% in the 51- to 64-year-old group to 53% for those 65+ years old—the level for men 18 to 26 years old; the percentage of Active women in the same groups increased from 32% to 41%.

Another statistic of great interest, for those same groups, emerged when we added the third (weekly) category to the first two, forming the category At Least Weekly. Although there was a decrease for men (from 81% to 69%), there was an *increase* for women (from 65% to 74%). All these findings obviously contradict a common belief in the existence of a later-years sexual twilight zone. The elderly were supposed to be satisfied with only *thinking* of sex, and perhaps—just perhaps—having sex once a month, or once every two months, assuming they hadn't forgotten about it completely. Comparing the two oldest groups surveyed, the men in the monthly-sex category increased from 11% to 20% and the women decreased from 8% to 4%. The percentages of men who reported rarely having sex actually *increased* from 8% to 11%; responses from women showed a decrease from 27% to 22%.

Our impression from our interviews is that persons who become widowed spend a reasonable period of time in mourning and celibacy. Their desires are then reawakened, and earlier inhibitions regarding sex outside of marriage are not seen as barriers to sexual liaisons and trysts. Married postmature persons usually limit their sex lives to their spouses. However, our interviews of call girls indicated that many men in the higher income brackets are their regular customers, and that these men function well, though perhaps a bit more slowly than their younger customers. Older men, many of them widowers or divorced, in the middle-income class or above, and in good health, tend to seek out for sex women who are from 5 to 25 years younger than themselves. Depending on the man's children (if any) and his attitude, his sex partner may simply share a long-term intimate friendship, or may become a new marriage partner.

A most critical finding uncovered in our research on age and sexual activity was the large numbers in the oldest group (65+ years) who were in the Active category (lines a and b in Table 2.1): 53% of men and 41% of women were having a reasonably active sex life. Compared to the crescendo during their middle years, the men had a slight diminution of sexual experiences. However, the interactions they did have were reported in our interviews to be more deeply gratifying; being unhurried, they shared to a greater degree with their partner(s) and had more time to spend on a seductive buildup. They also reported that they experienced more warmth and intimacy after the sex act.

To some extent, this same kind of unhurried sex-for-joy was reported by those 51 to 64 years old. The 39- to 50-year-old group seemed to have mixed feelings. Some respondents still emphasized numbers of conquests and speed of climax; their youthful urgency mimicked the rushed intensity of adolescence. Others were beginning to enjoy lavishing time and attention in maximizing unhurried sexual situations.

ORGASM

Estimations of orgasm range from the ultimate sexual fulfillment to nothing more than hype. For some people, orgasm is the only way they know to be fulfilled sexually; a smaller number of people of both sexes feel gratified by the qualities of the sexual experience without orgasm. Women view orgasm as important; men regard it as crucial.

Table 2.2 indicates the different rates of orgasmic achievement found for men and women; the rates for the Frequently category remained

TABLE 2.2   **Survey Item D.6.**

I HAVE ORGASM DURING LOVEMAKING:									
	Ages (Years)								
	18 to 26		27 to 38		39 to 50		51 to 64		65+	
	M	F	M	F	M	F	M	F	M	F
N =	254	265	352	373	283	293	226	231	213	221
a. Always	68%	18%	68%	16%	60%	14%	77%	21%	55%	8%
b. Often	25	39	26	51	34	52	18	44	38	42
c. Sometimes	3	22	3	18	4	22	1	22	4	37
d. Rarely	1	8	1	9	1	7	2	10	1	4
e. Never	3	13	2	6	1	5	2	3	2	9
Frequently = lines a + b	93%	57%	94%	67%	94%	66%	95%	65%	93%	50%
At Least Sometimes = lines a through c	96%	79%	97%	85%	98%	88%	96%	87%	97%	87%

fairly constant for all age groups. Male sexual biology must be kept in mind. For men to be fully satisfied in their sexual function, three aspects must all work together—erection, ejaculation, and sensation of orgasm. Our interviews indicated that many women contend that they can find sexual relations deeply gratifying without experiencing orgasm—an almost inconceivable notion to men, for whom orgasm and ejaculation are synonymous. (Men who have had prostate surgery and experience retrograde [diminished] ejaculations are a notable exception.) For all age groups, there was at least one 27% difference reported between men and women (ages 27 to 38) in their ability to achieve orgasm Frequently (lines a plus b in Table 2.2). However, looking at line a (always) by itself, we found that the differences between men and women ranged from a low of 46% for the 39- to 50-year-old group to a high of 56% for the 51- to 64-year-olds. We share the view of many experts that a woman often fails to achieve orgasm because her prior sex life has not given her sufficient "practice" in the stimulation of the clitoris and surrounding areas. In only a relatively small number of cases would gynecologists and sex therapists suggest that the failure is physical. Social emphasis on a woman's right to have orgasm is fairly new. Among our respondents, the percentage of women achieving orgasm At Least Sometimes increased with age from a low of 79% (lines a through c) for the 18- to 26-year-old group to a high of 88% (lines a through c) for the 39- to 50-year-old group. Between 93% and 95% of men in all age groups had orgasms Frequently. When we combined lines a and b (always, and often), we found that men did not decline in an ability to achieve orgasm during sex, in any significant numbers, over the entire span of the ages surveyed. The youngest and the oldest groups had the same percentage: 93%. Our findings clearly contradicted the popular myth that males reach their sexual peak in their late teens. Not only was there no decline in the ability to reach orgasm among the men between ages 27 and 64, but the frequency of their sexual activity was actually higher overall than that of the 18- to 26-year-old group (see Table 2.1).

POSTMATURE SEX

It became very clear to us as we conducted our interviews that men and women over the age of 65 did not want to be relegated to the rocking chair and were often as sexually driven as they were in their youth. As we have shown in Table 2.1, their frequency of all sexual activity declined somewhat from the level attained in their 30s and 40s, but when they engaged in sex, their ability to reach orgasm and have "functionally" successful sex diminished very little from their earlier years (Table 2.2). Their desire to continue a relatively active sex life was unchanged as described in an amusing manner by a recently remarried 73-year-old businessman.

✦ *IN THEIR OWN WORDS* ————————————————————————

After my late wife's death, I was down, no question about it. For a while, I didn't see any reason to live. Friends, even well-meaning friends, told me I had done all I had aspired to do in life, so I should just sit back. Sit back for what? To wait to die? That's stupid. People don't know how they can hurt you, even with good intentions. Anyway, it went that way for a while. Someone suggested I get into psychotherapy, and I laughed. At my age? They said "yes." Well, I did, and that was what helped me change my life around. At first my kids were pleased with the changes. I wasn't calling them in my depression to keep me company, or just to hear their voices. But it all changed when I started dating again.

I'll never forget. My older son and his wife were horrified. They were saying the most hostile things. I really felt they thought their inheritance would go out the window if I became attached to another person. They might not mind an old woman, as a friend, but a younger woman made them see red. Even good friends were telling me it was inappropriate, that I should sign myself into a nursing home, that I was into a second childhood. Some even hinted that my socializing was an early sign of senility. These were friends. Imagine what the people who openly disliked me were saying?

Anyway, I have been to many doctors in my life, both for myself and my late wife. I became friendly with their receptionists. One of them was so understanding. She would give me early appointments so that I wouldn't have to wait all day, offer me coffee in the office and, more importantly, listen to me. You can tell when a person is really listening, you know. She happened to be a young widow. Her husband was killed in a tragic car accident and she was left with one child. We would commiserate, and I was surprised how comfortable I was with her. There is, of course, a big difference in our ages. What to do about it? I asked her out to dinner. She hesitated and then said okay, but she didn't want the doctor to know. I said okay. We went out for six months. It was great, but I was afraid to try to have sex with her. It had been years since I had had sex with my wife, and it was over fifty years since I had even touched another woman. Could I make it successfully? One night she came to my boat; the moon was out, and to my amazement, I hadn't forgotten how to do it. She was surprised and delighted. In fact, sex has been a wonderful highlight for both of us. I am not seventeen anymore, but we are able to have an excellent sexual relationship, and I mean excellent for both of us.

—A recently remarried 73-year-old businessman

In the course of our survey, we found that personal stories such as this were not rare. Most of the mature and postmature men and women who responded were still seeking active sex rather than just handholding—well-meaning relatives notwithstanding.

MASTURBATION

As we have seen, sexual activity involving partners, among all age groups, is frequent. What about the individualistically private sexual experience of masturbation? Do the more mature age groups engage in this activity, traditionally seen as part of adolescent sexual experimentation? Masturbation fulfills different needs for different people, at various ages in life. For a few, it is all the sex they ever have; for others, it is a personal, occasional sexual statement, or it supplements interpersonal sex. Not everyone has sex partners, and, among those who do, the partner may not be totally adequate, and the sex with the partner may not be satisfying. What about autoeroticism and masturbation? Does the level of need for it distinguish young from old? How does its practice change with age, and for men and women?

The old research question "Do you masturbate?" has been answered. We know that people do. What has been only minimally researched is the intensity of the sex urge that accounts for how often adults masturbate. Earlier research was concerned with whether adults masturbate. With evidence that they do, we explored the larger dimension of how often, by age and by sex.[6]

It has long been known that there are men who masturbate daily, but our survey found that some women, even at a young age, have a similar frequency. As shown in Table 2.3, in the 18- to 26-year-old group, 6% of the men and 2% of the women masturbated daily. When we combined lines a and b of the table (daily, and several times weekly), however, we found a considerable difference between men and women in our youngest age group: 24% of young men compared to 8% of young women were Active masturbators. The percentage difference, between men and women, of Active masturbators dropped from 16% among the 18- to 26-year-olds to 14% and then to 9% in the next two age groups surveyed, and climbed to a high of 24% for the 51- to 64-year-olds. The sharp increase in percentage difference in the latter group was caused by frequency changes for both sexes: Active masturbation reached a high of 32% among men and declined to 8% among women. For men, the turnaround toward decline in the practice seemed to occur around the age of 65. For older females, the decline was constant in the three oldest groups studied (from 14% to 8% to 2%).

At the other end of the spectrum, 26% of men and 44% of women in the youngest group (18 to 26 years old) reported that they never masturbated. We believe that these numbers are unusually low because of a skew caused by data from the South (see Table 12.10). Reports of At Least Monthly masturbation among men (lines a through d in Table 2.3) had a jagged pattern: an increase from 51% to 62% in the two youngest groups (18 to 26, and 27 to 38 years old, respectively); a decline to 54% among the 39- to 50-year-olds; an increase to 58% for the 51- to 64-year-olds; and a decrease to 50%

TABLE 2.3   **Survey Item D.8.**

I MASTURBATE ON AVERAGE:									
	Ages (Years)								
	18 to 26		27 to 38		39 to 50		51 to 64		65+	
	M	F	M	F	M	F	M	F	M	F
N =	253	266	353	378	281	294	226	233	214	213
a. Daily	6%	2%	9%	3%	7%	2%	9%	1%	1%	0%
b. Several times weekly	18	6	19	11	16	12	23	7	16	2
c. Weekly	19	10	25	16	19	16	22	12	27	2
d. Monthly	8	9	9	17	12	17	4	16	6	23
e. Rarely	23	29	26	33	30	37	18	34	27	38
f. Never	26	44	12	20	16	16	24	30	23	35
Active = lines a + b	24%	8%	28%	14%	23%	14%	32%	8%	17%	2%
At Least Monthly = lines a through d	51%	27%	62%	47%	54%	47%	58%	36%	50%	27%

for those 65 and over. The percentage for women increased from 27% in the youngest group to 47% in the next two groups; declined to 36% in the 51- to 64-year-old group; and dropped to 27% among the 65+ group. Older men (65+) were much more likely to masturbate At Least Monthly (lines a through d) than women (50% and 27%, respectively), a situation that apparently parallels the At Least Monthly reports for the 18- to 26-year-olds (51% for men and 27% for women).[7]

Much of the literature of sexology has restated a belief that, by the time a person reaches 39 to 50 years of age, orgasm from masturbation, especially for men, becomes more difficult to attain alone, and that people need more extended social interaction (and, by implication, increased stimulation from those other persons) to achieve orgasm. Our findings indicated that, regarding this belief, the sex literature may be off by a couple of decades. No dramatic decline seems to occur until at or near the age of 65, the traditional retirement age. Further research would be needed to determine the degree to which a real decline in desire, need, or response ability occurs or whether we are seeing a reflection of cultural expectations surrounding retirees, which consign to "retirement" all aspects of life including sexuality. Is this most senior group supposed to exercise their memories but not their bodies sexually? Attitudes of the aging may be a factor in the responses on masturbation in the 65+ age group. Only 17% of the men in the 65+ group are Active masturbators (lines a and b of Table 2.3), and only 2% of the women. Further refinement of the survey for this age category would need to investigate whether those who say that they never masturbate are actually involved in mutual interpersonal masturbation and are unwilling to categorize it as masturbation. Mutual interpersonal masturbation, involving two persons, is a commonly accepted outlet both inside of marriage and between two unmarried partners. In Chapter 3, we will see that some men and women prefer masturbation to intercourse (Table 3.42) and do not consider themselves to be masturbating if someone else manipulates their genitalia during the sexual experience.

Age does take some toll on sexuality. In our informal interviews, many people reported that sexual arousal has become more difficult for them as they have aged. They need more interpersonal stimulation, and masturbation may not be enough. Yet, the erotic appeal of masturbation transcends the youthful years. To varying degrees, it is a basic and extensive part of adult sex life.

Although masturbation has particular appeal for many people, others, in all age groups, reject it, and it cannot be the only measure by which to evaluate changes in sexual activity during life stages. Because masturbation is a self-performance activity, it offers advantages to those who avoid interpersonal sex because of religious beliefs, shyness, lack of partners, or fear of sexually transmitted infection.

CAUTION IN SEX

The long history of sexually transmitted diseases has made caution in sex one of the facts of life. In the late 1980s, the AIDS epidemic made caution in sex a fact of life or death.

How have people reacted on this side of panic? When a desired experience of sex is moments away but the partner's past liaisons are not known, to what degree are Americans prudent and self-protective about their sexuality?

Caution, as expressed in the responses in Table 2.4, is not clear and consistent across the age groups surveyed. Among males, at the extreme of strongly agree, we found that, with the exception of the 51- to 64-year-old group, the older the men, the *less* they endorsed caution. Young males, often stereotyped as indulging in sexual excesses, were 5% to 10% more concerned than men in the older groups. This pattern of strongly agree was repeated among women 18 to 64, but the youngest group was 17% more concerned than the 51- to 64-year-old group. In the 65+ group, the possibility exists that the upswing among the women (31%) reflected not so much caution as an avoidance of painful intercourse after their natural vaginal lubrication had become dysfunctional. Not surprisingly, the youngest age group—presumably, the most vulnerable because they were less frequently in monogamous relationships—were least likely to be Negative (disagree, or strongly disagree) about the perceived need for caution. Among those who were Affirmative (strongly agree, and agree), the youngest group reflected the most caution.

TABLE 2.4   **Survey Item A.14.**

| IN THE PAST FEW YEARS I HAVE BECOME MORE CAUTIOUS ABOUT SEX: |

	Ages (Years)									
	18 to 26		27 to 38		39 to 50		51 to 64		65+	
	M	F	M	F	M	F	M	F	M	F
N =	256	274	357	380	284	302	229	234	217	224
a. Strongly agree	29%	31%	24%	29%	19%	20%	22%	14%	19%	31%
b. Agree	54	48	52	43	50	44	52	42	55	25
c. No opinion	10	14	7	13	11	16	8	18	5	21
d. Disagree	5	6	15	13	17	17	14	21	14	22
e. Strongly disagree	2	1	2	2	3	3	4	5	7	1
Affirmative = lines										
a + b	83%	79%	76%	72%	69%	64%	74%	56%	74%	56%
Negative = lines d + e	7%	7%	17%	15%	20%	20%	18%	26%	21%	23%

◆ *IN THEIR OWN WORDS* _____

I was the original love child. During the '60s and early '70s, Haight Ashbury in San Francisco, and the East Village in New York were my homes; I grew up there. It was in New York that I experienced Woodstock, as well as that whole generation. There's nothing like it now. Maybe there never will be. It wasn't just sex and drugs, it was love. People cared for each other. There was protest and hope in the air. We were the generation that said, "You can't trust anyone over 30." Now that I am into my 40s, I have modified my views somewhat, but not all that much. My parents were horrified when they heard that I had had an abortion. They really had no idea at all of how we, that whole generation, lived. We thought marriage was passé—that if you liked someone, you slept with them as a sign of your love.

My parents' generation seemed to hold no relevance for us. We had Timothy Leary and Mark Rudd at Columbia University as our mainstay people. Most of society's institutions seemed totally out of date and unnecessary, so we wanted to do away with them.

I don't see any generation gap anymore at all. I think I've become less radical. My heart is still in the right place, but I don't have time to go to demonstrations and I don't sleep around. I've built a life. It might have been easier if my parents had been able to communicate their values to me, but I believe that where I am now is not too far from their ideas of where I should be. We each have to find answers for ourselves.

—A 40-year-old single mother

Does everyone have some concern about caution? Do some life-styles, cultures, and individuals go counter to the prevailing wisdom as a way of life? Not everyone given the same information, however threatening, will respond in the same way. Sex is a personal issue and a personal expression, but sexuality can also be used to make a political statement, to defy or support almost anything that society or the family as an institution might say. In that context, personal pleasure takes second or third place.

Table 2.4 indicates that most people are indeed more cautious sexually. How has this caution been exhibited? Have concerned individuals greatly diminished their sexual contacts and activity? How has each age group changed in terms of frequency in sexual involvement? To find some answers, we examined opinions regarding changes that have occurred during the past 3 years. Our findings are reported in Table 2.5.

Where did all the caution go? Certainly not to the side of abstinence. Although our questionnaire respondents indicated that they had become more cautious about sex (Table 2.4), they were having much more sex than they had been having 3 years before. In the youngest group, 62% of the men and 66% of the women reported that their sexual activity was Increased (much more, and more, lines a and b in Table 2.5) as compared to 3 years before. Serious diminution of sexual activity was shown by only 5% of the men and 9% of the women in the youngest group. A decade ago, this information might have been received with "They're young" and a shrug. Now, we have to see the picture in its totality and wonder about the effectiveness of a national campaign, occasionally

TABLE 2.5   **Survey Item D.9.**

COMPARED TO 3 YEARS AGO, MY SEX ACTIVITY IS:									
	Ages (Years)								
	18 to 26		27 to 38		39 to 50		51 to 64		65+	
	M	F	M	F	M	F	M	F	M	F
N =	255	274	356	382	282	300	229	233	215	222
a. Much more	37%	43%	16%	22%	23%	13%	24%	7%	18%	8%
b. More	25	23	22	21	20	16	20	16	11	31
c. Same	22	15	33	27	32	34	24	39	37	21
d. Less	11	10	21	16	21	21	20	23	22	31
e. Much less	5	9	8	14	4	16	12	15	12	9
Increased = lines a + b	62%	66%	38%	43%	43%	29%	44%	23%	29%	39%
Decreased = lines d + e	16%	19%	29%	30%	25%	37%	32%	38%	34%	40%

bordering on hysteria, that is urging Americans to cut down on sexual activity, to practice only safe sex, and to take fewer sex partners.

Table 2.5 shows generally less increase of sexual activity (lines a and b) among those age 27 and older. This lower increase was particularly noticeable among women, whose sexual activity declined from a high of 66% among the youngest group to a low of 23% for the 51- to 64-year-old group. These findings are not surprising, given the fact that, as people move into their late 20s and beyond, their work, family pressures, and decreasing amounts of leisure time make an expansion of the time available for sexual activities less likely. This is borne out when we look at the Decreased activity (less, and much less, lines d and e). As respondents' ages increased, a higher proportion reported that their sexual activity had decreased. For women past the age of 39, the percentage of those in each age group who reported a decrease (lines d and e) was larger than those reporting an increase (lines a and b). The downward trend may not be attributable to caution, but rather to a diminution of sex in their marriage and/or sexual contacts. We were surprised that so large a percentage of those in the mature groups reported an increase in their sexual activity. It would be interesting to know how many of these respondents were persons who have become divorced or widowed and have developed a renewed interest in sex with new partners. Time may take some toll among older persons, but Americans are not relinquishing sex to the younger folks alone. Full sexual activity continues for the great majority of those 65 and older (see Table 2.1). In our informal interviews, many of those in the 65+ group stated that tenderness and passion are still present, but the urgency of sexuality in their younger years has mellowed. As noted earlier, our results among the 65+ group were considerably higher than those generally reported in the sex research literature. In future research, this entire subject of age and sex will have to include new considerations and outlooks, and will require much more study of the sexually active postmature population.

SEXUAL INITIATION

Several age-related characteristics of sexual activity during the adult years have been explored so far in this chapter. A fuller picture can be drawn by considering the age of sexual initiation: At what age did individuals have their first full sexual experience? The responses we received required that we include in Table 2.6 a category for under 10 years of age.

A comparison of the youngest group surveyed, those 18 to 26 years old, with the oldest group, those 65 years and older, tells a dramatic story. Of those in the youngest age group, 21% of the men and 15% of the women had already had full sex by age 14. When the oldest group was growing up, the mores and standards of their day dictated that women

TABLE 2.6   **Survey Item H.15.**

SELF-IDENTIFICATION: AGE AT FIRST FULL SEXUAL RELATIONS:									

	Ages (Years)								
	18 to 26		27 to 38		39 to 50		51 to 64		65+	
	M	F	M	F	M	F	M	F	M	F
N =	254	266	357	378	284	300	228	231	214	216
a. By age 10	3%	2%	2%	1%	2%	0%	3%	1%	1%	0%
b. 11 to 14	18	13	17	10	16	7	16	2	16	1
c. 15 to 18	70	68	54	61	51	43	58	47	43	40
d. 19 to 25	9	16	24	26	25	48	21	49	38	55
e. 26+	0	1	3	2	6	2	2	1	2	4
By age 14 = lines a + b	21%	15%	19%	11%	18%	7%	19%	3%	17%	1%
After age 18 = lines d + e	9%	17%	27%	28%	31%	50%	23%	50%	40%	59%

were to remain virgins until marriage: only 1% of the women had had full sex by age 14, compared to 17% of the men. The traditions of boys will be boys and girls will be virgins were simultaneously kept intact.

It is informative to examine the percentages of women who had had full sex by age 14 (lines a and b of Table 2.6). The highest percentage (15%) is found in the youngest group; a steady decline occurs across all the other age groups. The older our female respondents were, the more likely that they abided by traditional norms regarding the initiation of full sex.

With the experience that young people report today comes far less distortion of sexual matters, and greater and more accurate knowledge of the biology and participative responses of the other sex. Our research unearthed some gothic fears and beliefs that were widespread among today's grandfathers when they were young and uninformed—none of which was mentioned by any of today's young male respondents. The most deplorable were "vaginum dentatum," a belief that the vagina had teeth and could bite the penis, and "penis captivus," the power of a female sex partner to "clamp up" and hold the penis captive in the vagina. Even as generations of young American males plotted how to get an illicit sex partner to permit them to enter her vagina, their sense of guilt involving such a conquest allowed a true panic at the thought of not being able to remove their organ when the act was complete. In interviews, older men reported various ingenious ways that were advised to "make the girl let go": "pinching her nipples," "pleading," and, if all else failed, "punching her in the stomach." This peer-to-peer fantasy is history, but our interviews brought an actual report of the penis becoming caught on IUD wires during intercourse, with the couple needing to be taken to a hospital emergency room to be separated. All of these seem minor anxieties compared to the traditional fear that one goes crazy when one masturbates, to which even early teen males, having nocturnal emissions, were not immune.

In Table 2.6, the 15 to 18 age category of sexual initiation consistently has the greatest number of sexual initiates. This is not necessarily a sign of liberation; rather, in these years, particularly among the two oldest age groups, many people were traditionally married and others began cohabitation or had sex with their future marital partners. From their high in the youngest group, the percentages of those 15 to 18 who experienced sex initiation diminish somewhat among those under 50; to some degree, older ages at marriage have been a factor during the past few decades. However, the high rates for those 15 to 18 indicate that changes in mores have made premarital sex an increasingly viable option for both men and women. Today, by the age of 18, most Americans have graduated from high school. In our interviews, a number of our respondents told us—about their friends, of course—that if they were still virgins, they were carrying a final burden that should be gotten rid of. A familiar agreement involved receiving a class ring or an engagement ring in exchange for the hymenal ring.

Sexual experience comes much earlier today, for more people, than in any previous era of our history. Comedian David Brenner maintains that, to find a certified virgin these days, one has to be standing outside the delivery room of a hospital. Some children under 10 have moved from the vicarious sex play of the past to full sexual relations (see Table 2.6).

SEX ROLES: PRAGMATIC OR PASSÉ?

Appreciating or depreciating one's own sex or the other sex is a product of traditional values and sex roles. To examine the extent of acceptance or rejection of these traditional sex roles, we asked respondents to give their opinion of this statement: "Traditional sex roles have no place in modern society." We deliberately made this survey item (A.13) strongly negative, in order to elicit an emotional response. How much of society is still involved in maintaining traditional sex roles? Many people would like to see a brave new world, swept clean of prejudicial stereotypes, even though they know that time—often, much time—is needed for people to grow into changing attitudes and relations.

Table 2.7 allows us to see how the different age segments of society are still involved in maintaining Traditionalist sex roles, and how many people disagree with them and advocate change (Feminist). Men 65 years and

TABLE 2.7   Survey Item A.13.

TRADITIONAL SEX ROLES HAVE NO PLACE IN MODERN SOCIETY:									
	Ages (Years)								
	18 to 26		27 to 38		39 to 50		51 to 64		65+	
	M	F	M	F	M	F	M	F	M	F
N =	255	274	356	382	284	299	229	234	216	223
a. Strongly agree	6%	7%	3%	9%	6%	9%	8%	3%	11%	4%
b. Agree	21	24	24	32	18	32	24	22	28	35
c. No opinion	19	16	14	10	14	10	16	6	15	13
d. Disagree	42	47	51	45	54	43	42	58	36	42
e. Strongly disagree	12	6	8	4	8	6	10	11	10	6
Feminist = lines a + b	27%	31%	27%	41%	24%	41%	32%	25%	39%	39%
Traditionalist = lines d + e	54%	53%	59%	49%	62%	49%	52%	69%	46%	48%

older had the highest rate of Feminist responses (39%) and men 51 to 64 were second (32%). A majority of men in each age group under 65 supported Traditionalist sex roles. In our informal interviews, we found that men 65+ were not the competition for young career women; in fact, they supported them. They were often fathers and grandfathers of young women seeking their futures in the personal gratification of a career. The sex roles of traditional society had little value for these particular men, and they perceived that the larger image of traditional sex roles would confine their daughters' and granddaughters' career pursuit.

If the Feminist responses (lines a and b in Table 2.7) are taken to indicate a truly feminist perspective, then, for men and women in all age groups, this perspective is in the minority. In the three younger age groups (spanning ages 18 to 50), women were more likely to have a feminist attitude; in the 65+ age group, there was no difference between the sexes (39% for both men and women). Women ages 27 to 50 were most opposed to the traditional roles. It seems no coincidence that these women were in age groups that must deal with the pressures of family life, which often place a greater stress on the mother/wife than on the father/husband.

✦ IN THEIR OWN WORDS

I'm very glad to speak to you because I have thought about most of the issues—older people dating, and how it would be different if I were young again and could live my life the way the young women do now. If the truth be told, by golly, I envy these girls today. Don't let any of the other women tell you otherwise. They too, at least most of my friends, do. Young women today work hard, and some of them have trouble having babies because they start so late, but they have a life of their own. I have no complaints about my husband. We spent 52 happy years together, and there is no use crying over spilt milk. But my life was his. His life was mine too, but he also had his business as an avenue of stimulation, and I had nothing of my own.

Being a mother, and now a grandmother, is a blessing. It's an experience that every woman should have. Doesn't the good book say, "Be fruitful and multiply?" But there were times when I found myself getting so bored playing card games and canasta with the other women my age—and hoping that something exciting could come into our lives—that I could have gone loco. I mean, it could have made a person cry. My life wasn't wasted, far from it. I just mean that there were, and should have been, many more things I could do. I remember the battle over giving women the vote. Well, now I write little stories and poems that the local newspaper publishes, and I write poems to my grandchildren on their birthdays. It's nice. You may be shocked, but I've joined NOW. That's right, the National Organization for Women. I want to help every young woman I can. It's a big world out there, and it's a shame not to partake in God's world to the extent that you have the ability to give.

—A 72-year-old grandmother

With a majority of respondents favoring the traditional sex roles (Table 2.7), we reasoned that an examination of their attitudes toward the double standard in sexual behavior could be very informative. The double standard was part of tradition, and people learned to live with it. It handicapped women sexually and put undue demands on them that were not placed on men. How many respondents would agree that a double standard in sex, regarding men's and women's behavior, was still in existence? Table 2.8 shows the responses we received.

The strongly agree category showed large differences of perception between men and women up to the age of 65. The largest discrepancy (23%) occurred in the 27- to 38-year-old group, which also had the largest percentage of women (44%) who strongly agreed that a double standard exists. An interesting study for further research might match these percentages, again by age groups, with the percentages of women who file for divorce or obtain a legal separation. No statistics on breakups of cohabiting unmarried couples in any age group would seem to be available.

With the exception of those over 65, women are consistently more aware than men of the sexual double standard that disfavors them. Interestingly, although most women were very aware of the double standard (generally, over 90%), the youngest group of women, those 18 to 26 years old, viewed the double standard with the lowest level of concern or awareness. We

TABLE 2.8   Survey Item A.15.

| THERE IS STILL A DOUBLE STANDARD IN SEX REGARDING MEN AND WOMEN: | | | | | | | | | |

	Ages (Years)								
	18 to 26		27 to 38		39 to 50		51 to 64		65+	
	M	F	M	F	M	F	M	F	M	F
N =	256	274	355	382	283	299	227	230	214	221
a. Strongly agree	19%	36%	21%	44%	22%	36%	21%	40%	28%	25%
b. Agree	56	51	64	48	56	60	54	51	50	67
c. No opinion	18	8	8	3	15	3	17	6	19	4
d. Disagree	6	3	6	4	6	1	6	1	3	2
e. Strongly disagree	1	2	1	1	1	0	2	2	0	2
Affirmative = lines a + b	75%	87%	85%	92%	78%	96%	75%	91%	78%	92%
Negative = lines d + e	7%	5%	7%	5%	7%	1%	8%	3%	3%	4%

believe that several reasons account for this. Members of this group may not yet have had the life experiences that are evidence of a double standard. Another possibility is that the sexual standards within the youngest age group really *are* more equal for men and women. We were unable to determine from our data which possibility is more likely; this is an area for future research.

SEXUAL SOPHISTICATION BEFORE MARRIAGE

Premarital sexual experience is a significant issue that touches on the sexual equality of men and women. In the past, young men were generally encouraged to explore sex and young girls were discouraged from any sexual experience. Men discovered their bodies' sexuality by experimentation with masturbation and interpersonal sex; women learned about their bodies from lectures on menstruation or from the man they married. A man who had had sexual experience was considered a source of valuable information; a woman with much sexual experience, or even sexual knowledge, was often considered immoral. To maintain respectability, the traditional or stereotypical Victorian woman was expected to blush at even the mention of sex or the use of terms outside of an accepted sexual vocabulary. A lady was defined, by implication, as a virgin who was innocent of sexual feelings. A woman who was not a virgin had to offer the most extreme reasons: she had been engaged to a cad who backed out of marrying her; or she was drunk or drugged when she made the mistake of sleeping with a man. Several transitory phases have passed since the Victorian era. How does the American public now react to premarital sex? Our questionnaire offered two parallel statements—one pertaining to men's sexual experience and the other to women's—to explore whether Americans differentially value male and female premarital sexual experience. Tables 2.9 and 2.10 indicate the respective responses we received.

The *difference* between men's and women's views with regard to the Positive value (very important, and important, lines a and b of Table 2.9) of men's premarital sexual experience increased with the age of the respondents. In the 65+ group, a more traditional view of male sexuality was expressed by the men, who were more likely than the women to consider premarital sex for males to be very important. This is underscored in the Positive percentages (lines a and b): 63% of men (versus 40% of women) in the 65+ age group considered male premarital sex to be important. One possible explanation is that, for some older men, whose potency may be diminishing, sexual performance becomes a strong male identification, a way to claim more sophistication and prowess—with women other than the spouse—in spite of advancing age, and an identification of the aging body with younger vitality and a more pleasing self-image. To widowers or single men who are dating during these years, self-image must be maintained and enhanced. Many of the women in this age group, however, have traditional values and may prefer companionship to life with a human counterpart to a peacock. Male strutting and preening seem to have been unappealing to these women; those over 65 whom we later interviewed still yearned for a passionate and warm sexual relationship. Women, however, are hindered in seeking a suitable

TABLE 2.9   **Survey Item B.7.**

FOR THE MAN, SEXUAL EXPERIENCE BEFORE MARRIAGE IS:									
	Ages (Years)								
	18 to 26		27 to 38		39 to 50		51 to 64		65+	
	M	F	M	F	M	F	M	F	M	F
N =	255	268	355	381	284	294	229	230	215	221
a. Very important	15%	19%	17%	15%	17%	14%	21%	22%	26%	17%
b. Important	37	33	31	40	44	40	41	24	37	23
c. Not sure	15	19	17	16	14	19	11	19	10	21
d. Unimportant	25	20	34	23	23	23	21	26	26	23
e. Very unimportant	8	9	1	6	2	4	6	9	1	16
Positive = lines a + b	52%	52%	48%	55%	61%	54%	62%	46%	63%	40%
Negative = lines d + e	33%	29%	35%	29%	25%	27%	27%	35%	27%	39%

TABLE 2.10   **Survey Item B.8.**

FOR THE WOMAN, SEXUAL EXPERIENCE BEFORE MARRIAGE IS:

	Ages (Years)									
	18 to 26		27 to 38		39 to 50		51 to 64		65+	
	M	F	M	F	M	F	M	F	M	F
N =	254	271	354	379	283	296	227	230	215	221
a. Very important	8%	10%	10%	14%	13%	12%	12%	11%	19%	3%
b. Important	30	33	30	42	41	40	38	30	31	22
c. Not sure	20	15	23	13	16	15	18	17	10	29
d. Unimportant	33	30	34	26	27	28	24	34	36	30
e. Very unimportant	9	12	3	5	3	5	8	8	4	16
Positive = lines a + b	38%	43%	40%	56%	54%	52%	50%	41%	50%	25%
Negative = lines d + e	42%	42%	37%	31%	30%	33%	32%	42%	40%	46%

partner by a greater sense (than men) of appropriateness in selecting partners and by maintenance of their dignity in the eyes of their friends and family. Men are not similarly hindered. An old rogue will still bring forth from his peers smiles of admiration and congratulations on his sexual conquests.

Let's take a look at the distaff side. How important did our respondents think premarital sex is for women?

The Positive data presented in Table 2.10 (very important, and important, lines a and b) are particularly interesting. For the two younger groups, females were more likely than males to consider premarital sex for women to be of value. Differences in responses were 5% and 16%, respectively, for the 18- to 26-year-old and 27- to 38-year-old groups. In the three oldest groups (spanning ages 39 to 65+), we found that men were more likely than women to value female premarital sex. The differences between males and females for these three oldest groups were 2% (ages 39 to 50), 9% (ages 51 to 64), and 25% (ages 65+).

When contrasting the men and women in the oldest age group (65+), 25% of the women gave Positive responses (very important, and important), expressing their view that women's premarital sexual experiences were of value; 50% of the men surveyed had the same view. Is it possible that many men believe that if their spouses had had some sexual experience before marriage, they may have had a more interesting sex life during the course of the marriage? Maturational differences that develop as we age and grow are reflected in sexual attitudes, but these differences are minimally visible from one age group to the next older or younger one. The generation gap, created by outmoded beliefs that sex was solely a youngster's domain, has been closed. Sexual activity is frequent and goes on through the 65+ age group. All age groups are in the same chorus now; some may have different harmonies to contribute, but they are all singing the same lyrics.

→ *IN THEIR OWN WORDS* ———————————————————————

What overwhelmed me at first was the sheer pressure for drugs and sexual activity. Everyone seemed to be having sex—maybe not great sex, but copious sex. When I spoke to my sorority sisters or asked any of my roommates about it, they seemed to be perfectly at home with sex and guys. I wasn't a virgin when I got here, but barely so. At first I really valued my freedom and wouldn't let myself get attached—you know, go steady and all. But, nowadays, I prefer to have one guy at a time, and that's not easy; the pressure may seem subtle, but it's pervasive.

The sex didn't bother me so much. In fact, I am really into it now. But the drugs did. I'm very health-conscious and don't like taking foreign substances into my body. Anyway, I now have a group of friends who don't do drugs, or do them only minimally. I have learned a great deal about sex and feel that I am really sophisticated. I'm embarrassed at how little I knew in high school, when we all thought we knew everything. Guys don't see you a lot of times and then slowly build up to having sex. The first or second time you get together it's simply expected as part of the socializing routine. The university's health service is good about letting us know the dangers of stupid sex. That's what I call it, because anyone with half a brain can be intelligent, have sex and not get burned. I am only now insisting that guys I don't know real well use condoms. And just to be extra cautious, I use vaginal cream. It doesn't feel natural to use condoms, and when I am involved seriously with a young man, I use only my diaphragm and cream. I am not sure that I trust the Pill fully. None of the girls in my dorm have had any of the scary stuff like herpes, and certainly not AIDS or anything. I believe the panic about sexually transmitted diseases is greatly overblown. Out of about 35 girls I know, only two have had abortions. We stood by them and so did their boyfriends. Of course, they didn't tell their parents.

—A 19-year-old female college student

THE LOVERS' KNOT

A poignant piece of medical history, the "lovers' knot," illustrates the extreme measures taken by some women who are now in the grandmother age group, in order to be "virgins" when they married. A "lovers' knot" was a minor surgical procedure performed by some gynecologists between about 1920 and 1950. They would place several stitches in the labia of young women who were engaged and about to marry, and were not virgins. On their wedding night, when consummating their marriages, these women would feel pain, and bleed, convincing their new husbands that they were pure and virginal. Times change; to most Americans today, this procedure seems nothing short of barbaric. However, women endured it to satisfy the intense pressure placed on them to conform to the protocols of that time period.

Sex roles ascribed to men were also restrictive, but, primarily, only lip service was given to them, no real adherence was expected, and no punishment was meted out for transgressions.

THE TRADITIONAL FAMILY AS AN INSTITUTION

The traditional family was the dominant institution in forming and perpetuating attitudes toward sex. These attitudes were preached and exemplified as life-styles to children. The traditional views dealt with in tables presented earlier in this chapter have been attributed, by most experts, to the family and, secondarily, to the churches. (As we shall see in Chapters 6 and 7, the relationships, roles, and functions of family members have undergone enormous, but socially acceptable, changes and, in the 1990s, a family can have several definitions of membership.)

The experience of living in a family structure tells a child a great deal about value, gender, and sexual identity, and the role that the child is to play in life. Table 2.11 indicates how our respondents of different ages felt about the traditional family as an institution.

TABLE 2.11   **Survey Item A.1.**

THE FAMILY IS THE MOST IMPORTANT INSTITUTION IN SOCIETY:									
	Ages (Years)								
	18 to 26		27 to 38		39 to 50		51 to 64		65+	
	M	F	M	F	M	F	M	F	M	F
N =	256	274	356	383	284	301	228	233	215	222
a. Strongly agree	52%	55%	49%	56%	50%	48%	53%	58%	59%	68%
b. Agree	39	40	41	35	37	43	37	31	33	26
c. No opinion	3	3	6	3	4	3	3	1	5	5
d. Disagree	5	2	3	5	8	5	5	6	3	1
e. Strongly disagree	1	0	1	1	1	1	2	4	0	0
Positive = lines a + b	91%	95%	90%	91%	87%	91%	90%	89%	92%	94%
Negative = lines d + e	6%	2%	4%	6%	9%	6%	7%	10%	3%	1%

We anticipated that older people would strongly advocate the importance of family, because they were raised and socialized in a more traditional, family-centered era. Overwhelmingly, they did. Less expected was the slight difference across age groups. The young people in the 18- to 26-year-old age group were divided between those who still live in their parents' homes, making the nuclear family an immediate reality, and those who have ventured out for careers or schooling. Because our youngest group consisted of young adults, we expected from them the most rebellion and distancing from the family. Not so; our data indicated that the obituary of the traditional American family has been prematurely written. This youngest group may rebel against family values and authority and/or run away from home, but, even in absentia, the family as an institution is valued. Rejection of the family is scarcely present, across all age groups, in the responses reported in Table 2.11.

The strong pro-family responses recorded among the young mature group—those 27 to 38 years old—show little change from those of the youngest group. Men and women 27 to 38 have, for the most part, left their parents' homes, although some may still live with their parents while awaiting marriage, obtaining a graduate degree, or saving to afford a residence of their own. Some individuals in this group are returning to their parents' homes and refilling the empty nests. The reasons given are usually economic, but future research might investigate whether the original nuclear family, which may not have been appreciated when adult children were younger, may have taken on a new luster.

In the 39- to 50-year-old group are people who are parents and grandparents themselves; their basic and overwhelming approval of the family as an institution remains firm. However, the men have slipped a few points from their earlier solid commitment. Men ages 39 to 50 expressed a 9% Negative (strongly disagree, and disagree, lines d and e) response. Do some men of this age *need* to question the importance of the family? Possibly so. Some of them have undoubtedly faced and coped with their own midlife crisis. To what degree have women, in surviving their midlife problems, derived support from the family and their changing roles in it? Do the attitudes of this group reflect a reaction to their own nuclear family of origin, or to the families they themselves head? Do their responses regarding the family begin to reflect their approval or disapproval of marriage and the family as they have lived it? If they are in a good marriage, do they rate the family higher than those in a bad marriage do? These and other similar questions await further investigation.

The youngest and the oldest groups are almost identical in their agreement. Those who aspire to or are just beginning a new family life and those who are looking back on the family they have formed and raised are most Positive. Among the three groups in the middle, only slightly less idealism is evident. On the whole, responses showed little question about the role of the family and its relevance. Whether its values were lived on a daily basis or it was seen as a haven for all its members, the family, however defined, was apparently as vital for the young adults in our sample as for the grandparent generation.

THE BREADWINNER

Earnings and husbands' egos have long been cited as roadblocks in the path of women's professional progress. A pervasive male belief extending into the 1950s was that the man, the head of the household, should be the primary, if not the only breadwinner. A wife's part-time work at a hobby was acceptable, as were the professions of teaching and nursing. It was always very important for a "family man" to be able to say, "I can take care of my family!" In fact, a man's status was measured by how well he took care of his family and his wife. Times have changed for all Americans, regarding the question of primary breadwinners and providers. The new term developed in the past several years to exemplify this concept is "househusband"—a married man who takes care of the household while his wife provides for the family by working outside of the home. Responses to the provocative question about one spouse earning more than the other are given in Table 2.12.

With the exception of the 65+ group, Table 2.12 shows that the women surveyed were consistently Negative (disagree, and strongly disagree, lines d and e), or less likely to be bothered by the fact that their husbands might earn more than they do. A substantially large percentage of men in all groups also felt that their spouses' earning more than they did

TABLE 2.12									Survey Item A.7.	

IF MY SPOUSE EARNED MORE THAN I, IT WOULD BE A SERIOUS PROBLEM:										
	Ages (Years)									
	18 to 26		27 to 38		39 to 50		51 to 64		65+	
	M	F	M	F	M	F	M	F	M	F
N =	255	272	355	381	284	302	230	234	216	222
a. Strongly agree	2%	1%	2%	1%	2%	1%	3%	2%	2%	0%
b. Agree	2	1	9	1	7	1	8	1	1	4
c. No opinion	5	2	8	2	8	3	10	4	10	13
d. Disagree	44	40	48	42	42	50	46	49	49	55
e. Strongly disagree	47	56	33	54	41	45	33	44	38	28
Positive = lines a + b	4%	2%	11%	2%	9%	2%	11%	3%	3%	4%
Negative = lines d + e	91%	96%	81%	96%	83%	95%	79%	93%	87%	83%

would not be a problem for them. As a reflection of the changing times, the youngest male respondents were the least concerned about which spouse made the larger wage.

A husband's earning more than his wife has never been a problem; the question here addresses the fact that approximately 30% of working wives make more money than their husbands. Although it is not surprising that the youngest group, born during or after the women's liberation movement, have few problems accepting economic equality for women, it is revealing that this acceptance extended to all the other age groups.

Among the 27- to 38-year-olds, we found people launched into their careers and moving up the professional or business ladders toward whatever degree of success they would eventually attain. Men in the 39-to-50 age group were at the earning peak in their work life, and some were in the professions. They did not yet have to face early retirement or part-time work, and were in a position to be fully in charge of family income. Yet, even in these comfortable circumstances, the two-income family seemed to be acceptable. Considering where the people in this age group are in their careers, the similarity between this group's responses and those of the other groups was surprising. One might almost have believed that this is a no-debate issue, between and among men and women. This group included older, male professionals who, in some instances, had had to stand by as women—their wives and others—passed them by on the promotion ladder.

In the 51- to 64-year-old group, we interviewed senior executives who were early retirees; some were on disability and others had accumulated a nest egg. Respondents told us that nest eggs today are not what they used to be. Responses similar to those of the younger groups showed up here as well. A tiny minority of the respondents depended on the ability of the one-income male in the household, and the nest-egg concept was gone; others desired to expand their previously considered definition of the "good life" and in doing so they expanded their horizons. Many Americans are worried about social security's continuance and reliability. Families are scrambling to keep up economically, and, even for the middle class, years of hard work and saving during a lifetime of employment may not be enough to get by on one income. Necessity has replaced pride and male-dominated tradition, and two paychecks are now widely accepted in all groups, including those earning low and medium six-figure incomes. This generation grew up hearing the term "lady boss" given a negative connotation. Economic reality has stepped in to drive away the ghosts of old stereotypes of male/female competence or incompetence. More often now, husbands take pride in and nurture their wives' careers. It is not uncommon for some of the men in this age group to retire or semiretire while their wives go on working.

Those in the 65+ grandparent generation are still among the most accepting of women's economic equality. Some of our male interviewees in this group expressed their feelings about women's work—not only about their wives, but about their daughters' and granddaughters' career efforts. For many in this group, retirement has not meant financial independence. In some families, particularly those in which the husband is considerably older than the wife, his health does not permit him to work, so the wife supports the two of them. This group has almost no naysayers (1% of men strongly agreed that unequal spousal earnings would be a problem).

People seem to have put aside the stereotypes of conflict between men's and women's earnings. Past masculine representations and beliefs, in which the nature of work and family economic care made them only a man's job, are no longer true. Financial muscle is no longer regarded as a male prerogative, and the role of breadwinner is no longer an extension of a man's masculinity. In all age groups, men and women accept the reality of partnership between the spouses and their mutual financial contributions to the home.

Two more items are of interest. First, this is, surprisingly, a nonissue for all age groups: a maximum of 11% of any group agreed or strongly agreed that unequal spousal earnings would be a problem. Second, in most age groups, males—who traditionally and even today usually earn more than their spouses—are more likely than females to consider a higher income by the spouse to be a problem. The relatively high consensus among men in all age groups, and women in all age groups, as reflected in the Negative responses (disagree and strongly disagree, lines d and e in Table 2.12) is also interesting. In all age groups except the oldest, the percentage of women who disagreed was somewhat higher than the percentage of men. For many traditional women, the concept of entering the outside world of work was frightening. They were unprepared for it psychologically and professionally. Yet, even the women in our older groups clearly opted for economic respect or professional fulfillment, and may not resent working. Traditionalists have no problem with a man's making more money than his spouse; we wanted to evaluate their acceptance of the spouse's earning more than the man. Over half of all married women now work outside the home, and as much as one-third of these women earn more than their husbands do. The women's movement has apparently liberated men in this area as well.

✦ IN THEIR OWN WORDS

> I clearly remember the embarrassment my parents felt when I had to have my wife work. She worked to help me through graduate school. Now I know lots of couples in which the wife helps put her husband through professional school, but back then, it was a problem. My parents were immigrants and couldn't give me much financial help. Although they lacked

money, they were big on opinions and values. A wife who works, they used to say, will have the last word, because he who has the cash decides things. It was hard for them to believe that we decided things jointly, and that I valued my wife's opinion.

Anyway, now that we have children and they have grandchildren, my parents have forgiven my wife. They were horrified because my wife went out to work while the kids were quite small. "You leave them with strangers?" my mother asked in shock. (The strangers were qualified nursery school teachers.) I find that, among nearly all of my friends, there is absolutely no problem about who brings in the bigger share of the bacon. In fact, most of the couples I know need two incomes to have even a few of the luxuries we aspire to. Strangely, my wife now works in my office and runs a tight ship, but my folks are okay about it because they see her in the role of secretary; in that role, she is serving me. Old habits die hard . . . I get very upset with them, but my wife tells me to take it easy. They are who they are and we are who we are. I hope I don't pass on such nonsensical attitudes to my children.

—A 48-year-old married male medical professional with two children

SUMMING UP

Age and aging are a specter for Americans, who spend billions of dollars each year on beauty products that purport to make the user more sexual or younger looking. No longer are women the exclusive customers for plastic surgery and cosmetics. However, our greatest fear connected with increased age is fear of diminished sex. Products available as remedies range from hormones to keep women and men sexually active, to surgery, to having implantations in men that permit them to have sex and reach orgasm. We do not gracefully leave the field of sexual interaction, nor are we willing to let sex become only a memory. This chapter has presented some important information indicating far greater, prolonged, and active sex lives for American adults, with only slight changes occurring at later ages. Society seems to be beginning to accept the fact that older people can have active sex lives. Even if tinged with reluctance, there is acceptance that children, at ever younger ages, have become sexual beings. No one group dominates sexually, and with intergenerational sex, we see in headlines of the rich and famous that many Americans have also adopted some interesting combinations of the ages of sex partners.

As we have seen in this chapter, the concept of "age-appropriate" sex behavior is in shambles, particularly at both ends of the age continuum. For all age groups, there is a blurring of limits and a striving for greater and more varied sexual performance—more subtly by women, and more overtly by men. Growing up in a free society, finding one's place in it, resolving the ego-identity question of "Who am I, what am I, and where am I going?" and achieving comfortable sex roles are far more difficult because there are almost no consensual sex guidelines. Everything from the age of sexual initiation into emotional/sexual commitment seems left up to the individual. Where once parents and religion provided markers and guidelines, peers and the media now provide a confusing and contradictory landscape.

For all age groups, there is overwhelming belief that the family, however individuals define it, is still the most important institution in society. Despite a large-scale desire to fully participate in what had once been seen as almost exclusively a man's domain, women have entered a man's world of work, without abandoning the family.

Although not easy for either men or women, the strain seems much heavier for women, particularly those between the ages of 27 and 50. Men do basically the traditional tasks; the Second Sexual Revolution places women in many new situations when compared to their family of origin, yet leaves them some uncertainty about their sex practices—one-night stands, delayed commitments, marriages, and childbearing. Increasing numbers of single women, uncertain of when to marry, or not wishing to marry, opt for single parenthood.

Significant findings, throughout this chapter, reflected the fact that sexual liberation has freed Americans of all ages, including the postmature population, both psychologically and physically. This freedom must be looked at and understood in the context of the great advances during the past two decades in the treatment of the health problems of older Americans. The importance of diet, exercise, and sociability is touted as contributory to both longevity and the quality of life as we age. Older Americans have a greater self-awareness that they must abandon old role stereotypes: creative life does not end with menopause and grandchildren are not all one has to live for in elderly years. This major shift in persons' self-image has had a great impact on the social acceptance of a wide variety of behaviors for the postmature that run counter to the traditional "rocking chair" image of previous generations. There is an increasing awareness that those over 65 may have a life that includes socializing and continued full sexual activity. Recognition of elderly persons' sexual existence is, even now, slowly becoming a reality. Even widowhood has been freed of traditional protocols and is no longer a mandated entry into the lonely world of bingo games and being alone in a crowd.

For many seniors, widowhood has brought an opportunity for a reawakened sexual drive that lay dormant for many years during a marriage that had become more of a habit than a vital source of joy in life. For some older Americans, the widening horizon of new social and sexual involvements in their golden years has placed them in conflict with their own children and grandchildren, who may find it difficult to let go of the traditional image of the parent whose life used to be solely directed to spouse and children. The new image of an independent and sexually vibrant person (or couple) who is free to create a new and sometimes private life may be too much for some children to accept. As many persons have observed, it is as if the child as adult wishes to control the sexual and private life of the parent in much the same way that the parent had controlled the child's sexual and private life years before. Are elderly parents receiving thoughtful concern or unconscious revenge?

Those too young or too old—or too timid—to have sex partners can find an outlet in masturbation. Ages for this activity seem to get ever younger. Among the oldest age group, masturbation is thought to be an activity of those who are "the wrong age" for interpersonal sex. However, respondents age 10 and below reported having full sexual relations, and even in this age of liberation, many respondents of all ages identified autoeroticism as an additional or exclusive outlet. Sexual behavior is found in all the groups in this chapter, although the definition of what is age-appropriate has broadened greatly. What appears to be a major change in behavior—even within marriage (see Chapter 6)—is the relative acceptance of masturbation as a common and even routine part of adult sexuality among men and women, and not just an activity of teenagers with raging hormone levels. Men and women still believe that there is a double standard, and women are more likely to perceive a double standard at all age levels.

Interest in sex may vary at each age level, but a consistent, broad-based interest in extensive sexual activity is very obvious at all age levels. From teenagers to the postmature, men and women are very sexually active. Some persons deplore teenage sexuality because they are appropriately concerned about pregnancy among preteens; others adore or deplore George Burns as the ultimate "dirty," sexually active nonagenarian who leers at Hollywood starlets with his symbolic unlit cigar in hand. Our data showed that all groups are more intensely involved in sex and sexual activity than was previously assumed. Because there is increased acceptance and participation in sexual matters, it is no longer possible to predict with any accuracy the type or frequency of sexual experiences of individuals simply by age. At least in the area of sexuality, we no longer have to follow a social script—not of our own making—that would increasingly limit our choices and activity as we get older. This makes for an exciting sexual future for all of us—if we so choose.

CHAPTER THREE

Men and Women: A Study in Contrasts

SOME SIGNIFICANT FINDINGS ABOUT MEN AND WOMEN

✦ Simultaneous orgasm is a must for 25% of men and 14% of women.

✦ When asked whether they had had at least one homo-sexual experience, 22% of men, 17% of women, and twice as many career women as women who were homemakers said Yes.

✦ 11% of men and 23% of women reported having been sexually molested as children.

✦ 56% of men, but only 44% of women, felt that they were functioning at their biological maximum sexually.

✦ 10% of men and 18% of women reported a preference for oral sex to achieve orgasm.

✦ Over 80% of our respondents were seriously con-cerned about sexually transmitted diseases, but more respondents reported *increased* sex activity in the past 3 years than reported *decreased* sex activity.

✦ Women, more than men, feel that traditional sex roles are no longer appropriate to modern society.

QUESTIONNAIRE SUBJECTS TABULATED IN THIS CHAPTER

	Table
The Family as a Social Institution: Current Views	3.1
Marriage and Fulfillment	3.2
Easy Divorce	3.3
Delaying Careers for Child-Rearing	3.4
Equal Care of Babies by Both Sexes	3.5
Abortion	3.6
Traditional Sex Roles in Modern Society	3.7
A Double Sexual Standard	3.8
Conflict Between the Sexes	3.9
The Importance of Love	3.10
Personal Professional Fulfillment	3.11
Male Premarital Sexual Experience	3.12
Female Premarital Sexual Experience	3.13
Homosexual Experience	3.14, 3.15
Sexual Orientation	3.16
Incest	3.17
Child Molestation	3.18
One-Night Stands	3.19
Attitudes Toward Masturbation	3.20
Masturbation Frequency	3.21
Age at First Masturbation	3.22
Variety of Sex Techniques	3.23
Simultaneous Orgasm	3.24
Sex and Intimacy	3.25
Sex Partner's Pleasure	3.26
Initiation of Sexual Activity	3.27
Orgasm During Lovemaking	3.28
Sexual Experience Before Marriage	3.29
Comparative Sexual Activity, Three Years Ago Versus Now	3.30
Oral Sex	3.31
Profane Speech During Sex	3.32
Anal Sex	3.33
Relationship with Spouse/Partner	3.34
Sensuous Nature of Sex	3.35
Self-Ratings of Sexual Activity	3.36
Biological Sexual Maximum	3.37, 3.38
Number of Sexual Partners	3.39
Sex Education	3.40, 3.41
Personal Preferences for Achieving Orgasm	3.42
Views on Personal Sex Practices	3.43
Sexually Transmitted Diseases	3.44
Sexual Harassment	3.45

W e've all heard of the "new woman." Is there really a new woman? Yes, there is! She is seriously involved in her career; she is also a lover and a mother. Her sense of empathic identification with men can bridge the gap between men and women. She is autonomous, has relationships of parity, is able to express herself sensually, and appreciates her network of women friends. For too long, sexist stereotypes substituted for reality; women are no longer pinups—they live, breathe, have opinions, and can take charge of a wide range of personal and professional situations.

In Germany, prior to and during the Second World War, a doctrine of the National Socialist Party openly advocated the traditional folk-view of women's roles: their province should be restricted to children, the kitchen, and the church (*Kinder, Küche, Kirche*). As a Nazi doctrine, this view is denounced and denied by Americans, but many endorse it in spirit, in their continuing attitudes toward women's conduct and capabilities. To this day, we hear the fallacy that women cannot be trusted in important decision-making situations because women are "too emotional," and the generalization that PMS (premenstrual syndrome) is scientific evidence that women are hyperemotional and capricious. The sexual and social roles assigned to women remain different from, and inferior to, those assigned to men.

In the emergence of sexual liberalization, there has been a residue of uneasiness; our society has ambiguity toward the basic sexual and familial changes that transformed the First Sexual Revolution of 1948 to 1988 into the Second Sexual Revolution, which began in 1989 and still continues. Our study has documented many levels of sexual and social changes for both women and men in the early 1990s, but we acknowledge that women's, not men's, sexual attitudes and behavior have drastically changed within the past two decades.

The enormous and ongoing change in women's social and sex lives has separated women into entirely different groups. Work-life and a workplace outside the home have given a new focus to many women's lifestyles. The innovations transcend income earned or the nature of the work performed; more significantly, they involve a personal sense of identity that sets these women apart. To get a clear picture of these differences, in this chapter we have organized our survey data for a comparison of the responses of men with three samples of women. In each table in the chapter, in the column alongside the data for men are the data for the entire sample of women who responded to the survey item. Next are data for the group we have designated women-C, career women employed full-time outside of the home. Data for women-H, homemakers who are not employed outside of the home at all, appear in the final column. Age had no part in these groupings, and there was no sorting for status as wives and/or mothers. In the women-C and women-H groups, we found that we had two distinctly different populations, regarding sex life and life-style in general.

Women who work part-time outside the home offered responses that were almost always between those of the women-C and women-H groups. Data on the part-time workers have not been separately tabulated.

One of the most striking indications of our data involves the unprecedented levels of agreement between men and women-C (those who work full-time outside of the home), as compared to women-H, who do not work outside of the home at all. New levels of sexual affinity and relatedness can also be observed, in sharp contrast to the stereotypical sexual roles men and women have had assigned to them in the past.

Despite doubts about the viability of the family unit because of the enormous changes of the recent past—the vanishing American father, the majority of married women working outside of the home, and the highest rates of divorce in American history—the view of the family as an important institution has survived (see Table 3.1).

On the question of whether the family is the most important institution in society, women (92%) and men (90%) overwhelmingly and almost equally agreed. Not surprisingly, among women, the homemakers—who are often likely to have chosen home over career because of their belief system—were even more likely to agree (96%). We acknowledge the possibility that their strong agreement reflected a need to justify their decision. Nonetheless, there is no question that, although each group has an investment that may differ from those of the other groups, the family is still seen as pivotal. The roles of men and women have changed. No

TABLE 3.1   **Survey Item A.1.**

THE FAMILY IS THE MOST IMPORTANT INSTITUTION IN SOCIETY:				
	Men	Women	Women-C	Women-H
N =	1,345	1,415*	641	285
Strongly agree	52%	56%	52%	67%
Agree	38	36	38	29
No opinion	4	3	3	2
Disagree	5	4	6	1
Strongly disagree	1	1	1	1
Strongly agree + Agree	90%	92%	90%	96%
Disagree + Strongly disagree	6%	5%	7%	2%

*Throughout the chapter, the total number of women is more than the number of women-C (career women employed full-time outside of the home) plus women-H (homemakers not employed outside of the home at all) because women working part-time outside of the home, or volunteering, are not included in either the women-C or the women-H category.

longer is it only the man who ensures the financial security of the family; today, in most marriages, both partners work. No longer does the man alone decide the mode of sexual gratification; most often, the couple decides together. If the sexual adjustment within marriage is not satisfactory, sex counselors and sex clinics are available for advice. In very basic ways, the Second Sexual Revolution is changing the roles and lives of Americans, even in marriage.

FULFILLMENT

Can an individual who is alone be fulfilled? The traditional doctrine, that only in marriage could a person be fulfilled, no longer carries the day. Thinking has changed about marriage and fulfillment; those who are single are no longer regarded as just waiting to marry. The responses to our survey statement about fulfillment are reflected in Table 3.2.

Only a small minority of men (20%) and women (13%) were in agreement with the traditional concept. It is interesting to note, however, that, among those in agreement, men were almost twice as likely as women to associate true fulfillment with marriage. Further, it was not surprising to see that homemakers' responses were more like those of the men surveyed than those of the career women. Combining disagree and strongly disagree, the percentages were: 69% for men and for women-H, and 84% for women-C. Fulfillment comes in many forms; however, for years, it was accepted that feminine fulfillment consisted of being a wife and mother. Now, even those women who do not work outside of the home disagree with this concept, although to a lesser degree than women who have careers.

TABLE 3.2   **Survey Item A.6.**

TO BE TRULY FULFILLED, ONE MUST BE MARRIED:				
	Men	Women	Women-C	Women-H
N =	1,338	1,412	638	282
Strongly agree	4%	3%	3%	7%
Agree	16	10	7	18
No opinion	11	6	6	6
Disagree	51	56	51	53
Strongly disagree	18	25	33	16
Strongly agree + Agree	20%	13%	10%	25%
Disagree + Strongly disagree	69%	81%	84%	69%

DIVORCE

Along with the traditional roles of men and women in marriage, the question of perpetuating marriages—sometimes, very imperfect marriages—became an issue. To get an idea of how the ending of a marriage was viewed by respondents, we posed a specific statement that echoed comments we had heard from some individuals who thought that divorce is too easy these days. Table 3.3 shows how respondents reacted.

Few issues are more bitterly fought between men and women than divorces. Most attorneys, as well as many individuals who are divorced, insist that "the friendly divorce" is a myth. In light of our findings in Table 3.1, indicating that both men and women value the family very highly, it is somewhat of a surprise that only 53% of the men and 60% of the women surveyed either strongly agreed or agreed that divorce is too easy now. Only among the homemakers do we find an approximation (72%) of the strong profamily sentiment expressed in Table 3.1's statistics. The 22% difference in agreement between the homemakers and the career women magnifies some aspects of the attitudinal matchup between men and career women (53% and 50%, respectively). Are married women who do not work strongly opposed to easy divorce because it can end a marriage that provides economic security for them? There are women who are totally and emotionally committed to being good wives and mothers and centering their lives around their homes. Is the very thought of ending this way of life so distressing for them that they are understandably opposed to "easy" divorces? We assume that some of our findings concerning homemakers reflect a residue, although much diminished from earlier eras, of the traditional belief that if you marry, you stay married. Departure should not be easy; yet, divorce lawyers earn high-bracket incomes from their large caseload of couples who are relinquishing their marital commitment.

TABLE 3.3   **Survey Item A.3.**

DIVORCE IS TOO EASY NOW:				
	Men	Women	Women-C	Women-H
N =	1,342	1,411	637	279
Strongly agree	23%	25%	18%	33%
Agree	30	35	32	39
No opinion	20	13	15	12
Disagree	23	23	32	13
Strongly disagree	4	4	3	3
Strongly agree + Agree	53%	60%	50%	72%
Disagree + Strongly disagree	27%	27%	35%	16%

In our professional practice, we have noticed very recently, among parties to divorces, an increased sense of awareness of their former partners' material needs. Couples are attempting to work out (not "slug it out") mutually satisfactory arrangements jointly, rather than in a courtroom. We call this process *conditional empathy*. For many couples, the most traumatic issue in divorce is not the division of property, but child custody, which is of equal interest to both parties.

DELAYING CAREERS

Couples often make accommodations that involve what many consider to be sacrifices, both in the divorce process and in the rearing of their children. Particularly, mothers are asked to give up their career ambitions in order to create a traditional home for their children. We wanted to discover how respondents felt about women making career sacrifices for their children. This demand is placed almost entirely on women, and creates a major conflict in today's working woman—that of simultaneously balancing career gratification and the needs of her children. Women who can balance both, equally well, are today's "supermoms." Attitudes concerning the delay of careers are seen in Table 3.4.

There are still many men (53%, in our survey) who feel that women should delay their careers during children's early years. Only 43% of our women respondents agreed. However, the difference between career women's and homemakers' agreement rates is sharply delineated (36% versus 57%). The traditional view is that a woman's place is in the home and, even if she wants a career, she should sacrifice by delaying her career for her children's sake. This is a strong justification for homemakers' roles in their daily lives. By contrast, modern career women who have full-time work-lives outside the home have had few female role

TABLE 3.4   **Survey Item A.10.**

MOTHERS SHOULD DELAY THEIR CAREERS DURING CHILDREN'S EARLY YEARS:			
	Men	Women	Women-C	Women-H
N =	1,341	1,406	638	278
Strongly agree	12%	13%	10%	20%
Agree	41	30	26	37
No opinion	10	8	6	7
Disagree	30	39	44	29
Strongly disagree	7	10	14	7
Strongly agree + Agree	53%	43%	36%	57%
Disagree + Strongly disagree	37%	49%	58%	36%

models to look to for guidance and for justification of their choice. Instead, they have often had to gain support from women's groups and their husbands. Many of these women, in interviews, claimed that a successful career gave them a feeling of independence, both in their marriage and in the event that their marriage were to dissolve. There are far too many horror stories of women who have had no career and then lose their husband through death, divorce, or abandonment. Divorced or abandoned women, especially, are often left penniless, with children, long-term debts, and unpaid bills. Their life-styles quickly degenerate, even though their former or exited husbands may live in luxury. Whether the source is financial insecurity or the larger social changes that the women's movement has brought to the roles of women, there is no doubt that something real and powerful has dictated—or perhaps permitted—that women now can choose to move from being full-time homemakers to being full-time career persons.

SHARING PARENTING

If we assume that both parents' incomes are required to maintain a household, and that the mother must work outside of the home, does this obviate the traditional belief that only women can do mothering? There is a price to be paid for removing a mother from the home to pursue a full-time career; that price is the father's increased involvement with child rearing. As reported in Table 3.5, men and women overwhelmingly agree that both sexes can take care of babies equally well. In what may be perceived as either a vote of confidence in men's parenting capacity or a push toward men's increased involvement with fathering, women feel, even more strongly than men do, that both sexes can take care of babies equally well.

TABLE 3.5 Survey Item A.12.

BOTH SEXES CAN TAKE CARE OF BABIES EQUALLY WELL:				
	Men	Women	Women-C	Women-H
N =	1,341	1,412	637	277
Strongly agree	21%	31%	31%	34%
Agree	52	50	55	40
No opinion	5	4	1	7
Disagree	20	14	12	19
Strongly disagree	2	1	1	—
Strongly agree + Agree	73%	81%	86%	74%
Disagree + Strongly disagree	22%	15%	13%	19%

It is not unusual for couples' relationships now to be founded on sharing, although some of this sharing is nontraditional. We have found, in our interviews and our practice, that men and women currently reflect a sense of shared life-tasks, an awareness of a new sense of parity, and mutual interdependence and respect that transcend sex delineation. Although the responses we received show overwhelmingly that men and women believe they can take care of babies equally well, there are sharp differences between the career and homemaker women's groups. Interestingly, men's opinions of whether men are just as capable as women, in nurturing babies, match those of homemakers (73% and 74%, respectively). Career women, whether because of ideological belief or practical experience, are much more likely to believe (86%) that men are equally capable of baby care. Is this difference between the two women's groups attributable to fewer opportunities for the husband of the homemaker to partake in the nurturing role, which, by traditional definition, is the mother's role? At issue is not simply who gets up to give the baby a bottle at night; rather, the whole *raison d'être* of traditional women had been that the mystique of mommyhood could be handled only by a female; it needed a deeply ingrained "special" sense of mission that only women had.

ABORTION

Not only the care of babies is at issue today; the balance of planned pregnancies and abortion is part of the most explosive controversy in our society. Controlling family size, through family planning that may include abortion, is a singularly controversial issue, as is abortion for an unwed mother. To get at their deepest feelings, we asked our respondents to reply to a statement that was positioned as unconditional: "Abortion is murder." Table 3.6 shows their replies.

TABLE 3.6   **Survey Item A.11.**

ABORTION IS MURDER:				
	Men	Women	Women-C	Women-H
N =	1,343	1,411	639	281
Strongly agree	14%	15%	12%	15%
Agree	16	15	13	14
No opinion	18	15	15	23
Disagree	32	26	26	29
Strongly disagree	20	29	34	19
Strongly agree + Agree	30%	30%	25%	29%
Disagree + Strongly disagree	52%	55%	60%	48%

The deep division that exists in American society concerning the abortion issue is evident in the table. A little over half of all men and women were in disagreement, aligning themselves with the pro-choice position that abortion is not murder. If we were to add, to those in the disagreeing group, those respondents who had no opinion—a reasonable assumption, because they did not hold to the position that abortion is murder—then we would be left with only 30% of both men and women who agreed that abortion is murder and, presumably, would be strongly opposed to abortion. It is not unreasonable to assume that this group probably consists of persons from religious denominations and political groups that are opposed to abortion. However, a comparison of the two women's groups indicates that 60% of the career women, but only 48% of the homemakers, did not agree with the proposition that abortion is murder. There is no reason to assume that significant differences in religious affiliation exist between these two groups. Do the varying attitudes toward abortion actually reflect the differences between older, more traditional beliefs and ideology, as represented by the homemakers—and indicated in previous tables in this chapter—and newer, emerging beliefs and ideology, as represented by the career women? For many homemakers, children are their *raison d'être*; consequently, their investment in motherhood is much greater than that of the career women. Are career women therefore more likely to accept abortion as a woman's right, especially because for some women-C, children may even be a liability?

The role of women is clearly changing and allowing more choices. The degree to which women who hold traditional beliefs will move toward those choices remains to be seen. In any event, as the role of women changes, so must the role of men. Is American society very resistant to these changing roles?

SEX ROLES

Our survey revealed that sexual choices and sexual gratification are very important to women. Along with striving for the best orgasm, women search for a meaningful permanent relationship. To achieve this type of relationship, women may have to interact and speak out in new ways, and play radically new roles. We decided to try and trace the actual dynamics of these phenomena. A statement posed to all respondents was: "Traditional sex roles have no place in modern society." The answers produced one unexpected and one unsurprising result, as shown in Table 3.7.

The unexpected result was that, despite the changes that have occurred and are still occurring in men's and women's roles, the majority of men (56%) and women (52%) surveyed disagreed with the proposition

TABLE 3.7   **Survey Item A.13.**

TRADITIONAL SEX ROLES HAVE NO PLACE IN MODERN SOCIETY:			
	Men	Women	Women-C	Women-H
N =	1,338	1,410	635	273
Strongly agree	6%	8%	8%	5%
Agree	22	29	32	24
No opinion	16	11	11	14
Disagree	46	46	43	52
Strongly disagree	10	6	6	5
Strongly agree + Agree	28%	37%	40%	29%
Disagree + Strongly disagree	56%	52%	49%	57%

that traditional sex roles have no place today. However, this does not necessarily mean that these people are traditionalists who have a long way to go toward change; it might mean that they see no reason for them to change *their* attitude concerning sex roles, which is coexisting with more traditional attitudes. If any profound change has occurred in our society in the past few decades, it is that an abundance of choices has become available for men and women of all ages. No longer is there a script for one and only one sex role. Each individual may carry out and be comfortable with a traditional sex role or may opt for a newer, more "modern," liberated role. As shown in Table 3.7, a woman who is a career woman, with all the ideology and rationales accompanying that choice, is more likely to be hostile to traditional sex roles (40%) than a woman who is a homemaker (29%)—not a surprising result.

DOUBLE STANDARDS

Another aspect of the dynamics of changing sex roles is the ancient phenomenon of the double standard. Other areas, such as economic opportunities, have opened up for women, but the barriers in changing sex roles still stand in the bedroom. They will be the last barriers to fall, not merely because of tradition, but possibly because of the fragile male ego. Men and women seem to want both their liberation and their tradition, although men have enjoyed their liberation all along.

In spite of the impact of both the men's and women's liberation groups and rhetoric, more than three-quarters (79%) of all the men and 91% of all the women surveyed (see Table 3.8) recognized that there is still a sexual double standard regarding men's and women's roles.

TABLE 3.8   Survey Item A.15.

THERE IS STILL A DOUBLE STANDARD IN SEX REGARDING MEN AND WOMEN:			
	Men	Women	Women-C	Women-H
N =	1,340	1,411	637	275
Strongly agree	22%	38%	40%	38%
Agree	57	53	54	51
No opinion	14	5	3	9
Disagree	6	3	3	1
Strongly disagree	1	1	—	1
Strongly agree + Agree	79%	91%	94%	89%
Disagree + Strongly disagree	7%	4%	3%	2%

The double standard is a major cause of friction between the sexes. Inequality, no matter how slickly packaged or justified, destroys self-esteem, creates a sense of doubt about one's value, and ultimately leads to anger. Concomitant with the double standard is some recognition by Americans that its effects are ammunition for continuing the "battle of the sexes." The responses to our survey statement about this issue were very revealing. As shown in Table 3.9, most respondents were aware of the battle, and, for one of the few times in our study, there was almost no difference between the answers of the career women and the homemakers.

Surprisingly, almost as many men (82%) as women (89%) acknowledged a conflict between the sexes. With men's dominance in our society for so long, and change coming very slowly, we would have supposed that they would notice conflict less, because they were more used to getting their way. This was not the case.

TABLE 3.9   Survey Item C.13.

I FIND THAT THE BATTLE OF THE SEXES STILL EXISTS TODAY:			
	Men	Women	Women-C	Women-H
N =	1,342	1,409	640	280
Strongly agree	19%	24%	26%	24%
Agree	63	65	62	64
No opinion	12	7	8	7
Disagree	5	3	4	4
Strongly disagree	1	1	—	1
Strongly agree + Agree	82%	89%	88%	88%
Disagree + Strongly disagree	6%	4%	4%	5%

Another expected finding was that career women—because they are out of the home and competing with men—would notice more of a conflict between the sexes than homemakers would. Again, the data said Not So. What do we make of this? As evidenced in previous tables, the homemakers were much more traditional than the career women. However, the homemakers' recognition of inequality was not dimmed; they may prefer the home, but is a good deal of conflict between the sexes still manifested in even the most traditional and loving homes? Where is this "battle" fought: in the bedroom, in decisions on child rearing or finances, in an imbalance of daily responsibilities for maintaining the household, or in silence? We don't know. However, we believe that, when 88% of the homemakers surveyed recognize an ongoing battle between the sexes, all is not well in our traditional homes today.

LOVE

Is the need for love a myth? Is it less important in this age of changing sex roles? Is love still, as traditionalists believe, more of "a woman's thing"? The answers on love, shown in Table 3.10, were overwhelmingly one-sided. When we combined the very important and important categories, the responses for both men and women could not have been much higher, or much more alike: 96% for men and 98% for women. Only 1% of each group in the survey felt that love was not important.

Only when we looked at the extreme of very important, taken alone, did we notice a difference between the sexes: 72% of the men said love was very important, compared with 85% of the women. Among the women, a slight edge in the commitment to love was given to the homemakers—89% compared to 83% for the career women. Again, the ideological configuration of the homemakers is consistent with their more traditional orientation.

TABLE 3.10   **Survey Item B.4.**

HOW IMPORTANT IS LOVE TO YOU?				
	Men	Women	Women-C	Women-H
N =	1,336	1,411	640	279
Very important	72%	85%	83%	89%
Important	24	13	14	8
Not sure	3	1	2	2
Unimportant	—	1	1	1
Very unimportant	1	—	—	—
Very important + Important	96%	98%	97%	97%
Unimportant + Very unimportant	1%	1%	1%	1%

Several other sections of the book indicate what love meant to our respondents in terms of sex, romance, and commitment. Often, our data indicated, the need for love has been a burden, not a gift.

PROFESSIONAL FULFILLMENT

Our data about the battle of the sexes and the double standard reflected on the interpersonal aspects of the sexual/social relationships of men and women. We knew it was important to also have information about individuals' inner self, personal life, and aspirations for their lives. We therefore juxtaposed and compared responses of two significant, basic statements about life: one on the importance of love, detailed in the preceding section, and one on personal professional fulfillment (see Table 3.11).

Personal professional fulfillment was ranked as very important or important by men and women equally (95%). In response to the question "How important is love to you?", the percentages were nearly the same: love was very important or important to 98% of the women and 96% of the men (see Table 3.10). We interpreted these findings as confirmation that virtually everyone needs and appreciates love, and that most people would like to attain career success. What does the relatively high statistic of 93% for the homemakers mean? In recent decades, partly as a consequence of and a reaction to the women's movement, the status of homemaker has taken on new meaning and pride for those who choose this marital life-style. They are indeed involved in personal professional fulfillment. When we note that 51% of the career women said their professional fulfillment was very important to them, we have to be aware that, despite the movement of women-C into a workplace outside of the home, many of them are still expected to continue the major tasks of their roles

TABLE 3.11   Survey Item B.3.

MY PERSONAL PROFESSIONAL FULFILLMENT IS:				
	Men	Women	Women-C	Women-H
N =	1,344	1,412	641	269
Very important	45%	49%	51%	48%
Important	50	46	47	45
Not sure	2	3	1	4
Unimportant	2	2	1	3
Very unimportant	1	—	—	—
Very important + Important	95%	95%	98%	93%
Unimportant + Very unimportant	3%	2%	1%	3%

as homemakers and, in some cases, mothers. These doubled and tripled responsibilities have resulted in the creation of "superwives" and "supermoms"—career women who strive to achieve their best in two additional realms. Our grandmothers', and probably our mothers', way of life was much simpler. Home was where they found whatever fulfillment their lives offered; theirs was a subordinated role in a less complex society. Today's homemakers have gained recognition as decision makers, child rearers, managers of the home environment, and, in some cases, community catalysts to improve that environment. Seeking gratification in the home and the workplace, as many of today's women do, involves a far more complex agenda than existed even one generation ago.

✦ *IN THEIR OWN WORDS* _____

> I love my job, and I find it rewarding, but I will tell you something I have decided, and I don't care if NOW disowns me. If the right man came along, I would marry him tomorrow. I've had sexual experience, and I've had all the networking and the new contacts that I may ever be interested in. It took me to the ripe old age of thirty-two to be able to say it. I'm tired of having my consciousness raised; I would rather have my body stroked. There is nothing wrong with having babies; even some of my militant friends have them.
>
> —A single, 32-year-old female Wall Street account executive

SEXUAL EXPERIENCE

Along with love and professional fulfillment, sexual behavior and attitudes toward sex have been modified by today's changing sex roles. What are some of the changes revealed in our data? In Tables 3.12 and 3.13, we summarize our examination of a long-standing, traditional issue: the importance (or lack of importance) of premarital sex for men and women.

Within each of the two tables, the percentages for each category, across all groups, show few variations, an indication that the men and women surveyed had a fairly similar set of attitudes concerning premarital sex for both males and females. Comparing attitudes toward premarital sexual experience for males (Table 3.12) and females (Table 3.13), there was only a slight difference in men's and women's views of its importance. Regarding males, 56% of the men surveyed, and 52% of the women, thought the premarital experience was very important or important for men; 46% of the men, and 46% of the women, put premarital sexual experience at the same level of importance for women.

TABLE 3.12 Survey Item B.7.

FOR THE MAN, SEXUAL EXPERIENCE BEFORE MARRIAGE IS:			
	Men	Women	Women-C	Women-H
N =	1,338	1,390	630	272
Very important	18%	17%	15%	26%
Important	38	35	39	29
Not sure	14	18	17	19
Unimportant	26	23	22	21
Very unimportant	4	7	7	5
Very important + Important	56%	52%	54%	55%
Unimportant + Very unimportant	30%	30%	29%	26%

However, comparing the women-C and women-H, the traditionally oriented homemakers agreed with the other groups that male premarital sex was very important or important, but differed considerably from career women (38% versus 54%, respectively) on the issue of female premarital sex.

The liberated attitudes of the homemakers toward premarital sex for males showed two interesting comparisons. In Table 3.12, their very-important-for-males rating (26%) exceeded that of the career women *and* the men. By contrast, in Table 3.13, their very-important-for-females rating was only 10%. Were they giving greater liberation to their sons, but reluctant to extend it to their daughters? In being more traditional than the men interviewed, the homemakers were, we believe, reflecting their ideological system, which contains the notion that the male will be the

TABLE 3.13 Survey Item B.8.

FOR THE WOMAN, SEXUAL EXPERIENCE BEFORE MARRIAGE IS:			
	Men	Women	Women-C	Women-H
N =	1,338	1,400	638	274
Very important	12%	11%	12%	10%
Important	34	35	42	28
Not sure	18	17	13	22
Unimportant	31	29	26	34
Very unimportant	5	8	7	6
Very important + Important	46%	46%	54%	38%
Unimportant + Very unimportant	36%	37%	33%	40%

initiator and teacher of sex and therefore should have some experience to bring to his bride.

HOMOSEXUALITY

When Kinsey and his colleagues[1] reported that 37% of men and 19% of women had had homosexual experiences to the point of orgasm at some period in their lives, many Americans were shocked. For some of the men (4%), their first experience was the beginning of a life-style of exclusive homosexuality. The statistics are not as clear for continuing exclusive lesbian activity among women, but most experts concede that the percentage is probably somewhat lower than for males. Table 3.14 indicates the proportion of men and women in our survey who reported having had homosexual experiences, and Table 3.15 profiles, for a much smaller sample, the frequency of the homosexual experiences.

Twenty-two percent of the men and 17% of the women said that they had had homosexual experiences. When career women were compared with homemakers, there was a larger contrast; the career women were far less traditional than the homemakers. Our data cannot explain the origin of the higher rate of the women-C homosexual experiences. Did a less traditional personality emerge during early childhood and predispose these women to being more sexually adventurous and to breaking out of traditional social roles? Or, were they exposed to a wider variety of attitudes and beliefs about sex experience through their business-world contact?

Because we had often heard the statistic of 10% given as an estimation of the number of male homosexuals in the United States, we attempted to provide (see Table 3.15) some up-to-date indication of the size of the homosexual population, from those who had answered Yes in Table 3.14.

Table 3.15 exhibits some of the difficulties in defining the term "homosexual." Although the figure of 4% of the adult male population is generally used to indicate the number of male homosexuals (gay groups use the figure 9% to 10%), does this mean that anyone who has ever had a homosexual experience is to be classified as a homosexual? If so, then

TABLE 3.14   **Survey Item H.17.**

HAVE YOU HAD HOMOSEXUAL EXPERIENCES?			
	Men	Women	Women-C	Women-H
N =	1,335	1,384	635	263
Yes	22%	17%	23%	10%
No	78	83	77	90

TABLE 3.15   Survey Item H.17.

HAVE YOU HAD HOMOSEXUAL EXPERIENCES? YES RESPONSES:				
	Men	Women	Women-C	Women-H
N =	294	235	146	26
a. Once	5%	6%	7%	4%
b. Occasionally	56	67	63	84
c. Frequently	13	6	4	7
d. Ongoing	26	21	26	5
Active = lines c + d	39%	27%	30%	12%

the correct statistic would be found in Table 3.14: 22% for men and 17% for women—much larger than most estimates. On the other hand, if we use only the category of ongoing, then we have a much lower finding.

The most accurate percentage of homosexuals may be found by combining frequently and ongoing into the active category. By doing this, 9% (39% of 22%) of the men and 5% (27% of 17%) of the women may be considered homosexuals—a more reasonable estimate. When we compare career women with homemakers, the consistent traditional pattern of homemakers remains true—7% (30% of 23%) of career women and 1% (12% of 10%) of homemakers may be considered lesbians.

The difficulty of extrapolating from data on homosexual acts to an estimate of the size of the homosexual population arises from the fact that many persons are bisexuals—they have sex with partners of both sexes. As we have noticed in other areas of sexual involvement, there is often a looseness of labeling relative to any particular sex activity. In our interviews, we found that, although there were respondents who identified themselves as heterosexual and reported having homosexual relations, there were also a number of respondents who identified themselves as homosexuals and reported that they have heterosexual relations as well. One bisexual man expressed this opinion about varied sex: "Why cut out

TABLE 3.16   Survey Item H.3.

SELF-IDENTIFICATION: SEXUAL ORIENTATION:				
	Men	Women	Women-C	Women-H
N =	1,333	1,411	638	278
Heterosexual	91%	95%	91%	98%
Homosexual	4	2	4	1
Bisexual	5	3	5	1

half of the population?" Many Americans seem to act out the popular injunction "Do your own thing," without taking labels seriously.

To clarify the preference lines, we asked respondents to self-identify their sexual orientation. As Table 3.16 shows, the number of persons who have engaged in homosexual acts either frequently or ongoing almost equally identify themselves as homosexual or bisexual.

INCEST

Several sex-related issues are sources of contention today. One is the issue of one-night stands (discussed later in this chapter) and another is the problem of incest. Incest is viewed as "a woman's problem" because the vast majority of incest victims are young girls; most become victims before the age of 10. Only recently has American society begun to recognize the enormous problem of sexual child abuse, including incest. To what degree is the American public specifically aware about the problem of incest? We asked for opinions on a strong statement in our questionnaire: "Incest is a major problem in American society now" (Table 3.17).

Responses showed that women were more aware of the problem than men. One reason for this difference may have been that more women than men had personally experienced incest as children. On this issue, there is no disagreement between career women and homemakers; this is not an issue of ideology or tradition or values. A large share of respondents offered no opinion, and a small percentage disagreed. We believe that those persons who had no opinion were not so much lacking in knowledge but viewed the issue of incest as too threatening or too horrible to contemplate. Another possibility is that they may have seen suggestions of incestuous desires among themselves or their spouses. In

TABLE 3.17   **Survey Item C.4.**

INCEST IS A MAJOR PROBLEM IN AMERICAN SOCIETY NOW:				
	Men	Women	Women-C	Women-H
N =	1,341	1,411	638	270
Strongly agree	18%	29%	29%	30%
Agree	42	46	46	45
No opinion	28	16	15	18
Disagree	11	8	8	7
Strongly disagree	1	1	2	—
Strongly agree + Agree	60%	75%	75%	75%
Disagree + Strongly disagree	12%	9%	10%	7%

order to sample our respondents' experience with sexual abuse, including incest, we asked them to indicate whether they had been sexually molested during childhood.

CHILD MOLESTATION

The results on child molestation, presented in Table 3.18, reflect one of the major social problems in our society today. More than one out of every 10 men who responded admitted to being sexually molested as a child, and an astounding 23% of the women reported this early horror. A puzzling statistic is that half again as many career women (as compared to home-makers) reported early molestation. Table 3.16 indicated that more of the career women than homemakers claimed to be homosexual. Is a cause-and-effect relationship operating here? Our data do not provide an answer, but there may be reason to assume, from our interviews, that the childhood background of these two groups may have been different with respect to the degree of deviance of those around them. If so, then child-hood molestation and both homosexuality and the choice of a career (rather than a domestic life-path) may be related to the environment in which the child grows up. On the other hand, some subtle behavioral characteristics related to later sexuality may put some children at increased risk for molestation.

Most Americans mistakenly believe the stereotypical image of a child molester: a person wearing a trench coat, standing outside of a school, and asking: "Would you like some jelly beans, little boy [or girl]?" Sections a through e of Table 3.18 contradict that characterization: most child mo-lesters are known to the children they molest. They are either relatives or persons in positions of authority relative to the child—for example, a par-ent, uncle, cousin, teacher, scoutmaster, religious or guidance counselor. Sections d and e of the table give discouraging details on how the criminal justice system treats sexual molestation of both girls and boys.

The data in Table 3.18 are a revealing portrayal of the entire societal interaction, from the actual molestation to the role of the authorities when an incident of molestation is reported. As the data show, most inci-dents are *not* reported; even when they are, they are frequently handled with great indifference by the authorities.

According to our respondents, almost 60% of molestations were either often or ongoing for both sexes, and 12% were reported to the authori-ties, equally for both sexes. Yet, arrests were fewer than half for mo-lesters of girls, and convictions for molesting girls were only one-third the number for molesters of boys. In a 1983 study,[2] one of the present authors reported that, when the molester is over 55 and the child younger than 12, the molester is virtually never sentenced to jail.

Recent headlines have highlighted schools and day-care centers from California to New York—and in many cities in between—as having staff

TABLE 3.18   **Survey Item H.20.**

I WAS SEXUALLY MOLESTED AS A CHILD:				
	Men	Women	Women-C	Women-H
N =	1,318	1,371	631	269
Yes	11%	23%	28%	18%
No	89	77	72	82

Yes Responses:	Men	Women
N =	142	318
a. *Who was the molester?*		
Adult stranger	33%	21%
Relative	44	62
Person in authority position	23	17
b. *How often?*		
Once	42%	41%
Often	44	39
Ongoing	14	20
c. *Was the incident(s) reported to authorities?*		
Yes	12%	12%
No	88	88
d. *Any arrest?*		
Yes	12%	5%
No	88	95
e. *Any convictions?*		
Yes	9%	3%
No	91	97

or directors involved in molesting many children for many years. Other news articles have focused on the clergy. Having officially ignored the matter for a long time, religious leaders now recognize that a serious problem exists within their ranks. For example, in a *New York Times* article on June 16, 1992,[3] Cardinal Bernardin of Chicago said "that he would establish an independent board to investigate accusations of sexual abuse of children by priests in his archdiocese." Americans are increasingly becoming aware of the extent of child molestation as a serious and widespread national disease.

There are continuing reports of people so traumatized by molestation that they blocked it from consciousness for periods of up to 30 years. The courts have increasingly permitted individuals to sue alleged perpetrators and their institution many years after the event, under a rule that supersedes the statute of limitations. The clock begins to tick when the person remembers the molestation, whether in psychotherapy or when some event in his or her life jangles a memory bank. One now-adult child sex-abuse victim who had difficulty being believed, as happens with many who make such accusations, was indignant: "A child can be a legally credible witness in a murder trial, but not for sex abuse!"

These findings are consistent with data in the literature of sexology and psychiatry, but, because very little has been written about what happens after the rare child speaks up, we researched this issue. Among the women in our study who had been sexually molested, we found that about half were molested before they were 8 years old, compared to a median age of about 10 for the men. It has been estimated that 1 of every 12 adult rapes, but only 1 of every *200* child rapes, results in an arrest.

ONE-NIGHT STANDS

A highly contentious issue, one-night stands, represents a dramatic departure for some women from the sense of sharing love, romance, and the intimacy between men and women that develops over time in a relationship. "Liberated" women can be sexually more assertive in a relationship, but the "quickie" with a stranger—the essence of the one-night stand—has not been widely associated with the new role of women in America. However, as a reaction to traditionally defined interpretations of when and where women are supposed to have sex, there is now a well-honed and openly discussed sense of sexuality among some women that goes beyond the many new doors to sexual gratification for women in sexual relationships. Sharp criticism of these leaps toward new freedoms in sexual relationships has surprisingly come from new quarters; long denounced by traditionalists and conservatives, the opposition is now echoed by radical feminists as well. The feminists argue that, in the past, male/female sexuality has been phallocentric and based on the subordination of women. Their fear is that, while most women enjoy their expanded opportunities, they may not be experiencing true sexual liberation. In this instance, the feminists use liberation to mean the ability to enjoy sexual interactions without having to use the sexual interchange as a means to establish or to maintain a relationship with a male sex partner. Sex, they say, should not be bartered for a relationship. In a sense, Erica Jong, in her prescient way, wrote of this more than a decade ago, in her book *Fear of Flying*.[4] She presented, in fictional form, the ultimate depersonalized sex fantasy for women—"the zipless fuck," in which women may initiate sexual intercourse with a stranger without a word being exchanged between them. The one-night stand is not quite so radical, but it does begin to approach the extreme of totally depersonalized sex.

We felt that one-night stands were worth space in our survey. The answers we received are shown in Table 3.19.

TABLE 3.19

I FIND ONE-NIGHT STANDS TO BE DEGRADING:				
N =	Men 1,341	Women 1,411	Women-C 634	Women-H 273
Strongly agree	15%	37%	32%	41%
Agree	32	31	35	29
No opinion	23	15	13	18
Disagree	24	13	16	8
Strongly disagree	6	4	4	4
Strongly agree + Agree	47%	68%	67%	70%
Disagree + Strongly disagree	30%	17%	20%	12%

That a minority of men (47%) believed that one-night stands were degrading is no surprise, given the history of males' frequenting brothels and call girls, and going to bars to pick up women for sex while they are out of town or in military service. What may come as a surprise to many readers is that only about two-thirds (68%) of the women surveyed found one-night stands degrading and that there is only a minimal difference between the responses of the "liberated" career women and the more traditional homemakers. This means that nearly one-third (32%) of women either had no opinion or were not opposed to this depersonalized form of sex. Anonymous sex has apparently achieved considerable acceptance into the psyche of American women. Because a no opinion response may indicate a lack of experience with this activity or a lack of objection, the implications of our findings should be further studied and researched, considering the dangers for society in an age of AIDS.

MASTURBATION

There is a natural need for people of all ages to explore and to experiment, to find their bodies' sexual parameters, their levels of comfort, and their preferences. Some of this sexual experimentation is done alone, and some with others. The need to find the new and exciting continues from just after birth until very old age; in fact, it helps promote healthy sexual appetites and interaction. The first discovery by children is that their genitals feel different from, for example, their elbows. Then two things happen, often at about the same time: just when they discover that touching their genitalia feels good, their parents, to varying degrees, make the touching a taboo practice. For most children, this action continues under the sheets, for fear of discovery; they now have been initiated to the beginnings of sexual guilt, most often associated with the practice of masturbation. Traditionally, despite the taboo, men have practiced masturbation far more than women. The extent of sexual guilt today is seen in the title of a book by Marty Klein, *Your Sexual Secrets: When to Keep Them, When & How to Tell.*[5] Klein claims that masturbation, especially among those who are involved in a continuing relationship with a sex partner, is the most commonly kept sexual secret. Views on masturbation continuing on in marriage were requested in our survey. Table 3.20 shows the results.

As a sign of personal discovery, it is a revolutionary change that approximately two-thirds of all men and women surveyed (66% and 67%, respectively) saw masturbation as a natural part of life. However, in a comparison of career women with homemakers, traditional ideology showed up again: the homemakers were the least accepting (59%) of masturbation as natural.

Even though many women believe that masturbation is natural, do they masturbate or are they thinking only of male masturbation? In the past, female masturbation was a subject that did not exist; it was unknown. "Nice people" did not speak about it until recent years, and "nice" women, in contrast to "loose" women, were not supposed to know what their genitalia looked like. Decades later, in orgasm workshops, many women cringed as they were given mirrors and told to look at their genitalia. The emergence of women's personal and deep interest in sexual gratification has become, more than coincidentally, accompanied by a surge of publicly expressed interest in masturbation. Drugstores that were still hiding condoms under the counter seemed suddenly and ubiquitously to set up large displays of "feminine" vibrators. Audiences would laugh knowingly when Robin Tyler, a female comic who prefers

TABLE 3.20   **Survey Item C.5.**

MASTURBATION IS A NATURAL PART OF LIFE AND CONTINUES ON IN MARRIAGE:			
N =	Men 1,340	Women 1,396	Women-C 634	Women-H 273
Strongly agree	17%	20%	25%	17%
Agree	49	47	53	42
No opinion	22	21	13	33
Disagree	10	9	8	6
Strongly disagree	2	3	1	2
Strongly agree + Agree	66%	67%	78%	59%
Disagree + Strongly disagree	12%	12%	9%	8%

the feminist designation of comedian, would say, "This Xmas I'm sending a dozen roses to my vibrator." What is the status of masturbation in America, for both women and men? As shown in Table 3.21, we posed a statement designed to obtain the information needed on frequency of masturbation among adults.

When we grouped together all forms of Regular masturbation, from daily to monthly, we found that men, in keeping with traditional stereotypes, do masturbate more than women (55% versus 38%). However, to give an indication of the changes in sex-role stereotypes, when we compared career women with homemakers, we found a sharp difference: 50% versus 21% who regularly masturbate. Career women approximated the frequency of masturbation for men. This was one of the most dramatic differences we found between the sexual behavior of career women and homemakers. There appears to be an overriding increase of expressing and experiencing sex, both solitary and interpersonal, among those women who work outside of the home. However, when we compared frequent masturbation—daily plus several times weekly—we found much less contrast between career women and homemakers (13% versus 8%). We also noted that 40% of the homemakers reported not masturbating at all. One might be tempted to think that they have so much good sex in their marriages that "who needs to masturbate?" The experience of most sex therapists and marriage counselors suggests that this is not always the case. Have the more traditional women-H been classically unwilling to engage in or only to admit masturbatory habits? Our experience indicates that, sadly, many of these women who do not masturbate may need it to develop their orgasmic response system and bring some "good sex" into their lives.

TABLE 3.21   **Survey Item D.8.**

I MASTURBATE ON AVERAGE:				
	Men	Women	Women-C	Women-H
N =	1,327	1,384	623	270
Daily	7%	1%	2%	1%
Several times weekly	18	9	11	7
Weekly	22	13	16	5
Monthly	8	15	21	8
Rarely	26	34	30	39
Never	19	28	20	40
Frequent = Daily + Several times weekly	25%	10%	13%	8%
Regular = Daily to monthly	55%	38%	50%	21%

> Masturbation? You must be kidding! When I was 17, I still didn't know which end of the tampon went into me. My mother never showed me; she always told me that girls who used tampons were no longer virgins. Luckily, my boyfriend's sister is a nurse, and she showed me. I felt stupid—here I am a college student, and I didn't know my own biology. Now that I look back on it, it's funny. My boyfriends always touched me, and it was terrific. I didn't really care to find out how to do it alone, because what's the fun of doing it alone—until I was 24. Then I said to myself, now it's time to know, and truthfully, I still don't know, even now, why I decided at that time, but I sure am glad that I did.
>
> —A 30-year-old single woman

At what age do most people begin to masturbate? Table 3.22 shows that there are some differences between the sexes, in the age of initiation. An equal percentage of women and men began masturbating by the age of 10 (both 19%). However, at the time of puberty, the interest in males apparently awakens in force: 53% of the males, compared to 25% of the females, began masturbating during the years of 11 to 13. Thus, by the age of 16, 88% of the boys had already begun, compared to 62% of the girls.

Many more women than men (45% versus 23%) began to masturbate at age 14 or older. This activity would coincide with the expansion of the socialization experiences that females are involved with at this age; through school, peers, and boyfriends, they become more exposed to different ideas on the subject of sex.

When we compared career women and homemakers, we could find no consistent pattern. Although a slightly higher percentage of career women had begun masturbating before age 14 (43% versus 39%), women-C were

TABLE 3.22   **Survey Item H.16.**

AGE FIRST MASTURBATED:				
	Men	Women	Women-C	Women-H
N =	1,328	1,390	621	222
By age 10	19%	19%	19%	14%
Ages 11 to 13	53	25	24	25
Ages 14 to 16	16	18	17	22
Ages 17 to 21	5	15	17	15
Ages 22 to 30	1	7	11	7
Ages 31 and over	1	5	4	3
Never	5	11	8	14

also slightly more likely to begin at a later age (after 21) than homemakers did (15% versus 10%). Virtually all men who masturbated had started by age 21, but 12% of the women had not.

What accounts for this apparent increase of interest in masturbation among women? Is it attributable to public sale of vibrators, the popularity of women's pornography, and the availability of erotic books in most bookstores around the country? When we compare the regularity of female masturbation reported in our study to the apparent generations, over centuries, of women who tolerated sex rather than enjoyed it, the present extent of women's autoerotic behavior was unexpected.

VARIETY

A fairly common feature of modern sex manuals is discussion of numerous variations of foreplay, coitus, and afterplay. The rationale is that sexual boredom may be an underlying threat to many marriages. Although the expectations for sexual variety are evident, how strong is the belief that it is a must for marital bliss? Table 3.23 gives the responses that we received.

Slightly less than half (49%) of the men surveyed, and just over one-third of the women (36%) felt that a large variety of sex techniques is a must for sexual pleasure. One of our cultural myths about male sexuality suggests that, to keep their libido in high gear, men have a greater need for sexual variety than women do. Some women we interviewed said that they felt deeply hurt, and perhaps even betrayed, when they got that response from a lover or husband. They were miffed by the suggestion that whatever the male did should be sufficient for the female partner. Variety is obviously a very important issue for some women, because different perceptions may threaten even the best of marriages.

TABLE 3.23   Survey Item C.7.

A LARGE VARIETY OF SEX TECHNIQUES IS A MUST FOR MAXIMUM PLEASURE:			
	Men	Women	Women-C	Women-H
N =	1,336	1,395	638	277
Strongly agree	13%	7%	7%	8%
Agree	36	29	28	34
No opinion	17	16	15	15
Disagree	30	39	42	36
Strongly disagree	4	9	8	7
Strongly agree + Agree	49%	36%	35%	42%
Disagree + Strongly disagree	34%	48%	50%	43%

THE MYTH OF SIMULTANEOUS ORGASM

Are some expectations or "musts" sexually unrealistic, even when widespread? Are they valued for the intimacy they seem to promise? For many decades, sex manuals touted the virtues of simultaneous orgasms, and many persons were brought up to believe that this was the ultimate goal during a coital act. We wondered how many people really believed that simultaneous orgasm was a must. Table 3.24 was our best indication.

Despite cultural bias, our results indicated that the vast majority of both the women and men surveyed did not feel that simultaneous orgasm is necessary to have gratifying sex. We might speculate that the men's smaller disagreement with the statement represented a throwback to the chauvinistic belief that male dominance in sex was sufficient to provide the female with such sexual pleasure that the male was able to time his partner's orgasm to coincide with his own. Whatever their reasons, our respondents overwhelmingly disagreed with the statement posed. In agreement that simultaneous orgasm is a must for gratifying sex were not quite one-quarter of the men (24%) and only 14% of the women. When we compared the career women to the homemakers, it was interesting to see once again that traditional ideology—strongly embedded in the homemakers—continued to cause their attitudes to be more similar to the men's than the career women's: 22% of the homemakers and 24% of the males supported the value of simultaneous orgasms, compared with 12% of the career women. Does this difference reflect pressure by some husbands or partners in ongoing relationships, or are career women exhibiting greater autonomy in their sexual expression? Further research would be required to answer these questions.

Some homemakers reported in interviews that simultaneous orgasm is a male demand; they are uncomfortable with it, but their partners

TABLE 3.24   **Survey Item C.9.**

SIMULTANEOUS ORGASM IS A MUST FOR GRATIFYING SEX:				
	Men	Women	Women-C	Women-H
N =	1,338	1,398	635	270
Strongly agree	7%	3%	3%	4%
Agree	17	11	9	18
No opinion	12	10	7	14
Disagree	52	52	51	47
Strongly disagree	12	24	30	17
Strongly agree + Agree	24%	14%	12%	22%
Disagree + Strongly disagree	64%	76%	81%	64%

view it as such an imperative that the women fake orgasm in order to comply. To some of the women, this view seemed like an unrealistic demand on a reflexive response over which they may have no control—a demand that intrudes into the love relationship without promoting trust or intimacy. The men who appeared to need simultaneous orgasms seemed to believe that their skills in controlling their partners' responses and timing were on trial. However, many of the women we interviewed said that men are very wrong in the belief that they can bring a woman to orgasm on demand.

▶ *IN THEIR OWN WORDS* _____

You've heard of "Clockwork Orange"; well, I call this sham of simultaneous sex "clockwork sex." It's terrible. I don't know of a single woman who demands that her man climax the very instant she does, but men seem to take this as some kind of ritual affirmation of their macho. I personally refuse to fake orgasm and, while I have become very annoyed at men who insist on it, I appreciate those men who are confident of their sexuality, and enjoy the mutuality of lifting each other to the heights of orgasm when it is right for each partner. There was one very insecure creep that I was involved with who was very good looking, but oh, did he have hang-ups! One of his hang-ups was simultaneous orgasm, which I faked along with for a while. Then I decided I would get even. After we made love the next time, and I had faked my orgasm, and I knew he had climaxed, I waited about three minutes and urgently moaned, "Oh, you've got me so turned on, I will die if I don't come again with you now!" He looked stunned, because he assumed that when he is done, sex is done—period. He mumbled something like, "Can you wait a while?" I groaned even more urgently, "Oh please, I need you now, right now!" We stopped seeing each other after that, but it was worth it.

—A 32-year-old female executive assistant

This long-held belief in the male's ability to control the female orgasm has reinforced the view, endorsed by many women, that it is better to fake a response than to challenge the erroneous belief. To challenge it would be to open the door to the view that women are in control of their own sexual responses rather than being the passive recipients of male technique. Some married women we interviewed reported being married for over 20 years without having had a real orgasm, and faking simultaneous orgasms all those years for their husbands. The responses we received in interviews showed that younger women were less apt to be accommodating to this male need, and more likely to insist that they have orgasm when they feel ready for it—if necessary, masturbating to help the orgasm along. Some even demand orgasm, independent of whether the male has orgasm, through cunnilingus or the use of vibrators by their partners. This attitude is sharply in contrast to older women's beliefs that they should serve and gratify men in bed—a byproduct of the Victorian era of passive submission to a controlling husband. Today, intimacy and gratification often go hand-in-hand with mutual trust and caring.

We would hope that, at least for the sake of the American male, this type of revenge is not going to become a bedroom pastime for most women.

INTIMACY

Many people assume that having sex with someone promotes intimacy; to others, sex is simply sex while intimacy is something else. In our survey, we asked how respondents felt about the issue of intimacy and its perceived relationship to sex. As shown in Table 3.25, most respondents saw sex and intimacy as two different things.

It is interesting that, on this issue, there was very little difference between male and female attitudes and even less difference between career women and homemakers. Do these responses show maturity in understanding the essential differences between the complex psycho-social-emotive phenomenon of intimacy as compared to sex, which may at times be only a reflection of a physical need that disappears when satisfied? Have a majority of adults reached a level of sophistication where they recognize that intimacy may not even be required to have fulfilling sex, or that a high level of intimacy and love with a spouse is possible without a desire for sex?

Perhaps; however, the statistics in Table 3.25 are in conflict with those in Table 3.19, where over half of the men and two-thirds of the women

TABLE 3.25   **Survey Item C.12.**

SEX AND INTIMACY ARE TWO DIFFERENT THINGS:				
	Men	Women	Women-C	Women-H
N =	1,339	1,413	637	274
Strongly agree	21%	32%	36%	25%
Agree	48	43	42	49
No opinion	10	4	3	8
Disagree	16	16	16	13
Strongly disagree	5	5	3	5
Strongly agree + Agree	69%	75%	78%	74%
Disagree + Strongly disagree	21%	21%	19%	18%

believed that one-night stands were degrading. What can be considered degrading about a one-night stand or a "zipless fuck," if sex and intimacy are two different things? What more, other than intimacy, would a woman need to make one-night stands less degrading? Society has removed the former mandate that individuals must be married to have sex, and has progressed to the stage where being in love is not necessary, if one is attracted sexually to the other person. On the other hand, we constantly hear singles yearning for a "meaningful" relationship. Somewhere, the paths of intimacy and sex have to merge, to establish the milieu for growth-enhancing sexual relationships. It seems that these conflicting attitudes need much more exploration and consistency.

If sex and intimacy are often viewed as dissimilar, how are the sex roles themselves seen by today's men and women?

SEX ROLES

Strangely, to some people, great sex means sacrificing; to others, it means discomfort; to those who advocate sadomasochism, it means real pain. We saw a beginning of the sacrificial nature of sex in the responses to whether one's sex partner's pleasure was more important than one's own (Table 3.26).

Over half the men and one-third of the women surveyed (53% and 34% respectively) stated that their sex partner's pleasure was more important than their own. Are men still clinging to the old "ideal marriage" concept embodied in the sex manuals of the 1930s, 1940s, and 1950s, that the male must sacrifice his own pleasure to "awaken the female" to pleasure and thus carry out his manly sex duty? From another perspective, the ability to satisfy one's sex partner may be seen as the

TABLE 3.26   **Survey Item D.1.**

MY SEX PARTNER'S PLEASURE IS MORE IMPORTANT THAN MY OWN:			
	Men	Women	Women-C	Women-H
N =	1,340	1,396	635	274
Strongly agree	12%	6%	5%	8%
Agree	41	28	25	35
No opinion	15	10	8	11
Disagree	29	49	54	40
Strongly disagree	3	7	8	6
Strongly agree + Agree	53%	34%	30%	43%
Disagree + Strongly disagree	32%	56%	62%	46%

height of macho. For women, the survey results indicate that the traditional views—that they should cater to the demands of the lords and masters—have still not disappeared. It is somewhat encouraging to note that career women were less likely (30%) than homemakers (43%) to hold on to these traditional views. From the perspective of modern sexologists, each partner in a relationship must take responsibility for his or her own sexual satisfactions, and mutually and equally give as well as receive. For one partner to retain the dominant sexual role while the other has the passive role invites problems. Incalculable damage may have originated from the mistaken notion that "vaginal orgasm" was the desired orgasm, which perpetuated male dominant behavior in bed.

✦ *IN THEIR OWN WORDS*

> Freud certainly did a number on women with his vaginal vs. clitoral orgasm. I had no trouble having orgasm—okay, if you want to, I can call it unclassified orgasm. Then I read Freud. What a horror show. I have never felt as inadequate as a woman as I did then! I had to go into therapy with a Freudian, and he then convinced me that Freud didn't really mean it.
>
> —A 40-year-old divorcee

No one can transfer another person's orgasm and experience it as one's own; people experience their own orgasms or none at all! What can be the quality of sex between two people when it is based on subordination, with one person sublimating his or her pleasure so that the other's is enhanced? There are men who make the not-so-subtle demand on their sex partners that they, the men, *must* be able to pleasure their sex partners and to have the partners' pleasure run on the men's timetable, or the whole venture will end in disaster. To some extent, this dominance requires female sacrifice in the deprivation of sexual gratification, and creates fertile ground for female partners' faking orgasm on command. Increased sensitivity to a partner's sex needs, currently a much discussed topic, has led the move away from this kind of dominance.

In past eras, women waited for the men to lead sexually, to make the initiating moves. Female partners remained passive, showing little interest, or perhaps even awareness, of what was happening; then they were expected to seem surprised, and, at last, they reluctantly agreed to sexual activity. By contrast, many men we interviewed reported being shocked by questions from sex partners about their sexual history, their former sex partners, and their sex ailments. It is very common now for a woman to ask her sex partner whether he has condoms, and just as acceptable for her to supply condoms if he does not happen to have them immediately available. How far we have moved from the passivity of

TABLE 3.27   **Survey Item D.4.**

I ALWAYS PREFER THAT MY SEX PARTNER INITIATE SEXUAL ACTIVITY:				
	Men	Women	Women-C	Women-H
N =	1,338	1,402	632	273
Strongly agree	2%	4%	4%	4%
Agree	19	20	16	24
No opinion	25	9	4	15
Disagree	50	60	68	49
Strongly disagree	4	7	8	8
Strongly agree + Agree	21%	24%	20%	28%
Disagree + Strongly disagree	54%	67%	76%	57%

women can be seen in the responses we received regarding preference that the sex partner initiate sexual activity (see Table 3.27).

As shown in Table 3.27, for the men, this was a new idea, which most rejected. Women-H tended to reject it also, but a fair share were undecided—not yet fully liberated. Among those who preferred that their sex partners lead, there was very little difference between men and women, and the homemakers again showed their more traditional leanings, when compared to the career women (28% versus 20%).

SEX AND ORGASM FOR WOMEN

As the First Sexual Revolution gained momentum, many women began to seek better sex; pictorial sex guides, lotions, and vibrators were available over-the-counter. Scented douches and vaginal sprays became popular, and orgasm clinics were begun by women's groups and some avant-garde gynecologists, as an outgrowth of the Masters and Johnson publications. Sexual apparatuses were sold in homes to groups of women, at gatherings organized much like the waterless cooker "parties" held in the 1950s. Women wanted to begin to enjoy what they had been missing; orgasm was no longer going to be the sole domain of men. However, a woman still couldn't say No to sex without being branded "unliberated." Today's Second Sexual Revolution permits freedom, rather than coercion—even subtle coercion—to be the guide for mutuality in sex. With mutuality comes an increased quality of sharing and giving, along with the freedom to ask for both pleasure and orgasm. This is an important issue because, if both partners do not enjoy sex, then it is exploitive. Keeping this in mind, we asked our respondents how often they had orgasm during lovemaking (see Table 3.28).

TABLE 3.28   Survey Item D.6.

I HAVE ORGASM DURING LOVEMAKING:				
	Men	Women	Women-C	Women-H
N =	1,341	1,398	631	273
Always	65%	15%	18%	13%
Often	28	46	49	38
Sometimes	3	23	23	27
Rarely	2	8	4	10
Never	2	8	6	12
Always + Often	93%	61%	67%	51%
Rarely + Never	4%	16%	10%	22%

The percentages reported in Table 3.28 reflect the traditional differences between the sexes in orgasmic response training. Boys traditionally begin their masturbation at an early age and frequently masturbate to orgasm during adolescence, often with group support for masturbatory activities. Young girls, however, are not as likely to masturbate, and when they do, their feelings of guilt often affect their ability to reach orgasm. According to sex therapists and sex researchers, women are much more likely than men to report a problem with their ability to climax. Thus, it is no surprise that only 15% of the women surveyed reported that they always have an orgasm during lovemaking. The career women were slightly more likely to always experience orgasm than the homemakers were (18% versus 13%). However, when we combined the often and always responses, the picture changed. In this combined category, 93% of the men frequently reached orgasm but the percentage of women climbed to 61% and a larger gap appeared between career women's and homemakers' responses (67% versus 51%). Are career women having better sex or are they being more insistent with their partners? Perhaps even more dramatic is the fact that, while 10% of the career women reported that they never or rarely have an orgasm, more than twice as many (22%) of the homemakers were being deprived of this sexual experience in their lovemaking.

PREMARITAL SEX

In earlier generations, the traditional female offering of "I saved it for you" was a highly cherished social value. No longer; single women are openly candid about having sex. To profile the practice of premarital sex, we asked all respondents to describe their sexual experience before marriage. Their answers are shown in Table 3.29.

TABLE 3.29   **Survey Item D.10.**

I HAD SEXUAL EXPERIENCE BEFORE MARRIAGE:				
	Men	Women	Women-C	Women-H
N =	1,374	1,381	560	263
Very much	34%	22%	22%	20%
Much	33	24	27	21
Little	18	23	23	21
Very little	6	14	12	16
None	9	17	16	22
Very much + Much	67%	46%	49%	41%
Very little + None	15%	31%	28%	38%

It is not surprising that males were more likely to engage in premarital sex (67%), but women seem to have begun to close a long-time gap (46%). Perhaps equally significant is the relatively narrow difference found between the traditionally oriented homemakers (41%) and the career women (49%). Of interest is the fact that more women reported having premarital sexual experience (46%) than reported masturbating (38%; see Table 3.21). This comparison parallels the men's responses that they rarely or never masturbate, but that they have had very early and frequent full sexual relations with partners (see Tables 2.1 and 2.6). There are still women waiting for men to teach them about their sexuality, but their number is far smaller than it once was.

THE PAST THREE YEARS

What happened to our respondents' sexual activity during the 3 years preceding their response to our questionnaire, when mass media were constantly subjecting the American public to urgent warnings and dramatic headlines about AIDS and STDs (sexually transmitted diseases)? These recent years have been unlike any that American culture has had to live through sexually. Most "experts" predicted, and some reported, a slowdown and almost a stoppage of sexual interaction. Evidence that AIDS had invaded heterosexual middle-America had been verified, and we wanted to find out how our respondents had accommodated to the new threat. Our survey asked for a comparison of present sex activity with the level of activity 3 years earlier. Our results were not what the "experts" had predicted (see Table 3.30).

Approximately one-quarter of the men (24%) and one-fifth of the women (20%) had much more sex activity. When we combined those with much more and those with more sex activity, the percentages rose

TABLE 3.30   Survey Item D.9.

COMPARED TO 3 YEARS AGO, MY SEX ACTIVITY IS:				
	Men	Women	Women-C	Women-H
N =	1,344	1,413	637	274
Much more	24%	20%	18%	18%
More	20	21	19	25
Same	29	27	27	28
Less	19	19	21	16
Much less	8	13	15	13
Much more + More	44%	41%	37%	43%
Less + Much less	27%	32%	36%	29%

to 44% of men and 41% of women who said they had increased their sex activity. When we added on those engaging in the same level of sex activity, the totals were 73% of men and 68% of women who had *not* curtailed their sex activity in response to the AIDS and STD warnings. No information was available on their use of condoms or other protection during intercourse.

Perhaps not too surprisingly, the homemakers increased their sexual activity more than the career women did (43% versus 37%). We felt justified in assuming that more homemakers than career women were in ongoing monogamous relationships. Another possible factor, although not verified, may have been that, for fear of contracting AIDS, more husbands were focusing their libidinal energies on intramarital sex rather than on extramarital affairs. Americans seem to be not easily persuaded to defer or to cease sex activity in spite of any concerns they may have about AIDS and STDs. In our interviews, we learned that many of our respondents, especially those who faithfully watch nightly news programs, had begun to doubt the AIDS reports, suspecting that political motives were behind the reporting. Further research on attitudes toward AIDS, incidence of AIDS and STDs among those who increased or did not curtail their sex activities in recent years, and occurrence of AIDS among married and unmarried persons would seem a valuable source for information on future sexual conduct.

ORAL SEX

A broad-based population had been enlisted to respond to our questionnaire, and we felt that we could learn much about individuals' preferences and evaluations of certain sex acts. Three particular sex acts, each with a long history of usage, proved of interest in the analysis of our

TABLE 3.31   **Survey Item D.12.**

RATING SCALE: ORAL SEX:				
	Men	Women	Women-C	Women-H
N =	1,343	1,411	638	276
Very normal	59%	55%	65%	43%
All right	29	32	27	41
Unusual	5	4	3	3
Kinky	6	9	5	13
Never heard of it	1	—	—	—
Very normal + All right	88%	87%	92%	84%
Unusual + Kinky	11%	13%	8%	16%

data—oral sex, profane speech during intercourse ("talking dirty"), and anal sex. Would men and women feel differently about these? If so, how differently? Each is discussed here in turn.

Oral sex grew in approval during the First Sexual Revolution and the beginnings of the feminist movement, but it was practiced for many years as an exploitive demand on women. "Red-blooded men" would demand fellatio, but would often not dream of reciprocating with cunnilingus. In spite of concerns about the spread of various sexual diseases, oral sex continues to increase in popularity. Because it is a sex act that may be pleasurable but is not reproductive, it is viewed as a luxury by some, and a necessity by others; some women we interviewed reported that oral sex is the only way they can reach orgasm. The ratings we received on oral sex are indicated in Table 3.31.

Our men and women respondents believed almost equally that oral sex is very normal (59% of men and 55% of women). However, this observation must be tempered by the fact that the homemakers were far less accepting of oral sex than the career women were (65% versus 43%). Regarding this act, the traditional orientation of the homemakers seemed to far outweigh the widespread changes in attitudes in our society.

For many years before its current acceptance, oral sex was listed in medical and psychiatric books as a deviant act. Some researchers have reported that oral sex plays a role in 85% of the business of prostitutes, and many call girls, particularly those who are high-priced, now insist that their customers wear condoms if they wish to be fellated.

TALKING DIRTY

We determined that individuals who enjoy oral sex were no longer considered "freaks" or deviants, but what of those who enjoy profane speech

TABLE 3.32   Survey Item D.12.

RATING SCALE: TALKING DIRTY:				
	Men	Women	Women-C	Women-H
N =	1,341	1,410	633	267
Very normal	17%	21%	25%	16%
All right	41	36	37	38
Unusual	22	18	17	19
Kinky	19	24	21	27
Never heard of it	1	1	—	—
Very normal + All right	58%	57%	62%	54%
Unusual + Kinky	41%	42%	38%	46%

during sex? Talking dirty (scientifically called coprolalia) is a sex act that has suffered bad press. Once condemned severely by physicians and others concerned with sexual behaviors, mores, and norms, "talking dirty" has taken on new dimensions with "dial-a-porn" 900-numbers, and it appears to be one of the sexual preferences of women as well as men (see Table 3.32).

Unlike verbal humiliation, which is meant to degrade the sex partner and is seen as destructive of the recipient's self-image, talking dirty involves verbalizing the sexual fantasy and the sex action as it takes place. Men have traditionally dominated in uttering obscenities, but coprolalia is different; it is intended to enhance stimulation by verbalizing fantasies as the lovemaking takes place. It is interesting that women-C led the men surveyed, in this erotic practice (see Table 3.22).

ANAL SEX

How does the American public feel about anal sex? (Our survey item did not specify heterosexual or homosexual partners.) Anal sex is not exactly tabletalk, but virtually everyone has heard of it, and it is practiced widely enough to warrant investigation (see Table 3.33).

When we combined the very normal and all right categories, we found that 29% of the men surveyed approved of anal sex, compared with 24% of the women. Among the women, 31% of the career women approved, more than double the percentage of homemakers (15%). Anal sex has received a great deal of press coverage as a major route for the transmission of AIDS. Gay men are, of course, much more involved with anal intercourse than heterosexual couples are, and a great deal of effort has been devoted by the Gay Men's Health Crisis to the advocacy of "safe sex," using a condom when having anal sex. The popularity of anal sex

TABLE 3.33   Survey Item D.12.

RATING SCALE: ANAL SEX:				
	Men	Women	Women-C	Women-H
N =	1,332	1,402	638	272
Very normal	8%	5%	8%	3%
All right	21	19	23	12
Unusual	38	34	34	35
Kinky	31	40	33	49
Never heard of it	2	2	2	1
Very normal + All right	29%	24%	31%	15%
Unusual + Kinky	69%	74%	67%	84%

among our respondents in general came as somewhat of a surprise, but 84% of the homemakers echoed the traditional descriptions of unusual and kinky. Among the career women, who may be experiencing a greater variety of sex acts with more adventurous partners, 67%, or a classic majority, considered anal sex unusual or kinky. The same description was given by 69% of the men—an interesting statistic alongside Table 3.14's listing of responses: 22% of the men said they had engaged in homosexual acts and 78% said they had not.

SEX AND RELATIONSHIPS

One of the questions at the heart of female–male trust and relatedness is whether a spouse or partner is also a person's best friend. As shown in Table 3.34, despite an ongoing battle of the sexes (see Table 3.9), men and women are not mutually antagonistic.

Respondents were overwhelmingly affirmative that their spouse or partner was also their best friend. This item was one of very few in our study that had no difference between career women's and homemakers' responses.

TABLE 3.34   Survey Item E.1.

MY SPOUSE/PARTNER IS ALSO MY BEST FRIEND:				
	Men	Women	Women-C	Women-H
N =	770	802	328	135
Yes	85%	83%	83%	83%
No	15	17	17	17

TABLE 3.35   Survey Item G.2.

SENSUALLY, I FEEL THAT SEX IS:				
	Men	Women	Women-C	Women-H
N =	1,342	1,409	636	274
1 Deliciously sensuous	63%	51%	56%	40%
2	29	34	31	42
3	7	13	10	15
4	1	2	3	2
5 Grossly distasteful	—	—	—	1

FEELINGS ABOUT THE SENSUAL SELF

At some point, regardless of the spouse or partner a person is coupled with, an understanding of one's own libidinal drive—a sense that sex is appetizing or, conversely, is distasteful—is essential to being able to communicate and physically interact adequately in sexual relationships. We asked our respondents to rate, on a 5-point scale, their sense of their sexual self as being deliciously sensuous (1, the highest rating) or on descending levels, moving toward grossly distasteful (5, the lowest rating).

As indicated in Table 3.35, the majority of both men and women surveyed agreed that sex is deliciously sensuous. Among the women, there was a considerable difference between the percentages of career women (56%) and homemakers (40%) who gave sex the highest rating. However, adding together the two highest ratings, we found that 92% of the men and 85% of the women agreed with the sensual nature of sex, even if they were reluctant to endorse "deliciously." The gap between career women's and homemakers' ratings remained wide at the second level and finally narrowed to 5% at a rating of 3, the midpoint between deliciously sensuous and grossly distasteful. Only one homemaker found sex grossly distasteful.

SEXUAL ACTIVITY

In this era of change, with its attendant sexual confusion, we felt it important to ask how individuals saw their personal sexuality and how they would rank themselves in sexual activity. Our ratings ranged, at several levels, from very active to inactive, as shown in Table 3.36.

We found only a moderate difference (10%) between men and women when we combined the very active and active ratings, and even less difference (4%) between career women and homemakers. Roughly one-third

TABLE 3.36   Survey Item G.3.

I CONSIDER MYSELF TO BE SEXUALLY:				
	Men	Women	Women-C	Women-H
N =	1,341	1,399	636	273
Very active	20%	13%	13%	12%
Active	36	33	35	32
Average	32	29	29	31
Below average	7	16	14	16
Inactive	5	9	9	9
Very active + Active	56%	46%	48%	44%
Below average + Inactive	12%	25%	23%	25%

of our respondents, across all groups, felt they were average sexually. When we combined below average and inactive, the women were more than twice as likely as the men to rate themselves at this level. Did these ratings reflect the reality of their behavior or a negative self-image, held by many women, when they compared themselves to the fiery females on soap operas and prime-time television? We could not dismiss a possible connection between this negative self-image and the high percentages of women who felt they were not functioning sexually at their biological maximum (see Table 3.37), although the two results could not be scientifically correlated.

BIOLOGICAL SEXUAL MAXIMUM

Biological sexual maximum, a new concept that we have utilized as a working concept, is the level of sexual fulfillment that a person perceives as his or her physical peak. In a self-appraisal, how satisfied is the person with his or her sexuality, as evidenced by sexual functioning and orgasms? When we asked our respondents whether they were at their

TABLE 3.37   Survey Item G.4.

ARE YOU FUNCTIONING AT YOUR BIOLOGICAL MAXIMUM SEXUALLY?				
	Men	Women	Women-C	Women-H
N =	1,337	1,392	626	267
Yes	56%	44%	36%	48%
No	44	56	64	52

biological maximum sexually, the men's positive response was significantly greater than the women's (see Table 3.37): 56% of the men and 44% of the women responded affirmatively. The 12% difference between affirmative career women (36%) and homemakers (48%) was significant and puzzling. Data in Table 3.28 indicated that the homemakers were not having more satisfying sex than the career women. Were the women-H more physically tired, so that their bodies did not desire more sex, or were their expectations lower and more easily fulfilled? The career women may have had a more sophisticated capacity for libidinal desire than they were achieving; or, the women who were full-time homemakers may have been truly more contented. Another possibility is that the career women felt that they were committing so much of their resources and energy to their work that they were slighting their personal—and sexual—lives, or, quite simply, they may have had higher expectations for themselves as sex partners.

What about those who responded that they were not functioning at their biological maximum sexually? Assuming that people who are not functioning maximally also seek sexual fulfillment, are they seriously deficient in their biological or their psychological sexual function? This serious question is not examined sufficiently in the existing literature. We therefore followed with a quantitative question addressed to respondents who had answered that they were functioning sexually below their perceived maximum (see Table 3.38).

Almost half of the men (46%) and 58% of the women responded that they were at least 50% below their sexual maximum. As indicated in previous tables in this chapter, the career women surveyed seemed to be less satisfied with parts of their sex lives than the homemakers (59% versus 53%). Based on the interviews we had with our female respondents, we concluded that, on the whole, women are finally awakening to the world of sexual interaction and are credibly and increasingly asking for but not always receiving sexual fulfillment. It had been commonplace for

TABLE 3.38　　　　　　　　　　　　　　　　　　　　　**Survey Item G.5.**

HOW MUCH BELOW MAXIMUM SEXUAL POTENTIAL ARE YOU?			
	Men	Women	Women-C	Women-H
N =	589	783	400	138
10% below	19%	17%	17%	16%
25% below	35	25	24	31
50% below	33	34	33	27
100% below	13	24	26	26
At least 50% below	46%	58%	59%	53%

a man to end a relationship with a woman because she "just wasn't good in bed," but rare for a woman to drop a man for the same reason. However, changes are underway: we learned in our interviews that more women are terminating their relationships with men whose sexual functioning is not adequate, and both men and women are having extramarital affairs for supplementary sexual activity.

THE NUMBERS GAME

There is no way to gain a fully objective appreciation of the totality of American sexual behavior without knowing how many actual sexual partners people tend to have. We asked: "How many different individuals (including spouses) have you had sexual relations with?" Table 3.39 summarizes the replies we received.

Traditionally, narratives of great numbers of sexual encounters have been part of men's numbers game—how many women they "had in the saddle," or how many notches they had on their belts. With the emergence of sexual equality, having frequent sex partners is no longer only a male prerogative. As shown in Table 3.39, only 1% of the men and 3% of the women we surveyed reported never having had a sex partner. Among the women, 4% of the homemakers claimed never to have had sex. Some of these respondents may have been "virgin wives"—women who marry for convenience, with the understanding that they will not have sex with their husbands because of their husbands' homosexuality or lack of libido. Other homemakers may have been women who had assumed the role of homemaker after parental death.

TABLE 3.39   **Survey Item G.7.**

HOW MANY DIFFERENT INDIVIDUALS (INCLUDING SPOUSES) HAVE YOU HAD SEXUAL RELATIONS WITH?			
	Men	Women	Women-C	Women-H
N =	1,332	1,391	628	262
None	1%	3%	1%	4%
1 to 10	28	42	33	48
11 to 30	32	39	46	32
31 to 60	21	9	10	11
61 to 100	8	3	3	3
101 +	10	4	7	2
1 to 30	60%	81%	79%	80%
61 and over	18%	7%	10%	5%

Our respondents were in all age groups, from 18-year-olds to octogenarians; many were from prior generations, among whom large numbers of sex partners were unheard of. Considering the relatively free sexual environment of the late 1960s and early 1970s, if we had limited the sample for Table 3.39 to persons under 55 years of age, we probably would have had a much higher response in the categories of greater numbers of sex partners per respondent.

Ten or fewer sex partners were reported by 28% of the men and 42% of the women. In comparing the women, it comes as no surprise that more of the homemakers (48%), as compared with career women (33%), reported fewer than 10 partners. The most dramatic elements of the numbers game are seen at the high end. Those reporting many sex partners (more than 30) begin to show the male–female difference more vividly: 39% of the men but only 16% of the women are in this combined group. It is noteworthy that, among those who claimed 30 or more partners, we found very little difference between career women (20%) and homemakers (16%). A comparatively small group of men (10%) and women (4%) reported having had more than 100 sex partners. Our interviews indicated that, for these persons, numbers were important; many of them accumulated huge numbers of sex partners in group-sex activities. At the highest end, we found three women and nine men, all between ages 38 and 65, who each reported having had 1,000 sex partners. One woman remarked that she was a sex surrogate, so sex was her business. In contrast, a 20-year-old Midwestern woman critically remarked that she is a virgin in a society that does not seem to appreciate virgins, and that she was not the only one: "There are a good number of us left in the Midwest."

LEARNING ABOUT SEX

Sex education in the public schools has become a highly charged emotional issue in the past decade. With the problem of AIDS, and the conflict surrounding the teaching of "safe sex" and the distribution of condoms in some school districts, sex education is a more explosive issue than ever. It is often disguised by schools under course titles such as health education, family life instruction, and so on. Many of the same groups that are against contraception and abortion also oppose sex education. MOMS (Mothers Opposed to Mandatory Sex) and other small organizations object to children's learning about sex in school, even though all studies have shown that there is no other facility in society that can offer this education. The home and the church have not filled an increasing need. We were not surprised by the responses we received to our survey question on sex education (see Table 3.40). Women and men in all groups responded overwhelmingly with a definite Yes to sex education in the schools.

TABLE 3.40

SEX EDUCATION SHOULD BE TAUGHT IN THE SCHOOLS:			
	Men	Women	Women-C	Women-H
N =	1,341	1,412	636	282
Definitely yes	90%	90%	93%	89%
Maybe	9	9	7	10
Not at all	1	1	—	1

Sex education is not universally taught in the United States; where it is part of the curriculum, it is of relatively recent vintage. Thus, most Americans have not had the benefit of learning about sex from qualified sources and helpful adults. We wanted to know where our respondents picked up their knowledge, so we included a survey item intended to tap that information. (See Table 3.41.)

The men and the women who responded had received their sex information in different places. Significantly, more women than men said they had learned about sex at home. Is it easier for parents to talk to daughters about sex? Probably not. More likely, the first menses created a necessary situation in which the mother provided sex instruction to the daughter. For fear of their daughters' pregnancy, many parents feel more compelled to provide information and limitations to adolescent girls than to boys. One-quarter of the women and one-fifth of the men received sex instruction at school. For reasons that are not clear, more of the homemakers received sex education in school (28%) than did career women (19%). Was this because the more traditional women were more likely to go to religious schools, where sex rules and "don'ts" were taught, and they interpreted this as "learning about sex"? We cannot verify this possibility. The church itself was cited by only 2% of the

TABLE 3.41

I LEARNED ABOUT SEX FROM:			
	Men	Women	Women-C	Women-H
N =	1,339	1,411	636	281
Home	25%	40%	40%	40%
School	20	25	19	28
Church	2	2	1	2
Streets	53	33	40	30

women and men. "The streets" provided instruction for 53% of the men and 33% of the women. Considering the bravado and the macho attitudes of young boys in groups, we continue to wonder how much misinformation, mixed with sexist thinking, contributed to the destructive attitudes toward the marital relationship that men are accused of today, and encouraged lifelong insensitivity to women's needs.

WHAT PEOPLE DO SEXUALLY: IS IT NORMAL?

With the acceptance of a variety of sex acts today, is there a preferred way in which each individual enjoys sex and achieves orgasm? Variety in sex as an antidote to boredom is an ongoing theme in "sophisticated" circles and in the media. Respected, nonpornographic magazines now carry ads for sexual appliances, as well as for books, videos, and films intended to stimulate sexual interest and promote new techniques. Our research had led us to believe that, although most people have preferences, they are flexible, receptive to new techniques, and able to accommodate other sexual activity and get gratification from it. To determine the relative incidence of particular preferences, we posed an open-ended statement in our survey and listed several options (see Table 3.42).

Intercourse was preferred by all groups, more so by men (82%) than by women (69%). Among women, the preference for intercourse was different between career women (65%) and homemakers (81%), reflecting, we believe, the more traditional and conservative views that consistently appeared in the homemakers' responses. Oral sex was the preference of more than twice the number of career women, as compared to the homemakers. Interestingly, despite the frequently reported belief that many

TABLE 3.42   **Survey Item H.22.**

MY PREFERRED WAY TO ACHIEVE ORGASM IS:			
	Men	Women	Women-C	Women-H
N =	1,338	1,398	628	266
Intercourse	82%	69%	65%	81%
Masturbation	5	8	9	4
Oral sex	10	18	23	10
Sadomasochism	—	1	1	1
Anal sex	2	—	—	—
Fantasy	—	—	—	1
Fetish	1	2	1	1
Other	—	2	1	2

men go to prostitutes because they prefer oral sex and their wives won't cooperate, far fewer men than women surveyed preferred oral sex for their own gratification. The other options got very small ratings, except for masturbation. More women (8%) than men (5%) preferred this activity, a result that may come as a surprise to traditionalists. Many women we interviewed reported that the certainty of orgasm from masturbation, which they could perform alone or with a partner, was the reason it was their prime choice. A recent practice involves an exhibitionistic masturbatory experience in which one partner masturbates while the other watches. Men seem especially drawn to this practice. In our interviews, many male respondents admitted that watching their female sex partners masturbate to orgasm was a great turn-on for them.

As diversity becomes widespread and tradition is weakened, average individuals not only become aware of different sex acts that they didn't know about before but also become more open to experimentation. They may initially question the normalcy of something they had always believed was not OK, but when they learn that many others—perhaps friends or neighbors, or the nice people on the TV talk shows—engage in "bizarre" sex acts, what they had regarded as "normal" takes on new content. We queried our respondents about their feelings regarding their specific sexual practices, offering a range of possible responses (see Table 3.43).

As might be expected, all groups saw themselves as completely normal or normal, but, of the four groups, the career women consistently were the most accepting of their sex practices as completely normal. In both our interviews and the responses to our questionnaire, people who had the most diverse and esoteric sex practices overwhelmingly rated themselves as normal. The need to see oneself as normal is obviously very strong.

TABLE 3.43   **Survey Item H.23.**

I REGARD MY SEX PRACTICES AS:			
	Men	Women	Women-C	Women-H
N =	1,344	1,406	633	268
Completely normal	55%	59%	63%	54%
Normal	40	36	34	41
Slightly odd	4	3	2	3
Unusual	1	1	—	1
Kinky	—	1	1	1
Completely normal + Normal	95%	95%	97%	95%
Unusual + Kinky	1%	2%	1%	2%

THE BOTTOM LINE

To almost all who venture out into sexual partnerships in spite of to-day's warning headlines, there is always the need to balance sexual gratification against concern about contracting sexually transmitted diseases. There has been a great deal of speculation as to how Americans handle this balancing. Our survey included a statement to probe the depth of our respondents' concern.

As shown in Table 3.44, a minimum of 79%, across all groups, were seriously concerned. We found it interesting that the women-H, who do not work outside of the home and who have consistently reported having fewer sexual partners and less varied sex in general, were more worried about the threat of sexually transmitted diseases than the more out-wardly active women-C. In the very much category, homemakers (70%) were considerably more concerned than career women (59%). Their degree of concern is an example of a recurring theme that we identified in the course of our study: facts and fears were often only thinly bound together by reality or appropriateness. In our interviews, we learned that emotions and lust, more often than reason, led individuals into whatever sexual activity they engaged in. We were not surprised by the responses; a high degree of concern was to be expected, in light of heavy media attention and hype regarding STDs. However, most Americans have yet to realize that their concern alone will not be protection when they engage in risky sexual behavior. Prudence and passion may seem to be strange bedfellows, but that pairing *is* the bottom line. Most people said in our interviews that they were now "prudent" in their sexual choices and practices; men and women often cooperated in new ways. Men who felt that a condom would not sufficiently protect them from disease wore two and even three condoms. Women who did not trust the condom inserted their diaphragms with the most powerful antispermicidal

TABLE 3.44   **Survey Item H.28.**

I AM CONCERNED ABOUT SEXUALLY TRANSMITTED DISEASES (STDs):			
	Men	Women	Women-C	Women-H
N =	1,345	1,411	638	272
Very much	59%	60%	59%	70%
Much	27	20	20	13
Unsure	5	4	5	6
Slightly	5	10	11	5
Not at all	4	6	5	6
Very much + Much	86%	80%	79%	83%
Slightly + Not at all	9%	16%	16%	11%

compound they could find. The men and women who spoke openly to each other about this matter—a common practice now—reported that they were cooperating with their partners for safety's sake. When making love, they would ensure that the man used two condoms that had been pretested with water pressure by the female partner. For her part, the woman would wear her diaphragm and jelly, which the male lover would check for correct insertion. These procedures were often cited as an example of "trust." The love affair with sex goes on—maybe more prudently, but as passionately as the human libido needs.

Some respondents complained that all these precautions took the fun and spontaneity out of lovemaking; others saw the precautions as enabling them to relax and enjoy the sex experience with an easy mind. For some others, the procedures of the exercise in trust, the "playing doctor," and similar preparations for the sexual encounter heightened its eroticism and increased their excitement. Married couples who trust each other's fidelity, especially those married for over 7 years, are spared all this preliminary checking activity.

SEXUAL HARASSMENT

As 1991 drew to a close, the Senate Judiciary Committee's hearings on the candidacy of Clarence Thomas for an appointment to the Supreme Court swore in a surprise witness. Anita Hill, a law professor, brought unprecedented attention to the candidate, the committee members (all male), and the advise-and-consent process, when she accused Judge Thomas of sexual harassment in the workplace. Not only activists in the women's movement, but many women who had been nonpolitical made opposition to sexual harassment a cause célèbre. A number of issues were raised in regard to sexual harassment, but the chief issue of the hearings, which drew enough interest to displace daytime TV soaps, was credibility. Many women complained about Anita Hill's treatment by the all-male committee, which sat virtually as a jury and captioned the issue as whom should we believe, the man or the woman? Most women felt that the members of the committee exhibited a typical male bias of believing the man and not the woman. This bias, as much as the alleged sexual harassment, was galling to women across the political spectrum. We decided to probe the extent of sexual harassment in the workplace, and received the responses shown in Table 3.45.

A considerable number of respondents—45% of women and 19% of men—claimed to have been harassed on their jobs. In our interviews, the men attributed the harassment they experienced to both heterosexual and homosexual individuals; the women ascribed their harassment almost entirely to men. In an age of liberation, it is interesting that an issue so broad gained national attention so accidentally. Was there an underlying awareness of widespread sexual harassment, on the part of

TABLE 3.45   Survey Item G.10.

I HAVE EXPERIENCED SEXUAL HARASSMENT ON MY JOB:		
	Men	Women
N =	1,341	1,416
Yes	19%	45%
No	81%	55%

women, who had been loath to complain about harassment or found no receptive audience when they did? That assumption is readily supported by the intensity and speed of reaction to the charges. Sexual harassment has become a household topic across America, despite Anita Hill's failed efforts to prevent Judge Thomas from becoming Justice Thomas.

SUMMING UP

Today, men and women are freer than ever to explore their sexual beings in or out of marriage. Their transformed sex roles, born of the women's movement and the sexual revolutions, facilitate heightened communication about their mutual satisfaction. With a majority of women now working outside of the home, and the new institution of the two-paycheck family, career women are very different from the women who do not work outside of the home. In terms of sexual outlook, practice, and identification, career women often take roles that have traditionally been regarded as male roles. What we call the Second Sexual Revolution, in which these career women have evolved and matured as a very distinct entity, may well bring differences between the two groups of women that are as great as or greater than the differences between women and men.

As American society at last allows women to abandon assent in favor of assertiveness, and permits men to forgo machismo for equality, the gender gap may start to narrow, beginning an era of new acceptance and understanding between the sexes, at least in the sexual realm. More and more married partners are developing interrelationships of trust without the traditional formality and security that were formerly associated with marriage. However, these new agenda roles face some hard decisions: in an era of two-career couples, women and men must learn how to make their newly structured marriages beat the odds of divorce, all the while juggling quality time together with the pressures of financial responsibility. Even with the threat of disease, Americans are still expressing their healthy sexualities—perhaps a bit more prudently, but with undiminished passion, love, respect, and frequency.

CHAPTER FOUR

Sexual Deviance

SOME SIGNIFICANT FINDINGS ABOUT SEXUAL DEVIANCE

✦ 6% of the men and 3% of the women surveyed reported some personal experience with cross dressing; 14% of the men and 11% of the women had had some personal experience with sadomasochism.

✦ 35% of the men and 23% of the women agreed that making love is the best way to make up after an argument. However, 51% of the men and 65% of the women surveyed disagreed.

✦ 17% of the men and 8% of the women responding to our questionnaire thought group sex was all right or very normal; 43% of the men and 68% of the women thought it was kinky.

✦ 2% of the men reported personal experience with adult sex with children. None of the women reported having had this experience.

QUESTIONNAIRE SUBJECTS TABULATED IN THIS CHAPTER

	Table
Sadomasochism	4.1
Arguments and Lovemaking	4.2
Pain and Pleasure in Sex	4.3
Dominance/Bondage	4.4
Cross Dressing	4.5
Fetishes	4.6
Verbal Humiliation	4.7
Golden Showers	4.8
Brown Showers	4.9
Necrophilia	4.10
Group Sex	4.11
Adult Sex with Children	4.12

Freud described deviants as "poor devils who have to pay a high price for their limited pleasures," but much of what he considered deviant has become part of the everyday sex lives of many Americans. What is deviance, or *paraphilia*, its new synonym in the professional literature? Most simply, deviance is the violation of society's rules, norms, laws, or customs. Sexual deviance ranges from a personally idiosyncratic routine of having to use a particular perfume or needing to experience the feel of silk, in order to turn on sexually, to the practice of dangerous, life-threatening sex preferences, such as simulated (and, on occasion, accidentally completed) asphyxiation by hanging, to become turned on.

Is deviance necessarily bad for the individual or the sex partner, or for society at large? Some types of deviance are obviously criminal, harmful, wrong, and immoral—for example, rape, or the sexual molestation of young children. However, other types of deviance are relatively harmless and almost never impinge on anyone else's rights or liberties—for example, the man who gets some pleasure out of wearing his wife's panties under his three-piece business suit. Kinky, yes! Harmful? Probably not. This chapter examines and discusses the differences between the harmless and the damaging kinds of deviance. Harmless habits that affect one personally, but do not make demands on one's partner, tend to be limited in terms of their impact and potential peril. Sociologists and historians, most notably the classic theorist Emil Durkheim, have told us that, when societies are experiencing rapid change or are in a state of decline or decay, people adhere less and less to the societies' moral norms. Thus, we may infer that, if the rates of deviant acts begin to increase in a society, the increase may reflect, or herald, some major changes in the basic value structure of the society—in some cases, changes of which the society's members may not yet be aware.

Students of sociology and social change are aware of the axiom that today's deviance may well be tomorrow's norm. The present widespread approval of the practice of masturbation and oral sex is an example of a deviance of yesteryear that has changed into a norm. The definitions of what is or is not deviant behavior are established by various legitimate institutions, the most important being government and religion. In a pluralistic society such as ours, however, there are often wide differences between what may be considered deviant by government and what is considered deviant by religion or among different religions. The deeply emotional conflict and debate over abortion illustrate this point. Let us suppose that an adult woman is a devout member of a religion that considers abortion to be a sin or even murder. If she knowingly and willingly participates in an abortion, she may legitimately be described or labeled as a deviant, even though there are no statutes prohibiting abortion. However, if her religion does not define abortion as "abnormal" or "wrong," then she would not be considered deviant. This apparent contradiction comes about because deviance is always defined by the legitimate authorities or institutions. Thus, the definition of an act as deviant should always include the qualifying statement "relative to this or that religion or group or state."

What other legitimate institutions can define deviance? Perhaps the best known is the American Psychiatric Association (APA), which periodically publishes *Diagnostic and Statistical Manual of Mental Disorders* (DSM).[1] Currently, revised third edition is the authority for reference; a fourth edition is being prepared. How does the DSM determine what is deviant? It depends on the advice of a group of clinicians and scholars who examine different patterns of human behavior that some people have identified as "harmful"—either to oneself or to others. If a behavior pattern regularly consists of specific acts, it is considered an identifiable and definable syndrome and its characteristics are stated in the DSM. Behavior that most people vaguely disapprove of—for example, drinking excessively and habitually to the point of alcohol dependence—becomes categorized as an illness or disease or emotional disorder. For other behaviors, such as cashing a forged-signature check or cheating on our income tax, we do not need the APA to tell us that we have acted deviantly. Criminal codes in the different states, or the Internal Revenue Service, have made it clear that these are deviant and punishable acts. Deviance may be as minor as picking one's nose in a restaurant—which violates only traditional customs—or as emotionally charged and dangerous as treason in wartime.

There is even "good" deviance. When the founding fathers of our country broke many English laws by refusing to obey the orders of the English government and its legitimate designees, they were acting in a criminal manner, just as all revolutionary leaders do; they were "deviants." The great religions of history were founded and nurtured by people acting in defiance of established authority and refusing to obey existing religious or secular law. Similarly, great artistic movements were invariably begun by painters who refused to paint the "right" way and acted on what they believed in. They often were called "weird," "crazy," and even "dangerous."

However, for most people, the term "deviant" seems most closely identified with sexual practices. For sexual norms, Western culture has looked to religion, the institution that has historically considered the regulation of sexual behavior to be its realm. It is the province of Western religion to regulate and interpret the principles and commandments of the Bible and to set up ideals of what is thought to be God's will for human behavior. Government shares religion's concern with sex, but for its own reasons: social order and population expansion. Government sees a need to regulate sexual activity in order to provide economically for the continuity of the family into future generations.

A discussion of the many moral norms relating to sexuality is outside the scope of this book, but we should be aware that they have varied over the centuries and have meant different things in different places. Onanism (the practice of withdrawal before ejaculation) was condemned in the Bible (Genesis 38: 9–10) and punishable by death, as were male homosexual relations (Leviticus 18: 22 and 20: 13). Sexual moral norms are not absolute and constant among the major religions or in the history of religion and theology. The mores, as well as the standards and norms, reflected in the definitions issued by the mental health community have mirrored the enormous flux in the religious community with respect to sexual norms. Perhaps the most illustrative example is masturbation, which, in one generation's lifetime, has moved from being classified as an abnormal behavior that could result in madness, blindness, and impotence, to gradual acceptance as normal for children and teenagers. Today, it is the position of many therapists that masturbation is necessary and healthy for the developing sexual being and may be carried on in the marital relationship as well. Another sexual behavior that was formerly considered an illness is homosexuality. Psychotherapy once tried to "cure" the homosexual individual. However, several years ago, the American Psychiatric Association dropped the listing of homosexuality as an "illness"; it is now generally considered merely a variant of normal sexual behavior.

Regardless of the APA's or the formal institutional churches' classifications, most people have some strong views about what is or is not deviant. By and large, it seems that the commonly held view (rather than the institutionally defined view) is that deviant acts are found to be offensive and are thought to challenge basic established beliefs about sex and religion. People who have strong views about deviance often think that their views are shared by the majority of the population, and, because they view sexual "deviance" to be of such an unusual nature, they may feel compelled to attract attention to the problem. However, attitudes toward sexual practices and beliefs have been changing rapidly in the United States in recent decades, as a result of a broadening of American values and considerations, discussed in Chapter 1. Because of the rapidity of change of those values, it has been difficult for the mental health profession to keep pace.

Many sexual practices that were once deemed wrong or sick or forbidden appear to be commonplace today. What happens when many people are breaking the traditional rules and restrictions? If "everybody is doing it," or, in statistical terms, if the majority of people are engaging in a particular behavior, does that mean that the norm is changing and the behavior will now be considered "normal" and permissible? That cannot be answered easily. If we use lying as an example, we know that just about everybody will lie on occasion, but that does not mean that lying is morally correct and should not be condemned whenever it occurs. Similarly with sexual behavior: whether something is morally right or "normal," in the sense of being healthy or not dangerous, is for the legitimate institutions to determine. In some instances, the determination or consideration of changes in formal definitions reflects changing behavior, so it is very useful to first learn the extent of the behavior. For example, although premarital sex by consenting adults is still a violation of the norm in most religions, the American people seem not to view this practice with the same negativity that was prevalent several decades ago. In a sense, the public acceptance and widespread manifestation of this behavior seem to have reduced the anxiety these couples might have, in an earlier time, felt about their personal sexual normalcy.

Sexual normalcy appears to be a concern of many Americans, and for good reason. Many of us believe that we have moved, as a nation, from a solid, stable, consensual set of sexual norms—those of "the good old days"—to sexual chaos. This view merely romanticizes the past. Doubts about what is sexually normal, and conflicts between behavior and belief, have, as far as we can learn, been present in our history from the days of the Pilgrims. Individuals in government and the churches, past and present, have decided for themselves and for others what is *sexually moral and immoral*. Our intent here is to probe the limits of what is *sexually normal and deviant*, and to determine where one ends and the other begins.

In presenting a representation of deviances at a variety of levels, we found that it was best to be selective, not exhaustive. We did not include in our questionnaire such widely practiced sex interactions, commonly thought to be deviant, as exhibitionism, voyeurism, and frotteurism. We wanted to offer our respondents a set of deviances within a wide range of popularity, but found that we tended to choose practices that psychologically distanced the partners from each other. After consulting with sociologists, psychologists, and religious leaders, we delineated a variety of sexual practices that are engaged in by individuals, couples, and groups in America today. A major consideration in categorizing sex acts is the possibility of either partner's suffering hurt, pain, or danger. If no one is hurt or bothered by a behavior, should we consider it deviant? We reviewed behaviors ranging from the perfectly "normal," socially valued and accepted sexual practices, such as married, heterosexual, male-superior intercourse (the "missionary position," with the male on top) to some of the most extremely disapproved of behaviors, such as necrophilia (sex with dead bodies). In between, we considered various acts of deviance based on their degree of societal and individual disapproval. Practices that may be offensive to some people, but are not harmful unless they are coercive, were included in our review.

We arrived at two categories of deviant acts. The first consists of acts that are frequently disapproved of yet widely practiced: sadomasochism, dominance/bondage, cross dressing, fetishes, and verbal humiliation.

In the second category are acts that few people would openly acknowledge practicing because they are strongly disapproved of by society. These include: golden and brown showers, necrophilia, group sex, and adult sex with children. We must also point out that deviant sex includes anything that is nonconsensual: rape, forcible acts, and abuse of all kinds.

Even a harmless practice becomes damaging if it is obsessive. Trying something for a kinky kick is one thing, but being unable to perform sexually without the kinky behavior becomes something entirely different.

The Rating Scale we used to elicit our respondents' personal evaluations of our list of sexual practices was as follows (see survey item D.12, in Appendix B):

A. Very normal
B. All right
C. Unusual
D. Kinky
E. Never heard of it

Our purposes in offering these alternatives were:

1. To assess the awareness of and opinion about each of these practices among the general public;
2. To discover how many people were engaging in these acts in the different segments of the general population.

A number of response checks were built into the questionnaire to obtain maximum accuracy. For example, survey item H.22 (see Appendix B) lists four deviant practices, one of which repeats, in different wording, a question that is related to the Rating Scale. Other, similar questions were inserted in different contexts, in several sections of the questionnaire, where respondents were asked to supply information about various sexual issues.

SEXUAL PRACTICES

Survey item D.12 (see Appendix B), the source of our Rating Scale on sexual practices, lists four behaviors that we have not classified as being sexually deviant: oral sex, anal sex, masturbation, and talking dirty. Discussion of these practices, and related tabulations of respondents' attitudes and behaviors, can be found in Chapter 3. In the sections that follow here, we evaluate the responses we received on the remaining items in survey item D.12. As noted above, these are the behaviors we have categorized as deviant:

Sadomasochism	Golden showers
Dominance/bondage	Brown showers
Cross dressing	Necrophilia
Fetishes	Group sex
Verbal humiliation	Adult sex with children

Sadomasochism

There are two roles in this pleasure-in-pain practice: the sadist and the masochist. Individuals who practice sadomasochism generally prefer one role instead of the other, but will often take whatever role is available.

A *sadist* is an individual who inflicts harm and/or pain on another individual in order to gain sexual and/or psychological satisfaction. The word originates from the name of the Marquis de Sade (1740–1814), who was known for the cruelty and brutality he inflicted, especially on women.

The *masochist* achieves sexual gratification by experiencing pain, whether anticipatory, immediately before, or during the sex act. Sometimes, receiving pain is all that is desired, and it takes the place of sexual relationships. The term masochist derives from the name of a 19th-century Austrian novelist, Leopold von Sacher-Masoch (d. 1895). If the masochist is a male, there is often a need to undergo the masochistic experience while dressed in women's clothes. The inflicted pain might range from a simple flagellation to a serious beating that leaves marks on the subject's body. There are houses of bondage that have every conceivable type of apparatus for delivering "discipline." Not only does the masochist have to receive the precise type of punishment he seeks, but he also must be able to tolerate the pain and wring pleasure from the humiliation related to the pain. There have been reported cases of older men, or men with heart trouble, who have died during their requested physical torment and humiliation.

Love bites, more commonly known as "hickeys," are believed by many therapists to be a mild and innocent form of sadomasochism. Other therapists see them as expressions of deeply rooted unconscious drives that relate pain to pleasure.

Dominance/Bondage

Dominance can sometimes be only symbolic, but most often it is physically acted out as a sexual performance in which one partner has total physical and emotional control of the other. Suppliers of apparatus, and magazines catering to dominance/bondage (D/B) aficionados, claim that approximately 8% to 10% of American households have some D/B apparatus, in its simplest form (ropes, to tie the husband or wife to the bed), and practice some of the many varieties of play acting that offer dominant and submissive experiences.

Dominants are the people who place much emphasis on or have a need for the practice of dominance and bondage, and who play the dominant role in the interaction. They often own a great deal of apparatus and know many ritualistic modes of carrying out this sexual practice. Equipment may include masks and ropes or chains, which are used to render the partner helpless. A woman who specializes in this practice is called a dominitrix. The psychological connections between dominance and rape cannot go unnoticed.

Submissives are those who are restrained during the domination act. For some individuals, being tied up is exciting enough to give them spontaneous orgasm. For others, it relieves their guilt feeling about voluntarily performing a sexual act (which, they were taught as children, was "bad" and "dirty"), even with their spouse. Many people who practice D/B consider it an ultimate sexual experience; for others, it is just another variant in a wide repertoire of sexual activity.

Cross Dressing

Also known as transvestism, cross dressing is more frequently practiced by males (although this fact is greatly confusing, because women may dress as men in our society without any condemnation or negative connotation). On the streets of big cities, transvestites may be known as "screaming queens." They obtain sexual pleasure by wearing the clothing of the other sex. Some transvestites may masturbate to orgasm while in the garb of the other sex. Young boys who are drawn to transvestism may find that they need to utilize an item of female clothing, such as panties, bras, garters, or stockings, to achieve arousal as they get older. A small but significant minority utilize stockings in near-asphyxiation scenarios involving self-strangulation. They can achieve orgasm only at the height of asphyxiation, and then are able to cut themselves down without succumbing. However, in recent years, in a number of cases, almost all involving teenage boys, the individuals waited too long and died from strangulation during or shortly after orgasm. Their deaths have been termed "autoerotic suicides."

Fetishes

Fetishes are primarily male sexual agendas. A fetishist is quite removed from the person who is the object of his sexual desire. He is interested in the "sexual object" only through a displacement to some item of the person's clothing, such as a shoe, a stocking, or underwear, or to a body part. The most common fetishes are feet, silk, and rubber. There are two major types of fetishists, hard and soft.

The hard fetishist is involved with leather and rubber objects. For the stimulation process to work, the object must be near enough to be touched or the sex partner must wear the object to induce sexual excitement.

The soft fetishist prefers fur, feathers, silk, and similar objects and materials.

Fetishists often have a need to obtain the desired objects by stealing, whether from a family member or a store. Usually, a fetishist becomes attached to an object, such as his mother's panties, that is taboo, which helps to further enhance his sense of excitement. Unlike the transvestite, the fetishist does not need to wear the clothes or other object; rather, he craves any sensory perception of the object. Touching, holding, seeing, or smelling it are enough.

Verbal Humiliation

An individual who derives pleasure from this behavior is given a very abusive, crude, and thorough tongue lashing by his or her partner. Verbal humiliation can accompany other behaviors, and is often a component of sadomasochism. Some individuals—and some prostitutes—specialize in this area. Two, or more, parties who know each other in detail may be involved. To be effective, the humiliator must know the submissive well enough that the invective can be accurate, and therefore hurtful. A frequent theme is to condemn the submissive for wanting the forbidden sex in the first place, and to make very accurate references to the forbidden—but lusted for—person whom the submissive covets. Several madams whom we interviewed, who operate houses of bondage, indicated that they never perform humiliation until they have had some discussions with the "John," so that they know how to be most effective. In those instances when a dominant does not humiliate intensely enough, the submissive may become enraged and humiliate the dominant instead, hoping thereby to infuriate the dominant to the point of heavy retribution.

From the viewpoint of psychoanalysis, those who find verbal humiliation a must are carrying a huge burden of guilt. The struggle to successfully function sexually requires that the guilt be addressed each time there is a potential sexual interaction. Because the forbidden thoughts, or prior experiences, hamper any kind of effective or gratifying sex functioning, they must be dealt with before any sexual action can begin. Therefore, the verbal humiliation marks the beginning of the sexual interaction, almost as an integral part of the sex act. Verbal humiliation serves as a symbolic punishment that cleanses the individual of the guilt; having paid the price with the humiliation, he or she can then indulge sexually. For many submissives, the discussion of the guilt is in itself an obsessive turn-on that colors the whole sex act.

Golden Showers

The medical term for golden showers is urolagnia. In advertisements that practitioners of deviant sex place to find each other, it is colloquially called "the waterworks." In this practice, individuals achieve orgasm while being urinated on. Usually, men are the recipients in the interaction. Because few men can persuade their wives or girlfriends to accommodate them, most seekers of golden showers must go to a callgirl they can count on. Their excitement has two sources: the sound of the woman's voiding and the sight of the yellow stream of urine. A good deal of preparation must be done beforehand by the donor. When a regular customer (these clients remain as regular customers) calls, one to two hours ahead, the prostitute quickly drinks as much as eight to ten beers, or the equivalent, and retains the fluid until the customer arrives and the elaborate ritual action takes place. A woman needs a healthy, strong bladder to succeed in this practice.

Brown Showers

The scientific term for brown showers is coprolagnia; those involved in this deviance, which is almost exclusively favored by men, achieve orgasm by being defecated on. There are psychoanalytic theories that this form of gratification has much to do with the time when, as a child, the individual was learning to control his sphincter muscles. Of all the perversions, this is probably one that is least openly discussed. Many men may brag about their sexual prowess and tastes, but few will announce a preference for brown showers. Most ordinary houses of prostitution do not accommodate this deviance because of the special equipment and people needed.

Necrophilia

In this perversion, an individual becomes sexually aroused by corpses. This socially repugnant practice is rarely acknowledged openly as a sexual stimulus. Some sex killers are also necrophiliacs. A variant of this deviance is seen in a genre of pornographic films called "snuff" films. In this type of film, the woman dies or is killed at the conclusion, after or during sexual intercourse. The action of killing the woman is a grossly fascinating perversion for a surprising number of men. These films, in which deaths were simulated, were gaining popularity until a film of an alleged actual death was shown in New York, commanding a $50 admission fee. This film received such massive condemnation that "snuff" returned to its under-the-counter status.

Group Sex

Group sex involves a number of people having sexual relations together, with several individuals, at the same time and place. Both single and married persons may be involved. In addition to the physical interaction with new partners, this practice has a strong voyeuristic and exhibitionistic appeal. There are publications and organizations that list individuals and couples around the country who are looking for new partners to engage in group sex.

Adult Sex with Children

The practice of adult sex with children is called incest if it involves blood relatives too close to marry, or child sexual molestation if it involves more distant relatives, or strangers. Statistics show that 80% to 85% of sexual attacks on children are not by strangers, but by relatives or acquaintances who have access to and are in a trust position with children, such as teachers, scout leaders, clergy, and counselors. The typical incest victim is under 10 years of age. Below that age, it is as likely that the victim is a boy as it is a girl.[2] Unlike a one-time rape, child sexual molestation is ongoing and frequently continues for years.

It is impossible to list every kind of personal sexual aberration. The many "girlie" magazines, like *Playboy, Penthouse,* and *Hustler,* have combined sales of more than 35 million copies each month. Voyeurism, the major appeal of these magazines, is obviously well entrenched, accepted, and institutionalized in our society. Many smaller magazines and organizations cater to the multitude of deviations that small groups and cults devise and/or practice. Voyeurism and exhibitionism can be harmful.

When innocent nonparticipants are forced to join in, the action may not be just a private viewing of pornography.

ATTITUDES TOWARD RATING-SCALE PRACTICES

The preceding section described a selection of sexual practices considered by mental health professionals and sexologists to be deviant. But how do most Americans view these practices, as normal or deviant? We surveyed our respondents, first, on what their attitudes were about these practices, and, second, on whether they had experienced them. The results for each practice follow here. Several of the tables indicate the percentages of respondents for each opinion on the Rating Scale (see survey item D.12, in Appendix B), and the percentages of men and women who said they had engaged in each practice.

Sadomasochism

Sadomasochism (S/M) has a long history, but only recently has it become openly discussed. As indicated in Table 4.1, very few of our respondents had never heard of it.

S/M houses need lots of equipment, including stocks, ropes, masks, boots, whips, black stockings, bras, and much more, to accommodate individual fantasies of their customers. Everyone we interviewed who sells sadomasochism insisted that, before having sex, they have a long talk with the potential client to determine his or her specific requisites. There are also clubs where individuals meet to act out sadomasochistic scenarios. Those who seek this action are, in the literature of sexology, classically seen as purging themselves of guilt; some claim that it feels good to test themselves. Sellers of equipment for dominance/bondage,

TABLE 4.1   **Survey Item D.12.**

RATING SCALE: SADOMASOCHISM:		
	Men	Women
N =	1,336	1,406
Very normal	2%	1%
All right	6	4
Unusual	19	15
Kinky	60	67
Never heard of it	13	13
Personal experience with sadomasochism	14%	11%

whom we interviewed, and magazines that promote sadomasochism, claim that at least 8%, and probably 10%, of American homes have S/M equipment. When we compared questions in other sections of the questionnaire (discussed later in this chapter), which were designed to show attitudes toward particular deviances and practices, the numbers were even higher. While still relatively small, the number of people who find pain to be an aphrodisiac is growing. In terms of actual experience, 14% of the men and 11% of the women surveyed reported having engaged in S/M.

◆ IN THEIR OWN WORDS

I get people here who have been all over looking for the right kind of pain they feel they deserve. Don't ask me why they want pain, I'm not a psychologist; but when they have found us, they usually don't go elsewhere. It may take some of the other girls an hour or even two hours to make these guys feel like they've had their treatment—I can achieve that in about 20 minutes. . . . Remember, these are businessmen, and they are not only buying my time, but they have to get back to work, so time is important.

Among the things I do, that work really quickly and well, are: I put clothespins on their nipples, or pins in their balls. Some of them need to see their own blood to be able to get off, and, when I service them, they do. Also, I've shoved ice cubes up many a guy's ass. That won't kill them, but it sure wakes them up. I have also shoved vibrators up their asses and turned them on—these were the battery-operated type—and some guys actually like that. I think they're nuts. . . .

. . . All the time that a torture scene is going on, there is constant dialogue. . . . I scream at the guy, and tell him what a no-good rotten bastard he is, how this is even too good for him, that he knows he deserves worse, and I begin to list his sins. It works every time. Hey, I'm not nuts, I know what I'm doing. I act very tough and hard, but I'm really a very sensitive woman. But you have to watch out for a guy's health. . . . you must not kill him, or have him get a heart attack . . . . I know of other places that have had guys die there. I've never lost a customer to death, though they may have wished for it during my "treatment." Remember, these are repeat customers. I have a clientele and a reputation that I value.

—A 34-year-old divorced mother (one child), college
graduate (B.A.), and operator of an S/M house

Typically, the ultimate desire for pain is also the danger: it could lead to death. Masochists enjoy pain and tease their tormentors so that they will inflict pain on them. A great deal was written in the mid-1980s about the fact that, although most Americans have little or no objection to sadomasochism, they—spurred on by leaders of the women's movement—do object strenuously to it because it most often humiliates and inflicts pain on women simply because of their gender. Some argue that it harms and dehumanizes men also, by presenting a caricatured macho image that is simply impossible for most men to live up to, even if they are so inclined.

Concern about children is increasingly expressed by parent and school groups, which claim that pornography and sadomasochism have invaded the home. Parents have, for the past decade, been complaining about cable television's presentation of violent and pornographic programs. Special devices have been marketed to prevent children from tuning in to such programs. With the advent of telephone sex, many children find that, by just dialing a telephone number, they can hear the most horrendously violent and degrading sexual messages.

Simeon Feigin, M.D., Psychiatrist and Medical Director of The Sterling Mental Health Clinic in New York, believes that men who seek repetitious and dangerous sex, including physical humiliation and sadomasochism, are attempting to ward off castration anxiety. Only by enduring pain, and surviving it, are they able to develop fantasies of omnipotence and enable themselves to function sexually, even if only in this limited manner.

Making Love as Making Up

There are individuals who may not know that they are practicing sadomasochism; rather, they believe that they are simply responding to their feelings of anger, rage, or need. These people find that they can relieve hostile tensions and settle arguments with their sex partners by using sex; or, they may need violence and hostility to function sexually at all, albeit under the guise of peacemaking. To investigate further the actual practices of S/M, we included several survey items, in other sections of the questionnaire, about various sex practices and deviances. Table 4.2 shows the results of one of these scattered survey items, which dealt with an example of what we call "deviance in daily life."

Thirty-five percent of the men and 23% of the women strongly agreed or agreed that making love is the best way to make up after an argument. Just a bare majority (51%) of the men were in disagreement, compared to 65% of the women. Many people and couples are often unaware of the implications of the facts of their sexual lives. Mental health workers whom we interviewed claimed that argue/make love is an addictive situation that will often be used as a subtle (or not so subtle) device to act out hostility against each other sexually. Needing the sexual release, many couples will provoke a fight to attain the subsequent sex.

In another survey item probing deviance in everyday life, we used the word pain, rather than making reference to sadomasochism: Table 4.3 indicates that 16% of the men and 12% of the women surveyed associated pain and pleasure—higher percentages than those in Table 4.1, which mentions

TABLE 4.2   **Survey Item C.8.**

MAKING LOVE IS THE BEST WAY TO MAKE UP AFTER AN ARGUMENT:		
	Men	Women
N =	1,343	1,413
Strongly agree	9%	5%
Agree	26	18
No opinion	14	12
Disagree	42	48
Strongly disagree	9	17
Strongly agree + Agree	35%	23%
Disagree + Strongly disagree	51%	65%

sadomasochism by name. In Table 4.1, the combined scores of very normal and all right totaled only 8% of the men and 5% of the women.

When sadomasochism is clearly identified (Table 4.1), the percentage of those in its favor is low. There seems to be a reluctance to acknowledge planning for or expecting S/M to be a part of sexual pleasure. When given a bit of disguise by calling it "pain and pleasure in sex," S/M seems to be much more palatable. Respondents to both survey items did not have to fake answers to sound "normal"; they had confidentiality. Instead, we believe that many people hide their hostile impulses, seen as unacceptable feelings, from themselves as well as others. Although most respondents rejected pain *and* sadomasochism, a substantial minority felt comfortable in approaching and practicing S/M in a variety of different settings

TABLE 4.3   **Survey Item C.11.**

PAIN AND PLEASURE REALLY GO TOGETHER IN SEX:		
	Men	Women
N =	1,343	1,414
Strongly agree	4%	2%
Agree	12	10
No opinion	13	9
Disagree	44	40
Strongly disagree	27	39
Strongly agree + Agree	16%	12%
Disagree + Strongly disagree	71%	79%

One practitioner of masochism was fairly unhappy with the obsession that demanded he be spanked when he was about to have sex. He sought therapy, after having tried and failed many times on his own, to force himself to stop. He was a bright, highly achieving professional whose life was going well, except for his humiliation of needing pain. He had long since known not to ask his wife to spank him. In their dating days, when he did try to involve her in this activity, he tried to make it out to be a game. They would alternately say or do something "naughty" and take turns punishing each other. This mild penalty, coupled with fun and laughter, was not enough for him. His sexual response was poor, long in coming, and frustrating for him and his wife. He was always making excuses of being tired, or having a lot on his mind. Asking her to take a hairbrush, or leather belt, to spank him hard in order to produce a vigorous sex response, failed. He became a regular buyer of commercial sex, in a house of prostitution that specialized in pain.

At age 34, this well-functioning professional had only marginal sexual function. As part of his therapy, he mentioned that his father had died when he was quite small, and his mother had found it hard to manage him, although there were no siblings. He was a very active child, and, to instill some "discipline," she resorted to quite severe spankings. At first he tried to fight back, but she overwhelmed him; she was outraged with his resistance and would hit him harder. He learned to take pleasure from the pain and began to enjoy the spankings. Later, he provoked incidents that would anger his mother and ensure that she spanked him. The nanny who watched him was a kindly soul who would not strike him hard, so it became an interaction shared with his mother alone. When this information surfaced, and he was able to see that the spanking was perhaps not his choice of sexual outlet, but that of his mother, he was startled. By coincidence, his mother passed away at about this point in his therapy. More information flowed from him, as if he had been keeping family secrets. His mother apparently would barge into the bathroom, and also into his bedroom, ostensibly to make sure that he was not masturbating. She strongly condemned masturbation, and when she saw any indication that he was even touching himself, she beat him severely. Sex and violence became an irresistible match. Shortly after revealing his family's sex secrets and developing awareness that he was being used in the sexual needs of his mother, he moved entirely away from the need for pain. However, after six months, he went back to the call girls who spanked him. "I had to try it once more, to see if it turned me on." He smiled as he related that he stopped the spanking halfway through, felt no turn-on at all, gave the surprised call girl an extra-large tip, and told her she could take his name out of her file because he wouldn't be back again. His marriage, which he had always valued, improved, and, although he did not confess to his wife, she sensed that he was somehow freed to enjoy himself with her.

Dominance/Bondage

Another practice with a long history and only recent emergence into open discussion is that of dominance/bondage (D/B). Dominance and bondage may be regarded as first cousins to sadism and machochism, or even as another form of S/M, although D/B and S/M differ stylistically. Dominance/bondage is much more directly involved with total control and subsequent humbling of the submissive individual, through pain, words, or a host of ingenious and degrading mechanisms. At its core is a demand for absolute and total control of the submissive. Specific code words are used among D/B aficionados, who have specific publications and a wide variety of equipment to select from. According to our interviews, and information received from those who are involved commercially in D/B, numerous husbands and wives practice D/B at home. Most couples reported that they made sure their children were asleep before they put on their gear and entered the fantasy world of D/B. Others, who were not embarrassed, performed in front of their children, and some even included the whole family. Dominance/bondage is a sex fantasy. For some couples, in mild forms, it is a prelude to sex. For others, the acting-out of the dominance scenario replaces the need to have normal sexual interaction. Even the need for orgasm is eliminated by many practitioners, who view D/B as a more gratifying outlet for their sexual needs. What did our numbers show, regarding opinions and practice of D/B? Table 4.4 gives an itemization.

Feminist and humanist groups have pointed out that the practice and philosophy of D/B feed into the mentality of men who beat their wives to attain dominance. The ultimate dominance that some strive for relieves them of responsibility for their sexuality. Much of this same mentality is credited for the newly publicized phenomenon of "date rape," a much discussed problem on college campuses. D/B provides a fantasy stage for men and women who need to exercise their compensatory

TABLE 4.4   **Survey Item D.12.**

RATING SCALE: DOMINANCE/BONDAGE:		
	Men	Women
N =	1,331	1,403
Very normal	2%	1%
All right	6	6
Unusual	22	17
Kinky	63	67
Never heard of it	7	9
Personal experience with dominance/bondage	11%	11%

sense of superiority and dominance. Most practitioners insist they have no political agenda and are simply indulging in a sexual practice that gives them great pleasure.

In light of the strong views Americans seem to hold concerning dominance/bondage, it may be surprising to learn from Table 4.4 that 8% of the males and an almost equal proportion of the females (7%) were accepting of D/B. Only 7% of the men and 9% of the women surveyed had never heard of D/B.

Cross Dressing

Cross dressing is generally regarded as a male problem, and it is among the most recent to have gone public. Women who cross dress have no problem; so-called "tomboys" are fully accepted, but "sissies" are not. Therefore, it is important to note that cross dressing refers primarily to men, although women also dress in the garb of the other sex. However, although women whose clothes imitate men's styling are accepted, women who dress in men's clothes are felt, by mental health professionals, to have psychological problems.

The term transvestites applies primarily to men who dress as women. Some wear women's clothes openly in public; others do it only in the privacy of their homes. There are different degrees of involvement. For some men, putting on outer garments of the other sex, such as blouses and skirts, may be enough, but many male transvestites also wear female undergarments. Most of the transvestites interviewed for our study stated that they had begun quite early—during, or even before, puberty—to try on their mothers' clothes secretly. Having done this several times, they found that they were hooked, and kept coming back to their mothers' clothes more and more frequently, and wearing more of them. Dressing in clothes of the other sex is called "dressing in drag"; one who

TABLE 4.5   Survey Item D.12.

RATING SCALE: CROSS DRESSING:		
	Men	Women
N =	1,329	1,404
Very normal	2%	1%
All right	6	4
Unusual	23	24
Kinky	55	54
Never heard of it	14	17
Personal experience with cross dressing	6%	3%

does it is called a "drag queen." In total, 6% of the men surveyed and 3% of the women reported experiencing cross dressing.

Few respondents (men, 2%; women, 1%) found cross dressing very normal, and only 6% (men) and 4% (women) said it was all right. A large percentage (14% of the men and 17% of the women) reported never hearing of it.

✦ *IN THEIR OWN WORDS* ─────────────────────────────────

I have been told that when I dress in drag, at times I look like Whistler's Mother [laughs], especially when I haven't shaved closely. I usually am good at detail, and I make sure when I dress as a woman that I have my nails done just so, and that my colors match. Honestly, it's hard to pin a date on when I began cross dressing, ... If pressed, I would have to say it began when I was about 10 years of age, fooling around with and putting on my mom's clothes. . . . I was always careful to put everything back in its exact place, and in 18 years of doing this in her home, my mother never, I mean *never*, suspected, or questioned me about putting on her clothes. I belong to a transvestite support group . . . , a group for men who cross dress. Some of the group are homosexuals, but most are not. A true transvestite—and I am one, so I know—is not homosexual. We don't discriminate against them in the group at all; hey, we have enough trouble getting acceptance as normal people and not just a bunch of weirdos ourselves. They are a bunch of nice guys . . . , really. Most of them are like me.

Most of them have told their families about their dressing inclinations, but those that are married are a mixed lot; some wives know and some don't, they just suspect. I believe in honesty, and told my wife about this before we were married. We're separated now, but I don't think it's because of my cross dressing. She may have thought that she would get me to change after we married. That is silly; you have to accept a person as they are. I wear my nicest female outfits on special occasions like Halloween, and go out to my favorite bars to celebrate. At home, I do find a need once or twice a week to dress in my female clothes, and to bring out the woman in me. We all have a masculine and feminine side . . . , you know. I have been asked many times why I cross dress, and it's hard to explain, other than it makes me feel good. There is something deep down that it gratifies. Some of my friends, when I was growing up, suggested psychotherapy, but I don't regard this as a problem. If it bothers someone else, then they have the problem. . . . I function perfectly well sexually with my wife, though it took her some time to be comfortable with me wearing feminine underwear; yes, sometimes I wear it while making love, it just makes it more exciting.

—A 42-year-old married father who is a high
school graduate, and has attended college
classes for a number of years

Fetishes

Fetishes include a broad range of activities, and, although both sexes are affected, mental health professionals consider fetishes primarily a male problem. Fetishes may take many forms and may involve obsessive fixation on a particular preference or on objects such as feet, or materials such as silk or rubber. For example, silk, or a silky feeling material, may become a must for an individual to function sexually; he may need to hold the silk, stroke it, or rub his face against it, to have a sex experience. If the fixation is a specific scent, the affected individual needs to be able to smell that scent in order to function. Those who have obsessions about feet (or other body parts) become aroused and ejaculate when they handle and fondle the sex object's feet, without needing genital contact at all. We did not attempt to make a catalog of obsessive objects and practices; rather, we sought to discover how, and how strongly, Americans feel about fetishes in general. Our Rating Scale's results are shown in Table 4.6.

The responses indicate that fetishes are considerably more acceptable than cross dressing (see Table 4.5). Twenty-two percent of the men surveyed and 18% of the women were generally approving (very normal or all right) of fetishes. Comparable figures on cross dressing were 8% and 5% (Table 4.5). Even though fetishes are primarily a male sexual behavior and few women have fetishes, there appears to be considerable female acceptance of it. Eleven percent of the men and 6% of the women reported having had experience with fetishes. Some women we interviewed reported that they felt more secure with their partner or spouse *because of* his fetish, because it would be difficult for him to find another woman who would keep his secret, understand, and gratify him.

TABLE 4.6   **Survey Item D.12.**

RATING SCALE: FETISHES:		
	Men	Women
N =	1,329	1,399
Very normal	5%	5%
All right	17	13
Unusual	31	31
Kinky	33	35
Never heard of it	14	16
Personal experience with fetishes	11%	6%

I thought it was a joke, really a great joke, until I discovered that the joke was on me. My ex-husband . . . and I were only married for two months before we got the so-called marriage annulled. That bastard lied to me. . . . I thought it was the luckiest day of my life when I met him. I wondered why he hadn't been snapped up by some woman before. He is a big executive, has his own airplane, a Porsche, a gorgeous huge house, and he's beautiful to boot. It's still such a shock and embarrassment, but not as devastating as it was then. It's now over a year, so I can talk about it.

When we met, he was a perfect gentleman. He knew the right wines to order, the right restaurants, and the right words to make my heart flutter. As soon as we met, he complimented me on my legs. He . . . said, "I bet you're a perfect size-six shoe," and I am. I wondered how he knew, and he told me . . . he used to be a shoe salesman. And then he made a strange comment, that when he was bored or felt down, he would go into one of his company's shoe stores and work there for a day. That was clue number one, which went right over my head. Also, his belt buckle had a shoe engraved in gold on it, and he made a point of showing it to me, and commenting on how rare it was to find a perfect foot. . . . I am fairly well endowed and men often make comments about my appearance, . . . but it felt strange when he didn't comment on my breasts, but on my shoe vamp! . . .

Anyway, to make a long story short, it was a whirlwind courtship, with a lot of affection but no real passion. . . . We gave each other lots of massages. He called it "good touching," and, truthfully, it felt good. I started to notice that, after a perfunctory back or neck rub, he'd go right to my feet, and spend a lot of time massaging and kissing them. Somehow, we weren't having sex—nothing that I could recognize as sex, but a lot of "good touching." . . . Well, comes the wedding day—that was beautiful and romantic! But the wedding night was unbelievable. . . . We got to the hotel room; he had reserved a palatial suite. . . . We were drinking and laughing. I was looking forward to a really passionate introduction to marriage, and feeling light-headed. I took my clothes off and put on sexy lingerie. He said something like, "Darling, you've been on your poor tootsies all day, let me take care of them." He went into the bathroom—he had a large pan that he had somehow gotten into the room—and came back with some warm water, scented soap, nail clipper, emery board, scented powder, and other such items. He gave my feet the attention of a lifetime. He must have spent a good half-hour washing, clipping my toe nails, filing my toe nails, caressing my toe nails, waxing my feet, perfuming my feet, kissing and licking my feet. Now, for the first time, I saw him doing this without his clothes on. He had a huge erection, and I thought to myself, "Well, whatever turns you on is fine." I waited and waited, and he kept touching, almost like pawing my feet. I tried, at first subtly, and then more obviously, to let him know there was more to me. Finally, uncontrollably, I blurted out, "Make love to me, I want you!" He replied, "I am making love to you" and he ejaculated. . . . The next morning and afternoon again, the same routine with the unbelievably obsessive foot loving. Whenever I would try to pull him up from my feet, to get on top of me, he would start to go soft, and if I tried to have him enter me, he would lose his erection entirely.

What made me totally freak out was what he tried to do with my toes. You know the way guys hold a billiards cue stick between their fingers? Well, Mr. Foot started putting his penis between my toes and moving it back and forth, and got all worked up. That was too much. I managed to jump up and stop this action. . . .

. . . This jerk was just getting off with my feet. . . . I tried to discuss it with him, but I quickly found out that there was no negotiation to be had. He finally let me know that he felt "differently" about women than other men did, and showed his "love differently." . . . Next, he said that he could be perfectly happy with me, and would take good care of me financially and in every way, if I would just be understanding. . . . But it was too weird and I couldn't live in a setting like that. I had my attorney arrange an annulment, and I have been getting over that trauma.

—A 33-year-old divorcee

Verbal Humiliation

Only fairly recently has verbal humiliation come to be recognized as a form of sexual gratification for some people. Verbal humiliation can be regarded as a subspecialty of sadomasochism. Instead of physical pain, it uses symbolic language to inflict harsh disapproval. People will often do "tests" on new sex partners to see whether—or how—the newcomers will act-out a sex scenario that these people need for their fulfillment. The exchange will usually start with mild criticism, warranted or unwarranted, which the aggressor evaluates as to whether the subject will or won't join in the scenario. A man using verbal humiliation might call his sex partner a whore, ridicule her body, and, in general, look for areas in which he can attack her with some accuracy. Women we interviewed, who were aggressors in verbal humiliation, were frequently at least as expert as men, and many reported that they could give at least as well as they got. The scene becomes one of flying putdowns, obscenities, and not a little venom. To be effective, the attacking language must be related to the life of the individual (for example, knowing that he peeked at his mother undressing, or watched his sister bathe). Table 4.7 summarizes how this activity rated with our respondents; the prevailing reactions were negative.

Only 5% of the men and 7% of the women reported having been involved in verbal humiliation as a sexual practice. In many ways, verbal humiliation, for the individual who is on the receiving end, is a purging for forbidden thoughts or for physical acts that he or she may have committed that need punishment. The individual who is dishing out the verbal humiliation needs to know specific, guilt-inducing facts, which can be used effectively against the recipient of the humiliation. When performed by a true sadist, this verbal act can be excoriating. In its own

TABLE 4.7

RATING SCALE: VERBAL HUMILIATION:		
	Men	Women
N =	1,342	1,411
Very normal	2%	2%
All right	6	3
Unusual	34	35
Kinky	51	52
Never heard of it	7	8
Personal experience with verbal humiliation	5%	7%

bizarre way, it is a massive turn-on for the recipient, who feels that, by being verbally punished, he or she is not only cleansed, but, having paid the price of humiliation, now has permission to enjoy sex. The frequency distribution in Table 4.7 indicates that verbal humiliation was not high on our respondents' list of acceptable deviances. Only 8% of the men and 5% of the women we surveyed regarded it with any level of approval.

Golden Showers

Golden showers ("the waterworks") is generally viewed as an odd outlet that is acceptable to only a small number; it is not a practice with wide appeal (see Table 4.8). However, people we interviewed who were practitioners reported being unable to function well, or at all, without it.

When we combined very normal and all right responses, only 6% of our male respondents and 3% of our female respondents considered

TABLE 4.8

RATING SCALE: GOLDEN SHOWERS:		
	Men	Women
N =	1,291	1,381
Very normal	2%	1%
All right	4	2
Unusual	17	8
Kinky	55	46
Never heard of it	22	43
Personal experience with golden showers	6%	4%

golden showers acceptable. Not surprisingly, 22% of the men and 43% of the women had never heard of the practice. Only a small subgroup engages in this deviance; it is not as widespread as the practices discussed earlier. Moreover, those who practice it are generally not given to talking about it. Only 6% of the men and 4% of the women responding to our questionnaire reported having experienced golden showers.

Brown Showers

The experience of brown showers is even more rarely sought than that of golden showers. Our statistics revealed that only a very minute number of our respondents (1% of the men) practiced this deviance (see Table 4.9).

Brown showers ranks lower than golden showers for acceptability as a sexual outlet. Combining very normal and all right responses, we showed only 3% acceptance among men and 1% among women. Unusual and kinky scores combined totaled 66% for men and 48% for women, and the balance of our respondents indicated that they had never heard of it. It is interesting that such a high percentage of women (51%) had never heard of it. None of the men or women we interviewed reported having experienced brown showers. This perversion is not new to Western culture, but it has not caught on with any degree of acceptance or popularity in America.

Necrophilia

Necrophilia is rare. Almost universally, Americans regard it as objectionable and firmly reject it. Necrophilia seems to be not only a nonacceptable sexual outlet but a rejected possibility. In interviews, when individuals expressed their opinion, it was always strongly negative. In the questionnaire responses, only 1% of the men and none of the women considered it acceptable (see Table 4.10). The respondents were trying to distance themselves

TABLE 4.9   Survey Item D.12.

RATING SCALE: BROWN SHOWERS:		
	Men	Women
N =	1,241	1,310
Very normal	1%	0%
All right	2	1
Unusual	17	6
Kinky	49	42
Never heard of it	31	51
Personal experience with brown showers	1%	0%

TABLE 4.10

RATING SCALE: NECROPHILIA:		
	Men	Women
N =	1,291	1,367
Very normal	0%	0%
All right	1	0
Unusual	18	10
Kinky	47	45
Never heard of it	34	45
Personal experience with necrophilia	0%	0%

from the concept: 65% of the men and 55% of the women considered it unacceptable. As with most of the deviances reported here, women were more likely than men to be unaware that people practiced such behavior. None of our respondents reported any experience with necrophilia.

Group Sex

Group sex seems to be a temptation for many Americans. Some try it, others wonder about it.

As can be seen in Table 4.11, group sex was viewed more favorably by men than by women in our survey: 17% of the men, compared with 8% of the women, felt it was very normal or all right. The activity is well-known: few respondents had never heard of it (2% of the men and 2% of the women). Fourteen percent of the men and 8% of the women indicated that they had experienced group sex. The respondents we interviewed

TABLE 4.11

RATING SCALE: GROUP SEX:		
	Men	Women
N =	1,342	1,412
Very normal	3%	1%
All right	14	7
Unusual	38	22
Kinky	43	68
Never heard of it	2	2
Personal experience with group sex	14%	8%

reported that group sex starts out as an area of great interest and drive among men. Most wives initially have to be urged, cajoled, and bribed to "try it." When couples continue with the activity, the wives become slowly, but definitely, the more ardent champions of the practice. They seek novelty and new partners, and their husbands then begin to lose interest in group sex.

Adult Sex with Children

National headlines have, for several years, been focused on this issue, as sex scandals have erupted in a number of major nursery schools, and, in fact, in schools that enroll all ages of children. Each new accusation brings an indication that adult sex with children is a highly negatively charged issue.

The responses we received, shown in Table 4.12, reflect the general negativism: no one chose the very normal or all right category. Admittedly, advocates of child sex abuse are not about to make public admission of their interest, so the negative responses were not surprising. The unusual category was chosen by 31% of the men and 25% of the women. Kinky, reflecting much of the opposition to child sex abuse practice, was chosen by 63% of the men and 73% of the women. Six percent of the men responding and 2% of the women had never heard of it. Only 2% of our male respondents, and none of the females, had experienced sex with children. Was there a need to "look good," to oneself and others, in this response? Most of our respondents rated themselves as romantic and sensual (see Table 5.11), both considered socially positive sexual attributes. A parallel situation may surround this response. Few persons may wish to acknowledge that they are involved in sex with children, even on an anonymous questionnaire. A high rate of incest and child abuse has been making its way into recent headlines. Questions involving socially very desirable or undesirable practices are often slanted by

TABLE 4.12   **Survey Item D.12.**

RATING SCALE: ADULT SEX WITH CHILDREN:		
	Men	Women
N =	1,340	1,413
Very normal	0%	0%
All right	0	0
Unusual	31	25
Kinky	63	73
Never heard of it	6	2
Personal experience with adult sex with children	2%	0%

the respondents to make themselves acceptable—often, to themselves. Against their denials is the sizable number of respondents who report having been sexually abused in childhood. Can we believe that such a remarkable number of those abused have *not* become abusers?

In an earlier study,[3] we reviewed over 10,000 cases of child sex abuse and found a very distressing pattern. In broad terms, child abusers come in two groups: those who have been having sex with children since their own childhood, and never stopped after they grew into adulthood; and those men who are over 55, had never touched a child sexually before, and suddenly become involved with young children. This group is the most distressing to their families, because they are often the uncles or grandfathers of the children they are molesting. These adults seem to be reverting to childhood and to childhood sex play. In general, sex offenders have a high recidivism rate, although therapists who work with them report that those who have become attracted to children recently, as adults, respond better to therapy and have a lower recidivism rate. There are several groups in the United States that advocate what is called "intergenerational sex." Among them are the René Guyon Society, whose motto is "Sex before eight and then it's too late," and the Pedophiliacs Information Society, which advocates intergenerational sex at even younger ages. For the most part, these male (an overwhelming number of these advocates are men) child sex abusers, are seductive, rather than threatening. Sergeant Lloyd Martin, formerly head of the Juvenile Vice Bureau of the Los Angeles Police Department, related to us that, when he sees a man who is much nicer to a child than any father would be, "I know I have a child sex abuser."

In that study, we also found that when the offenders are over the age of 55 and the abused child is younger than 12, the offenders almost never (less than 4%) are sentenced to jail. Instead, they are sent to "counseling": to a member of the clergy or perhaps to psychotherapy. Over 85% of child sex abuse is by relatives or by people in an authority situation who have power over the abused child. Our earlier research showed that less than 15% are strangers offering a child candy, a ride, or some other inducement outside a school. What makes the lack of stiff jail terms more contradictory is that, in most child sex abuse cases, there is physical evidence of sex abuse and maybe even a confession. Worse, the child is most often sent back to the same abusing home, where the live-in relationship with the offender continues.

OTHER FRINGE SEXUAL ACTIVITIES

Institutionalized Incest

In interviewing psychologists, sociologists, and police officers around the country, we have uncovered information about entire geographic areas where incest seems to be widespread. In these areas, an institutionalized pattern seems to have gone on for generations, and is accepted by both men and women within the community and in the surrounding communities. Professor Donald Schneller, a sociologist at Middle Tennessee State University, calls these areas "cut-off communities." They exist in isolated or "backwoods" areas in various regions of the country.

Sergeant John Johnstone, formerly of the New York State Police, described to us his frustration at making multiple child sex abuse arrests of the same family members. No one in the family calls for the police; most often, a school nurse or a guidance counselor reports the crime. One respondent we interviewed related how startled he was, while painting a house in an isolated area in the South, to have the housewife comment to him that "she hoped her husband would do for her daughter what her daddy had done for her," meaning break her in sexually. Individuals who live in these cut-off communities have their own values about sex, about education, and about life in general. The characteristics of these areas vary somewhat, but they share being cut off from the mainstream culture and preserving an uncanny ability to resist outside pressures directed at curtailing what outsiders consider unacceptable sexual practices.

Commercialized Sex

Why do we include consideration of prostitution in a chapter dealing with sexual deviance?

One of the usual criteria in determining whether an act is deviant is an assessment of whether the person engaging in the act has freedom of choice in deciding to perform or not perform it. Does he or she control the act, or is he or she compelled to perform it, whether willingly or unwillingly? Can the individual volitionally refrain from doing it, or stop it once it has begun?

In 1977, Janus and Bess showed that prostitution is an addiction,[4] and that prostitutes frequently talk about eventually leaving "the life," in spite of how rewarding it is at present. Janus and Bess studied a group of prostitutes who were young, intelligent, successful at their trade, and sufficiently educated that they had been able to initiate careers other than "the life." Upon followup about one year later, the majority had resumed their sexual careers, some full-time, some part-time; very few had stayed away for a year or more. What makes these findings especially compelling is that these women realized that their careers in prostitution were dangerous; some were giving all their money to their pimp, in essence endangering themselves for nothing, and some had lost their children to child care agencies—yet they could not leave "the life."

When their histories were examined, 85% of the prostitutes were found to have been sexually molested in childhood—most by age 10. The sex business is seen by some mental health workers as a repetition compulsion in which prostitutes have little or no control. They have no alternative to counteract the sense of degradation at having their bodies rented for a fee or a per-hour rate. Social scientists, commenting on prostitution, have questioned whether it is a victimless crime. In our judgment, it is not; the prostitute is the victim. With the knowledge that this victimization, which seems voluntary, is in fact compulsive behavior beyond the control of the person, we conclude that prostitution must be considered a deviance.

In most big cities, the success formula for prostitution and other sex-related commerce imitates the practices in New York and Los Angeles. New York City is considered by most experts who study prostitution to be the prostitution capital of the United States. We interviewed vice squads, prostitutes, and madams in America's major cities, to study the function of commercial sex and the communities' responses. In most states, prostitution is considered a crime. In a seeming contradiction, prostitutes do not want prostitution to be legalized; they would then have to pay taxes, as all other professions do. Instead, they simply want decriminalization of prostitution, so that they are not considered criminals. The other party in commercial sex is the "John," who is not arrested, and is seldom publicized the way his prostitute partner is. When the New York Police Department conducts raids on street prostitutes, they are chained together in long lines and brought to jail. The unit that chases and arrests the street prostitutes is popularly known in the trade as the "pussy posse."

Most prostitutes are organized into small, protected groups, new members need referrals. A small number of prostitutes operate independently. Each group of women (and/or young men) has its pimp or madam. Most prostitutes claim that they entered the field voluntarily, for the money, but the very young "baby pros" have often been shown to have been coerced into "the life." Most prostitutes plan to leave the business "just as soon as I get enough money"; few do so because there is seemingly never enough money. For some prostitutes who have a higher education and a less damaged ego, an event that we have come to call "the end-of-the-line syndrome" will cause them to leave. A welfare department may threaten to take their child(ren) from them, they may take a life-threatening drug overdose, or their pimp may beat them up once too often. The few who finally leave "the life" frequently manage very well in the "straight world." They are verbal, sociable, and attractive.

Women who belong to a "stable," or group of prostitutes, refer to each other as in-laws. Women who do not have a pimp and operate solo, which is a dangerous practice, are called outlaws. With a madam, the split of fees is either 50/50 or 60/40 (favoring the house). With a pimp, there is no split—he takes it all, giving the woman only enough to keep herself in clothes and to share a communal apartment with other women. Prostitutes refer to themselves as "working girls." Men who are customers of prostitutes are called Johns, and women who frequent male or female prostitutes are called Janes.

Many mental health professionals have tried to determine why prostitutes work so hard, endanger their lives to earn money, and then give it all away to the pimp. There is no solid or easy answer. The pimp takes the role of an exploitative father, and prostitutes have a need to belong to some kind of family, even an exploitative, illegal one. There is a hierarchy in each house: a "main woman" (the pimp's favorite), middle-level women, and trainees. There is no upward mobility in prostitution. At whatever age a woman or young man becomes involved, his or her career, with time, only goes steadily downward.

The vice squads in large cities do not attempt to stop prostitution. Instead, they direct their efforts toward controlling and shifting commercial sex activities, like prostitution, off main streets and out of the sight of tourists. This is a difficult job. Prostitutes, especially streetwalkers, seek customers in tourist areas and places with a heavy flow of street traffic. The standard fine for prostitution, in many cities, is $50 or $100. If a prostitute is a repeat offender and the fine is too high for her to pay immediately, a judge will frequently let her pay it off over time. The prostitute is generally released immediately and goes back to the streets to earn the money to pay the fine. This cycle prompts many prostitutes and feminists to note that prostitutes are supporting the courts with their work. A common joke among prostitutes is that the fines imposed are society's way of collecting rent from them.

Living dangerously, with only minimal concern for the consequences, seems to be a driving need for many prostitutes; they see the exploitation in "the life" as part of the package. To safeguard themselves, most prostitutes now request that clients use condoms as protection against AIDS; however, some do not. Other dangers, such as physical violence and abuse, are more immediate.

Our research in the past 10 years—much of it in New York—has indicated that, contrary to conventional wisdom, the prevalence of commercial sex has increased. According to Lieutenant William McCarthy,[5] former head of the Vice Squad of the N.Y.P.D., many houses of prostitution advertise in the New York Yellow Pages under "Escort Services." In Manhattan alone, in 1992, judging by the comparative numbers of individual escort services (many supplying call girls who go to the Johns' homes or offices) listed in the borough's Yellow Pages, call-girl prostitution has increased over 400% since 1983. Big-city commercial sex caters to those who want to go beyond the acceptable level of deviance in society. The range of services offered, in addition to prostitution, includes drugs, pornography, and "kiddie porn." Commercial sex is a big business with a nationwide network of contacts. In contrast to the fun-and-games aspect of deviance at home, commercial sex is exploitative of both the client and the prostitute.

Lieutenant McCarthy believes that the "victims of vice" are people for whom hope is absent. He compared vice to people going to a theater. They are already interested in the product and the performance; the vice operator acts as an usher. McCarthy feels that people involved in these commercial sex activities are "selfless human beings who are caught up in anonymous commercial sex acts." Concern for personal safety has no place in their world.

SUMMING UP

Sexuality in America became unleashed, went public, and turned experimental as a result of the First Sexual Revolution. Americans may not have invented deviance, but they have gone a long way to develop it and create its mass appeal. We call this process the eroticization of America. Many experts predicted the demise of American sex in the wake of the panic generated by AIDS. We found, instead, a continuous and increasing variety of marginal sex.

Americans today, in general, put a premium on innovation in sexual experience. Some sexual practices that were once deemed esoteric and/ or weird have become more desirable as an in-group experience. Sexual sophistication demands an increasing repertoire of unusual sexual acts that are personally experienced, as well as the knowledge of many other sexual acts still to be tried. Variety is constantly desired, to enrich the sexual experience.

As suggested in this chapter, the search for novelty may lead many persons into deviance. The obsessive nature of their sex drives does not offer them the freedom to choose other sexual outlets. Some sexual practices that are *au courant* today were only recently considered quite deviant by religious, mental health, and medical authorities.

Ingenuity has surfaced in the area of sexuality, both in society and in the lives of individuals. There is no national consensus on morality, or sexuality, and the role of the family as a guide for sex practices has declined. The preferences of marginal groups have had a growing influence, and the mass media can claim some minimal influence. The media have shocked and titillated Americans, but rarely have they been a useful source of information to grow with. There is a thin line between deviance and novelty; Americans cross that line frequently. The conflict between deviance and morality seems increasingly to have become downgraded from a life-and-death struggle to a skirmish. Organized religion no longer serves as an effective arbiter of American morality, and individuals are left to chart sexual courses of their own. Deviance in daily life has become a personalized part of sex life in America, and some people choose deviance as an ongoing part of their sexuality. The eroticization of America continues.

CHAPTER FIVE

The Singles' Scene

SOME SIGNIFICANT FINDINGS ABOUT THE SINGLES' SCENE

✦   The majority of singles do not find their life-style gratifying, but only one in three would prefer being married.

✦   Men find sex more sensuous than do women.

✦   38% of single men and 45% of single women would
like to become parents even if they do not marry.

✦   More than half again as many singles report an increase in their sexual activity in the past 3 years, compared to those who report a decrease.

✦   Divorced people have a larger incidence of divorce
among their parents than do married people.

✦   Only 40% of singles feel free to approach the other sex
for sex.

QUESTIONNAIRE SUBJECTS TABULATED IN THIS CHAPTER

	Table
Sex and Intimacy	5.1
Singles' Life-Style	5.2, 5.3, 5.9
Marriage and Fulfillment	5.4
Initiation of Sexual Activity	5.5, 5.6
Attitudes Toward Parenthood	5.7
Attitudes Toward Divorce	5.8
Traditional Sex Roles in Modern Society	5.10
Self-Ratings on Feelings of Romance	5.11
Sensuous Nature of Sex	5.12
Self-Ratings of Sexual Activity	5.13
Biological Sexual Maximum	5.14, 5.15
Frequency of Sexual Activity	5.16
Masturbation Frequency	5.17
The Importance of Love	5.18
Number of Sexual Partners	5.19
Comparative Sexual Activity, Three Years Ago Versus Now	5.20
Parents' Marriage	5.21

PERSONALS

BEAM ME UP, SCOTTY

I have been around the world and then some. Beautiful, intelligent, funny, sensuous 31-year-old gal with a sound appreciation of the finer things of life, looking for a partner to share my space capsule. Can you face up to a healthy challenge? Can you share completing the *New York Times* crossword puzzle? Can you enjoy a well-made quiche? Are you ready to try a zero-gravity relationship? Your age should be 30–39, educated (no nerds need apply), well-built, and capable of loving and laughing. Call . . . .

C.E.O. IN EARLY RETIREMENT

I—highly educated, in excellent physical shape, and a financially secure 55+, 6'2" man. I love to cook and to fly kites. Have lots of time to sail my boat and the means to live a life of luxury with the right "her." She—must be over 5'7", 29 to 38, a well-built head turner, with at least one college degree, capable of loving a big hunk of a man, and making him feel good. We can do great things together. Call . . . .

E ach week, *New York Magazine, California Magazine, Living Single* (a Midwestern magazine), and several hundred other magazines across America publish thousands of ads like these in their "Personals" or similarly named columns. The way to meet another single has become less a matter of luck and more a plan for successful marketing. Our research has ascertained that, on average, a man between 30 and 56 who places an ad with reasonably appealing copy will receive from 175 to 300 responses during the first week after his ad appears in a major city's publication, and only slightly fewer responses during the following weeks. Women, ages 25 to 43, who place an ad that has creative copy, will receive approximately 45 to 125 responses in the first week, but the number of responses tends to decline slightly more rapidly than responses to men's ads, as weeks of publication pass. Outlandish claims of status, money, and sex in the ad copy will increase the number and earnestness of responses.

Singles are a large, varied, and growing segment of today's American population; in fact, 41% of Americans over 18—some 73 million people— are unmarried. This is a dramatic increase from 1970, when singles made up only 28% of all adults.[1]

IN THEIR OWN WORDS

A couple of friends and I were comparing notes. Among us, we've had men in about 65 different life-styles and careers. We're all turned off to jocks— they just don't seem real, and many are impotent! We're trying to find out where and who the real men are. We're turned off by doctors and engineers, too. I think they like to play with their instruments more than they do with women. They are so wrapped up in themselves that it's hard for them to really give emotionally. I enjoy great sex with a guy I care about, and I've had some terrific lovers. I don't have to sleep with a lot of men, but I do have to sleep a lot with my man.

—A 28-year-old woman who has never been married

✦ ✦ ✦

I know I have to get on with the business of living today and not in the past. Friends, even my in-laws, tell me I am not cut out to be alone. Truthfully, I don't feel much alone. I throw myself into my work and my research and my children, and it's enough. I'm a scientist and can be very objective, but I haven't seen a woman to compare with my late wife. I have attractive graduate students and even assistants in my lab but I'm really not interested. I just don't feel ready yet.

—A 49-year-old widower

What do we really know about the singles in our society, those who are unmarried and not living with a partner? Many of them are financially secure, religiously and politically active, and educated; all of them are alone. Is the very nature of their aloneness a factor in determining their needs, frustrations, and behaviors? Does living alone (at times) cause these solitary individuals to display differing attitudes and desires regarding sex and sexual habits? Not all singles are never-been-married people; some are divorced or legally separated, some are widowed, and some may yet marry. Some of their responses during our interviews provided revealing answers to the above questions.

Singles are no longer predominantly in the 18- to 25-year-old age group, traditionally considered the proper time of life for being single; today, more than at any time in the past, singles are likely to be adults of middle or older age. Singles may be heterosexual or openly homosexual. Whether younger or older, wealthy or poor, many are actively seeking marriage or some kind of stable relationships with other persons. Almost desperately, some singles seek contact and relatedness in newspaper ads, video dating clubs, bars, resorts, church socials—almost anywhere.

In recent years, being single has become, if not the norm for our society, at least not an aberrant pattern. The number of individuals living alone has grown from 18.3 million in 1980 to 23.0 million in 1990.[2] (Our classification categories are slightly different from those of the Census Bureau, which lists as permanently divorced anyone who has been divorced. Our classification is based on the person's present status. A divorced person who is now remarried is listed by us as married.) A number of factors account for the growth of the number of singles: the higher divorce rates since the early 1970s; the increased financial and emotional independence of women in the past quarter-century; the postponement of marriage and childbearing to later ages, by both men and women; and the bulge in the population of adults in the middle-age groups—the "Baby Boomers," who were born following the Second World War and are now in their 40s.

WHO ARE THE SINGLES?

From the time they were born, the "Boomers" changed America's way of thinking about young people. In the years of their births, roughly from 1945 to 1950, the nation became child-centered. As these children grew, adolescents' demands for freedom in thought, activity, and expression increased in intensity and created friction with the parent generation. A subculture of youth developed, with needs, mores, and market influence of its own. The music teens listened to became the music heard everywhere; the movies they liked were the only ones playing in town. The clothing of adult women of all ages and sizes was "mini-mized" to clone the short-short skirts being worn by those who were sweet sixteen.

When they reached the college campuses in the late 1960s, the Boomers became famous for sit-ins and demonstrations—many of which were pro-civil rights and against hidebound organizations and military–national priorities. The Boomers gave us Woodstock, marijuana, love-ins, a crafts revival, and rural communes. "Do your own thing" became their slogan and their guide for activity. Disapproving of the adult world around them, and perhaps believing that they could somehow avoid entering it, the young created a unique rallying cry: "Don't trust anyone over 30!" Although only a minority of young people participated in any of the highly publicized, generation-labeling protests and mass demonstrations, these events encapsulated the mood of an era, and the majority of young people and adolescents embraced the desire to exhibit and enjoy their own individualities.

Eventually, the Boomers discovered they had to earn a living and needed skills for the jobs that awaited them. They gave community colleges a new population spurt, acquired undergraduate and, often, graduate degrees, and entered the real world of work. They encountered the new tool of the workplace, the computer. They migrated to cities, got good jobs, and began to earn high salaries. They learned to dress for success, and they continued to do their own "thing," however it was identified by then. Protected with widely available and effective means of birth control, they practiced living together, seeking new if temporary relationships. When they chose to, they had children, inside or outside of marriage.

The new life-style of the Boomers' children was envied by many older adults, even while they threw word-rocks at it, such as Yuppies (young urban professionals) or Yumpies (young upwardly mobile professionals). The acronyms DINKS (dual income, no kids) and SNAG (single new-age guy or girl) became popular among a number of singles. Some slightly older folks tried on new labels, such as Muppies (mature urban profes sionals), but these imitations didn't fit very well.

The children of the people who had experienced their own adolescence during the 1950s were coming of earning-age. Entire new industries came along to meet the needs of this most pampered generation of Americans. Designer jeans and nail salons catered to their desire to look expensively attractive but not extravagantly overdressed. Bars serving limited menus of newly chic ethnic foods—pasta salads, Tex-Mex tidbits, sushi, Cajun, and nouvelle American—sprang up in the neighborhoods where the young set worked or lived. Squash and tennis clubs, gyms, and health clubs offered fitness at a price, and many singles, not all young, signed up for memberships. Not infrequently, they joined out of a sense of obligation. As one young woman on her way to her gym explained, "I'm not looking forward to the next hour and a half, but I'm single and under 30, so I have to work out."

The personal goal of previous generations of young adults had been to find permanent mates and make marriages that would start families. The Yuppies of the 1970s and 1980s simply enjoyed themselves. By their very numbers and their relative affluence, they pioneered a new life-style for singles that set the social tone and economic standard for more than a decade. Singles had all the fun; they could date and enjoy a constant variety of sex partners without having to worry about spouses, or children, or accounting to anyone—or so it seemed to many married people.

Responses from singles contributed to one of the most striking findings of our research: Single adults *at all ages* have attitudes about sex, love, and marriage that are remarkably similar to those expressed by people born in the post-Second World War years (1945 to 1950) who are still in the singles' scene. This similarity was particularly apparent in responses to questions about the problems of being single.

RELATING

Although the term may be vague, a "relationship" is the new goal. The many creative pleas found in singles' ads ask for relationships, not marriages. No matter how ill-defined, a relationship beats loneliness, named by single people as their most major problem (see Table 5.9). However, in spite of the loneliness, a core of "permanent" singles remains committed to the singles' life, opting to remain unmarried (see Tables 5.2 and 5.3). These singles shy away from situations designed specifically for singles, such as singles' bars or singles' tours, because most people who frequent these kinds of environments *want* to get married. Hard-core singles, both men and women, cite a variety of personal reasons to remain single: money, control of one's own personal life, and—for women—fear that marriage will consign their careers to second place.

✦ *IN THEIR OWN WORDS* _____

> Let's face it, if I can't pay the alimony, then I have no business getting married. I know all about research and statistics, and one of two American families ends up getting divorced; with my luck I'll be in the splitsville group. And, I haven't even mentioned child support. How am I going to pay for two homes, my potential future ex-wife's and mine, when I have a hell-of-a-job getting by, paying one rent and taking fairly good care of myself right now?
>
> —A 34-year-old male high school teacher, who has never married

The singles' life has abundant benefits regarding sexual choice and variety of partners, but certainty is not one of them. For many singles, sex is the sought-for gratification; for others, sex is the way to beat loneliness.

Does a sexual relationship promote intimacy? Or, does it merely promote more sex? If the latter, then sex and intimacy may be seen as distinctly different. Many of our sample of respondents (not delineated as single or married) agreed that they were different (see Table 5.1).

Our interviews revealed that sincerity, caring, and even commitment often arise when single people have sex. What may be casual sex for one partner may be viewed by the other as a form of sharing, a very personal and intimate experience that will draw the couple closer. There is an almost classic dialogue that represents the tradition of pre- and early sexual revolution. While having sex, the man asks the woman if she loves him. The de-rigeur response is, "Would I let you do this if I didn't love you?" Singles are skilled in reading between the lines, when they have sex in uncommitted relationships. Table 5.1 indicates that men (69%) do not distinguish sex from intimacy as strongly as do women (74%). The percentages of men and women who disclaim a unity of sex and intimacy are close (17% and 21%), but women, overall, are more assertive in their opinions.

Among the major sexual changes that have taken place in American society is the fact that assertiveness regarding sex is now a prerogative exercised by women. The Second Sexual Revolution has enabled most women to fulfill themselves in many ways, not the least of which is assertion of their sexuality rather than passive acquiescence to sex. In many relationships today, women take the initiative for sex. Faked orgasms are fast disappearing and are being replaced by authentic orgasms. This would appear to be a benefit for both sexes, but some men have had difficulty adjusting to the liberated single woman.

Singles overwhelmingly speak of, and seek, love (see Table 5.18). Love is still considered the experience that makes life most fulfilling. Although the ways in which love weaves itself into the fabric of individual

TABLE 5.1 Survey Item C.12.

SEX AND INTIMACY ARE TWO DIFFERENT THINGS:		
	Men	Women
N =	376	438
Strongly agree	21%	34%
Agree	48	40
No opinion	14	5
Disagree	12	15
Strongly disagree	5	6
Strongly agree + Agree	69%	74%
Disagree + Strongly disagree	17%	21%

lives has changed, our research clearly shows that love is highly valued and is here to stay.

A new specter has appeared on the singles' scene: sexually transmitted diseases (STDs). Nonetheless, many singles, while expressing anxiety about STDs, maintain active sex lives by utilizing defensive measures, exercising increased caution in selecting sex partners, and otherwise practicing "safe" sex.

WHERE DID ALL THE SINGLES COME FROM?

We noted earlier in this chapter that the singles' population has continued to grow rapidly. Many singles actually prefer to remain single, for any of a number of reasons. How did we develop such a huge singles' society? Single men have always been more socially accepted than single women. The First Sexual Revolution, liberalized divorce laws, reduced social pressures to marry, and the women's movement explain only part of the phenomenon. The number and quality of career opportunities for women have continued to grow, causing more women to postpone marriage for the personal gratification of careers. However, as women's freedom of choice has expanded, new problems have arisen.

✦ *IN THEIR OWN WORDS* _____

> Being vice president of a marketing company at 32 is exciting, but many measure it against home and family. I earn $85,000 annually. This is more than 90% of men in America earn. I dress well, belong to a posh gym, take tennis lessons from great pros, travel extensively, and have terrific friends. The problem is that very few of them are men. Maybe my standards are too high? Sometimes it's hard to find someone to talk to who can understand me—not a stereotype of what they think a "professional woman" should be, but just me. I've been very successful professionally; I have a great many social skills and I'm not really worried about men and marriage, though many of my friends are. When I reach 36, I'll start to worry.
>
> —A 32-year-old businesswoman

Other singles, however, worry more about their futures. In 1986, *Newsweek*[3] reported that, statistically, a woman of 35 was more likely to be killed by a terrorist than to find a husband. A woman might indeed be looking for a husband, but she is more likely to be looking for a loving relationship, whether inside or outside the context of marriage. The marital potential of the single woman in her late 30s or her 40s may have been grossly minimized.

The "what's next" syndrome haunts many singles. Throughout our interviews, single individuals, both men and women, asked, "Well, I've got a good life now, and I enjoy it, but what's next?" "Where am I going to be three years, or five years, from now, and where *should* I be three years from now?" The unknown "what's next" causes anxiety, no matter how well placed the single person is in terms of present work or love relationships. Without an ongoing, committed relationship, many singles find it difficult, if not impossible, to plan a future.

LOVE, SEX, AND/OR MARRIAGE

We found a major role reversal in our interviews: a great many single men among our respondents disclosed that they and their male friends were looking, sometimes desperately, for commitments from women, and that the women wanted to play but not to commit. The ability to seek love, and to experience erotic gratification to its maximum potential, without having to pay even lip service to marriage, is new. There has been an ongoing debate, particularly in the professional mental health community, about the desirability of this development. In the First Sexual Revolution, many Americans shied away from marriage; in the Second Sexual Revolution, the status and desirability of marriage are growing. The traditional man viewed marriage as confining: he would have to be committed to one woman, caring and providing for her. The traditional woman viewed marriage as freeing her to do things she could not do as a single woman. Some women now give up more than men do when they marry. Many women love their careers, and an increasing number earn more than their potential spouses. Unfortunately, trying to maintain their careers while involved in relationships represents a crisis for many successful women. Couples are under considerable pressure when they attempt to work out relationships that meet the needs of both partners. A "liberated" approach by both is often required if the relationship is to succeed.

Relationships are both exciting and terribly anxiety-producing for this generation; there are simply no appropriate role models for the "new man" who can cry and diaper babies, or for the "achieving woman" who is successful and more comfortable in the workplace than the home. Our interviews showed that, although many men have gained an appreciation of the newly competitive female as a full economic and social partner, many others still remain intimidated. A general consensus among sociologists and feminists is that playing a comfortable role will be easier for the daughters of these women, and perhaps even for young women now in high school and college, because of the awareness and role models that the present pioneering generation of women has provided.

BUILDING ON THE FAMILY MODEL

The singles' life has traditionally been presented as being in direct opposition to family life. Many significant changes in the singles'—and the family's—life-style, however, have narrowed and minimized the differences. Sociologists use the term "family model" to indicate a social structure modeled after the traditional family organization and the roles of its members. A close look at the social lives of the singles' groups reveals ongoing associations that closely imitate family intimacy and relatedness and, in essence, become surrogate families.

How do adult singles' surrogate families function? From our interviews with those involved in this type of singles' pseudofamily, we learned of some interesting life-styles. Often, committees interview prospective applicants for the sharing of a summer house, for compatibility and similarity on a number of important issues. The committee takes into account age, religion, social status, physical attractiveness, and professional standing. Ironically, these are the very characteristics that traditional parents would have asked of a potential mate for their child. Generally, the gender of the individual must fit a predetermined ratio, to give the house's roster a sense of balance. Each member pays in advance for the entire season, thus making a solid commitment not to leave the "family." Members shop for food, cook, serve, clean, and live together. They become emotionally involved and intimate with each other in the same way that biological families do—maybe even more so, because these people relate by choice, not by chance. House rules generally are rather stringently imposed regarding dating or sleeping with other members of one's own house (it's felt to be too incestuous), although these rules are sometimes not observed. "Outside" guests are discouraged from sleeping over. It is common for a whole house to socialize together at a favorite pub, or to participate in regular social functions in the vacation community, as well as in their home community. Members also socialize as a group with other houses ("families") seeking friends. For some, the socializing is enough intimacy; they don't seek potential spouses. In effect, the "family" is enough for many of the members.

At the end of each season, "family" members pledge to return the next year, and most do. Members keep in touch regularly, helping each other shoulder career problems, family problems, alimony payments, illnesses, and so on. Some members may leave to marry, but this social group remains an ongoing family unit; even new spouses will be introduced to this "first" family.

Winter family groups are reportedly also growing rapidly in many areas of the country. The summer homes focus on beach and bikinis; the winter groups concentrate on skiing, winter sports, and fireplaces. Some members have little interest in skiing, but they love to put on ski sweaters, sit around the fire, socialize, and feel the sense of camaraderie all about them. Some men and women belong to both a summer home and a winter home, with different "families" in each. In other parts of the country, newly emerged singles, such as recent high school or college graduates, band together in single-sex households that clearly serve familial functions such as those described above.

Networking is often correctly perceived as a way to advance careers; however, networking also plays a significant role in a single person's social life. Networks are formed, both informally and formally, by professions, tenants' associations, religious or educational institutions, and combinations of all of these. Singles' networks exist in all major cities in the United States. Our research revealed that there are a variety of options allowing singles to cope with, if not downright enjoy, their life-styles.

Are most singles happy with their lot? An in-depth look at the data painted an interesting picture, as described in the next section.

HOW GRATIFYING IS THE SINGLES' LIFE-STYLE?

Throughout the following exploration of the substance of the singles' life-style, we have provided comparisons of single men and women and have matched our single respondents against the divorced group whenever relevant. Where applicable, we have included data from married couples, for comparison of their responses with those of the single and divorced individuals.

Tables 5.2 and 5.3 examine attitudes toward the state of being single. Is it a preferred, actively joined way to live, or a life-style in which some people happen to find themselves and to which they accommodate? Table 5.2

TABLE 5.2   **Survey Item F.1.**

THE SINGLES' LIFE IS THE MOST GRATIFYING LIFE-STYLE:		
	Single*	Divorced
N =	817	245
Strongly agree	7%	5%
Agree	19	11
No opinion	22	19
Disagree	46	55
Strongly disagree	6	10
Strongly agree + Agree	26%	16%
Disagree + Strongly disagree	52%	65%

*Signifies "never married" in the tables in this chapter.

TABLE 5.3   **Survey Item F.1.**

THE SINGLES' LIFE IS THE MOST GRATIFYING LIFE-STYLE:		
	Men	Women
N =	377	438
Strongly agree	8%	6%
Agree	21	15
No opinion	25	19
Disagree	42	52
Strongly disagree	4	8
Strongly agree + Agree	29%	21%
Disagree + Strongly disagree	46%	60%

contrasts divorced individuals, who were single when surveyed, with those who have never married. (Widows, widowers, and "separated" individuals are not included in the tables in this chapter.)

We wanted to find out whether there was a difference—and if so, how much—between single men and women on this issue. The responses we received are reflected in Table 5.3.

Just over one-quarter of the singles surveyed (Table 5.2) answered affirmatively, but more than half (52%) disagreed; the divorced group (65%) was even less favorable. The differences between single men and women (see Table 5.3) show that more men (29%) favor the single life than do women (21%), but a much larger percentage of men (46%) do not find it gratifying. Some reasons for this may be, as we heard from our interviewees, that women are conscious of their biological clock, and that men have greater social freedom of movement, which permits them to more fully and freely enjoy single living. Income is an additional factor affecting life-style, and men, on average, have considerably higher incomes than women.

FAMILY RESURGENCE

The obituaries that have been written about the American family may well have to be scrapped during the Second Sexual Revolution. The American family structure has imperfections, but it still seemed viable and attractive to most of our respondents. Gone are some radical social theories of the 1960s and 1970s, to which some of our highly educated interviewees alluded. For example, one proposal suggested one-year or five-year marriage contracts that would automatically expire unless renewed; another advocated "open marriages," in which the couple was

TABLE 5.4   **Survey Item F.2.**

IF I COULD LIVE IT OVER AGAIN, I WOULD DEFINITELY BE MARRIED:		
	Single	Divorced
N =	813	242
Strongly agree	9%	7%
Agree	24	41
No opinion	38	27
Disagree	22	19
Strongly disagree	7	6
Strongly agree + Agree	33%	48%
Disagree + Strongly disagree	29%	25%

free to have sexual affairs. Both of these proposals are variants on the singles' life-style.

The two groups of currently single individuals (those never married and those divorced) held different attitudes regarding marriage. (See Table 5.4.) For some singles (29%) and divorced persons (25%), the singles' life was still the more gratifying life-style. Given another chance, they would definitely *not* be married. The major difference in attitude among respondents who are now divorced was that nearly half (48%) thought that being married was better. This is a striking finding. Sadly, one-third of the singles (33%) said they would definitely be married if they could relive the choices or life-events that led to their single status.

Has the perception of the "swinging singles'" carefree and highly desirable life, as portrayed in some media, become worn and thin? Responses showed a greater popularity of marriage, although there was no majority pro or con. Are individuals increasingly searching for their personal fulfillment in marriage rather than in the singles' scene? This area deserves followup and future research.

SEX AND THE SINGLE LIFE

Several questions in our survey were designed to elicit information about attitudes toward sex and about sexual practices. On the ability to connect with others for the purpose of engaging in sexual activity with them, we separated the data for singles and divorced persons (Table 5.5) and by gender (Table 5.6).

The responses in both tables did not vary by more than 5%. Agreement and disagreement each claimed about two-fifths of the responses and, among the divorced persons, the percentages were the same (45%).

TABLE 5.5   Survey Item F.3.

I AM STILL INTIMIDATED ABOUT APPROACHING THE OTHER SEX FOR SEX:		
	Single	Divorced
N =	811	245
Strongly agree	8%	10%
Agree	34	35
No opinion	17	10
Disagree	27	36
Strongly disagree	14	9
Strongly agree + Agree	42%	45%
Disagree + Strongly disagree	41%	45%

(See Table 5.5.) Interestingly, 19% of women surveyed said they had no opinion on this issue. (See Table 5.6.) These results seem to indicate that tradition and restraint, and perhaps some indecision on the part of women, are still very much with us. Although the sexual environment has become dramatically open since the 1960s, fewer than half of today's singles are comfortable about broaching the subject of sex to a member of the other gender. A separate breakdown of our data, in Table 3.27, showed that men and women share very similar attitudes and anxieties about proposing sex. How times have changed!

If so many people have qualms about making first approaches, how then do people get together?

TABLE 5.6   Survey Item F.3.

I AM STILL INTIMIDATED ABOUT APPROACHING THE OTHER SEX FOR SEX:		
	Men	Women
N =	376	435
Strongly agree	6%	9%
Agree	37	31
No opinion	16	19
Disagree	24	31
Strongly disagree	17	10
Strongly agree + Agree	43%	40%
Disagree + Strongly disagree	41%	41%

I love coming into a room, having heads turn to me. I get a charge out of seeing the desire in the men's eyes, but I act cool while they die for me—at first. I take my time and look around. Then, if I am interested in anyone, I let it be known, ever so subtly—just a nod of my head, so our eyes meet; that usually does the trick. Then I wait for him to approach me. The whole initial drawing together, the first eye contact, the first words spoken between us—always reminds me of an adagio movement in a symphony. The sensuous implications are below the surface but the intensity steadily, at a measured pace, keeps growing.

—A 29-year-old female investment banker

If all men had qualms about making the first move, this woman would never have an opportunity for any kind of relationship! One wonders how she would fare if she were the one who was initially attracted to a man and he was "playing it cool." What will she do when she loses her ability to turn men's heads?

One never-married man whom we interviewed seemed to sum up the ambivalent feelings of many singles toward making the first approaches. He had lived with each of two women for several years, and had made it clear that he did not hesitate to approach a woman for sex—he said he had slept with about 90 women. Yet, he told us, he "hates the seduction game." Then he went on heatedly: "Let's face it, no one gets seduced unless they really want to be. Since both parties want the same thing, why do we have to play games?" When singles' needs are in conflict with others' expectations, frustration is the result.

Why can't women express their desires like men do? Why must we all play this stupid game of seduction? I couldn't believe it. We were lying in bed, we had great sex early in the night, and I still felt horny. I wasn't sure if he was still sleeping, but I figured it would be a nice way to wake up. I reached over and touched his penis . . . he pushed my hand aside, and rolled over, turning away. Away from me! Now you've got to admit that I am not hard to look at. I was homecoming queen at college, and I was a model for a while before I got into the business end of advertising. Here I am, offering myself to this jerk, and he pushed my hand away! At first I thought that perhaps he didn't realize what was happening, so I rolled over against him, kissed him, and reached around to touch his penis again. This time he not only pushed my hand away, but he muttered, "No, leave me alone, I'm tired." Well, this confirmed some prior experiences with doctors as lovers. Herbie—I'm sure that his mother calls him Dr. Herbie—a great looking young surgeon with an irresistible body and a firm tush, was too tired to make love! Making love once, the night before, made the poor baby tired. What was I to do, force him? Knowing what a baby Herbie is, he might even tell his mother I raped him. So I crept out of bed, then suddenly realizing what was happening, I said to myself, "Stupid, why are you sneaking out of bed like a thief, this is your apartment!"

I enjoy great sex with a guy I care about. The question in your questionnaire asked if sex is sensual. I answered truthfully that it is deliciously so. So I've had some terrific lovers, and then there are the guys like Herb. Herb was one more doctor; my mother always urged me to go with educated men, especially doctors. Women's roles have changed so much, so quickly, my ego-ideal was waffling somewhere between Gloria Steinem and my mother, and was I confused! Yes, there are some guys who don't like the new woman I represent, and you know what I say to that? TOUGH!

—A 28-year-old career woman, who has never married

Beyond attitudes toward assertiveness—or, in the eyes of the traditional man, aggressiveness—and how approaches should be made, there is still the issue of the products of sexual encounters: children. Some singles wish to have sex with no further commitments; others are willing to become parents without wanting to become spouses.

The New Age Woman often experiences growing apprehension when she reaches her 30s and early 40s and her biological clock is ticking away. Some women express regret at not having children; others report that they are fine without children. Even in these times of postponed childbearing, the question of parenthood looms up for men as well as women. Singles with no plans to marry do become single parents—some by adoption, and others biologically, through sperm banks; but most still enter parenthood the old-fashioned way. Table 5.7 shows the importance of parenthood among single people.

Strivings for parenthood can be seen in the responses of both the men and the women surveyed. The numbers seeking parenthood are close, but they still show women being more interested than men in becoming parents. Although the percentages of those desiring parenthood are slightly lower than those rejecting it, they are still notably large for the singles population. It is no surprise that the 1990 Census reported that there were 13.9 million single-parent households maintained by the mother, and 2.0 million maintained by the father.[4] The strength of the need for creating a family, perhaps even a unique kind of family, remains very strong in our culture, without regard to marital status. Our interviews confirmed that, although many in the singles group clearly desired to become parents, most would prefer to do this in the context of marriage.

Another factor in the decision to remain single is purely economic. Money is something that singles worry about. Among men, there is fear regarding the potential burden of having to pay alimony for a failed

TABLE 5.7   **Survey Item F.4.**

I WOULD LIKE TO BECOME A PARENT EVEN IF I REMAIN SINGLE:		
	Men	Women
N =	374	437
Strongly agree	6%	10%
Agree	32	35
No opinion	20	9
Disagree	26	28
Strongly disagree	16	18
Strongly agree + Agree	38%	45%
Disagree + Strongly disagree	42%	46%

marriage. We questioned our respondents about the prevalence of this fear. (See Table 5.8.)

Some singles used the excuse of real or anticipated financial problems to remain single, but, combining the two levels of agreement, we found that those in both groups who showed concern for the potential negative financial consequences of divorce were hardly the majority. The singles, who had never been married, were more concerned about being trapped in a financial marital web than were the divorced. Potential money problems associated with divorce did not figure largely in the minds of either group.

What *are* the perceived problems in the single life? Lack of shared experiences, solitary meals, lack of conversation, and the problems listed in Table 5.9, are profound issues for many singles. Loneliness was cited by both single men and women as their major problem.

TABLE 5.8   **Survey Item F.5.**

FEAR OF DIVORCE AND ITS MONEY PROBLEMS KEEPS ME SINGLE:		
	Single	Divorced
N =	809	246
Strongly agree	7%	4%
Agree	15	14
No opinion	15	12
Disagree	39	42
Strongly disagree	24	28
Strongly agree + Agree	22%	18%
Disagree + Strongly disagree	63%	70%

TABLE 5.9   Survey Item F.6.

WHAT IS YOUR MAJOR PROBLEM, IF ANY, IN BEING SINGLE?		
	Men	Women
N =	374	437
Loneliness	41%	41%
Family pressures	2	5
Finances	4	5
Social pressures	5	4
Finding a spouse	12	17
None at all	36	28

Our interviews with single men and women showed that loneliness is a burden that mature adults and the younger singles have in common. Our interviews also disclosed that single women are more successful than men at networking and at making and maintaining relationships (of whatever kind), possibly because of strong cultural support of such women's networks. Men are expected to be able to "tough it out" alone. However, according to some respondents whom we interviewed, recent developments involving male networking seem to promise some support for single men's socializing needs.

Finding a suitable spouse, the next problem cited in order of importance, was slightly more a concern of women than of men. Family pressures and social pressures were minor for both groups. Thirty-six percent of the men and 28% of the women surveyed claimed that they had no problem with being single. The 8% difference between the two groups indicated that the women were less at home with their single status.

A more personal and intimate look at the emotional makeup of single and divorced persons follows. The material is drawn from the responses we received to questions that examined the import of romance and sensuality in the lives of our respondents.

VIEWS AND EXPERIENCES

When we began to compare singles with marrieds on several issues relating to romance and sex, our first question was: What do singles think about the value of traditional sex roles? Table 5.10 compares the singles' answers with those of married and divorced respondents.

Interestingly, all groups felt that traditional sex roles have a place in modern society (disagree and strongly disagree). The singles and marrieds responded almost identically, indicating that the singles identified with family values. The divorced group, who had experienced the

TABLE 5.10 Survey Item A.13.

TRADITIONAL SEX ROLES HAVE NO PLACE IN MODERN SOCIETY:						
	Single		Married		Divorced	
	Men	Women	Men	Women	Men	Women
N =	376	437	769	802	119	124
Strongly agree	6%	6%	6%	8%	11%	9%
Agree	20	26	23	29	27	34
No opinion	16	14	14	10	20	9
Disagree	47	48	47	46	37	45
Strongly disagree	11	6	10	7	5	3
Strongly agree + Agree	26%	32%	29%	37%	38%	43%
Disagree + Strongly disagree	58%	54%	57%	53%	42%	48%

trauma of family breakup, supported traditional roles less than the others. All three groups seemed aligned with some societal reminder of what their status was and what roles they were to play. Often, even when they acknowledged that there is a sexual double standard, people we interviewed still indicated that they preferred traditional sex roles, or, as Archie Bunker would frequently orate, "Boys are boys and girls are girls." With the exception of the divorced group (42% of men and 48% of women), our respondents were quite close (within 5 percentage points) in their disagreement with the questionnaire statement. Those who responded that they reject tradition (strongly agree and agree) mustered their highest percentages among divorced men (38%) and women (43%), but were distinctly in the minority. Twenty percent of divorced men indicated that they had no opinion on the questionnaire statement. Many values have changed, but the need for tradition, the need for guidelines on how to behave sexually like a male or female, still persists in American society.

Is there a discernible difference, between those married and those not married, in feelings of romance and sensuality? Table 5.11 shows responses based on self-description.

Differences emerged among the responses of the several groups. Not surprisingly, the single women led in seeing themselves as very romantic. This self-image came out often in interviews as a reason to remain single; their love had been unrequited, and they were optimistically holding out for their Prince Charming. Sharp differences showed up between men and women, both married and single. Women saw themselves as very romantic considerably more than did men. However, men led by a wide margin in the romantic self-view. Responses of realistic, for both men and women, were higher for the marrieds than the singles,

TABLE 5.11   **Survey Item G.1.**

ROMANTICALLY I AM:				
	Single		Married	
	Men	Women	Men	Women
N =	377	439	769	801
Very romantic	28%	41%	17%	33%
Romantic	54	36	55	46
Realistic	13	14	23	17
Cautious	4	7	4	3
Cynical	1	2	1	1
Very romantic + Romantic	82%	77%	72%	79%

which seemed to us to be a natural outgrowth of the widening experience of marriage. Psychotherapists and marital therapists consistently find that reasonable, realistic expectations and a willingness to compromise are major factors in stable and rewarding relationships. A member of our research team characterized our groupings of "the singles, divorced, and marrieds" as "the dreamers, the disillusioned, and the practical" respectively.

With their idealistic vision of being "romantic," many single people embark on a heedless and compulsive search for intense continuing romance, which often causes them much disappointment and hurt. For some, the search for "romance" becomes their raison d'être, a "cause" to justify repeated painful relationships. Their search is really an unrealistic desire for the euphoria and ecstasy of the infatuation stage of relationships, and an inability to accept the natural ending of that stage. Our data showed that the singles, especially the single women, were the more cautious group. Did the married people need less caution because having a partner gave them a sense of security and less anxiety about being personally vulnerable? Cynics were few in all groups, with only a slightly higher rate in the responses of single women.

Romance is the material that dreams and poems are made of, but, as we heard repeatedly in our interviews, it may not work as well with real people in real situations. When interviewed, the "hard core" singles, the ones who are repeatedly hurt each time romantic feelings do not flower into lasting relationships, expressed the most desperate need for love. They were not consciously turned off to intimate relatedness, but their need for it was so great, and their expectations so unreal, that they repeatedly set themselves up for disappointment. Unfortunately, their expectations are encouraged by films and other popular media.

I always ask myself the question, "Why am I 43 and still single?" The answer is heartbreak and disappointment. I am successful, have money, and have a great future. Why am I being tortured like this? I have been in love with quite a number of women, and, in fact, I was engaged to four. They were always the ones who broke off the relationship. Women are great at brinksmanship; they are the emotionally strong ones, not the men. To prove the point, one of my former fiancées called off the marriage the day before the wedding. Am I doomed to forever be the "bridesmaid" and never the "bride"? Each time something like this happened, I was crushed. I think I should buy stock in the company that makes Valium. Every time I experience a disastrous relationship I get a new therapist, hoping that maybe this one can tell me what went wrong, tell me that I am too vulnerable, that I wear my heart on my sleeve. One therapist, in fact, told me that by being so gung-ho for a total commitment, I was frightening women away. Call it by whatever name you will, when my dreams are shattered by a woman, it's heartbreak city for me.

—A 43-year-old single man

While personal agonies go on, romance is very much alive and doing well on the American social scene. Individuals are now able to customize their romantic desires and eroticism to suit their personal needs. Romance is what most people still build their lives on, and, in the case of both the singles and the divorced, what they build their hopes on as well. In a progressive move from the abstraction of romance to the eroticism of sex, Table 5.12 examines self-assessments of sensuality.

From these data, one can see dramatically important living patterns emerging. The group that sees themselves as more deliciously sensuous

TABLE 5.12   **Survey Item G.2.**

SENSUALLY, I FEEL THAT SEX IS:				
	Single		Married	
	Men	Women	Men	Women
N =	376	437	770	799
1 Deliciously sensuous	70%	55%	57%	46%
2	23	30	32	38
3	6	12	9	14
4	1	2	2	2
5 Grossly distasteful	0	1	0	0
Line 1 + Line 2	93%	85%	89%	84%

than the other is, not surprisingly, the singles. They led all respondents as being very romantic, and they led all others as being deliciously sensuous. The fact that marrieds, especially married women, have the lower ratings on deliciously sensuous confirms some cynics' theory that romance and eroticism are incompatible with marriage. Indeed, many "hard core" singles make the same claim. Regarding the significant difference between the singles and the marrieds, some might call the higher responses of the singles *wishes* and the lower responses of the marrieds *realism*. Those married respondents whom we interviewed claimed that romance and sex were plentiful and were sufficient to their needs and desires; many of them strove for sensuality, even if they did not feel it intensely. Perhaps when they were single the marrieds too would have responded in the extreme in favor of romance and sex. Few respondents found sex to be distasteful (see Table 5.12). Therefore, another interpretation of the responses of marrieds is that they, once again, were willing to exchange idealism for a pragmatic, but enduring and rewarding, realism.

As for the less sensuous, our interviews established that many of them did strive for sensuality; even if they did not feel it intensely, their attitude toward it was far from negative.

Having found that romance and sensuality were important as part of the persona of both single and married persons, it was now time to look into the actual functional level of their sex lives. Our analysis distinguished between what respondents hoped for and how they viewed themselves. Shortly, we will examine what they actually *did*. Table 5.13 addresses a self-view of sexuality. Our questionnaire offered respondents five choices as answers to a statement on personal sexual activity.

The married, contrary to expectation, reported the highest level of sexual activity. One obvious reason is the availability of a sex partner near at hand. For the singles and divorced, sexual urges may frequently go unfulfilled for lack of a partner. The possibility also exists that self-assessment

TABLE 5.13   **Survey Item G.3.**

I CONSIDER MYSELF TO BE SEXUALLY:			
	Single	Divorced	Married
N =	814	244	1,567
Very active	18%	15%	16%
Active	29	30	38
Average	25	26	33
Below average	15	15	10
Inactive	13	14	3
Very active + Active	47%	45%	54%
Below average + Inactive	28%	29%	13%

on this issue may be a matter of expectation: singles and divorced, who may have the same frequency of sexual activity as the marrieds, may interpret their activity level as below par. To be fair, some singles, particularly older persons, complain that their problem is finding sex partners, not a lack of sexual desire or ability. These findings paint a new picture of marriage: while not a constant scene of "shells bursting in air" sexually, it is a sexually consistent and gratifying way of life for some people. This theme, which we touch on frequently, is supported by many marriage counselors who have found that the causes of divorce include over-romanticized dreams and impossible demands for sexual and other kinds of gratification.

The divorced group is interesting. Its responses are sometimes similar to those of the marrieds and, at other times, similar to those of the singles. Divorced people tend to see themselves as cynical, as a result of their experience with marriage failure. This self-identification may make it harder for the divorced to socialize and spontaneously enjoy sexual and/or romantic interaction. However, their relationships may be more successful in the long run, if they can modulate their cynicism and overcome their cautiousness enough to take basic relationship roles.

Sex and romance are important ingredients to success in marriage; they are not part of the fireball ferocity of anxiety or desperation, but they bring a long-term slow burn that is reported as gratifying by marrieds but is put down by our instant-gratification-dominated culture. Singles led the way with their self-estimation of intensity for sensuality. However, marriage seems to have come a long way to dispel a notion that many American children have—that their parents do not have sex with each other. Comedian Sam Levinson's joke said it all: "Poppa maybe, mama never!"

Americans are romantic and they accept sensuality readily, and these two precepts form the basis for sexual fulfillment. But do most Americans feel they are functioning at their biological maximum sexually? If not, how far below their perceived maximum do they feel they are? Tables 5.14 and 5.15 show these self-ratings. We have included the married respondents in these tables for comparison. Sex, we had found, was often viewed in extremes; in Table 5.15, we offered respondents the opportunity to express intense disappointment with their sexual activity level by

TABLE 5.14   **Survey Item G.4.**

ARE YOU FUNCTIONING AT YOUR BIOLOGICAL MAXIMUM SEXUALLY?			
	Single	Divorced	Married
N =	814	244	1,561
Yes	53%	43%	49%
No	47%	57%	51%

TABLE 5.15   Survey Item G.5.

HOW MUCH BELOW MAXIMUM SEXUAL POTENTIAL ARE YOU?			
	Single	Divorced	Married
N =	384	142	784
10% below	23%	9%	17%
25% below	27	29	32
50% below	27	29	37
100% below	23	33	14
50% to 100% below	50%	62%	51%

including a response of up to 100% below their sexual potential. As our early pilot studies had shown, including that alternative made sense for the small number of respondents who felt that they had to list, in the extreme, their frustration with their sex lives.

About half of the singles (53%) and marrieds (49%) responded that they were functioning at their sexual biological maximums; the divorced group's response was 43%. By combining the two lowest levels of sexual activity in Table 5.15, we confirmed much of what already had been made clear by the other data in this chapter: A tiny minority (14%) of marrieds said they were functioning 100% below their sexual capacity; 23% of the singles and 33% of the divorced said the same. The divorceds' sexual function level indicated that they were lacking sexual fulfillment more than any other group. The question then became: Do the singles or the divorceds suffer from lack of sex partners, or do they have libidinal problems?

Specifics were required to determine the actual frequency of sexual activity. Our first need was for information on the totality of *all* sexual activity in which they were involved. Those data were gathered in Table 5.16.

By a very significant margin, the married group reported having sex much more frequently than the other two groups. Fear of STDs may play a part in suppressing the numbers of sex partners for the two nonmarried groups, although Table 5.19 and Table 5.20 give this theory little support.

Throughout this chapter, there is consistent confirmation of the fact that, although single and divorced people may have a greater variety of sexual partners, they do not have sex with the frequency that married persons do. Marrieds' easier accessibility to sex partners obviously affects these results. However, the variety and novelty of having different sex partners is the counterbalance for singles and divorced.

The fact that such frequent sexual relations are occurring within marriage might come as a surprise to those cynical singles who see marriage as the doom of sexual spontaneity and longevity and wave a banner for "Variety beats monotony." Sex in marriage today is not sex as an obligation;

TABLE 5.16   Survey Item G.6.

FREQUENCY OF ALL SEXUAL ACTIVITY IS:			
	Single	Divorced	Married
N =	815	246	1,552
Daily	11%	9%	14%
Few times weekly	32	33	44
Weekly	21	26	27
Monthly	17	10	8
Rarely	19	22	7
Daily + Few times weekly	43%	42%	58%

married sex in this era of the Second Sexual Revolution combines sexual activity with romance and mutual sensuality. The new sexual awareness by women, their altered roles, and their diverse life-styles have wrought great changes. To further define the sexual activity practiced, we queried respondents on their frequency of masturbation. (See Table 5.17.)

The singles responded most frequently to the never option, which seemed to indicate that they must have satisfying interpersonal outlets for their sexual needs. Nonetheless, their daily-to-weekly masturbatory activity levels were slightly higher (48% for men, 28% for women) than the marrieds' (44% and 16%) and significantly lower than the divorceds' (68% and 37%). Our singles seemed to have active interpersonal sex lives, but they still needed supplementary solo activity.

TABLE 5.17   Survey Item D.8.

I MASTURBATE ON AVERAGE:						
	Single		Married		Divorced	
	Men	Women	Men	Women	Men	Women
N =	374	432	768	797	120	122
Daily	9%	2%	5%	1%	8%	4%
Several times weekly	17	12	17	5	29	15
Weekly	22	14	22	10	31	18
Monthly	6	11	10	19	5	20
Rarely	23	24	26	40	21	32
Never	23	37	20	25	6	11
Daily + Several times weekly + Weekly	48%	28%	44%	16%	68%	37%

Masturbation represents a personal expression of sex. Dramatic results became evident in Table 5.17. Men, in each group, reported greater incidence of masturbation, but women's percentages were also substantial. However, the divorced group's percentages were dramatically different, with the largest percentages of men and women reporting daily-to-weekly masturbation. Their loss of readily available partners explained much of this activity. In interviews, they indicated that they had supplanted interpersonal sex relations with masturbation. Our interviews clarified that the never responses were not to be taken as meaning that these individuals had no sex life, but only that some other avenue of sexual expression was being taken. Again, there was a greater similarity between the singles and marrieds than between either of those groups and the divorced group. Our data probably underestimated the true incidences, because we found, in our interviews, that some individuals were shy about reporting masturbation.

SEARCHING

As the singles population has grown, so have the number and variety of services meant to provide the opportunity to initiate and maintain social contacts. Such facilities include dating services, singles resorts, singles housing complexes, and singles tours—all directed toward meeting and mating. Reality and romantic fantasy commingle in such settings, permitting some participants to anticipate long-term relationships, and others, short-term sexual interactions.

As we saw in Table 5.5, many people reported having difficulty in approaching others for sex. Table 5.14 revealed the numbers of people who have identified themselves as functioning below, or even far below, their sexual capacity. How do individuals accomplish successful sexual approach scenarios? Some researchers have examined how people approach prospective partners and, in essence, ask and/or bargain for sex. The "exchange theory" seeks to explore how males and females initiate relations. Scanzoni,[5] for example, employed this framework to suggest that singles are definitely goal-oriented and they intentionally seek to obtain something in a relationship by exchanging something else in return. Bargaining for sex and companionship seems gauche, particularly to sensitive singles, and this deal making makes them feel even more vulnerable and socially exposed. Nonetheless, bargain they inevitably do, although their trading methods may not be obvious or even conscious. They are aware, however, that they can offer what others seek from potential partners. The part of the exchange theory that is most interesting—and most upsetting to some bargainers—is what each, male and female, has to exchange with the other. Men exchange social status as their value, and women offer expressive qualities, according to the exchange theory. Like many other theories, much of the substance on which these models were built has diminished or evaporated totally. As women have advanced and modified their status in modern society, the changes in their roles have accelerated and deepened. An interesting alternate view was offered by Hendrix,[6] who pointed out that one characteristic of dysfunctional relationships is that they tend to be seen like a commodities market. Hendrix advocated an approach in which partners work to overcome an exchange-based relationship and focus on genuinely giving to each other, with no strings attached and no expectations of a commodity (often love, nurturing, or sex) in return.

What price do singles pay to find and to establish new relationships, and how much of themselves are they willing to invest? Responses to our statement about commitment to love (Table 5.18) shed a good deal of light on this question.

As the table shows, both groups believed that love was worth a risk of hurt. The no opinion responses represented an interesting contradiction for the singles group, however. Generally, singles are the more needy and passionate of the two groups, yet 6% remained undecided on the issue of love versus hurt. Combining the disagree and strongly disagree responses revealed that 9% of singles would not risk being hurt for love. The more conservative divorced group felt this caution much more strongly (15%).

The people in both groups have the same basic needs for love. Yet there are, according to our interviews, many singles who will never marry because they cannot feel enough urgency about forming a relationship to enable them to offer a lasting commitment. Most singles claim simply that they have not found the "right" person. This explanation eases one's ego and puts the responsibility on an absent "other."

Our interviews illustrated both the ambivalence of many singles toward relationships, and their trials and disappointments.

TABLE 5.18   **Survey Item A.2.**

IT IS BETTER TO LOVE AND BE HURT THAN NOT TO KNOW LOVE:		
	Single	Divorced
N =	816	245
Strongly agree	37%	35%
Agree	48	47
No opinion	6	3
Disagree	7	12
Strongly disagree	2	3
Strongly agree + Agree	85%	82%
Disagree + Strongly disagree	9%	15%

I know a great many sharp women—I mean, smart, beautiful, with great careers—who really move a lot socially, and when we talk, most of them say the same thing; they have been hurt by some men. I have found that the strong ones are not the ones who claim that they were not hurt, but the ones who recover quickly, and remember that they may also have broken some guy's heart in the search for love.

One guy, a surprisingly bright man who was 41, an executive type, told me how he had broken up with six different women he was engaged to. There was a long story why each relationship had come unraveled, but in each case he reached a point where he felt that he had to commit himself "forever," and he freaked out, and walked. This he told me on the first date! I figured this guy is weird. If this is the message he is giving me, I don't even want to get started. I told him to get lost!

It would be okay if he was the only strange man I knew, but he's not the only guy I've met who has serious problems. My question is how can you find out just what a person is like before you say "I Do"?

—A 33-year-old woman who is a manufacturing executive

✦ ✦ ✦

Look, I know I have looks, and I do have the figure, unlike some of my friends who have had babies and let themselves go to pot. I'm also smart. Attractive men have always wanted me, and vice versa. Some of them were my students, though rarely so. But this is not a big town. There came a time when it looked like there were no more men in the town or the school who would appeal to me.

Finally, when it got too quiet I decided to place an ad in *New York Magazine*. I'm close enough to New York City to get in easily, and I spend most of my free time there anyway at the art galleries, so distance didn't matter. But what to say was the problem. I had never defined myself in cold facts. I came up with things like "art devotee, sensuous lady, and financially secure," which I am. After the initial unease of meeting people this way, I got to like it. Yes, I am a modern woman, and I have had affairs, long-term affairs with married men.

I think there is more passion and caring in these relations than in marriage. Two people hunger for them so much they're willing to deal with the problems. My goodness, I never realized the sheer numbers of men that were lonely, but some of them are so depressed they depress me. I've become kind of an expert at this game so I started putting in phrases like, "good man wanted—high on life, enjoys the good life, etc." This worked, but I had to take out the financially secure part of the description of myself, because I started getting a lot of men who were interested in my money, and not my body. I could take it if they were equally passionate about each. In fact, if I ever found such a man I'd never let him go!

—A 41-year-old female administrative assistant, who has never married

THE NUMBERS GAME

What about all that wild fun and funky sex that singles are supposed to enjoy? Is sex really varied for them, and do the numbers and reported variety of sexual partners singles supposedly enjoy ring true? Some singles claim their reason for singleness is enjoyment of the freedom and the fun. We found that most respondents were surprised themselves, when they tallied up the number of sex partners they had had in their lives. Table 5.19 summarizes the numbers of sex partners that were reported to us.

Some comments regarding this question, and the responses we received, are in order. In creating our computer program, we initially set the maximum number of possible responses at two digits, assuming that we would get responses no higher than 99 sexual partners, except for a very few individuals. As the responses to our questionnaire began pouring in, we quickly learned, to our surprise, that we had been too conservative. We had to modify the program to accommodate three digits, up to a maximum of 999 partners. Even this did not encompass everyone. We had 12 respondents who reported having had sex with 1,000 different partners! Of these 12, only 3 were in the sex business as call girls or sex surrogates.

Further investigation revealed that the largest tallies were coming from individuals who had been practicing group sex, in which numbers of sex partners accumulated rapidly.

The divorced group, we learned in our interviews, had much more sexual experience with a variety of partners, or frantically sought a larger supply of partners, or simply had been around longer.

TABLE 5.19   **Survey Item G.7.**

HOW MANY DIFFERENT INDIVIDUALS (INCLUDING SPOUSES) HAVE YOU HAD SEXUAL RELATIONS WITH?			
	Single	Divorced	Married
N =	810	242	1,561
None	4%	0%	0%
1–10	26	20	42
11–30	40	46	32
31–60	16	12	15
61–100	5	7	6
100 +	9	15	5
1–30	66%	66%	74%
61 and over	14%	22%	11%

At the lower end of the scale, the percentage of those who had had 10 or fewer partners was significantly greater for marrieds. Although the marrieds reported having sex most frequently, compared to the other groups (see Table 5.16), 42% had had 10 or fewer sex partners. We could not interpret from the range given on the questionnaire (1–10) how many monogamous marrieds were responding. If further research indicates a majority of monogamous marriages within this group, that result would support the perception of many marital therapists that availability and security are as aphrodisiac as novelty and variety. However, our results showed that, when the next larger category (11 to 30 sex partners) was added, the total percentage for marrieds shot past the other two groups (74% had 1 to 30 partners, compared to 66% in the other two groups). More research on these findings is in order.

THE SINGLES: MORE SEX OR LESS?

Has the sexual life-style of singles flourished or withered in the past few years? Table 5.20 provides some relevant information.

The responses of the single men and women were very similar; even on this question, the women reported only slightly less activity than the men. It is striking that, in both groups, almost half of those surveyed reported increased sex activity in the past 3 years, and only 25% and 29%, respectively, reported less sexual activity. Yet singles are the most vulnerable candidates for what society is supposed to be fearing most— STDs. In interviews, many of our respondents expressed confidence in their ability to protect themselves by selecting healthy partners, taking prudent contraceptive measures, and practicing "safe" sex. In a development that dates back only a few years, women and, to a lesser extent,

TABLE 5.20   Survey Item D.9.

COMPARED TO 3 YEARS AGO, MY SEX ACTIVITY IS:		
	Men	Women
N =	375	435
Much more	28%	23%
More	20	22
Same	27	26
Less	17	15
Much less	8	14
Much more + More	48%	45%
Less + Much less	25%	29%

men are increasingly interviewing their potential sex partners about their prior sex lives, to determine how many partners and what kind of people each individual has had sex with. No verification of the information given is possible, of course. A number of respondents told us that they had rejected partners whom they "felt" were not safe.

THE NEGATIVE AFTERMATH OF PERFECTION

Sex among the singles may serve multiple purposes. It can be sex as its own reward; it may serve to measure the compatibility of a potential long-term mate; or, sometimes, sex may even be used to promote a compatibility that will lead to marriage. However, factors that interfere with a person's psychological readiness for marriage may be present.

Some singles we interviewed stayed single for what seems to be an odd reason: They reported their parents' having "a marriage made in heaven." These people anticipated great difficulty in duplicating such a marriage for themselves on earth. In order to explore this belief and the family experience, we felt that individuals' prior family history regarding divorce would contribute to our understanding. Mental health practitioners know that, frequently, parental divorce affects children as they make their own choices as adults. To shed some light on this possibility, we examined responses of all three groups to a survey item about their parents' marriage (see Table 5.21).

The results were impressive in tracing clues to the life-scripts these respondents were following. A convincing segment of the puzzle surrounding their choice of life-style—single, divorced, or married—was seen in the numbers of parental divorces for each of the three groups. The singles and the divorced group led in having come from families of divorce or separation. Do a significant number of singles and divorced persons remain unmarried for reasons they may not consciously be aware of—reasons traceable to their being products of broken homes? Most of the marrieds surveyed had come from intact families. The divorced group had had the

TABLE 5.21   **Survey Item B.10.**

MY PARENTS' MARRIAGE WAS:			
	Single	Divorced	Married
N =	818	246	1,569
Always intact	65%	67%	76%
They separated	9	5	7
They divorced	23	27	16
Never married	3	1	1

courage to try marriage, and, statistically, divorced people remarry at higher rates than the never-married singles marry.

SUMMING UP

One of our unanticipated discoveries in researching singles was that, as seen through the eyes of single people, marriage still looks good! Gone are the jokes everyone has heard about marriage, such as: "The three rings of marriage: the engagement ring, the marriage ring, and the suffering." Most single and divorced people aspire to marriage and family. Their not being married is regarded as a matter of timing—it's not the "right" time, or they haven't met the "right" partner—rather than an enduring commitment to a carefree and swinging life-style. However, singles tend to be more romantic and probably less practical than married people. Less willing to settle for the real, they maintain a fantasy of perfection.

The American family has suffered too many premature obituaries in the mass media and even in social science journals. The family is functioning and is awarded increasingly high status by all groups. There is no question of the presence of a very large group of mobile, professionally successful singles who have deferred marriage and children. There is also a large group of formerly married, now divorced people looking to become attached again. Along with other incentives, the reality of sexually transmitted diseases has made it more urgent to be married and to have a safe sex partner.

Perhaps a more surprising finding is that the three groups are not as disparate as may have been assumed. They are all cut from the same cloth, with the same basic needs. To understand the singles' scene, one must be aware of the phenomenon of singleness, view divorce or marriage as an evolving and not a fixed situation, and look at relationships as a continuum. At any given time, some people are moving toward one state of being and others are moving away from it. Personal social freedom, coupled with security, is what singles claim to strive for; some find it in marriage, some in other relationships, and some relentlessly pursue it as an unattainable ideal.

Most of the singles we interviewed expressed the feeling that they were successful in their careers. Many, though, proclaimed that they always are still seeking that "someone special." Singles, particularly young singles, continue to experiment with relationships and with expressions of love and romance. Some hit and some miss. For many singles, the search for personal fulfillment is drawn against a backdrop of parental divorce. Some of the singles are not youngsters: many are over 30, and quite a few are in their 40s and 50s.

The divorced group is an amalgam that resembles both marrieds and singles but has somewhat more cynicism about relationships. Divorced persons are still open to trying again, in the hope of having a good marital relationship. "I've learned from the past, and I don't think I will repeat my original mistake," is how many express themselves and their expectations. Their confidence is high with regard to most other life areas. But marital therapists consistently caution that the divorced, as well as singles recovering from a breakup, will be destined to recapitulate, over and over, troubled relationships that can be remarkably similar, if they don't learn from their relationship experience. However, the therapists also offer the hope that learning from these experiences can help an individual's relationships evolve in an increasingly satisfying manner.

With patience, time, and support, individuals go a long way toward liberating their inner selves, as only they can do best. Networks and support groups, religious and educational institutions, political organizations, and special interest groups (feminist groups, fathers against confiscatory alimony, and others) make for a very full basket of resources for both singles and those presently unmarried. Through such groups, as they learn from others' experiences, many singles and divorced people get support and find importance, meaning, satisfaction, and, perhaps, love in their lives.

CHAPTER SIX

Marriage and Divorce

SOME SIGNIFICANT FINDINGS ABOUT MARRIAGE AND DIVORCE

✦ Women who lived with their spouses before marriage are more likely to be divorced than women who didn't; men, less likely. Couples still married had lived together, on the average, for a shorter period of time before marriage than those who are now divorced.

✦ More than one-third of men and more than one-quarter of women admit having had at least one extramarital sexual experience, but extramarital affairs account for fewer than one-quarter of all divorces.

✦ More than twice as many women as men, married or divorced, report never having masturbated.

✦ Among the divorced, men cite sexual problems as the primary reason three times more frequently than women. Women cite extramarital affairs twice as frequently as men. But both cite emotional problems as the most frequent cause of divorce.

✦ The divorced, both men and women, had more premarital sexual experience than those still married.

✦ Divorced women have had more abortions (33%) than either married (25%) or single women (23%).

```
┌─────────────────────────────────────────────────────────────┐
│        QUESTIONNAIRE SUBJECTS TABULATED IN THIS CHAPTER       │
└─────────────────────────────────────────────────────────────┘
```

	Table
Reasons for Attraction to Spouse/Partner	6.1, 6.2
Sexual Experience Before Marriage	6.3
Cohabitation Before Marriage	6.4, 6.5
Honeymoons	6.6
Relationship with Spouse/Partner	6.7, 6.9
Sexual Gratification in Marriage	6.8
Marital Status	6.10
Variety of Sex Techniques	6.11, 6.12
Personal Preferences for Achieving Orgasm	6.13
Masturbation Frequency	6.14
Self-Ratings of Sexual Activity	6.15
Ratings of Sex Partner's Sexual Activity	6.16, 6.17
Self-Ratings of Marriage	6.18
Reasons for Divorce	6.19
Extramarital Affairs	6.20
Abortion	6.21
Length of Remarriages	6.22

✦ IN THEIR OWN WORDS ─────────────────────────────────────

I can't believe how happy I am; it's like a dream come true. Sometimes I have to pinch myself to make sure I am awake. If this is a dream, then I hope I don't wake up. Truthfully, I was scared of marriage—not really scared, rather terrified. I always valued my independence, and my friends. I think I always had an ideal marriage as a fantasy in the back of my mind, but didn't believe that it could come true. Well, was I wrong! Jim is that dream. If I had known that two people giving to each other, in the context of love and security, could feel so good, I think I would have married at eighteen.

—A 41-year-old professional woman, married one year

✦   ✦   ✦

I am divorced now, coming out of a marriage of 24 years' duration; we never made it to 25. It wasn't a real marriage; I see lots of people who have gotten married, but very few real marriages. We had known each other since high school. After we married, she decided very quickly that she didn't like all the things we had done together before. I had heard horror stories from friends of mine, how a spouse turns on you and renounces all the things that you thought you shared jointly. Well, it happened to me. Soon we weren't talking too much together either, except for arguing.

—A 47-year-old professional man, recently divorced

In his 1970 book *Marriage Observed*, J. H. Wallis[1] observed that "we have still not quite come to grips with what it is that makes marriages last, and enables them to survive." More than 20 years later, many social scientists are still trying to understand the mystique of lasting marriages, but the final answers are still light years away.

How could anyone easily discover solutions to this complex problem? People are multifaceted, and the marriage relationship is the most private and personal of affairs. A definitive study of lasting marriages would require analyzing a multitude of events, interactions, and conflicts over the course of numerous adult lifetimes. Such a study would, in fact, have to begin even before the marriage, with the paired-off individuals themselves—their personalities and backgrounds, their family situations and socioeconomic environments, the circumstances of their meeting and courtship, and much, much more. It would not only be impossible to look at every potentially contributing factor, but it would be hard even to decide where one should begin.

Our examination of American marriages looked at selected relevant factors. We began fairly close to the onset of a relationship, in the hope of identifying what attracts people to one another in the first place. After that, in more or less logical progression, we examined some common premarital and honeymoon experiences. Finally, we looked at some aspects of divorce, and especially at factors that we suspected might contribute to marital success or failure.

Before we detail our findings, we believe it would be helpful to examine some marriage experiments of the American past. We feel this is important because there is always the temptation to believe that events of the present are new and original. In fact, Americans have long experimented with alternative forms of marriage, and some attempted to do away with marriage altogether.

UNTRADITIONAL AMERICAN MARRIAGE EXPERIMENTS

In the 19th century, our forebears really let their sexual imaginations loose. Historians have pointed out that, although America retained its basic puritan outlook on sex and sexuality through the 19th century, the period after the War of 1812 saw some loosening of official moral restraints. Indeed, the second quarter of the 19th century saw the start of a 50-year heyday of sexual and marital experimentation.[2] Sometimes, this took the guise of religious fervor; at other times, it was justified as social improvement. The range was enormous: from celibacy—for example, among the Shakers—to polygyny (the form of polygamous marriage in which a man has more than one wife) among the Mormons, to a variety of shifting or "free love" arrangements, pioneered by the Oneida Community.

The Shakers practiced total celibacy, even for converts who had been married before joining the community. Children and adults lived together in sex-segregated dormitories, and males and females sat on different sides of communal areas for dining and worship. Children entered the community when one or both of their parents joined, or—and this was most often the case—as orphans. They were free to leave, if they so chose, when they reached adulthood; but because relatively few left, membership was replenished.

The Shakers were noted for their diligent work habits, practical approaches to designing tools and furnishings, and joyous celebration of their devout faith. Their communities, largely in Ohio, New York, and New England, continued to thrive into the early 20th century, but few young converts have rejuvenated them in recent decades, and most communities have now ceased to function.

The Mormons, formally known as the Church of Jesus Christ of Latter-Day Saints, are the notable example of polygyny. The marriage ceremony required women to vow obedience to their husbands. After 1852, most men had more than one wife by the time they reached middle age. That was the year when the charismatic Brigham Young, who led his flock to settle in Utah in 1847, announced that plural marriages had been dictated by Joseph Smith, the faith's founder, a decade earlier. In Utah, the Mormons became noted for their industriousness, and they soon became the dominant population in the territory.

A Mormon woman who, with her husband, ultimately defected, recounted in an 1875 autobiography[3] that "many men [had] married [second or subsequent] wives, and [had] brought them home, before their first wives knew even that they were in love. They had not had courage to introduce the subject, but believed that when the wife found that it was done and could not be undone, she would see the uselessness of feeling badly, and would soon get over it. But no wife who has been thus treated ever did 'get over it.'"

In her account, polygamy is depicted as a source of constant backbiting and envy: "Each wife finds pleasure in telling all the little weaknesses of the other wives to her [friends] . . . [and] each notices every article of clothing that the others wear. . . ."

Dissatisfied or mistreated wives could, however, easily obtain divorces, simply by asking Brigham Young, the Prophet. If he agreed, a bill of divorce was drawn up, which had then to be signed by the husband, in the presence of two witnesses. After divorcing, a former wife was eligible for remarriage, and, while some men had a large number of wives at one time, there were some women who, by arranging divorces strategically, were able to have a number of husbands in series.

Toward the end of the century, it became apparent that the Mormons' adherence to plural marriage was interfering with their political efforts to achieve statehood. In 1890, they officially decided to forgo the practice. Utah was admitted to the Union as the 45th state in 1896, on the understanding that the state would forever prohibit polygamous marriages. A few men continued to insist on their right to have more than one wife; some such efforts reappeared in the news and the courts as late as the 1980s.

Perhaps the best known 19th-century American commune was the Oneida Community of upstate New York, founded in 1848 and run by John Humphrey Noyes. The community engaged in a number of social experiments devised by Noyes, a religious idealist who believed in spiritual perfectibility. Noyes held that women were the spiritual equals of men. From this, economic and sexual openness followed logically.

The community soon became economically self-sufficient and prosperous. Members lived in individual rooms in a large mansion house, which was expanded several times as more members joined. The mansion also contained a number of large common areas where people worked and dined together, studied, were entertained, and socialized.

Noyes is credited with originating the term "free love" to describe the practice of sexual equality, although he himself preferred to use the phrase "complex marriage" instead. For all members, there was equal sexual access to all opposite-sex members. Theoretically, all men and women at Oneida were potential conjugal partners.

Here's how it worked. A man who was attracted to a woman applied to a special committee for permission to visit her for sexual purposes. Permission was usually granted after someone, usually an older woman, had sounded out the chosen female on her willingness. The idea was to make sure the liaison was mutually desired; no woman was required to have sex with a man if she did not wish to. If the woman agreed, the man would visit her room for a few hours after the evening's activities. There was no requirement for continued relations; a woman would not accept further visits from a man if she chose not to.

These arrangements were for sexual enjoyment only, not for conceiving offspring. An important component of the Oneida idea was to separate sex-for-pleasure from sex-for-procreation. An effective means of preventing conception, known as coitus reservatus, was practiced. Men were permitted to have sex only with older women, past childbearing age, until they learned how to control ejaculation in a not-for-procreation relationship.

We can only describe the sexual and marital customs of the past; no statistical data on them are available for us to analyze. However, as we examine the sexual and marital experiences common today, it is useful to realize that some of our forebears also enjoyed variations on the mainstream theme.

TABLE 6.1   **Survey Item E.8.**

I WAS INITIALLY ATTRACTED TO MY SPOUSE/PARTNER BY HIS/HER:

	Married or Formerly Married*	
	Men	Women
N =	890	928
Looks	27%	16%
Personality	48	43
Sexiness	8	8
Wealth	2	1
Warmth	13	25
Power	1	3
Humor	1	4

*Single, separated, and widowed groups are not included.

MODERN MARRIAGE

Starting at the beginning of any relationship, our first topic is attraction. When we compared initial attraction to a partner, among married and formerly married men and women,* we got the results shown in Table 6.1.

To both the men and the women responding, personality was the most important attractant. Men and women differed most in the significance of appearance (looks): 27% of the men were attracted by their partner's or spouse's appearance; 16% of the women were captivated by their man's appearance at first acquaintance. The fairly high proportion of men's responses stressing the physical appearance of women is not surprising; it confirms the general impression that men are more visually turned on to sex and sexiness than are women. It also underlines the extent to which our culture stresses women's physical attributes and purveys women as sex objects. Because men's physiques are "sold" to women far less pervasively, women are able to probe beyond the appearance of a man. When they do, they are most likely to look for his ability to relate. A man's warmth attracted one-fourth of all women, but a woman's warmth held negligible appeal for men. These reactions are perhaps not surprising either: Women are traditionally concerned with building relationships, and these data indicate that they are attracted to men who appear to share a concern for human interactions and a capacity for genuine interest in other people. Men would probably be quite

*Widowed respondents who have not remarried were excluded from tabulations in this chapter because they tend to be predominantly older women, whose responses, if included, would have skewed the results reported.

TABLE 6.2   **Survey Item E.8.**

I WAS INITIALLY ATTRACTED TO MY SPOUSE/PARTNER BY HIS/HER:				
	Married		Divorced	
	Men	Women	Men	Women
N =	770	803	120	125
Looks	26%	17%	33%	15%
Personality	49	44	42	39
Sexiness	9	5	4	21
Wealth	2	1	0	1
Warmth	12	26	16	20
Power	1	3	1	3
Humor	1	4	4	1

surprised to realize how few women are attracted to power and wealth, both traditional characteristics of masculinity. Indeed, women expressed as little attraction toward these characteristics in men as did men for power and wealth in women.

Were there any differences, we wondered, between the sources of attraction among people who remained married versus those among people who subsequently divorced? We separated out the data for the two groups, as shown in Table 6.2.

The divorced women we surveyed were four times as likely to be attracted to a man because of his sexiness, and only one-fourth as likely to be attracted by a sense of humor, compared to women who are still married. Comparing the married and divorced men, looks were 7% more important to divorced men, and personality, 7% less. Sexiness rated higher with married men (9%) than with divorced men (4%), who gave warmth and humor higher ratings than did the marrieds.

PREMARITAL SEX AND LATER DIVORCE

Is there a relationship between premarital sexual experience and the likelihood of divorce? Table 6.3 gives some possible clues.

In assessing sexual experience before marriage, there were significant differences in responses, especially between men who are presently married and those who are divorced. We will see elsewhere in this chapter that sex difficulties do account for some divorces; one of the partners often complains that what his or her mate regards as "liberal" or "sophisticated" sex is actually an imposition. The intriguing notion here is that the seeds for later sexual problems may get planted before a

TABLE 6.3 Survey Item D.10.

I HAD SEXUAL EXPERIENCE BEFORE MARRIAGE:				
	Married		Divorced	
	Men	Women	Men	Women
N =	772	802	122	127
Very much	31%	16%	37%	20%
Much	34	21	39	21
Little	18	29	13	26
Very little	9	18	1	17
None	8	16	10	16
Very much + Much	65%	37%	76%	41%
Little + Very little	27%	47%	14%	43%

couple even marries. Many couples seek counseling before marriage, and this would seem to be an area that counselors could fruitfully explore, to help with the adjustment of both partners in a future marriage.

COHABITATION AND MARITAL SUCCESS

Cohabitation that is open and undisguised is becoming a widespread social custom and is usually accepted by the couple's family and community. In colonial days, couples found opportunity for sexual relations before marriage—but not without penalty. Court records have shown that even married couples were punished—by being fined, and sometimes by being lashed as well—for discovery of premarital "misconduct." In Connecticut, the punishment for unmarried sexual relations could include a compulsory sentence to marry, according to researchers William Kephart and Davor Jedlicka.[4] The U.S. Bureau of the Census has developed an official definition for cohabitation: Two unrelated adults of opposite sexes, sharing the same living quarters, with no other adult present. Following this definition, the Bureau counted 2,856,000 cohabiting couples in 1990, an increase of 44% over the number recorded six years earlier. Most had never been married; almost one-fourth were under 25 years old.

With so many couples, especially young and unmarried couples, living together, a natural question is whether living together before marriage helps the couple to know each other, to learn to communicate about sexual as well as other matters, and to negotiate with each other. Does cohabiting make any difference at all? Our questionnaire asked about having lived with a future spouse, and for how long (see Tables 6.4 and 6.5).

TABLE 6.4   **Survey Item E.4.**

DID YOU LIVE WITH YOUR SPOUSE BEFORE MARRYING?						
			Men		Women	
	Married	Divorced	Married	Divorced	Married	Divorced
N =	1,571	245	770	120	801	125
Yes	43%	56%	47%	44%	39%	67%
No	57%	44%	53%	56%	61%	33%

About two out of three divorced women cohabited with their mates before marrying them, compared to about two out of five still-married women. More divorced women (67%) than divorced men (44%) had cohabited before marrying; more divorced men (56%) than divorced women (33%) had not cohabited before marriage. The range of differences between divorced and still-married men was only 3 percentage points.

We inquired about the length of cohabitation of those who had answered Yes (see Table 6.5). Almost half of all still-married people who had cohabited were married within one year. However, less than one-fourth of those who subsequently divorced had married within one year. This suggests that those still married had decided to marry before cohabiting, and that their cohabitation was directly connected to their decision to marry. For the divorced, on the other hand, more than three-fourths had long-standing (more than one year) cohabiting relationships before marriage, suggesting that the decision to marry was a consequence of the living-together experience. The failure of their marriages seems to indicate that an extended period of cohabitation can be in some way detrimental to a resulting marriage.

Living together in itself, then, is no guarantee of success in future marriage. As F. Philip Rice concluded in 1989,[5] "No study has presented

TABLE 6.5   **Survey Item E.4.**

HOW MANY YEARS DID YOU LIVE TOGETHER (BEFORE MARRYING)?		
	Married	Divorced
N =	676	139
One year or less	49%	22%
2–5 years	44	72
6–10 years	6	5
More than 10 years	1	1

objective evidence to show that nonmarital cohabitation increases or decreases subsequent marital satisfaction." Two studies that compared premarital cohabiters and noncohabiters found that, after cohabiters marry, there is significantly less communication and satisfaction.[6] It was not clear, however, that cohabitation was the only factor that made the difference in the cases cited in those studies.

Many people cohabit for long periods of time, but the living-together experience is not always a step on the road to marriage. Indeed, it may well be a step in the opposite direction. R. R. Clayton and H. L. Voss,[7] for example, found that at least two-thirds of cohabiting couples in the 1970s did not marry. Our study revealed that, among those who had cohabited, almost three-fourths of all who subsequently divorced had lived together from two to five years. In light of their later marital difficulties, this may have been more of a prolonged trial run than a solid commitment.

HONEYMOON EXPERIENCES

What actually happens at the start of marriage, when partners go off on long-dreamed-of honeymoons intended to be filled with erotic loving? Are honeymoons truly idyllic experiences, as they have long been portrayed in the movies and in the fantasies of Americans? Table 6.6 details the honeymoon outcomes for our respondents.

We offered no neutral choice; our intent was to nudge respondents into deciding whether their honeymoon had been a positive or negative experience.

Our most interesting finding here was that married women's and men's responses were generally very similar—within 5 percentage points—but the responses of divorced men and women were widely divergent. Responses for traumatic honeymoon, which may have very complex and intimate causes, were almost the same for married and divorced respondents; women reported this experience significantly more than men.

TABLE 6.6   **Survey Item E.9.**

MY HONEYMOON WAS:				
	Married		Divorced	
	Men	Women	Men	Women
N =	769	802	117	123
Thrilling	52%	47%	38%	19%
Boring	6	10	5	37
Traumatic	4	9	1	7
Very sexual	33	30	51	18
Asexual	5	4	5	19

Early in life-as-a-married-couple, the first inkling of distinctions between lasting and failed marriages appears. Almost all of the divorced men found their honeymoons thrilling or very sexual, but less than two-fifths of the divorced women gave those responses. Taking in more than just sex, thrilling implies the many expectations, discoveries, and personal intimacy that two people share in the honeymoon's special setting. (That is, in fact, why we asked separately about the sexual component of the honeymoon.) People on their honeymoons often report *trying* to be sexual because it is expected of honeymooners. Perhaps this effort to make the wished-for experience happen accounts for the high percentage of both divorced and married people who reported thrilling or sexual honeymoons.

Especially for women, the honeymoon mood seems to be a reliable forecaster of the fate of the marriage. More than one-third of all divorced women reported being bored on their honeymoons—a markedly higher percentage than married women, or men of either marital status. Almost one-fifth of the now-divorced women—nearly four times as many as respondents in other categories—experienced asexual honeymoons. Asexual does not mean good, bad, or boring sex. It means mere token sex or perhaps no sex at all.

FRIENDSHIP AND SEX IN MARRIAGE

What is the "glue" that holds good marriages together? This complex question continues to intrigue researchers. Historian Jeanette Lauer and her husband, sociologist Robert Lauer,[8] determined to look for common threads in relatively long-lasting unions. In 1985, as the divorce rate zoomed, they examined 315 marriages that had lasted for 15 years or more. The results were extracted in several journals; the original article appeared in *Psychology Today*. The Lauers found that there was significant agreement, between the women and men in these long-lasting marriages, about what it was that kept them together. The leading reasons these veteran partners gave for what keeps a marriage going are listed below in descending order of frequency:

Men:	Women:
My spouse is my best friend.	My spouse is my best friend.
I like my spouse as a person.	I like my spouse as a person.
Marriage is a long-term commitment.	Marriage is a long-term commitment.
Marriage is sacred.	Marriage is sacred.
We agree on aims and goals.	We agree on aims and goals.
My spouse has grown more interesting.	My spouse has grown more interesting.

Men:	Women:
I want the relationship to succeed.	I want the relationship to succeed.
An enduring marriage is important to social stability.	We laugh together.
We laugh together.	We agree on a philosophy of life.
I am proud of my spouse's achievements.	We agree on how, and how often, to show affection.
We agree on a philosophy of life.	An enduring marriage is important to social stability.
We agree about our sex life.	We have a stimulating exchange of ideas.
We agree on how, and how often, to show affection.	We discuss things calmly.
I confide in my spouse.	We agree about our sex life.
We share outside hobbies and interests.	I am proud of my spouse's achievements.

The first seven items on each list are the same and, even more signifi-cant, they appear in exactly the same sequence. For those married for long periods of time, this duplication is no surprise. Unanimity of thought seems basic for them.

Our survey asked about some of the same factors—specifically, views of sexuality, and whether the partners considered each other best friends. Table 6.7 compares the responses of the married men and women with those of the divorced men and women.*

A noticeable difference exists between the response patterns of those who are still married and those who have been divorced. More people in a lasting marriage recognize the role of friendship within their relation-ships. The Lauers' study produced the same finding, that the partners within a long marriage become increasingly close. Because about three-fourths of divorced people remarry, there is cause for concern that those who remarry may still not know how to become "best friends" with a spouse. Thus, most of those who are more likely to say that their partner is *not* their best friend may marry again and, quite possibly, repeat a self-destructive pattern in successive marriages, and find no more satisfying degree of friendship with the new mates.

---

*Questionnaire respondents indicated their *present status* as married, single, divorced, or widowed (survey item H.6). Divorced persons' responses have been interpreted as apply-ing to their relationship with their former spouses; we cannot know whether some di-vorced respondents had new partners at the time they completed the questionnaire.

TABLE 6.7   **Survey Item E.1.**

MY SPOUSE/PARTNER IS ALSO MY BEST FRIEND:						
			Married		Divorced	
	Married	Divorced	Men	Women	Men	Women
N =	1,572	245	770	802	119	126
Yes	86%	61%	89%	83%	71%	53%
No	14%	39%	11%	17%	29%	47%

SEX—IN AND OUT OF MARRIAGE

It's not easy to get at the exact role of sexual gratification in contributing to overall marital satisfaction. We tried to pin it down by offering a group of five possible responses. (See Table 6.8.)

Nearly three-fifths of the married people in our survey found sex much better (35%) or better (24%) after marriage. This is about the same proportion that Morton Hunt[9] found, a decade or so earlier, when 60% of women and 66% of men rated their marital intercourse as highly pleasurable.

In our survey, the divorced people expressed significantly less satisfaction with sexual interaction than the still-married. Because the divorced people were responding for the situation in their previous, failed marriage, negative hindsight may have contributed to their responses. More than one-third of the divorced women reported sexual relations that were worse (31%) or much worse (4%) after marriage. Were the women more sensitive (than the men) to ungratifying sexual experiences in their marriage, or were they giving a sour-grapes reappraisal of the situation, following their divorce?

TABLE 6.8   **Survey Item E.2.**

SEX IS MORE GRATIFYING SINCE MARRYING:						
			Men		Women	
	Married	Divorced	Married	Divorced	Married	Divorced
N =	1,566	242	770	122	769	120
Much better	35%	20%	34%	21%	37%	19%
Better	24	22	25	33	24	11
Same	29	36	30	38	28	35
Worse	10	18	10	4	9	31
Much worse	2	4	1	4	2	4

✦ *IN THEIR OWN WORDS* _____

I have no regrets at all about my prior life. Working my way up the corporate ladder, the traveling, being one of the guys, fighting off unwanted passes, it was all okay. Anyone I slept with, I wanted to, and I feel that it was a justifiable part of my life. Sex is fine, and even sex for fun is fine, but I draw the line at selling myself.

The thing is, this is better, infinitely better. I feel that Tim is my man, and I am his. Sounds corny, but it makes sense. We belong to each other, and yet we are in a nondemanding relationship. It's so nice to know he'll be there. I don't have to plan who to get to go with me New Year's Eve, or who to go to Club Med with in the Spring. I always felt that I was a sophisticate, but sex is even more terrific now. It's not technique, it's trust. When I hold Tim, or he holds me, it's different. I have changed. I mean my political views, my feelings about the need for equality for women and the women's movement are still the same, but I feel differently about men. I no longer see them as a group, especially as a group that looks down on women. I see them now as individuals, as feeling, caring people, some nice, and some jerks. Having my own man, and knowing he feels pretty much as I do is a kick.

—A 44-year-old marketing director, married one year;
first marriage for both partners; no children

Timing, frequency, type of sex, expertise, knowledge, who initiates, who is the aggressor, variety of sex acts—all are cited by sex researchers as part of drawing closer to, or away from, a mate or sex partner. We decided to focus on the role of sexual novelty in maintaining the freshness of marriage (see Table 6.9).

At first glance, there was minimal difference among these respondents, regarding their interest in sexual experimentation; whether divorced or married, male or female, they were interested in sexual variety. This matchup was somewhat surprising. The demand for constant variety, or

TABLE 6.9   Survey Item E.5.

IT IS IMPORTANT TO ME THAT MY PARTNER BE OPEN TO SEXUAL EXPERIMENTATION:					
			Married		Divorced	
	Married	Divorced	Men	Women	Men	Women
N =	1,564	243	769	795	120	123
Yes	52%	55%	56%	49%	52%	58%
Slightly	38	41	36	39	44	39
No	10	4	8	12	4	3

TABLE 6.10   Survey Items H.6, H.8.

SELF-IDENTIFICATION: MARITAL STATUS OF THOSE MARRIED OR FORMERLY MARRIED:		

	Number	Percent of All Respondents Ever Married
Divorced (not currently married)	249	9%
First marriage	1,182	75
Second marriage	315	20
Third marriage (or later)	79	5

experimentation—often borderline or "kinky" types of sex—is often reputed to be a serious irritant between partners whose tastes differ. Consequently, we would have expected consistently higher levels of interest in sexual experimentation among the divorced than the still-married. The relatively high rate of importance given to experimentation, among our married respondents, suggested that their sexual variety needs were being adequately met within their marriages.

The most notable distinction we found related to those who did not consider experimentation important: two and a half times as many marrieds (10%), compared to divorced people (4%), seemed sexually content and had no need for embellishment. Was the extremely low (4%) response for the divorced an indication that these people may have been unable to accommodate the variety needs of their former partners?

The marital status of respondents to our survey is defined in Table 6.10. For a number of questions, we compared responses based on whether our subjects were divorced, were still married, or had remarried.

SEXUAL VARIETY

Are the divorced more, or less, adventurous in their approach to sex? We sorted the data we had gathered on participation in five sex-adventure practices, and compared them in Table 6.11. It's important to note that the responses were life-reports and not indications of participation while in the current marital status. Respondents were asked to give multiple answers if they applied.

The practice of threesomes had the highest percentage of participation among all respondents, even those in their first marriages, who were less adventurous than those who were divorced or remarried. Was the need for unusual sex the cause of marriage dissolution for those who were divorced or remarried? No definitive answer could be determined, but we decided to profile the same data according to the gender of the respondents. (See Table 6.12.)

TABLE 6.11   Survey Items H.26, H.27.

SELF-IDENTIFICATION: I HAVE PARTICIPATED IN:			
	First Marriage	Divorced	Remarried
N =	1,171	243	386
Sex for money	8%*	19%	17%
Group sex	9	21	9
Threesomes	11	24	27
Sex slave	0	2	5
Open marriage	3	8	10

*In Tables 6.11 through 6.13, responses do not sum to 100% because respondents were permitted more than one choice.

Both the men and the women who were past their first marriages had been more adventurous than those still in their initial marriages. Men generally engaged in more varied practices than women, but, among the remarried, women's participation in group sex far exceeded men's. Our interviews indicated that some women may enjoy group sex because it affords an opportunity for them to fondle and generally display affection toward women as well as men.

How did the still-marrieds achieve the excitement they claimed they wanted? Sex for money, group sex, and threesomes had the highest percentages of participation among this group, but, because the questionnaire was directed toward gathering a life-report on these practices, we could not determine whether these adventures were premarital or ongoing. Comparisons spanning prerelationship, cohabitation, and first-marriage years would be valuable for further research.

TABLE 6.12   Survey Items H.26, H.27.

SELF-IDENTIFICATION: I HAVE PARTICIPATED IN:						
	First Marriage		Divorced		Remarried	
	Men	Women	Men	Women	Men	Women
N =	575	596	120	123	189	197
Sex for money	14%	3%	24%	13%	31%	4%
Group sex	13	4	24	17	3	16
Threesomes	14	8	29	18	42	14
Sex slave	0	1	1	2	7	2
Open marriage	3	3	10	5	13	7

TABLE 6.13   **Survey Item H.22.**

MY PREFERRED WAY TO ACHIEVE ORGASM IS:				
	Married		Divorced	
	Men	Women	Men	Women
N =	769	784	119	119
Intercourse	89%	75%	85%	64%
Masturbation	1	7	1	10
Oral sex	6	16	13	22
Sadomasochism	1	0	0	1
Anal sex	2	0	1	0
Fantasy	0	0	0	1
Fetish	0	0	0	0
Other	1	2	0	2

To determine what sexual variation appealed to our respondents, we asked about their preferences for achieving orgasm and found some surprising results. (See Table 6.13.)

We have avoided showing entries with 0 responses in every column, but we thought it particularly important for the reader to see the entire range of options offered in the questionnaire. Despite our respondents' high interest in sexual experimentation, hardly any of them preferred to achieve orgasm by "kinky" means. Sadomasochism, anal sex, fantasy, and other approaches combined, accounted for only 1% to 4% of orgasmic preferences.

Popular wisdom is confounded in these data. Isn't fantasy considered important in sexual satisfaction—indeed, isn't this technique highly recommended by most of those who give advice on the subject? Yet, among our respondents, only 1% of divorced women, and *no one else*, relied on fantasy as the primary means to achieving orgasm. Similarly, fetishism is often talked about, and there is widespread popular belief that many people, especially men, require one or another repeated cue to become satisfactorily stimulated—yet not one of our sample selected this option as preferred.*

The largest share of all respondents—about three-fourths of married women and two-thirds of divorced women, and close to 9 out of 10 married and divorced men—reported a preference for achieving orgasm through traditional intercourse. Coupled with our findings that the vast majority of both married and divorced persons expressed an interest in sexual experimentation, we can only assume that they are somehow

---

*Our question dealt only with *preferred* means. We did not ask about the use of these techniques as adjuncts.

finding ways to provide stimulating variations, perhaps by arranging the immediate environments or wearing intriguing cosmetics and garments for intercourse occasions.

Also notable was the strong showing for oral sex as a preferred means of achieving orgasm, particularly among women. Our data are consistent with findings of other researchers in recent years. For example, a 1983 study by P. Blumstein and P. Schwartz[10] found that two-thirds of couples practiced oral techniques at some times; a decade earlier, Morton Hunt[11] had found that half of all couples did.

Whether divorced or still married, the women we interviewed reported that oral techniques are an important turn-on in their lives. Married men relied relatively little on either oral sex or masturbation as the preferred means of achieving orgasm. Few men in our entire sample relied on masturbation (see Table 3.42), a strong indication that they had adequate opportunities for traditional intercourse, whether within or outside of marriage. The women in our sample, more than the men, preferred masturbation.

That significant numbers of women enjoy masturbation is not particularly surprising. Divorced women often have difficulty finding sexual partners, and masturbation is a recognized and appropriate solution to that problem. Research, starting with Masters and Johnson's[12] report on female sexuality in the 1960s, has indicated that women can learn to control their own sexual response exquisitely by masturbating; since the 1970s, the feminist health movement has been quite active in explaining to women all aspects of how their bodies work. It is notable that almost as high a proportion of married women as of divorced women regularly prefer to achieve orgasm by masturbation (Table 6.13).

Paradoxically, we found (see Table 3.42) that the proportion of women who had never masturbated was about the same as the proportion who chose masturbation as their preferred means of achieving orgasm. We decided to refine our data further, to distinguish current marital status for those who had never masturbated. (See Table 6.14.)

TABLE 6.14   **Survey Item D.8.**

I MASTURBATE ON AVERAGE: NEVER:							
Divorced		First Marriage		Second Marriage		Later Marriages	
Men	Women	Men	Women	Men	Women	Men	Women
N = *Respondents reporting that they had never masturbated—divorced, married, or remarried*							
119	116	576	582	150	151	36	34
4%	12%	6%	12%	0	12%	0	0

Significantly more women than men, whether divorced, married, or remarried, had never masturbated. However, by the time the men were in their second marriages, and any parties were in their third or later marriages, all had experienced orgasm through masturbation. The most striking statistic here is that about the same proportion of women, across the three very different marital statuses, had not masturbated. Which means, of course, that similarly equal proportions *have* achieved orgasm through masturbation.

How do individuals see themselves in terms of their sexuality? Do some view themselves as purely sexual beings? We set up a continuum so that there would be a place for everyone, men and women, in assessing how proper or liberal they were in their personal sexual views (Table 6.15). We also asked them to evaluate their partners' places on the sexual spectrum (Table 6.16).

The combined very proper and proper responses of all males (17%) and all females (23%) in our sample were surprisingly close. More than half of the males surveyed considered themselves liberal or very liberal, compared to just over one-third for the females. The difference between men's and women's perceptions of their places on the sexual spectrum accorded well with the traditional stereotype of men being more adventurous and open than women, in sexual matters. Against that tradition, perhaps what was most surprising here was that the difference between men and women wasn't greater. When we added the men who regarded themselves as sexual moderates (31%) to those who said they were very proper or proper (17%), we saw that less than half of all the men did *not* consider themselves sexual liberals. For the women, the equivalent combination totaled 65%.

TABLE 6.15   **Survey Item E.6.**

SEXUALLY, I CONSIDER MYSELF TO BE:		
	Men	Women
N = Total married and divorced groups of respondents	892	927
Very proper	3%	4%
Proper	14	19
Moderate	31	42
Liberal	44	27
Very liberal	8	8
Very proper + Proper	17%	23%
Liberal + Very liberal	52%	35%

✦ *IN THEIR OWN WORDS* _____

Mac and I gave up swinging four years ago. Not that it wasn't exciting. It was, but we just got tired of getting everyone else's social diseases. The group we got together with was really quite nice, and there was always some new people who happened to be passing through town, you know. I don't know if all of the visiting couples were actually married, but they said they were, or were about to get married. But I suppose it doesn't matter.

We found you could have much more intensely exciting times with other people around. We used to discuss whether making it with eight or ten people around makes us jaded now, when we are left with only a spouse. I'm not sure, but it's still okay with Mac. We do occasionally go to a nudist camp, or to nude beaches with the kids, but we don't have other sex partners.

I have done some crazy things, like having four men working on me at one time, cramming into every orifice in my body. I have never felt so incredibly overwhelmed. Since I am an expert on fine art, I would pose like a classical statue and the men would come on to me. At some point, when I got turned on, I would respond. Some man once said that it felt like necrophilia; that was creepy. But we didn't go for the kinky stuff, you know, the S/M and the whacko masks and boots and all. We met some lovely people and we've become good friends. You would be surprised at the type of people, and how many very successful people swing. It's amazing how you can get close to people who are not family, and yet you experience the most intimate things with them, but when you see them in the supermarket you act as if nothing happened.

—A 45-year-old married female executive
who holds a Master's degree

TABLE 6.16   Survey Item E.7.

SEXUALLY, I CONSIDER MY PARTNER TO BE:				
	Married Now or in the Past		Married Now	
	Men	Women	Men	Women
N =	892	927	770	801
Very proper	7%	11%	7%	13%
Proper	25	12	26	12
Moderate	38	22	38	21
Liberal	26	47	25	46
Very liberal	4	8	4	8
Very proper + Proper	32%	23%	33%	25%
Liberal + Very liberal	30%	55%	29%	54%

TABLE 6.17   Survey Item E.10.

MY SPOUSE/PARTNER IS SEXUALLY SOPHISTICATED:			

| | | Married | |
	Married	Men	Women
N =	1,572	770	802
Yes	60%	58%	62%
No	40%	42%	38%

At this point, it might be helpful to take a look at people's perceptions of their partners' sexual attitudes (Table 6.16).

About one-third (30%) of the male but more than half (55%) of the female respondents considered their partners liberal or very liberal. Were they jeering or cheering their liberal or very liberal partners?

It is highly significant here that Table 6.16 shows close similarities between male and female response patterns in a number of categories. For example, married men and women considered their partners moderate in almost precisely the same proportion as did the total sample; indeed, at almost every response level, the opinions of married men and women about their partners were remarkably similar to the sample. This suggests that marital status is more significant in assessing the partners' sexual views than is gender.

Our questionnaire also asked about the sexual sophistication of the respondent's partner. (See Table 6.17.) The designation of sophistication generally has positive-approval status.

The traditional stereotype of men is that they know more about sex, or think that they do, than women. The married women credited their partners with sexual sophistication, with a fairly high rating (62%). What is of interest here is the small gap between men's and women's ratings of their partners. Married men's rating of their partners (58%) was only 4% lower than the rating they had received in return.

SELF-RATINGS OF MARRIAGES

Of great interest and importance to our study was to determine how today's Americans see their marriages. We decided to use very colloquial, brief expressions in our questionnaire to capture our respondents' spontaneity of personal interaction as much as possible. Table 6.18 summarizes their answers.

TABLE 6.18   **Survey Item E.3.**

I RATE MY MARRIAGE AS:						
			Men		Women	
	Married	Divorced	Married	Divorced	Married	Divorced
N =	1,576	247	772	122	804	125
Great	38%	17%	40%	40%	36%	1%
Good	45	39	45	25	44	50
Fair	13	13	12	5	15	19
Poor	2	13	2	10	2	15
Terrible	2	18	1	20	3	15
Great + Good	83%	56%	85%	65%	80%	51%
Poor + Terrible	4%	31%	3%	30%	5%	30%

Not surprisingly, the married people rated their marriages more positively than did the divorced. Even with a combined rating of 56% of great and good marriages, the divorced group still terminated their marriages. Good was apparently not good enough. By the same token, bad may not be bad enough for some people. Four percent of the marrieds had remained in what they acknowledged to be poor or terrible marital relationships. Nearly one-third of the now-divorced respondents reported that their marriages were poor or terrible. Over half of the divorced men (65%) and women (51%) described their marriages as great and good.

DIVORCE TIME

The two major factors repeatedly cited by marriage counselors and mental health practitioners as having the potential to destroy marriages are sex and money. Some people divorce for reasons that have nothing to do with a lack of sexual happiness, but it is rare for a couple to get divorced when their sex life is excellent. Morton Hunt,[13] for example, found a high correlation between couples' ratings of their sex lives as highly satisfying and their marital relationship as emotionally close. The converse held, too: Three-fifths of women and two-fifths of men who rated their marital relationship as emotionally cool reported unsatisfactory sexual relationships as well.

Marriage and divorce have become so related in people's minds that, in ordinary conversation, when most Americans talk about one, they will invariably refer to the other. When planning marriage, many couples discuss the "what if" question—"What if we don't like being married to each other? How will we settle matters?" Divorce attorneys whom we interviewed confirmed that a growing number of people of all ages are drawing up prenuptial agreements before any marriage—their first, second, or later tries. Younger people, in record numbers, are consulting lawyers before taking vows, probably anticipating the future worth of their career paths. For the many women and men who are now marrying at later ages, many of whom have accumulated wealth that they are reluctant to throw into joint ownership in marriage, such agreements make particular good sense. This caution does not necessarily mean that they are entering into marriage resigned to its failure; probably no one marries with the intention of getting divorced. However, no one with any awareness today can ignore a side effect of the First Sexual Revolution: one of every two marriages in this country ends in divorce.

♦ IN THEIR OWN WORDS _____

> Sometimes she drives me crazy; she is obsessive, has to be told that she is good, and needs everything to be perfect. Her career needs are tremendously important to her, and she is doing well. Though she drives herself hard, she manages to look attractive, and to dress chiquely, and though she is not what many would call a beautiful woman, she is, to me, a handsome woman. I am very uncomfortable with her need to be aloof—she tries to look cool, you know, all business, and disdains public gestures of affection; in bed she is the hottest, most exciting woman I have ever known. We have been married seven years, and any number of times, when I get upset at her for having her head in the business, and making up her monthly, weekly, or semiannual report, I'm to the point of thinking divorce. I mean that I feel sometimes like I'm second fiddle, and her career comes first. But then, when we get to bed, and she lets herself go, we go wild together, and I forget what I was angry about in the first place. There are probably other things we have in common as well, I'd hate to think it was only sex, but it certainly makes an incredible impact.
>
> —A 36-year-old engineer

Popular discussion of divorce tends to assume that the number and rate of divorces began to increase in the 1970s and are continuing to do so. The facts are somewhat more complex. According to U.S. Government sources,[14] the statistics for some key years in the 20th century were as follows:

| Year | Divorces | | Year | Divorces | |
	Number	Number per 1,000 Population		Number	Number per 1,000 Population
1900	56,000	0.5	1970	708,000	3.5
1910	83,000	0.9	1975	1,036,000	4.8
1920	171,000	1.6	1980	1,189,000	5.2
1930	196,000	1.6	1985	1,190,000	5.0
1940	264,000	2.0	1986	1,178,000	4.9
1950	385,000	2.6	1988	1,167,000	4.7
1960	393,000	2.2	1990	1,175,000	4.7

Both the number and the rate of divorces rose steadily from the turn of the century to 1950, dropped a bit in 1960, then started shooting up dramatically. The high point of 5.2 divorces per 1,000 persons was marked in 1980, but then the rate declined steadily to 1990 and the number of divorces fluctuated. Perhaps the "backlog" has been cleared out, with most of the long-married couples who were divorce material finally being divorced. If that's the case, we may expect to see the divorce rate continue to fall until it stabilizes at a lower level. Some experts believe that this stable divorce rate has already been reached. The rate will probably never dip as low as it was before 1970.

Most states have instituted no-fault divorces. People generally, and women in particular, increasingly refuse to be dead-ended in any aspect of their lives. These and other trends will ensure that most of those living through unhappy marriages are unlikely to endure them indefinitely.

◆ *IN THEIR OWN WORDS* _____

Often, I wonder how we made it to 24 years. She started college, but education wasn't her top priority; she was more interested in an MRS. than in a B.A. We were both young, and foolish, but I believed in love.

At first it was wonderful; our honeymoon wasn't very sexual, but I credited that to her being a virgin. We had never had sexual relations before. In those days the thing to do was petting, and my first wife would pet "only above the neck." I told her that was necking, not petting, but she didn't care. In a way, I admired her morals. The problem was that she didn't do much more after we got married, either. If I were ever to believe in miracles, I would have to say that the conception of my four children was miraculous. We had intercourse so infrequently—she always had headaches, periods, and stomachaches—that it is amazing she conceived at all. I used to think there was something wrong with me because I couldn't get her turned on.

Anyway, marriage had never been presented to me as a wild orgy you have with your wife, so I took the crumbs that I could, and spent my energy building my career, writing papers, giving lectures, and taking lots of cold showers. You can't just up and leave a wife and children easily, and remain respectable in a residential college community.

At some point, I became aware that students, and even some of my fellow faculty were, as the kids say, turned on to me. I didn't notice it, actually; my wife did. She attended a lecture series where I was being honored. After the speeches, people came over to me to congratulate me and comment on my talk. When we left, she startled me with, "You know those young things were dying to sleep with you. I was watching them make goo-goo eyes at you." Of course, I protested that I didn't know what she was talking about. I really didn't. She said, "I'm a woman, I know that look. You can't fool me. Have you been fooling around with any of them?"

"Well, of course not," I told her. It was the first sign of life regarding anything sexual that I had seen in her. It started me thinking. Had I been so blind, and negatively conditioned to sex by my marriage, that I didn't spot seductive looks? Why was I the last person in the world to know I was sexy?

Soon afterward, I had my first affair, with a young faculty member who was divorced. We had known each other for several years, and there was no great passion, but she was a woman and I a man. It was strange how it came about. We were both out of town at a professional conference. I naively thought, what a nice coincidence, now I can talk to someone I know. Anyway, the very first night, after some drinks, I found myself in bed with her. The sex was fine, but the guilt was awful. She kept telling me, "Grow up, we're both adults, and if we can give each other some pleasure, what's the sin in that?" It wasn't easy; I could see my poor sad-sack wife, and the dread of my kids ever finding out. The conference lasted a week but I carefully avoided my colleague for the rest of it.

Back at the college I made sure not to be alone with her for weeks. Finally I decided that was silly and started talking to her again. She was certainly not the tramp that my primitive conscience trumpeted at me. Growing up, there had been only two kinds of girls—nice girls who shunned sex, like my wife, and tramps who liked sex.

Then I dated some other women, too, even some graduate students. To my surprise, I could be passionate. I felt like a kid again. Sex wasn't bad; we had been sold a bill of goods. I began to see that I had gotten trapped in a marriage built on guilt, not fulfillment. I left about six months after that. My wife asked if I was leaving because of another woman. I told her it was because there was no joy or life or sex in the marriage. She shook her head, and said I was acting like a fool, told me what financial arrangement she wanted and walked away. The lawyers did the rest.

—A 47-year-old educator and Ed.D.

This couple had been sexually naive at marriage; they had become engaged at a time when people did not live together before marriage. The world changed dramatically during the 24 years they were married.

Would they have been more sexually compatible if they had been able to live together before marrying? Would they have discovered their incompatibility and avoided the marriage pitfall that lay in wait for them? Countless older people, divorced in the 1970s and 1980s after marriages of 15 to as many as 30 years' duration, are asking themselves these questions that can never be answered.

THE CAUSES OF DIVORCE

What accounts for divorce? What causes a marriage and/or a family to disintegrate, to descend into disharmony and from there into disunity?

The many causes of divorce are not as easy to categorize as most people—especially the nondivorced—tend to believe. Greater evidence of sexual mismatches leading to divorce was revealed in our in-depth interviews than in the tabulated responses to our questionnaire. One after another, our interviewees told us that the major reason for their divorce lay in the elements of a sexual relationship. When partners find each other too demanding sexually, or when one prefers to obtain sexual gratification in a way that turns the other off, there is bound to be antagonism in the bedroom. This type of marital friction may leave little room for negotiation. Conversely, our interviewees told us that, no matter what other problems may beset them, when their sex life was excellent, they rarely considered divorce. Instead, they found various ways to negotiate their nonsexual differences.

Basic disagreement on such personal issues as a couple's preferred methods of sexual gratification can overwhelm other attributes needed for relating, such as trust, care, and feelings of security. The inability to feel unity with the marital partner sexually is so personal and so profound that it often dooms relationships that seem objectively to have otherwise good qualifications, such as similar ages, religious attitudes, educational backgrounds, and economic statuses.

Marriages break up for a variety of reasons. Table 6.19 lists those cited by our respondents who were divorced as being their *primary* reasons for breaking up.

Traditionally, the problems cited most as causes for divorce have been sex and money. Our findings agreed only in part: Money was close to the bottom of the ratings, among our male and female respondents alike. Sex was an important issue for the men surveyed but was markedly less so for the women. However, for women, the incidence of extramarital affairs was an important primary reason for breakup. The two issues are likely related. Men who have sexual problems in their marriage are at risk for trying extramarital affairs, which women then see as their justification for terminating the marriage. We learned in our interviews that, for some respondents, sexual problems were seen as emotional problems, which may have inflated the number of responses

TABLE 6.19   **Survey Item H.18.**

IF DIVORCED, THE ONE PRIMARY REASON WAS:		
	Men	Women
N =	122	127
Sex	17%	5%
Money	7	7
Rejection	12	13
Children	1	1
Emotional problems	31	27
Extramarital affairs	11	22
Open marriage	1	2
Other	20	23

to emotional problems. Men, particularly, may have great difficulty admitting to sexual problems, preferring to classify them as emotional, rather than sexual, difficulties. Extramarital affairs seem, therefore, to be a moderately important divorce factor for both women and men. Combining responses for sex, extramarital affairs, and open marriage (by definition, sexual experience outside of the marriage), women and men both totaled 29%.

The primary reason our respondents cited most frequently was emotional problems, a term we heard frequently from the divorced women and men we interviewed. Emotional problems and rejection (a specific type of emotional problem) were together blamed by 40% of the women and 40% of the men. Emotional problems encompass that very large category of "incompatibility," as well as situations in which one or both partners are indeed in some sort of psychological distress.

To sum up these significant results, two-fifths of our divorced respondents, both female and male, blamed emotional problems (including rejection) in their relationships, and more than one-fourth cited sex-related problems (sex, extramarital affairs, and open marriage) as the primary cause of the failure of their marriages. For our respondents, emotional and sexual difficulties were the two major contributing factors to divorce.

EXTRAMARITAL AFFAIRS

The role of extramarital sexual activity in divorce is paradoxical. Whereas about one in five divorced women and one in ten divorced men in our study (see Table 6.19) cited extramarital affairs as the primary cause of their divorce, some extramarital sexual activity apparently can occur within an otherwise stable marriage without causing a breakup.

We found that, among the married men and women, 28% had had more than one extramarital sexual contact without their marriages dissolving. (See Table 6.20.)

In the only once category, the differences in responses between the still-married and the now-divorced are striking. No data were available, among the now-divorced, on whether their single extramarital encounter contributed to their eventual breakup. Forty percent of all the divorced women and 45% of the divorced men reported having had more than one extramarital sexual relationship while they were still married.

The often-told stories about the sexual exploits of the traveling salesman may have had a good deal of truth in the past; today's stories go beyond the traveling salesman and the farmer's daughter. Both women and men travel on business, and trade shows, conventions, and sales calls provide opportunities for varieties of networking, albeit not intentionally of the sexual kind.

Despite the enhanced opportunities for interactions in our mobile society, it is known that extramarital affairs are poor ingredients for a trusting marriage. Given the frequency of such affairs, it seems likely that many spouses, consciously or unconsciously, overlook their mates' straying.

Our data showed (Table 6.20) that about two-thirds of the married men and three-fourths of the married women surveyed claimed never to have had extramarital sexual relationships. That leaves one in three married men and one in four married women who *have*, at least on one occasion. This adds up to a significant number. Extramarital sex seems to figure significantly in American marriages.

Researchers in recent years have noted an apparent increase in extramarital sex, particularly for women. Rubenstein,[15] for instance, found that 50% of the married women in her 1983 study had had at least one sexual encounter with men other than their husbands; Hunt's[16] 1974 study had placed the percentage at about one-fourth, as had Kinsey[17] and his associates in 1953.

TABLE 6.20   **Survey Item D.5.**

I'VE HAD EXTRAMARITAL AFFAIRS:				
	Married		Divorced	
	Men	Women	Men	Women
N =	768	787	121	123
Never	65%	74%	44%	41%
Only once	7	8	11	19
Rarely	14	11	24	27
Often	12	4	17	8
Ongoing	2	3	4	5

Marriage has always been wonderful to come home to. Well, you may ask, if that is the case, why then did I get divorced three times? Because I believe in marriage. My first wife and I were childhood sweethearts and we thought we were madly in love. . . . In those days, you had to promise the girl that you'd marry her if you did anything more than necking. Or at least that you loved her, and you would marry her when you grew up.

One night her parents were out of town, and I slept with her. I literally slept with her—we didn't have sex. Just a little kissing and very light petting. But I felt guilty as hell the next morning. Even though she was still a virgin, I felt I had compromised her. So I did the right thing. She was 16 and I was 17; I forged her birth certificate, borrowed a car, and we went off to Baltimore (where there was no waiting period) to get married. We didn't tell anyone. Then she went back to her parents' house to live and I went to mine.

After a year of this, the strain was too great for her. She cracked and told her parents. What a scene! They made us get married all over again, this time with a minister. The marriage was a disaster, but I stayed in it for 15 years. We had four children, and I was always a good provider.

She simply was not sexual. She felt sex is an unnecessary burden, that I want and need sex every night—which was a slight exaggeration. What kept me with her were other women. I really believe that more marriages have been kept together by extramarital affairs than by all the marriage counselors in the country. I must have had affairs with at least 45 women, some of them fairly long-term relationships, and some were even caring relationships. . . . When marriages number two and three didn't work out, I said, no good! I didn't work hard to build up a business empire, and come home to find an enemy in my house. I said out. Hey, I have good lawyers, and I had made prenuptial agreements, so I sent them on their way, a little richer, to frustrate some other guy.

My new wife knows this, and she says that she doesn't let me out of the house in the morning without making love, because that's how she got to be my present wife. Now and then we skip a day. I think the experts who say that if you devote too much of your energy to sex, it takes away from your need to achieve in business are nuts; I'm living proof. What's best in this marriage is that I haven't had to look for much extracurricular activity.

—A self-made entrepreneur, now in his 60s and his fourth marriage

We have been talking, up to now, about clandestine sexual activities outside of marriage, or "nonconsensual extramarital relationships." "Open marriage,"[18] a consensual extramarital sexual encounter, requires the acquiescence and knowledge of one's spouse and thus is a very different matter. Often, but not always, a mutual exchange of partners takes place at the same time. A time and place may even be assigned, by agreement between two or more couples, for their interchange to take place. Despite popularization in a book of that title in the early 1970s, open marriage has never become as prevalent as nonconsensual extramarital activities, and its popularity seems to be waning even further today.

One of the major marks of the First Sexual Revolution was the breakdown of traditional taboos against the "sin" of sex outside of marriage. Many of our male and female respondents reported having had extramarital affairs. Indeed, we suspect that the actual total may be even higher than reported, because many who have had such relationships are probably reluctant to admit it. No one can know for certain whether these episodes represent a search for better sex, a rebellion against tradition and authority, or hostility to and conflict with the marriage partner.

ABORTION

In the present social context, we can't speak of marriage and divorce without considering the issue of abortion. Do divorced women have more abortions than married women? Is abortion more prevalent as a birth control procedure among the nonmarried than among the married? When we asked our respondents, they answered as shown in Table 6.21.

While the never married (23%) and the married (25%) were close, in the percentages who had had abortions, the divorced reported a much higher incidence (33%). To some, it may seem surprising that a married woman is slightly more likely to have an abortion than one who has never married, because they assume that abortions are primarily for single women who cannot afford socially or financially to have a child. We found that issues relating to sex and money are only two of many reasons for women having abortions. Many pregnant women and couples anguish through decision making when there is medical evidence that a fetus has serious, even life-threatening medical problems, or when the relationship of the marriage is on the rocks, or when the woman falls ill, or when a host of other, personal grounds for choosing abortion occur.

TABLE 6.21   **Survey Item H.24.**

I HAVE HAD AN ABORTION:			
	Single	Married	Divorced
N =	441	804	127
Yes	23%	25%	33%
No	73	70	63
No answer	4	5	4

Authors' note: This table and the others relating to abortion contain a no answer category because the percentage of people not responding may be a meaningful indication.

REMARRIAGE

There is life after divorce, as hundreds of thousands of Americans have discovered. The Bureau of the Census[19] has estimated that one out of every three marriages is a second-time-arounder for one or both partners. Three-fourths of divorced women and four-fifths of divorced men are likely to remarry. At least half of the men who remarry will do so within 4 years of their divorce, and at least half of the women who remarry will do so within 3 years. Most people, according to Census officials, will be in their early or middle 30s when their second marriage takes place. Most sources estimate that between one-third and one-half of all marriages involve at least one previously married partner.

The score isn't in yet on the fate of those remarriages. Some researchers find that remarriages are more likely than first marriages to terminate in divorce. Other researchers suggest that remarried people have a high level of satisfaction and a sense of well-being. In a general way, we can assume that the longer a marriage has lasted, the more stable the relationship is. Table 6.22 gives the data we received for first, second, and third marriages.

The table shows that remarriages can be long-lived. About half of the second and third marriages had not yet reached a fifth anniversary, but about 30% had lasted longer than 10 years, and more than one in ten had passed the 16-year mark. From a cross-check of respondents' ages and length of present marriage (survey items H.2 and H.7; see Appendix B), we were able to determine that the divorced and remarried people tended to be somewhat older (in their 40s) than those who were in their first marriages, nearly half of whom were under 40.

Today's headlines attest that age difference—in marriages and in relationships in general—no longer carries the significance that it once did. The older woman–younger man relationship has become relatively commonplace but has not yet reached the level of acceptance of older men relating to younger women. There is, in general, less concern with age and more attention to the nature of the individual. We hear much more

TABLE 6.22   **Survey Items H.7, H.8.**

SELF-IDENTIFICATION: LENGTH OF MARRIAGES:			
	First Marriage	Second Marriage	Third Marriage
N =	1,182	315	79
Less than 5 years	25%	46%	53%
6–10 years	20	22	27
11–15 years	15	21	7
16 or more years	40	11	13

about personality, sense of humor, and similar qualities, when someone is attracted to an individual. Generally, where there is a wide age difference, there is also a great deal of family and peer pressure against the marriage; however, if the couple can overcome the pressure, some of these marriages are often highly successful.

MARRIAGE TODAY, AMERICAN-STYLE

How has marriage changed in the past several decades? Until relatively recently, divorce was extremely rare, although marital unhappiness was a commonplace. An extreme case from two centuries ago, reported by Nancy F. Cott,[20] concerned a marriage of 30 years' duration. The wife appealed to Massachusetts courts to let her divorce the husband who "had been cohabiting at home with her sister" and was no longer supporting her and their children, instead spending all his money at local taverns. His financial failings had led directly to the divorce proceedings, not his sexual peccadilloes, which his lawful wife had tolerated for 8 years.

Scholars today who study the reasons for divorce analyze such issues as the power structure within the marriage. For example, Willard Waller and R. Hill,[21] among others, hold that the spouse who has least to gain by staying married controls the future of the relationship. A related idea is that the most infatuated spouse is the one with the least power, because she or he has most to lose if the marriage breaks up. Generally, it is the spouse with the least power who attempts to keep the marriage going.

This may explain why a substantial proportion of divorces since the early 1970s has been initiated by wives. No longer powerless, today's women are educated, able to earn, and unwilling to put up with the kinds of unpleasant living arrangements that women too often had to settle for in days gone by. When we asked women who had brought suit against their husbands why they had decided to end their marriages, they usually said something like this: "I decided there was no reason to put up with his behavior," "I would rather be on my own than cook another meal or do another load of laundry for him," or even "I thought that whatever might happen couldn't be worse than living with that insensitive man."

✦ *IN THEIR OWN WORDS* _____

> Brad and I have been married for nine years, but there have been rocky moments from the very beginning. I think that we were both not really prepared for a modern marriage. By that I mean a marriage based on parity, respect, trust, and, yes, a good deal of exciting sex. The advice I got from my mother, who is a good bit older, and was concerned that here I

was 31 and single, was straight out of Currier and Ives, or maybe older. She was actually telling me that old saw about not having sex before marriage, because, why would a man buy a cow if he could get all the milk he wanted? My friends' advice wasn't much better either; it ranged from my feminist friends who warned me not to let him dominate me, and not to let myself be dragged into phallocentric sex, and that all men are pigs. My traditional friends and relatives gave me snippets of advice on how to please a man. I don't think men get that much advice when they marry. It took a bit of time to knock off the rough edges, and to realize each other's humanity. My goodness, trust is so important. Brad is basically a kind guy, but he had been raised in a very traditional home. Can you believe that his mother still serves herself last? After everyone else has been served, and well into eating, she will sit down and eat. Sexually, we had very few problems, since I didn't take my mother's advice; I was able to audition Brad before we were married, and we both make great music together. It was just in the many small, slighting ways that men make women, even professional women, feel like domestics that got to me. It took him a while to see what I was talking about, and even for me to be able to articulate exactly the frustration and anger I was feeling. Once I got my finger on it, it made sense to him. I think that this is a problem for many women; it's the kind of thing where they feel frustrated, and their husbands feel that they are being bitchy, or about to have their period. Talking it out worked for us. I don't know if it's perfection, all I can say is that I feel respect as well as love in this marriage with Brad.

—A 40-year-old professor of philosophy

SUMMING UP

In our professional experience, we have found that many people seek in marriage their own ideals of perfection, and, for some, this search can translate to an impossible dream. Based on that professional experience, as well as on interviews with people in long-lasting marriages, we believe that successful marriages are built by people with healthy egos, people who are flexible and who seek and need sexual intimacy and kinship. People who can adapt to the life-style and sex life of another without viewing it as an egregious invasion of their own ideas, values, or personal space will have the best chance of establishing a rewarding and lasting marital relationship.

The family, too, as we will see in the next chapter, has gone through enormous changes. Not all of these are a result of the sexual liberation of the previous generation. The advances of the women's movement toward equal treatment and opportunity, the economic need for two incomes, and a growing modification of traditionally restricted sex roles are among the contributing factors. Men can now cry, nurture babies and children, and in other ways be more rounded and fully contributing partners both emotionally and practically. Women can now aspire to the same education and the same kinds of professional careers that men have always had access to, and thus also be more rounded and fully contributing partners both intellectually and financially.

These many new options give men and women much more to negotiate and to agree on than was true for their parents' generation. The modern marriage relationship as a social structure is still evolving and will surely not settle into a single pattern. It differs from one couple to another, because each couple has its own way of resolving the many issues to be addressed to satisfy the needs of spouses and children.

Marriage may have been undervalued during the First Sexual Revolution. Today, it appears to have once more become highly valued as a haven from the "real world," only this time the haven is for the career-woman wife as well as the husband returning from a hard day's work.

CHAPTER SEVEN

Children:
To Have or Have Not

SOME SIGNIFICANT FINDINGS ABOUT CHILDREN:
TO HAVE OR HAVE NOT

✦ 19% of the single men and 23% of the single women surveyed reported using no contraception; among the divorced respondents, the same report came from 39% of the men and 27% of the women.

✦ 32% of the Protestant women, 29% of the Catholic women, 11% of the Jewish women, and 22% of the women who professed no religious affiliation reported having had at least one abortion.

✦ 96% of the men and 97% of the women who answered our questionnaire felt that family planning is important.

✦ Of the women who had had abortions, almost 20% had their first before they reached 18 years of age.

```
┌─────────────────────────────────────────────────────────────┐
│        QUESTIONNAIRE SUBJECTS TABULATED IN THIS CHAPTER       │
└─────────────────────────────────────────────────────────────┘
```

	Table*
Parenthood	7.1
Number of Children	7.2, 7.3
Delaying Careers for Child Rearing	7.4
Family Planning	7.5
Contraception Methods	7.6
Women Who Have Had Abortions	7.7, 7.9, 7.10, 7.11
Age at First Abortion	7.8
Reaction After First Abortion	7.12
Surrogate Mothers	7.13
In-Vitro Fertilization	7.14

*Authors' note: Some tables in this chapter duplicate data appearing elsewhere in the book. They are repeated here because they are relevant to the issues discussed in this chapter, and we feel their reappearance gives better continuity.

✦ IN THEIR OWN WORDS

I am thrilled with my baby. Yes, I finally had a baby. Has it changed my life? It has, and it hasn't. We are the same people, I hold the same job, and our marriage is wonderful. But the baby does something about making you feel for the future. There is something intangible and deep about motherhood that I find increasingly almost mystical.

My husband and I pretty much share the household and baby chores, though I am the one to more often get up in the night when she cries. I decided to nurse, but only for the first two months. I wanted the experience, and now that I've had it, it's enough. I believe that one can be professionally productive and also have the fulfillment of family. Many of my friends think that only dummies become mothers. If I had it to do over again, I would have gone for motherhood earlier.

—A 38-year-old female banking account executive

✦ ✦ ✦

I think kids are wonderful. I babysit for my younger sister's kids, and they love me, but I'm not cut out to be a mother.

—A 40-year-old public relations executive

✦ ✦ ✦

My family is nice, except for my little brother who is five, but he is a boy, and boys can be so pesty. I believe that my mom and dad are happy together. And the children—there are three of us—are happy too. My mom helps me with most of my homework, except for math or science when my dad helps me. Even though I can do most of it myself, it feels good that my folks help me and care about me.

There were times when mom and dad were not so happy about each other, and they used to yell a lot. We got past that and they smile and kiss each other, as well as us, as much as they can. I think I am pretty lucky, especially when I hear from my friends about how they live with their families which are divorced. It sounds terrible. I used to worry about that happening to my mom and dad.

The only thing that is maybe nice about divorced parents is that the kids always seem to have so many toys, and their parents take them to all kinds of shows and things. We don't go to that many shows, but sometimes my friends will ask me to come along with them when they go with their mom or dad, and I get to see these great shows, and eat anything I want in expensive restaurants. I guess they like to have me along because I am a good friend, and it makes them feel good. I like that a lot, and my friends and I whisper a lot, and tell each other about secret things that we don't tell adults, mostly because it is about the adults.

> —An 8-year-old girl who attends a school for gifted children

---

Marriage is not the only response to love, nor is it only a response to love. Beyond love, marriage involves decisions about practical matters, such as where to live, who does what chores and sees which friends, and how to spend money. The single most important decision made in a marriage, of course, is whether to have children.

Having children, making a family, is traditionally considered the focal task of adulthood. Isn't Nature's plan to perpetuate the species? The policies of governments everywhere encourage the nurture and training of the next generation. Part of the psychological definition of mental health in adults is readiness to assume responsibility for bearing and rearing children. Traditionally, childless couples have been viewed as selfish or hedonistic, and childless marriages, as less than complete.

FAMILY VERSUS HOUSEHOLD

What exactly *is* a family? Different types of family structure were attempted in the 1960s, and many of those communal experiments are still going strong. Nurturing families can be established in households of every variety. There are multifamily households of communes, single-parent families, families established by gay male couples who adopt children, and by lesbian women who arrange pregnancies through artificial insemination or other means and raise these children with their lovers.

Substantial numbers of couples are choosing to remain childless. National average household size and family size have dwindled steadily for almost half a century. In some neighborhoods, childlessness has become the norm and child rearing is the exception. Married couples are having fewer children and having them later in life—and, more than ever before, deciding not to have any children at all.

How did these changes happen? In what ways are childless marriages different from those that become child-oriented, and in what ways are they the same? Does having children put a damper on a loving marital relationship? What attitudes underlie these changing family patterns? How do these new family life-styles affect the adults and children living in them? How do they affect our communities and workplaces?

Before we look at what makes a family, we should first look at what constitutes a household. The Bureau of the Census makes a distinction: A household can be headed by a single adult and thus may possibly contain only one person; a family has at least two people related to each other by birth or marriage. In 1990, married couples with or without children constituted 56% of all families, down from 71% two decades earlier.[1]

"Only One U.S. Family in Four Is 'Traditional,'" headlined a *New York Times* article[2] in early 1991. Census Bureau data, said the report, showed "the decline of the traditional family—two parents with children" from 40% of all households in 1970 to 31% in 1980 and 26% in 1990.

A generation or so ago, most households in the United States consisted of traditional families; in the 1970s, there was a sharp spurt in the number of newly established households. Increasingly, these new units did not fit the definition of "family." Several demographic factors were responsible. Most dramatic was the movement of the first wave of "Baby Boomers" out of their parents' homes to set up homes of their own. (As we noted earlier, "Boomers" are generally identified as those born between about 1945 and about 1950.)

In the 1970s, the establishment of single-person households grew by 5% every year; in the 1980s, their growth was about half that rate. Meanwhile, other nontraditional-family households were being established by the large wave of the newly divorced. These were people who had married in the 1960s, 1950s, and even earlier. Throughout the 1970s, the number of divorced mothers increased 9% a year, slowing to 1.6% a year on average in the 1980s.[3] Increasing numbers of women were establishing satisfying and financially rewarding careers. As recently as one generation ago, almost all working women lived at home with their parents, and those who didn't braved scorn and scandal. It was not unusual for an employed and unmarried woman to live in her childhood home until the death of her parents, perhaps when she was just reaching retirement age herself. However, from the 1960s on, educated women who could support themselves began taking their own apartments and sometimes even buying a home—alone. As numbers increased, gossip decreased. These women, who were busy making careers and independent social lives, postponed marriage and lived alone.

The number of people living together in the average household has decreased sharply in the 20th century. The Bureau of the Census has reported that the average size of a U.S. household in 1989 was 2.62 persons, less than half the size of a mid-19th-century household. What's more, Census officials expect American households to continue dwindling, to approximately 2.5 persons by the year 2000. The current low rate is largely due to a decrease in the number of children per family and an increase in single and couple adult-only living units.[4] Recent Census data showed that there were 9.7 million single parents in 1990, an increase of 41% in each decade since 1970. American household size, which averaged 2.63 in 1990, had been 2.76 in 1980 and 3.14 in 1970.[5]

The actual *number* of traditional families changed little in those years: 25.5 million in 1970, 24.2 million in 1980, and 24.5 million in 1990. But because the total number of households was growing more rapidly in this period, the two-parents-plus-child family was becoming an increasingly smaller part of the whole. Because of population growth, there are today approximately the same number of households with children as there were when the post-Second World War Baby Boom ended, but these constitute only a little more than one-fourth of all households. The number of married people who do *not* have children—29% of all households— is slightly higher. Another one-fourth of the population consists of single-person households. Female-alone heads of households increased from 8.7% in 1970 to 11.7% in 1989; male-alone heads of household increased from 1.9% in 1970 to 3.1% in 1989. (The fourfold preponderance of female-alone households probably reflected the greater tendency for older women to be widowed.[6])

In the early 1990s, however, these trends began to reverse. Proportionately fewer new households were being established and the divorce rate was diminishing. With the end of the Baby Boom, there were fewer young adults left to move out of parental nests, and some of the earlier single-person-household Boomers had finally met a mate with whom to couple up. The marriage rate went up as the divorce rate went down. As more and more Boomers married, the "birth dearth" came to an end. The extremely low birth rate that resulted from peoples' postponement of childbearing was followed by an increase in babies born to Boomers. This "boomlet" or rebound baby boom produced 4 million babies in 1989, as many as in 1964.[7]

THE IMPORTANCE OF FAMILY

Sociologist Louis Lieberman, professor at the City University of New York, has identified the functions traditionally served by the institution of the family—sexual gratification, reproduction, education, transmission of religion, and social–psychological protection. He explained:

> By sexual gratification and reproduction, it was meant that children were supposed to be born only within a legitimate and socially recognized family structure, i.e., birth out of wedlock was not legitimate and the mother and child [were] subjected to much abuse and ostracism. Related to this, sex was permitted only between husband and wife, for the purpose of reproduction and not pleasure, at least not for women.
>
> By education, we meant that the role of teaching the child the basic skills of work and housekeeping, as well as the rudiments of social behavior, and the primary socialization skills had traditionally been carried out by the family.
>
> By the religious function of the family, we meant the legitimacy of the family in transmitting religious values to its offspring, to give a religious identity and religious education to its children and to act as an agency through which many of the religious norms of the society were to be carried out. In addition, many other religious activities such as ceremonies and rituals were frequently carried out within the family.
>
> By social–psychological we meant that the parents were the protectors of the children, especially the father who protected the entire family from physical danger. The father also gave status identity to the family by virtue of the various positions he occupied in society, and the parents were expected to provide for almost all of the physical, social and psychological needs of the children and of each other.

However, Dr. Lieberman concluded, "Today, these functions are a mere shadow of their past." He felt that the family has been so changed and its ability to perform these traditional functions is so weakened "that there is some speculation about the viability of the traditional structure as a permanent social institution."[8]

Another scholar who studies family dynamics, Stephen Fleck,[9] has observed that family goals and tasks are determined by the culture and society in which the family exists. As our society changes, we can expect the goals and tasks of our families to shift as well. Thus, the tasks of today's family are no longer primarily economic, as they were when even young children were expected to contribute to the subsistence of all family members. Even so, the goal of guiding the younger generation into adulthood remains as vital as ever, although the specific tasks to be performed by our youth on their way to that goal may be less clearly defined.

How important was family to the people we surveyed? Did our respondents reflect the trends identified by the sociologists, the Census Bureau, and other observers? As can be seen in Tables 2.11, 3.1, 9.1, and 10.2, our respondents overwhelmingly agreed that the family is the most important institution in our society. Further, the agreement held for both sexes and stretched across all age groups and all education levels. There was some difference in agreement among those identifying

TABLE 7.1   Survey Item A.8.

BECOMING A PARENT IS THE ULTIMATE HUMAN ATTAINMENT:		
	Men	Women
N =	1,341	1,413
Strongly agree	9%	9%
Agree	27	24
No opinion	17	13
Disagree	37	41
Strongly disagree	10	13
Strongly agree + Agree	36%	33%
Disagree + Strongly disagree	47%	54%

themselves as ultraliberals, which is covered in Chapter 9, and among those who had had postgraduate education, as discussed in Chapter 10. But, by and large, the agreement with this statement was universal among our respondents.

To assess our respondents' attitudes toward the importance of having children, we asked whether they agreed that parenthood was the ultimate attainment (Table 7.1).

Attitudes toward children are certainly relevant in a book about sexuality, because they are the product of sex. The main issue relating to children is whether to have them, and if so, when. Interestingly, by a small percentage, men responded more favorably than women to the statement that parenthood is the ultimate human attainment. This result may seem surprising, considering the traditional belief that women live just to become mothers. However, some other indicators show that this is a pattern geared more to a male preference for tradition, and perhaps to keep women from leaving the home. Responses in this vein can be seen in replies to other questions regarding traditional sex roles (Table 3.7), the double standard (Table 3.9), and the question of whether both sexes can take care of babies equally well (Table 3.5). We mention these tables here to round out our findings on this issue.

CHILDLESS MARRIAGE

According to the Census Bureau, one of every five women who are or ever were married was childless in the 1980s. A body of research on adults who do not have children suggests that the reasons are many and complex; these adults are not simply childless because they dislike children or fear parenthood. They may have other priorities. Many nurture children to whom they are related, or with whom they interact through career choices or volunteer activities. Others nurture a business enterprise or a career with the same level of involvement that parents devote to their offspring. About one-fourth of all childless women were raised in the kind of disturbed family setting that is called "dysfunctional" today, and they do not want to inflict even the possibility of a repeat performance on a child. Still others choose childlessness because of a hereditary defect, either physical or mental, which they have reason to believe would afflict a child they might conceive. The childless-by-choice are up against substantial pressure from society in general and from family, especially their own parents; they have made a decision, perhaps painfully, and may be forced to confront it frequently. That is not, incidentally, a bad idea: People change and situations change; many people who chose childlessness at one stage of their life find reasons to make the opposite decision some years later. It can be important to keep options open.[10]

HOW MANY CHILDREN?

What about the people we surveyed? If they were or had been married, did they have children? Tables 7.2 and 7.3 gave some indications, by marital status and gender.

An interesting finding was that the divorced respondents reported having had more children than respondents who were currently married. Aside from the possibility of a divorced person's having had several marriages, and children in each marriage, one other factor is involved. When a respondent represented a family group in which the mother was not married but had children from different fathers, that respondent was entered into the divorced group.

Tradition places the mother in the major role of child-nurturer and teacher. The social changes that have made it possible for women to follow

TABLE 7.2   **Survey Item H.9.**

SELF-IDENTIFICATION: NUMBER OF CHILDREN, BY CURRENT MARITAL STATUS:		
	Married	Divorced
N =	1,570	246
No children	20%	14%
1 child	20	18
2 children	36	29
3 children	15	18
4 children	7	10
5 or more children	2	11

TABLE 7.3 Survey Item H.9.

SELF-IDENTIFICATION: NUMBER OF CHILDREN, BY GENDER AND CURRENT MARITAL STATUS:				
	Married		Divorced	
	Men	Women	Men	Women
N =	770	800	121	125
No children	15%	23%	19%	12%
1 or more	85%	77%	81%	88%

different paths are still taking place. The debate over whether women more than men should have primary responsibility for child care rages in the popular press, in the boardroom, among women's groups, and even among men. Many women and men feel that, even for those women who enter the work force, a job should not take precedence over their traditional responsibilities as mothers; their children should still come first.

How did our respondents feel about mothers delaying their careers during their children's early years? Table 3.4 showed that 53% of the men felt that women should defer their career development while their children are small. The women were less so inclined; 49% felt that they should not have to interrupt their budding careers for child rearing. However, differences showed up between career women and homemakers: 57% of the traditional women agreed that a woman's place is in the home, and 58% of the career women disagreed. One must bear in mind that, for women who devote themselves full-time to the home, children are their justification. For some couples, income level dictates that both parents work full-time outside of the home; homemaking full-time is not an option for these women.

We were not surprised that, the more education respondents had, the less likely were both males and females to agree that child-rearing time should be borrowed from a mother's career (see Table 10.5). Nor were we surprised to find that women were more likely than men to *disapprove* of the mother's taking career time off for child care. Women, no matter what their educational attainments, are well informed, by the media and by other women, of the career problems that result from a prolonged absence from the workplace. They have heard many tales of the reentry difficulties—poorer pay, lower ranked position, less or different responsibility, and less interesting work all await women who take a few years' leave of absence to devote to raising their children.

As indicated in Table 7.4, the married and the divorced gave almost identical responses to this survey item, reflecting much about the economic reality that both groups faced. Not all women—and not even all

TABLE 7.4   Survey Item A.10.

MOTHERS SHOULD DELAY THEIR CAREERS DURING CHILDREN'S EARLY YEARS:		
	Married	Divorced
N =	1,569	245
Strongly agree + Agree	48%	49%
No opinion	10	7
Disagree + Strongly disagree	42	44

women who work—want a career. Most women who work have a primary goal of earning money; some believe strongly in the social usefulness of their occupations; and many enjoy the more varied social life of their work environment. Many women also claim that a successful career gives them both the reality and the feeling of independence. The new generation of working mothers, with full-time work-lives outside the home, is the first to have more than an occasional female role model to look to for guidance and for justification for its choice. Formerly, women often had to gain support from women's groups and supportive husbands.

The subject of whether mothers should work full-time outside of the home is complicated by the need for the mother's earnings in the two-paycheck middle-income family. (There is no question about the need for the mother's earning power when she is a single parent.) Corporate America is moving at a glacial pace toward accommodating the family needs of its working women and men. Parental leaves are often available, but men, who are more likely than women to fear a career interruption, seldom choose the child-care option. Even for women, a few weeks on disability-level pay is the norm after giving birth, and anything more is generous. Americans have a long way to go to achieve the level of support for family time that is provided in European nations, where six months of paid family leave for each parent is generally minimal.

Although child rearing has traditionally been almost exclusively a woman's domain, many recent family arrangements include the father's sharing domestic duties.

As reported in Table 3.5, the men and women surveyed overwhelmingly agreed that both sexes can take care of babies equally well. In what may be perceived as either a vote of confidence in men or an attempt to push them toward increased involvement with fathering, the women felt even more strongly than the men that both sexes can take good care of babies.

This is a bread-and-butter issue, not a fun-and-games competition about which sex can do something better. Women who wanted both a career and motherhood have, in the past, been trapped at home during the years when they might have been advancing in the business world. Many settled for reality, persuaded themselves that child raising was *the* major significant act of their lives, and found community organizations on which to lavish their administrative and practical skills. Perhaps later, when their children were in high school or college, these women would reenter the business (or academic) world they had left two decades earlier, only to find that the moving-up-the-ladder jobs were now held by people 20 years their junior. "Having it all" is still of concern to young women today, and it is a central issue for the women's movement. But child rearing is still seen as primarily a women's concern, as the responses to our survey item certified. Society has the task of creating new institutions—expanding child-care services would be a start—to enable those women with skills, interest, talent, and the will to excel in more than one role, to seek the most personally gratifying way to live their own lives. At the same time, those women who wish to focus on their home responsibilities should be free to do so without any pressure to conform to the paths others choose.

CHILDREN AND DIVORCE

Are marriages with children happier than those without? A woman we know, whose children are in the acting-out teenage years, recently remarked to us, "I wonder what long-married people who don't have children talk about." Most of the rest of life can be fairly repetitious, but children constantly present new challenges as they grow into new stages and activities. We wondered whether problems in child rearing contributed to marital disharmony and divorce. In our interviews, we asked divorced respondents who had children about the reasons for their divorces. Only one, a woman, cited problems with children as the primary reason for her divorce.

Not only have there been vastly more divorces in recent decades, but children were involved in a higher proportion of them than ever before. In 1922, the lives of 93,000 children were disrupted by divorce; by the 1980s more than one million children a year had parents who were divorcing.[11] In the early 20th century, only about one-third of divorcing couples had children, whereas almost two-thirds of recently divorcing couples did. Of divorced respondents to our survey, slightly over half (51%) had children. These figures suggest that, in earlier days, people who had children may have refrained from divorcing. Anecdotal evidence supports this conclusion: How often we have heard from people who put up with unhappy marriages "for the children's sake!" The large proportion of recent divorces involving children suggests that unhappy spouses are no longer willing to tolerate their marital difficulties, whether children are present or not.

Eighty-five percent of men and women ages 18 to 24 believe that couples in their generation will be more likely to get divorced than those in their parents' generation.[12]

✦ *IN THEIR OWN WORDS* ───────────────────────────────────────

I think divorce is terrible, it stinks, it breaks your heart. You love your mom and dad the most in the world, and then they make you choose who to live with. Then you don't get to stay with, or see one of your parents except on weekends. They tried to explain it all to us, and how they both loved us, but that they had to split up. I am never going to do this to my kids, and come to think of it, maybe I will never get married, so I don't ever have to do that. It was terrible, my mom and dad both cried, and me and my brother also cried when they told us that dad was going to move out, and that they were separating.

Divorce is a dark cloudy day in a kid's life. My best friend and I talk a lot about it, and that makes it a little better, but I almost didn't get to live near my best friend anymore. I had to make a really loud fuss to be able to stay with my mom so I could go to the same school and have the same friends. I felt bad seeing my dad living all alone, and I stay over his house sometimes, and we have fun, but then I feel terrible that my mom isn't here to enjoy it with us. I don't know why adults do that. How can you be in love with somebody and marry them and then decide that you have fallen out of love?

—A 12-year-old boy who attends junior high school

FAMILY PLANNING

Whatever the current marital status of our respondents, they were far more likely to have few or no children than to have a houseful. People who have no or few children (slightly less than three-fourths of our respondents had two or fewer children) are more likely to be making effective use of family planning methods. We asked a number of questions about this. First, we asked about attitudes toward family planning in general, and then about contraceptive methods used. One method used by some of our respondents was abortion, and we asked several additional questions about this highly sensitive topic.

Family planning no longer arouses strong emotions today. Some of the available means of birth prevention are condemned by the more conservative branches of the major religions, but few groups advocate constant childbearing. As indicated in Table 7.5, our respondents, male and female alike, overwhelmingly voted for the central importance of planned pregnancies.

TABLE 7.5   Survey Item B.1.

FAMILY PLANNING IS:		
	Men	Women
N =	1,342	1,414
Very important	56%	62%
Important	40	35
Not sure	2	2
Unimportant	2	1
Very unimportant	0	0
Very important + Important	96%	97%

The combined very important and important responses (96% for men and 97% for women) present us with another, particularly important area where males and females are in complete agreement.

An early advocate of family planning was the American physician Charles Knowlton, who earned notoriety in both the United States and Great Britain for his views on the subject. In his 1832 book, *The Fruits of Philosophy*,[13] he expressed some radical ideas that placed him in direct conflict with the establishment of his day. Knowlton held sexual interests to be normal, and believed that their reasonable indulgence was both satisfying and healthy. He called celibacy unwholesome and sexual denial harmful. To aid people in this "reasonable indulgence," he advocated several contraceptive practices, including the diaphragm, then called a vaginal tent, and the postcoital douche. What particularly outraged the moral guardians of the day was the realization that, "with knowledge of contraception in the hands of all, female virtue [would be] on the way out." The city of Cambridge, Massachusetts, imprisoned Knowlton for three months of hard labor for his views.[14]

It has been pointed out that many of the same people who oppose abortion are inconsistent and contradictory in that they also oppose the use of contraceptives, which offer an effective alternative to unwanted pregnancies that may end in abortion. In order to determine the extent of the differences between the religious and the nonreligious, we asked whether our respondents used contraceptives. Because traditional Catholics and Jews, as well as many other religions and denominations, disapprove of the use of some or even all contraceptives, we expected that more religious respondents would be opposed to the use of contraception.

In the next chapter, Tables 8.5 and 8.6 indicate that contraception was widely practiced by all groups we surveyed, across the entire religious spectrum. Approximately 65% of our respondents used contraception, and there was little difference based on religiosity. In our interviews, however, those who did not use contraception often referred to religious concerns or traditional values.

Yes, there are times when I am tired, when I would dearly love to lie down and take a nap. I can't do that often. The children are demanding, but I regard them as gifts of God. We are a religious family, and I guess that part of life is struggle. I believe that we are being tested. I had gone to a liberal college, and I knew of girls that had abortions, and I knew even then, that route was not for me. They said that having babies at that early point in their lives would mess up their careers. A career was of interest to me, but not an absolute must. Home and a family were more important. I figured that I would work until I got married, save some money, and have children. Truthfully, I didn't plan for six, very few people do. But that is the way it worked out, so who am I to question it?

We are not wealthy, but we have a lot of love in this family. My husband works hard, and we all try to work together. My oldest daughter is a wonderful little mother to the youngest children. I don't know what I would do without her. I am not sure that I will not have any more children. My life is governed by my religion, and I take it seriously. We use more natural ways of contraception, like the rhythm method, and for about a half-year we just abstain. Some friends from college think that I am some kind of a throwback to the past. But I don't see them that happy; they are depressed when they break up with their boyfriends, they are lonely, and all their money and their careers can't buy them the love I feel from my children. Being a mother is the most gratifying role in my life.

—A 34-year-old wife, and mother of six children,
who is a full-time homemaker married
to a clerk in a local business

We also looked at whether contraceptive use was in any way related to current marital status. Table 7.6 shows rates of use of particular contraceptive methods.

The dramatic finding here was that single people were more likely to use family planning methods than the other groups. Single men, especially, seemed to take responsibility for contraception. The married and divorced men showed similar rates of contraceptive use (53% and 58%, respectively); however, the divorced women were considerably more likely to use contraceptives (68%) than the married women (54%).

We sensed a synthesis between the men and women we interviewed—a strong sense of identification with the other sex's needs. Among the married and divorced, high numbers reported for vasectomy

TABLE 7.6 Survey Item H.19.

SELF-IDENTIFICATION: TYPE OF CONTRACEPTION USED:						
	Single		Married		Divorced	
	Men	Women	Men	Women	Men	Women
N =	379	441	771	805	122	127
Condoms	60%	22%	38%	15%	41%	16%
Pill	6	41	11	15	9	12
Tubal ligation	0	4	0	15	0	26
Rhythm	4	4	3	3	0	0
Abortion	0	2	2	3	1	2
Vasectomy	3	0	12	6	10	1
I.U.D.	1	3	1	2	3	4
Diaphragm	5	15	8	10	3	16
Cream/Jelly	4	6	4	5	6	5
None	19	23	44	42	39	27
No answer	4	4	3	4	3	5
None + No answer	23%	27%	47%	46%	42%	32%
Users (all methods)	77%	73%	53%	54%	58%	68%

Author's note: Widowed persons and those reporting themselves separated were not included in this tabulation. We did not include hysterectomy because it is not a contraceptive procedure. Because many individuals use several contraceptive methods, the numbers for the methods listed total to more than 100%.

and tubal ligation, techniques that permanently rule out children (unless a new and chancy surgical procedure proves effective). Many people listed their contraceptive as a couple; for example, where a man had a vasectomy, his wife or partner listed vasectomy. Other individuals similarly reflected what they and their sex partner jointly employed as contraceptive methods. There had been considerable publicity in the late 1980s and again in the early 1990s about a pill for men, but when we checked with medical experts, the message was that we no longer hear about it because research was stopped: the pill for men didn't work. Condoms for men and the pill for women were the most popular methods employed. Although the pill is the most widely used contraceptive by women, we heard some anxious questions about the pill's long-term hormonal impact.

The popularity of condom purchases by women has been a fairly recent concept. Some women justify carrying condoms in their purse "just in case," as teenage boys of prior generations did. The women are apt to cite the prevention of AIDS as their reason, as well as the prevention of conception.

ABORTION

At least 25% of our female respondents acknowledged having had at least one abortion (see Table 6.21). The percentage is less for the very religious and more for the not religious (see Table 8.3).

Abortion has been a public and political issue for at least the past quarter of a century. It is, obviously, a very complex personal issue as well. Repeated studies have shown that most pregnancies are unplanned and that about half of all abortions are performed on married women.

The Supreme Court's *Roe v. Wade* decision of 1973 had the effect of legalizing first- and, in some circumstances, second-trimester abortions throughout the country. The Court's essential consideration was that, in the early stages of pregnancy, abortion was a private matter for a woman to decide. Since then, there have been continual efforts to undo the decision. Indeed, in several states, restrictive legislation has already been enacted. If legal challenges to these restrictions fail, we could once again see women having to choose between expensive and perhaps surreptitious and dangerous operations or the burden of delivering and raising children they do not want or may be unable to care for.

Abortion, as we ourselves know from our own clinical experiences, is usually not an easy decision for a woman to make, no matter what her circumstances—well-off or financially constrained, young or mature, married or single, having a supportive family or a dysfunctional one. Objective as well as emotional factors enter into every abortion decision, and, in our research, we have learned of countless such decisions. We know that the factors considered, the others confided in, and the emotional costs, are never the same for any two women. Our experience has shown that a woman's judgment about her own circumstances and ability to care for a child should be the determining factors in the continuation of every pregnancy.

✦ IN THEIR OWN WORDS

I love my beach house; being near the ocean and nature, I often do paintings of the beautiful scenes. It is a requirement for me that I have control over my life. I love nature's creations, but in my own life, I can only handle a few of them at a time. I have had four abortions. I did some thinking about this before I had my first, and though I hadn't gotten pregnant to have an abortion, it was the only thing that made sense for me. I feel that since I had all of my abortions fairly early in the pregnancy, these were like cells a doctor was removing from my body. It really isn't any different than what my dentist does when he scales my gums, my beautician cuts my hair, or when I cut my nails.

I don't believe that it's a question of morality or sin. It is a matter of being able to care for the human being that will follow this pregnancy.

Certainly I am responsible; I feel that I am an excellent mother, and I love my son dearly. We're very close, closer than most kids I see with their mothers. What good is it to bring babies into this world to have lives of deprivation and pain? Most of my friends have had abortions, for good reasons, not frivolous ones.

I thought that I would feel terrible after the abortions; I didn't. There is a reflective period, once you get over the pain, and I knew I had done the right thing. When I was pregnant with my son, I knew this was something special and I would have this child, and I am glad I did. As much as I know that my baby was right for me, I knew the other pregnancies were not. I have absolutely no regrets.

> —A 38-year-old professional artist and single parent
> who lives with her child and her lover

How do Americans feel about the terms in which the antiabortion groups state their case? We gave our respondents an essentially emotional statement, "Abortion is murder," and asked whether they agreed or disagreed (see Table 3.6). Only 30% of our respondents agreed that abortion is murder. Many, although they felt undecided, would not agree that abortion is murder.

Our respondents clearly reflected the chasm that exists in our society concerning abortion. Some interesting sidelights were seen in Table 3.6. Men's and women's opinions on this issue were *very* similar. Indeed, there was more difference of opinion between career women and homemakers than between men and all women.

The situations of those who require an abortion vary. Some, like the woman just quoted, are unmarried but want a child, or more than one child, anyway—at a time that's right for them.

In Table 7.7 we see that the vast majority (84%) of our respondents who had abortions also had children. We know from other studies, as

TABLE 7.7   Survey Items H.9, H.24.

SELF-IDENTIFICATION: WOMEN WHO HAVE HAD ABORTIONS, BY NUMBER OF CHILDREN:	
N =	355
No children	16%
1 child	29
2 children	27
3 children	12
4 children	9
5 children	2
6 +	5

TABLE 7.8   Survey Item H.24.

SELF-IDENTIFICATION: AGE AT FIRST ABORTION:	
N =	355
Under 15 years	2%
15–17 years	17
18–21 years	42
22–25 years	13
26–30 years	13
31 and over	13

well as from personal interviews and professional experience, that women who choose abortion are very likely to have children subsequently, or they already have as many children as they can care for. Abortion was not chosen by these respondents to avoid childbearing; it was chosen to avoid childbearing at the wrong time or in the wrong circumstances for them.

We looked also at the ages of these women at the time they had their first abortion. As indicated in Table 7.8, about three-fifths had an abortion before they were 21, another one-fourth while still in their 20s, and only about 13% had their first abortion after age 30.

One of the most interesting findings we turned up in our analysis of the abortion data in our survey concerned the age at which women who had had abortions had become independent and sexually active.

In Table 7.9, we see that more than 80% of the women respondents who had had abortions were 21 years or younger when they left home and were on their own. Table 7.10 shows that, of the women who reported having an abortion, almost all (97%) had their first sexual experience before they were 21. It would definitely be a mistake to interpret

TABLE 7.9   Survey Items H.11, H.24.

SELF-IDENTIFICATION: WOMEN WHO HAVE HAD ABORTIONS, BY AGE MOVED OUT OF PARENTS' HOME:	
N =	355
Under 15 years	2%
15–17 years	22
18–21 years	58
22–25 years	16
26–30 years	1
31 and over	1

TABLE 7.10   Survey Items H.15, H.24.

SELF-IDENTIFICATION: WOMEN WHO HAVE HAD ABORTIONS, BY AGE AT FIRST FULL SEXUAL RELATIONS:	
N =	353
Under 15 years	12%
15–17 years	43
18–21 years	42
22–25 years	2
26–30 years	1
31 and over	0

these data as suggesting that early independence and sexual initiation make it likely that a woman will have an abortion. Rather, we believe that, taken together, these experiences represent the social and sexual world into which these women matured. This is the generation that came of age physically at a time when being on their own and having early sexual involvements was relatively new and definitely trendy. These social developments, which started in the late 1960s and mushroomed in the 1970s, coincided after 1973 with the legal availability of abortion. The women in our survey represented the life-style possibilities in the decades in which they came of age.

Is it possible to become pregnant without having had full sexual relations? Of all the women in our sample who had had one or more abortions, all but two reported having had full sexual relations as children, adolescents, or young adults; two other women, however, apparently required abortions following incomplete sexual interactions.

Another interesting set of findings related to the occupational status of women who had had abortions. (See Table 7.11.) The findings were striking, albeit not very surprising: Women with careers outside the home were about five times as likely to have one abortion, and nine times

TABLE 7.11   Survey Items H.14, H.24.

SELF-IDENTIFICATION: WOMEN WHO HAVE HAD ABORTIONS, BY CAREER OUTSIDE OF THE HOME:		
	1 abortion	2 or more abortions
N =	212	135
Have career outside home	84%	90%
Do not have outside career	16%	10%

TABLE 7.12   Survey Item H.25.

POSTABORTION REACTION WAS:	
N =	344
Relief	43%
Pleasure	4
No reaction	8
Sadness	29
Guilt	10
Regret	6
Relief + Pleasure	47%
Sadness + Guilt + Regret	45%

as likely to have more than one abortion, as women with no outside career. The data suggest that the economic necessity of working full-time often accompanies the inability, for economic reasons, to provide for a child. Additionally, the time constraints of a full-time career outside the home conflict with the time demands of pregnancy and motherhood.

How do women feel after going through an abortion? Pro-life advocates claim that such women are emotionally damaged and, psychologically and otherwise, are affected negatively by both the decision and the procedure. Our findings, shown in Table 7.12, do not confirm these conclusions.

As could be expected, very few women took pleasure in having an abortion, but it is interesting to note that very few expressed regret. Those women we interviewed who had experienced abortion made their choice very seriously; for them, it was something that *had* to be done. They had heard all the details about abortions from friends, the media, and their doctors. In most cases, we found that, married or single, women who have abortions get a good deal of support from their friends and loved ones. Abortion is occasionally a cause for disagreement, but mature decisions make the tension of the event less traumatic.

We have examined data relating to women who chose to end their pregnancies. What about the women who had the opposite problem—wanting children but unable to conceive?

NEW CONCEPTION TECHNOLOGIES

When people want children but for one reason or another are unable to conceive, there are a number of ways they can still have a family. Adoption and donor insemination have long been available. Hormone-based fertility treatments have been available for only a few decades. New in the past decade or so are surrogate motherhood and in-vitro fertilization. Every possibility has advantages and disadvantages. Treatments to enhance a woman's ability to conceive—using so-called "fertility drugs"—frequently result in multiple births, and often one or more of these infants is too frail to survive. "For adoption, there are long waits, deals that fall through, no control over genes. Intercourse with a selected partner or insemination by a known donor can open the door to future wrangles over custodial rights. Hence many women opt for insemination with the sperm of a faceless donor. The amount of information about the donor varies from clinic to clinic; a few provide detailed medical histories and personal profiles."[15]

Other couples may make an arrangement, through a lawyer, for a woman who will bear their child. For a fee, usually a substantial payment plus all medical and other related expenses, the surrogate mother will carry the fetus through pregnancy and, soon after birth, will release it to the contracting parents. In most cases, the surrogate will be inseminated with sperm donated by the husband/father-to-be. This arrangement, which has a number of variations, has led to several high-profile lawsuits, and there is as yet no legal consensus about the best way for the would-be parents to proceed. By mid-1992, commercial surrogacy arrangements had been banned in 17 states.[16]

To get an idea of whether there exists a public consensus on the subject, we asked our respondents for their opinion, men and women separately. (See Table 7.13.) The results were dramatic. Men and women reflected almost identical responses on this emotional issue, both in accepting and rejecting the idea of surrogacy.

In most cases, a surrogate mother's biological child has half the couple's gene pool, in that the father's sperm impregnates the surrogate.

TABLE 7.13   Survey Item A.4.

SURROGATE MOTHERS HAVE A DEFINITE ROLE IN AMERICAN FAMILY PLANNING:		
	Men	Women
N =	1,331	1,407
Strongly agree	5%	5%
Agree	31	31
No opinion	30	27
Disagree	23	26
Strongly disagree	11	11
Strongly agree + Agree	36%	36%
Disagree + Strongly disagree	34%	37%

Apparently, many women (36%) are willing to forgo their own biological input, or, more likely, they are convinced that the input would be impossible. A more recent development permits an egg removed from the mother to be fertilized by the biological father and then implanted in a surrogate's uterus to be carried to term. Respondents we interviewed who had resorted to surrogacy universally reported going through extensive and expensive tests and examinations and losing their sense of privacy. We found it most interesting that just below one-third of the survey population were unwilling or unable to express an opinion on the subject. The high no opinion ranking indicated that there was no common consensus on surrogacy. The publicity surrounding some of the litigation has undoubtedly left many people confused about how they stand on this issue.

One of the most successful of new techniques is in-vitro fertilization (IVF). In contrast to a natural pregnancy, in which the egg is fertilized by the sperm within the body of the mother, in-vitro fertilization takes place outside the body, in a test tube, where several eggs removed from the woman are exposed to the sperm donated by the man. A resulting embryo is then implanted in the mother's uterus, from which point the pregnancy proceeds much as any other. We were interested in whether this procedure was accepted as a viable option by both men and women. (See Table 7.14.)

In much the same pattern of response as to surrogate motherhood, men and women again had almost exactly the same scores. There was, however, a much higher (actually double) level of acceptance, with over three-fourths of the men and women approving of in-vitro fertilization. Although some religious groups find this procedure unacceptable, the overwhelmingly positive response shows again that Americans choose their level of conformity to dogma. Americans in general appear to have accepted the legitimacy of this technique and are willing to let science help where nature may have failed them for conception.

TABLE 7.14   **Survey Item G.9.**

IN-VITRO FERTILIZATION AND TECHNIQUES LIKE IT ARE:		
	Men	Women
N =	1,340	1,411
Vital	15%	17%
Beneficial	62	61
Problematic	19	21
Sinful	4	1
Vital + Beneficial	77%	78%

SUMMING UP

Families in the 1990s have several possible and socially accepted variations of personnel. However, the viability and value of the contemporary nuclear family's having a mother, a father, and one or more children is being rediscovered by today's young adults. Brought up in the exceptionally child-centered families of the 1950s and early 1960s, they rebelled for a while, living as singles or in childless pairs longer than any previous generation. Now, they use a wider variety of contraceptive methods than even their parents had available—and resort to legal abortion, if necessary—to more effectively plan and provide for the children they want. If nature is uncooperative when they decide it's time to conceive, they turn to a new set of sophisticated technologies to ensure conception. They're having fewer children and having them later, but they are having them as much as any more traditional generation did.

Our research has led us to believe that the family will be considered more positively in the 1990s than it has been in recent decades. The American family is enjoying a renaissance. Despite all the striking changes of life-styles—late marriage and later childbearing, more married women working outside the home, the highest rates of divorce in the world, and even the prevalence of abortion—the family has survived. We dare to say that it has become even stronger, because people make family decisions with more awareness of the range of options now available. We believe that people undertaking marriage and family today have more concern for the risks families face. They also have greater determination to avoid and overcome any obstacles that stand in the way of establishing a viable family unit.

CHAPTER EIGHT

Religion and Sex

SOME SIGNIFICANT FINDINGS ABOUT RELIGION AND SEX

✦ 61% of those who considered themselves to be very religious, and 66% of those who said they were religious, reported using contraceptives.

✦ More than 30% of the very religious respondents acknowledged having had extramarital sexual relations at least once; more than 70% had had premarital sexual experience.

✦ Protestants were least supportive of traditional sex roles, among the major religious groups represented in the survey.

✦ 32% of the very religious and 35% of the religious believed that women should have sexual experience before marriage. That view was shared by 41% of the Protestants, 42% of the Catholics, and 69% of the Jews surveyed.

✦ Catholics are the most passive sexually: 30% of the Catholic women and 27% of the Catholic men preferred that their partners initiate sexual activity.

✦ Jewish respondents, both men and women, had had their first full sexual experience later than any other group identified by religion.

QUESTIONNAIRE SUBJECTS TABULATED IN THIS CHAPTER

	Table
Abortion	8.1, 8.2
Incidence of Abortions	8.3, 8.4
Contraception Use	8.5, 8.6
Traditional Sex Roles in Modern Society	8.7, 8.8, 8.9
Sex Education	8.10, 8.35
Religion and Sex Practices	8.11, 8.12, 8.13
Female Premarital Sexual Experience	8.14, 8.15
Masturbation	8.16
Variety of Sex Techniques	8.17
Pain and Pleasure in Sex	8.18
Initiation of Sexual Activity	8.19, 8.20, 8.21, 8.22
Extramarital Affairs	8.23
Fantasizing	8.24
Comparative Sexual Activity, Three Years Ago Versus Now	8.25, 8.26
Religion and Premarital Sex	8.27, 8.28
Oral Sex	8.29
Self-Ratings on Feelings of Romance	8.30
Sensuous Nature of Sex	8.31, 8.32
Self-Ratings of Sexual Activity	8.33
Biological Sexual Maximum	8.34
Age at First Full Sexual Relations	8.36, 8.37
Sexually Transmitted Diseases	8.38

BE FRUITFUL AND MULTIPLY

For many centuries, religion has been the primary institution that regulates the sexual norms and conduct of the believers. Even in secular societies, we find that religious authorities act as judges and censors of all matters sexual; religions are involved in the marriage process, they baptize babies and confirm young people, and, for generations, had almost total control over the legal and social norms governing sexual practices. Their control has survived to a large degree in today's world, despite the great sexual and social changes our society has undergone. The result has been a widespread discrepancy between preachment and practice, particularly within the more affluent segments of Western culture.

Only recently in Western history has the state approached the traditional role of religion in legalizing marriages, registering babies, and legislating whether certain contraceptive practices, abortion, or heretofore "unnatural" sex acts are permissible. However, although the state has indeed assumed some of the prerogatives of religion, the church and the state often coexist as social regulators. Couples who marry, for example, usually choose to be married by a member of the clergy. In almost all cases, these marriages are procedurally registered with the state in which the marriage occurs.

A major impact of religion on social behavior is effected through the mechanism of "guilt"; that is, when placed in a possibly compromising sexual situation, one is able to retain self-control by feeling that somehow this sexual act is "wrong." Interestingly, many individuals we interviewed felt that, without at least a bit of guilt, sex loses some of its appeal; for some, the defiance of authority was a turn-on. With the sexual revolution has come personal sexual choice, a concept that is anathema to religion. This chapter explores how Americans experience their sexuality relative to their religious identification and influence.

Among the several items of personal information our questionnaire requested of our respondents was the item relating to religious affiliation (survey item H.4; see Appendix B), which included three types of groupings. One was a listing of the major religious identities in America: Protestant, Catholic, and Jewish. Another category for response to religious affiliation was *none*. For most questions, we found that there was very little difference among the responses of members of the three major religions. Only when there were significant differences did we include them as separate tables.

Other was the third grouping we included. Our assumption that such a grouping would prove useful in our analysis of the data proved to be fallacious. Other turned out to be a useless grouping because of the heterogeneity of the responses it attracted. We did not foresee the many and varied religions, religious groups, cults, and exotic pseudoreligious congregations that would present themselves. Common folklore suggests that most such groups originate and flourish in California, but our data indicted that they can be found all over the country. They may be based on foods, astronomy, astrology, charismatic leaders, foreign cultures, historical events, or any of a number of other organizing characteristics, but, when categorized together, the resulting mass had no homogeneous character and simply did not constitute a definable group. Consequently, although the individuals are included in other sections of our study, they do not appear in this chapter as a religious category of other.

Because, except for a few issues such as abortion, there is very little difference in sexual norms among the major Western religions, "religiosity" is usually considered a better indicator of the meaning and influence of religion in one's daily life. For this study, religiosity was measured on a scale of very religious, religious, slightly religious, or not religious.

ABORTION

Perhaps no subject tied to both sex and religion has raised more emotion, generated more laws, and produced more violence than the issue of abortion. We asked our respondents to state the degree to which they agree with the statement "Abortion is murder." The responses, on the scale of religiosity, are shown in Table 8.1

When we combined strongly agree and agree responses, we found a very strong correlation between religiosity and attitudes about abortion: the more religious respondents were, the more they believed that abortion is murder. Since it is women who have abortions, was it reasonable to hypothesize that their attitudes would be much stronger than men's attitudes on this subject?

As Table 8.2 shows, except in isolated pairings, our data did not support the commonly held belief that women have stronger views on this subject than men. When we combined the two categories of agreement we found that, with the exception of those who were not religious, women were only slightly more likely than men to agree that abortion is murder—but only by percentages ranging from 1% to 6%. Among the not religious respondents, women (9%) were less likely than men (15%) to believe that abortion is murder. Only at the extremes did we find some striking differences between men and women: very religious women were much more likely than very religious men to believe that abortion is murder (55% versus 37%), and nonreligious women were much more likely than men to strongly disagree with the statement (59% versus 33%).

TABLE 8.1   **Survey Item A.11.**

ABORTION IS MURDER:				
	Very Religious	Religious	Slightly Religious	Not Religious
N =	269	866	986	620
Strongly agree	46%	19%	9%	4%
Agree	15	21	15	8
No opinion	13	19	19	10
Disagree	12	26	34	32
Strongly disagree	14	15	23	46
Strongly agree + Agree	61%	40%	24%	12%
Disagree + Strongly disagree	26%	41%	57%	78%

TABLE 8.2   **Survey Item A.11.**

ABORTION IS MURDER:								
	Very Religious		Religious		Slightly Religious		Not Religious	
	Men	Women	Men	Women	Men	Women	Men	Women
N =	126	143	414	452	478	508	316	304
Strongly agree	37%	53%	18%	19%	11%	9%	5%	2%
Agree	22	11	23	22	12	15	10	7
No opinion	16	10	20	18	21	17	12	9
Disagree	12	11	25	26	37	32	40	23
Strongly disagree	13	15	14	15	19	27	33	59
Strongly agree + Agree	59%	64%	41%	41%	23%	24%	15%	9%
Disagree + Strongly disagree	25%	26%	39%	41%	56%	59%	73%	82%

For many persons who are religious, their attitudes may reflect great conflict in their lives at one time or another. When we looked at whether they had had an abortion themselves, 18% of the very religious and 21% of the religious said that they had. Table 8.3 gives further details.

As shown in Table 8.3, one's religious commitments can exert a powerful control over the decision to have an abortion. The not religious respondents were more than half again as likely as the very religious and religious to have had an abortion.

We decided to examine the religious affiliations of women respondents who said they had had an abortion. (See Table 8.4.)

We included respondents who categorized themselves as other, just to explore the possibility that those with less prominent religious affiliations have a different incidence of abortions. Americans pick and choose those aspects of religious practice that are comfortable for them. In regard to an issue as emotional as abortion, there is perhaps more zeal than surrounds

TABLE 8.3   **Survey Item H.24.**

I HAVE HAD AN ABORTION:				
	Very Religious	Religious	Slightly Religious	Not Religious
N =	144	453	508	305
Yes	18%	21%	27%	32%
No	77	74	69	64
No answer	5	5	4	4

TABLE 8.4   **Survey Item H.24.**

I HAVE HAD AN ABORTION:					
	Protestant	Catholic	Jewish	Other	None
N =	499	359	154	239	158
Yes	32%	29%	11%	18%	22%
No	63	66	85	78	75
No answer	5	5	4	4	3

other issues. Looking at the Protestant group, one must bear in mind that the many groups in the United States who are Protestant range from the fundamentalist in the Bible Belt to the liberal unitarians, with many combinations mixed in. Although abortion is contrary to Catholic doctrine, the proportion of Catholic women who had had an abortion was only slightly less than the proportion of Protestant women. The Jewish group reported the lowest number of abortions, and this seems to be in agreement with the fact that Jewish men and women have the latest sexual initiation of all groups (see Table 8.37). Additionally, Jewish men reported the highest use of contraceptives (see Table 8.6).

The question of abortion is obviously a very complex and personal one. Much of the sense of sexual freedom that singles feel, for example, might evaporate without abortion as a backup option, if they so choose. Husbands and wives might not feel as free about experimenting sexually, in group sex or mate swapping, if the termination of an unwanted pregnancy were not legally available. Fear of pregnancy is a real fear for many persons; studies show that 70% of all pregnancies were unplanned. Were the Supreme Court's *Roe v. Wade* decision to be overturned—and some observers on both sides of the issue say that a reversal is not impossible—abortion could once again become illegal in many states. A reversal could well make the country return to an era in which men would have to act more responsibly in sexual matters, to relieve women of the burden of delivering children they do not want or may not be able to care for.

CONTRACEPTION

A commonly held opinion among the pro-choice advocates is that the same religious persons who hold to the pro-life positions are inconsistent and contradictory in that they oppose not only abortion but also the use of contraceptives as birth control devices. After all, these advocates argue, should not all people, regardless of how religious they are, support the use of contraceptives as an alternative to unwanted pregnancies that could possibly result in abortion? In order to determine the extent

TABLE 8.5   Survey Item H.19.

DO YOU USE CONTRACEPTION?				
	Very Religious	Religious	Slightly Religious	Not Religious
N =	254	831	957	606
Yes	61%	66%	65%	66%
No	39%	34%	35%	34%

of the differences between the religious and the nonreligious, we asked whether our respondents used contraceptives (Table 8.5). Because traditional Catholics and Jews, as well as many other religions and denominations, disapprove of the use of contraceptives, our expectation was that we would find considerable differences depending on religious affiliation. However, when we analyzed the data on that basis (Table 8.6), the differences were hard to find.

Substantial numbers of people in all religions used contraceptives. Among both the Protestants and the Jews surveyed, men and women reported the same extent of contraceptive use. Among Catholics, women reported more use than men. The group that listed itself as not having any religion revealed an interestingly complex response: The men reported using less contraception than men in the other groups, and the women used it more than did the other women. Although the percentages differentiating this group from the others are not vastly different, we would have expected that the nonaffiliated none group should be the freest of religious restraint and therefore the one most likely to use contraception. This prediction was true of the women, but not of the men. We did find that the none group was amorphous, with no consistent belief, and that it contained people with the widest variety of practices, offering an extensive range of different, personal choices. In addition, as we discovered in our interviews, many respondents did not consider vasectomy or tubal

TABLE 8.6   Survey Item H.19.

DO YOU USE CONTRACEPTION?								
	Protestant		Catholic		Jewish		None	
	Men	Women	Men	Women	Men	Women	Men	Women
N =	471	483	320	344	141	150	138	150
Yes	64%	63%	64%	69%	69%	69%	60%	74%
No	36%	37%	36%	31%	31%	31%	40%	26%

ligation as contraception. Many assumed that contraception involved an ongoing use of some gadget, medicine, or technique, and if they were not using one of those methods, or anything similar, they were not using contraception.

Despite the official position of many religions that they are opposed to the use of contraceptives, we found very little difference connected to how religious the respondents were. Only among the very religious were people less likely—by only a few percentage points—to use contraceptives.

◆ *IN THEIR OWN WORDS* _____

> Hey, I feel that sex is great, it's important, but you got to think of the other person too, and you've gotta live within the rules that God instructed man to live with. I listen to my friends, guys like to brag, and some of them sound like they don't care about anyone, just their own pleasure. I never went with more than one girl at a time, and I have a girlfriend now, we've been going together for 3 years, we're going to get engaged in a couple of months on her next birthday. She is also religious, and it means a lot to her too. We both feel that it is a beautiful thing for a girl to be a virgin until she is married, and to give this as a gift to her husband. But what about nature; sex is a drive, and at my age it really demands attention, so we worked out a way to handle sex without guilt. When we have sex, we play around in a number of ways that feel good to us both. But when we are going to have intercourse, I always use a condom, and I enter her, but I withdraw before I ejaculate. She seems satisfied, and I don't mind coming later, but most important of all, she is still a virgin, because I haven't come inside her, and she is therefore pure.
>
> —A 24-year-old salesman

ATTITUDES TOWARD SEXUALITY

Sociologists have coined the phrase *sex roles* to describe the set of socially acceptable and expected behaviors and attitudes that men and women are supposed to have by virtue of growing up in our society. Among other functions, sex roles help people to feel comfortable when relating to persons of the opposite sex. Certain modes of relating in sex roles are characteristic of different cultures. Many cultures, both preindustrial and technologically advanced, believe that males must be taught to be men, and females to be women, through certain traditional ceremonies and customs. American rites of passage, if at all existent, have no such institutional base. One can hardly call a "sweet sixteen" party, or a boy's obtaining his first automobile, institutional rites of passage. Rather, except for formal religious rites such as the bar mitzvah among Jews, adolescents are unacknowledged as they enter the social pressures of the adult world.

In the absence of traditional and institutional rites of passage, with their more rigidly defined expectations for future adult behavior, we can expect that definitions of male and female social roles will vary over time. With the sexual revolutions and the women's movement have come changes in the traditional sex roles, or the ways in which men and women formerly interacted socially and sexually. Today, men can cry and not be perceived as weaklings; instead, they are seen as being sensitive. Women can be competent professionals and still be seen as feminine. However, definitions of male and female roles are not as fluid in the mainstream religions of America. Thus, we might expect religious people to be more resistant to changes—particularly changes that contradict traditional interpretations. To investigate this possibility, we analyzed responses to the statement "Traditional sex roles have no place in modern society" according to the religiosity of the respondents. The results are reported in Table 8.7.

As the table shows, the less religious respondents were, the more likely that they saw no need for traditional sex roles today (strongly agree and agree). This pattern is not surprising: the definition of traditional sex roles has historically come more from religion than from any other source, and these people have diminishing degrees of religious affiliation, or none at all. However, indicative of the changing times and the discrepancies between traditional roles—which would limit women to homemaking and child rearing—and the emerging equality of women as an intellectual, economic, and professional force in society, only 49% of the very religious and religious disagreed with the statement and supported the place of traditional sex roles, and only 12% and

TABLE 8.7   **Survey Item A.13.**

TRADITIONAL SEX ROLES HAVE NO PLACE IN MODERN SOCIETY:			
	Very Religious	Religious	Slightly Religious	Not Religious
N =	264	862	978	615
Strongly agree	7%	6%	5%	11%
Agree	20	22	29	27
No opinion	12	14	15	12
Disagree	49	49	45	43
Strongly disagree	12	9	6	7
Strongly agree + Agree	27%	28%	34%	38%
Disagree + Strongly disagree	61%	58%	51%	50%

9%, respectively, strongly disagreed. In the absence of traditional definitions of sex roles, religious individuals have very few options as sources
of new models. If their churches were to abrogate the responsibility to
set realistic standards, these individuals would have to grapple alone
with the growing divisions between traditional models and emerging
realities.

We next wanted to determine whether there were gender differences
within the levels of religiosity. The tabulation of responses, differentially
for men and women, is presented in Table 8.8.

As shown in Table 8.8, there is a relationship between religiosity and
males in disagreement concerning sex roles. Thirty-six percent of the
nonreligious men rejected traditional roles; the other three groups of
men who expressed agreement ranged from 26% to 28%. However, the
women, except for the very religious, were more likely than men to reject
traditional roles in all the remaining groups. It was interesting that the
slightly religious women rejected the traditional roles to the same extent
as the nonreligious women (42%).

Did the acceptance of traditional sex roles differ among the adherents
to the major religions? Table 8.9 supplies the data.

With the exception of the men in the none group, a majority, and at
times a large majority, of all the other groups rejected (disagree and
strongly disagree) the displacement of traditional sex roles. Catholic men
rejected it least, among the three religion-affiliated groups. Oddly,
Catholic and Jewish women were less rejecting of traditional sex roles
than Protestant women were. One could expect that the none group of
women would predominantly want to do away with tradition, but those
who expressed opinions were only 5 percentage points apart.

TABLE 8.8   **Survey Item A.13.**

TRADITIONAL SEX ROLES HAVE NO PLACE IN MODERN SOCIETY:								
	Very Religious		Religious		Slightly Religious		Not Religious	
	Men	Women	Men	Women	Men	Women	Men	Women
N =	123	141	413	449	475	503	313	302
Strongly agree	7%	6%	4%	8%	4%	7%	13%	9%
Agree	21	19	22	21	23	35	23	33
No opinion	9	15	16	12	18	11	13	11
Disagree	48	50	45	53	48	41	44	42
Strongly disagree	15	10	13	6	7	6	7	5
Strongly agree + Agree	28%	25%	26%	29%	27%	42%	36%	42%
Disagree + Strongly disagree	63%	60%	58%	59%	55%	47%	51%	47%

TABLE 8.9 Survey Item A.13.

TRADITIONAL SEX ROLES HAVE NO PLACE IN MODERN SOCIETY:								
	Protestant		Catholic		Jewish		None	
	Men	Women	Men	Women	Men	Women	Men	Women
N =	468	487	328	350	145	151	144	154
Strongly agree	2%	5%	9%	9%	1%	11%	14%	8%
Agree	17	26	23	26	33	27	30	41
No opinion	13	11	17	15	4	12	21	7
Disagree	57	50	43	46	55	42	31	41
Strongly disagree	11	8	8	4	7	8	4	3
Strongly agree + Agree	19%	31%	32%	35%	34%	38%	44%	49%
Disagree + Strongly disagree	68%	58%	51%	50%	62%	50%	35%	44%

SEX EDUCATION

Is the debate about sex education for children in the schools as fierce as it once was? Apparently not: Across the board, we found that most respondents favored sex education in the schools, possibly as an implied method of educating the young not only about sex, but also about sex roles. (See Table 8.10.)

Most respondents approved of sex education in schools; the less religious favored it more than the other groups. Noteworthy is the very small percentage of respondents—almost all among the very religious—who opposed it. Interestingly, the very religious also have the largest share of maybe responses, indicating some uncertainty even among those thought to be most negative.

It appears that most Americans favor sex education in the schools, but it has not gone without its detractors. Small numbers of objecting parents have formed groups with names like MOMS (Mothers Against Mandatory Sex education). They charge that, if sex education is part of the curriculum:

1. Children will be taught how to have sex;
2. Teachers do demonstrations in class, or so they have heard;
3. By teaching children about sex, the schools are giving their approval to sexual interaction.

Americans as a whole, on this issue and numerous others, still reveal strong conflicting attitudes toward sex. Van Harris, a popular comedian, has put this contradiction well: "We don't let children pray in school, but we put Bibles in motel rooms. How many of you have ever checked into a motel to pray?"

TABLE 8.10   Survey Item G.8.

SEX EDUCATION SHOULD BE TAUGHT IN THE SCHOOLS:				
	Very Religious	Religious	Slightly Religious	Not Religious
N =	267	866	984	619
Definitely yes	79%	88%	92%	93%
Maybe	18	11	7	7
Not at all	3	1	1	0

CONFLICTS WITH RELIGION

Because many persons who object to contraception and abortion base their objections on religious arguments, we posed a questionnaire item that would draw out how important it was to individual respondents to have their sex practices in harmony with their religion. In Table 8.11, the data gathered for that survey item have been resorted to match respondents' self-descriptions regarding religion.

In one of the strongest relationships we had found so far, the more religious respondents were, the greater the importance they placed on avoiding contradiction between beliefs and practices in the area of sex. However, before any conclusion that strong beliefs seemed to be translating into conforming sexual practices, this caveat: Because a person places great emphasis on the importance of his or her religious beliefs does not mean that, in that person's private life, there is no deviation. Sociologists have long reported the discrepancy between preachment and practice in

TABLE 8.11   Survey Item B.6.

THAT MY SEX PRACTICES ARE IN HARMONY WITH MY RELIGION IS:				
	Very Religious	Religious	Slightly Religious	Not Religious
N =	262	857	976	611
Very important	45%	18%	2%	3%
Important	36	38	24	8
Not sure	7	24	26	15
Unimportant	5	17	37	37
Very unimportant	7	3	11	37
Very important + Important	81%	56%	26%	11%
Unimportant + Very unimportant	12%	20%	48%	74%

American family life, particularly regarding sex practices. As virtually all researchers of mate swapping and group sex have reported, most participants are religiously conservative and active churchgoers. The desire to follow religious dictates faithfully is no doubt present, but to practice them may be difficult for some, in the face of practical considerations and peer group influences. Many persons in our sample reported that being part of the religious life and the secular social life of America was like living in two different worlds.

A widespread assumption is that women are more likely than men to feel that they want their sex practices to be consistent with their religion's teaching, because women are more likely to be closer to their religion than men are. Table 8.12 distinguishes the earlier data, by gender.

Women who were religious were only somewhat more likely to be concerned with conformity to religious teaching concerning sex than men were—a 4% difference among the very religious and a 7% difference for the religious. The contrast between the first two pairings (men and women who were very religious and religious) and the final two (slightly religious and not religious) was quite dramatic.

Our final analysis of responses to this survey item was based on whether there was a difference in attitudes among the adherents to the major religions. (See Table 8.13.)

In observing wide differences among the religions in Table 8.13, one must be cautious of erroneous interpretations. It might be easiest to suggest that Protestants are most likely to adhere to their religion's teachings about sex, with Catholics and Jews adhering only at much lower percentages, but one must realize that, except for some of the more

TABLE 8.12   **Survey Item B.6.**

THAT MY SEX PRACTICES ARE IN HARMONY WITH MY RELIGION IS:								
	Very Religious		Religious		Slightly Religious		Not Religious	
	Men	Women	Men	Women	Men	Women	Men	Women
N =	122	140	410	447	474	502	312	299
Very important	32%	56%	18%	18%	1%	4%	2%	4%
Important	46	26	35	42	26	22	8	9
Not sure	6	9	29	18	24	27	13	18
Unimportant	7	3	14	19	37	38	37	36
Very unimportant	9	6	4	3	12	9	40	33
Very important + Important	78%	82%	53%	60%	27%	26%	10%	13%
Unimportant + Very unimportant	16%	9%	18%	22%	49%	47%	77%	69%

TABLE 8.13   Survey Item B.6.

THAT MY SEX PRACTICES ARE IN HARMONY WITH MY RELIGION IS:			
	Protestant	Catholic	Jewish	None
N =	973	687	294	289
Very important	16%	6%	3%	5%
Important	35	26	13	9
Not sure	23	21	17	15
Unimportant	21	34	40	27
Very unimportant	5	13	27	44
Very important + Important	51%	32%	16%	14%
Unimportant + Very unimportant	26%	47%	67%	71%

fundamentalist churches, Protestants have far less doctrinaire interpretation as to the meaning and purposes of sex than do Jews and Catholics. According to Westheimer and Lieberman, in *Sex and Morality: Who Is Teaching Our Sex Standards?*,[1] most traditional Jews and Catholics grow up to believe that their respective religions teach that the only purpose for sex is procreation within the traditional marital structure, and that anything outside of this purpose is a sin. These authors also pointed out that Protestant sects vary greatly, from extremely conservative regarding sexuality to very liberal. Consequently, we would suggest that the findings in Table 8.13 for the combined categories of very important and important reflect only the percentage of traditionally oriented or fundamentalist members of the respective religions. With respect to the others—those who have religious identity but for whom harmony with religion is not important—many recent researchers, including Westheimer and Lieberman, have reported that, in the area of sexual behavior, mere religious identity is not a predictor of behavior or of attitudes regarding sex.

✦ IN THEIR OWN WORDS

> It may seem trivial to some people, but it's a serious problem for me. I love my boyfriend very much, and I know it's mutual, but for many good reasons, we can't get married for a number of years. We have been making love for a long time, and it's wonderful. I have learned so much that I feel I have learned about the whole world of sex. My problem is that I have no problem in having sex, but I feel guilty that we use contraception. Every time he uses a condom, I feel that we both have sinned.
>
> —A 21-year-old female student

PREMARITAL SEX

As we have discussed in other sections of the book, most Americans agree that sexual experience for men before marriage is important. On the other hand, in keeping with the traditional sexual double standard, the question of sexual experience before marriage for women is still a controversial issue. Historically, women have played a passive sexual role, and while male sexual meandering would be excused with "boys will be boys," women who meandered were labeled "whores" or "tramps." Because religious dictates might have colored our respondents' views, we decided to look more closely at this issue of women and premarital sex. Table 8.14 groups the data by religious commitment, and Table 8.15, by affiliation with each of the three major religions.

As we might have expected, the very religious group attributed the least importance to women's sexual experience before marriage (32%). The less religious the respondents, the more likely they were to believe that premarital sex for women is important (35%, 52%, and 59%, respectively). These findings confirmed what we have suggested earlier—that religiosity tends to be strongly correlated with traditional views.

We were also interested in seeing whether differences existed among adherents to the three major religions (Table 8.15).

In contrast to Table 8.13, where Protestants appeared to be more conservative than Catholics, in Table 8.15, we noted no significant difference between Catholics and Protestants in their assessment of the importance of women's premarital sexual experience. On the other hand, in interviews, the Jewish respondents strongly reflected what appears to be a developing consensus among most Jews, except the Orthodox—that premarital sex is a private concern rather than a community concern. Consequently, Jews generally feel more free to examine the function of

TABLE 8.14   **Survey Item B.8.**

FOR THE WOMAN, SEX EXPERIENCE BEFORE MARRIAGE IS:			
	Very Religious	Religious	Slightly Religious	Not Religious
N =	266	864	984	620
Very important	12%	8%	13%	15%
Important	20	27	39	44
Not sure	15	19	20	12
Unimportant	24	40	25	25
Very unimportant	29	6	3	4
Very important + Important	32%	35%	52%	59%
Unimportant + Very unimportant	53%	46%	28%	29%

TABLE 8.15   Survey Item B.8.

FOR THE WOMAN, SEX EXPERIENCE BEFORE MARRIAGE IS:				
	Protestant	Catholic	Jewish	None
N =	975	686	297	300
Very important	7%	10%	24%	16%
Important	34	32	45	42
Not sure	17	24	11	17
Unimportant	33	28	19	24
Very unimportant	9	6	1	1
Very important + Important	41%	42%	69%	58%
Unimportant + Very unimportant	42%	34%	20%	25%

premarital sex for women in the context of its value to later marital happiness. Apparently, in doing so, Jews are considerably more likely to approve premarital sex.

Why was the none group not more "liberated"? Those presently nonaffiliated may have once been in the ranks of Protestantism and Catholicism, where their customary view of sex was in constant contact with religious standards and their restrictions. Consequently, the none group has little experience with personal decision making, which sexual behavior requires. Put simply, liberated behavior does not always ensure liberated thought. It is also of significance that 42% of the Protestants and 34% of the Catholics found premarital sexual experience for a woman to be relatively unimportant.

MASTURBATION

The new thinking among the Christian religious groups, which was illustrated in the previous tables, was confirmed again in the percentages of those who indicated acceptance of masturbation. (See Table 8.16.) The statement posed in our questionnaire was one that reflected the opinion of mental health authorities and medical people: "Masturbation is a natural part of life and continues on in marriage."*

---

*The reader must keep in mind that many people interpret the Biblical story of Onan to suggest that masturbation is specifically forbidden. Although the Bible indicates severe punishment for men who "spilled it [seed] on the ground" (Genesis 38:9), Biblical scholars generally agree that this refers not to masturbation but to *coitus interruptus* and the fact that Onan did not fulfill his social and religious obligation to marry his dead brother's widow.

TABLE 8.16   **Survey Item C.5.**

MASTURBATION IS A NATURAL PART OF LIFE AND CONTINUES ON IN MARRIAGE:				
	Protestant	Catholic	Jewish	None
N =	972	681	297	298
Strongly agree	13%	18%	29%	29%
Agree	50	49	46	48
No opinion	23	21	18	16
Disagree	11	10	6	5
Strongly disagree	3	2	1	2
Strongly agree + Agree	63%	67%	75%	77%
Disagree + Strongly disagree	14%	12%	7%	7%

As others have noted, one of the most complete turnarounds in American sexual attitudes resulted from the publication of the Kinsey reports on American men and women.[2] Prior to Kinsey, masturbation was viewed as a sin by most, a sickness by some, and a vice by many. But the findings of Kinsey and his staff, that nearly all young boys and a large percentage of young girls masturbate, seemed to bury the myths that masturbation caused blindness, insanity, and hair on the palms of boys and on the faces of girls. Today, most sex therapists and physicians not only consider masturbation a "normal" behavior but even desirable to help train and activate the orgasmic reflex system. This is strongly reflected in Table 8.16, especially when we note how few persons in all religious groups strongly disagree with the statement.

◆ *IN THEIR OWN WORDS* ─────────────────────────────────

I felt so foolish I could die! There I was with my group of sophisticated friends talking about sex. Some of them were feminists, and some more traditionalists; we were a sharp group of successful young professionals. Somehow the topic came to masturbation and orgasm; someone brought up Masters and Johnson. Some of the girls didn't volunteer much, but of those who spoke, most said that they have orgasm, and how they insist that their partner be attentive to their orgastic needs. Somehow, I spoke up, and said that I had never masturbated, and didn't remember having an orgasm. This was followed by a lot of tch, tch and really? Even the girls who didn't talk were tch-ing. Someone used the word "pleasuring," and one of the girls asked me if I had any genital pleasure. Like a naive boob, I thought for a moment and said, "Well, every day, when I bathe, it feels good to direct a stream of water at my vagina." I felt that it was pleasurable and cleansing at the same time. As if electrified, one of the girls jumped and began querying me with questions about how it felt, like did I feel any excitement, etc. Then to my shock and embarrassment she said, "You have been getting your orgasms with the stream of water, in fact, that's a recommended way to masturbate, that the orgasm clinics recommend." I felt a deep, instant blush come over my face, and I stammered, but it registered with me, and I sensed that she was right. We talked a bit more, and I explained that since I was a very religious person I had been taught that masturbation was not right. They laughed loudly, but I didn't sense they were laughing at me. I had the feeling that many of them had traveled similar roads. That was a while ago; since then I've discovered that there are many ways to have orgasm, by whatever name. As far as my religiosity, I still identify myself as a religious woman, but I feel that the Lord has a big world out there to take care of, and I take care of my sexuality. I feel that some of the proclaimed rules that the churches have were made and interpreted by men, and they have no right to try to control my body.

—A 26-year-old professional woman

SEXUAL VARIETY

Most sex therapists and marriage counselors are aware that, even in the most loving of relationships, sex can begin to take on routine qualities and become boring. However, given that the missionary position (male on top during intercourse) has long been believed by many religious persons to be the only acceptable way to have sex, we wanted to see whether this attitude had also changed. We asked the respondents to react to a proposition that would indicate whether use of a large variety of sex techniques had become acceptable to them. (See Table 8.17.)

TABLE 8.17   **Survey Item C.7.**

A LARGE VARIETY OF SEX TECHNIQUES IS A MUST FOR MAXIMUM PLEASURE:			
	Very Religious	Religious	Slightly Religious	Not Religious
N =	264	863	982	619
Strongly agree	9%	9%	11%	12%
Agree	31	28	33	37
No opinion	14	19	17	13
Disagree	37	35	34	35
Strongly disagree	9	9	5	3
Strongly agree + Agree	40%	37%	44%	49%
Disagree + Strongly disagree	46%	44%	39%	38%

Although a large number of the respondents (ranging from 37% to a high of 49%) agreed with the proposition, there was not so dramatic a difference as one might have expected between the very religious and the nonreligious (40% versus 49%). These responses are another sign of the trend away from traditional religious attitudes toward sex. In this instance, many people apparently saw merit in enhancing the recreational or procreative functions of sex with a variety of sex techniques. Do varied sex techniques make sex frivolous? Not at all; they just change the sexual experience from functional to fun-filled. However, some still regard such diversity as a sin, reflecting their religious beliefs. As observed earlier in this chapter, for some persons, guilt—in this case related to sexual sinning—adds appeal or excitement to sexual activity.

SADOMASOCHISM

One of the most interesting aspects of research in general and research of sexuality in particular is that such research occasionally yields unexpected results. Some sex researchers had noted that the practice of sadomasochism had been increasing in popularity in recent times; nevertheless, it had not been accepted as mainstream sex practice. To learn whether attitudes had changed in this area, we asked for responses to questions that had several different approaches. Some of the questions were direct, and some indirect, about respondents' attitudes toward this type of sex. For example, one of the direct statements dealt with a relationship of pain and pleasure in sex. Our respondents' answers are given in Table 8.18.

Overwhelmingly, our respondents disagreed that pain and pleasure go together in sex. However, among the minority who agreed with the statement, there was a positive connection with religiosity. Twenty

TABLE 8.18   **Survey Item C.11.**

PAIN AND PLEASURE REALLY GO TOGETHER IN SEX:			
	Very Religious	Religious	Slightly Religious	Not Religious
N =	265	864	984	618
Strongly agree	6%	3%	2%	1%
Agree	14	12	11	9
No opinion	10	12	11	9
Disagree	32	40	44	47
Strongly disagree	38	33	32	34
Strongly agree + Agree	20%	15%	13%	10%
Disagree + Strongly disagree	70%	73%	76%	81%

percent of the very religious agreed, and percentages went on down to 10% of the not religious. Eighty-one percent of the not religious disagreed that pain and pleasure went together, compared to only 70% of the very religious. Were the very religious invoking the biblical judgment that women shall bear children in pain or did they believe that the more religious a woman is, the more she must submit to her husband's advances—painful though her submission may be? In interviews, our respondents described two types of pain: physical and psychological. However, some of them reported the need to couple pain with sex in order to be sexually satisfied. Our observations were that the number of those who subliminally sought pain in sex was higher than those who advocated or overtly practiced sadomasochism (S/M). We noted in Chapter 4 the claims that 10% of all American homes have some S/M equipment or paraphernalia, such as handcuffs, paddles, whips, and so on. Earlier in this chapter, we suggested that people who are religious but wish to function in the sexual mainstream have a difficult time balancing their conflicting values. They function sexually, but the need for pain evinced here may be indicative of a great deal of ambivalence. To address this inner dilemma, they associate pleasure with pain, and sex with punishment, telling themselves they must feel bad about feeling good.

◆ IN THEIR OWN WORDS

> Let's face it, there is no free lunch. You have to pay something for everything you get in this world. Sex is wonderful, but it doesn't come easily or cheaply. I believe that those people, like myself, who have the solid fiber to feel the strength and even the pain of sex are bigger people.
>
> —An industrial worker in his 40s

INITIATING SEXUAL ACTIVITY

When religious individuals are participating in sex, are they doing so hesitantly? Do guilt and ambivalence prevent them from expressing their normal, healthy sexual desires? To determine individual levels of activity and initiative, we placed before all respondents a statement about the initiation of sexual activity. In this instance, we will again look at the responses in two ways: in the context of religious intensity (Table 8.19) and according to particular religious affiliations (Table 8.20).

As shown in Table 8.19, with the exception of those identifying themselves as religious, there was virtually no difference in sexual initiation preference as a function of religiosity. All groups preferred to initiate sex rather than have their partner do so—in most cases, by a 3:1 margin.

TABLE 8.19   Survey Item D.4.

I ALWAYS PREFER THAT MY SEX PARTNER INITIATE SEXUAL ACTIVITY:				
	Very Religious	Religious	Slightly Religious	Not Religious
N =	266	864	983	618
Strongly agree	3%	3%	3%	4%
Agree	17	24	18	16
No opinion	18	20	16	12
Disagree	51	49	57	63
Strongly disagree	11	4	6	5
Strongly agree + Agree	20%	27%	21%	20%
Disagree + Strongly disagree	62%	53%	63%	68%

Approximately one-fifth of all our respondents, with or without fervent religious feelings, preferred to have their partners initiate sex.

Were there gender differences in the responses to this survey item? Table 8.20 shows that there were only slight differences between the responses of men and women, with the exception of very religious women, who preferred somewhat more initiating activity by their partners, perhaps in conjunction with this group's preference for the traditional role of women.

When we categorized the responses to the statement by religious affiliation (see Table 8.21), considerable differences showed up among the major religious groups, in practices and attitudes concerning sex. Nearly twice

TABLE 8.20   Survey Item D.4.

I ALWAYS PREFER THAT MY SEX PARTNER INITIATE SEXUAL ACTIVITY:								
	Very Religious		Religious		Slightly Religious		Not Religious	
	Men	Women	Men	Women	Men	Women	Men	Women
N =	124	142	413	451	474	509	315	303
Strongly agree	2%	5%	3%	4%	2%	3%	3%	4%
Agree	13	19	23	25	18	18	14	17
No opinion	23	14	29	10	24	9	19	6
Disagree	46	55	43	57	51	62	62	64
Strongly disagree	16	7	2	4	5	8	2	9
Strongly agree + Agree	15%	24%	26%	29%	20%	21%	17%	21%
Disagree + Strongly disagree	62%	62%	45%	61%	56%	70%	64%	73%

TABLE 8.21 Survey Item D.4.

I ALWAYS PREFER THAT MY SEX PARTNER INITIATE SEXUAL ACTIVITY:				
	Protestant	Catholic	Jewish	None
N =	971	684	297	299
Strongly agree	2%	5%	2%	4%
Agree	20	24	13	12
No opinion	16	17	11	16
Disagree	57	50	64	65
Strongly disagree	5	4	10	3
Strongly agree + Agree	22%	29%	15%	16%
Disagree + Strongly disagree	62%	54%	74%	68%

as many Catholics, compared to Jews and the unaffiliated group, preferred that their partners initiate the sexual activity (29% versus 15% and 16%, respectively). Protestants were in between, at 22%. However, the more dramatic finding was that the vast majority, across the three religions, preferred the active sex role to the passive—from a high of 5:1 for the Jewish group to a low of almost 2:1 for Catholics.

Again, we looked for gender differences, and summarized the findings in Table 8.22.

Protestants and Catholics, both men and women, appeared to be more passive sexually than the other two groups. Women in all groups, more

TABLE 8.22 Survey Item D.4.

I ALWAYS PREFER THAT MY SEX PARTNER INITIATE SEXUAL ACTIVITY:								
	Protestant		Catholic		Jewish		None	
	Men	Women	Men	Women	Men	Women	Men	Women
N =	476	495	329	355	145	152	143	156
Strongly agree	1%	4%	5%	4%	3%	1%	1%	7%
Agree	21	19	22	26	8	18	12	12
No opinion	24	8	29	7	14	9	23	9
Disagree	51	62	42	58	64	63	63	67
Strongly disagree	3	7	2	5	11	9	1	5
Strongly agree + Agree	22%	23%	27%	30%	11%	19%	13%	19%
Disagree + Strongly disagree	54%	69%	44%	63%	75%	72%	64%	72%

than men, preferred to have their partner initiate sexual activity; the Catholic women were the most passive of any subgroup. Except for Jewish men, close to one-quarter of all other men had no opinion. Was this an indication that many men have not yet adjusted to women's new freedom, resulting from the women's liberation movement, or is it a sign of a decrease in religion's control over sex, which formerly dictated men's primacy in sex?

SEX FOR THE INDIVIDUAL

Many of the survey items analyzed in this chapter have dealt with sexual issues that seemed to be directed primarily toward married or engaged couples. In a religious context, these questions imply commitment to one partner, as a prelude to sexual involvement with a partner who is available for or interested in marriage. Being in love (a state leading to marriage) and marriage traditionally justified all sexual activity for religious individuals. What about sex when there is no chance of or no desire for such commitments? We considered one of the representative areas, extramarital affairs, in Table 8.23.

The data are hardly comforting for those who would prefer to believe that adultery is a function of the nonbelievers. Although it is true that the nonreligious are most likely to engage in extramarital sex at least once (44%) and the religious are least likely (26%), the very religious were even more likely (31%) than the religious. Another finding may be even more disturbing, given the faith many Americans have in religion as the strongest curtailer of illicit passion: the very religious were **most likely** to report often and ongoing adultery (16%).

TABLE 8.23				Survey Item D.5.
I'VE HAD EXTRAMARITAL AFFAIRS:				
	Very Religious	Religious	Slightly Religious	Not Religious
N =	173	563	642	406
Never	69%	74%	64%	56%
Only once	7	8	9	10
Rarely	8	10	16	19
Often	14	6	9	12
Ongoing	2	2	2	3
At least once	31%	26%	36%	44%

TABLE 8.24   **Survey Item D.7.**

TO SUCCESSFULLY FUNCTION SEXUALLY I FANTASIZE:				
	Very Religious	Religious	Slightly Religious	Not Religious
N =	264	863	980	617
Not at all	35%	24%	24%	21%
Slightly	47	51	55	53
Much	14	15	16	17
Very much	3	8	4	8
Totally	1	2	1	1
Have ever fantasized	65%	76%	76%	79%
Much + Very much + Totally	18%	25%	21%	26%

FANTASY

Is fantasy a significant factor in the sex lives of religious people? If so, this would provide some answers in the individuals' personal search for and justification of the type of sex they find gratifying. Table 8.24 shows our respondents' admissions about fantasizing.

When we grouped together all persons who had ever fantasized during sex, we noted that the less religious were more likely to fantasize—from 76% to 79%, compared to 65% of the very religious. Of greater interest was the finding that even the very religious and religious fantasized a great deal (18% and 25%). Because sexual fantasy often entails mental scenarios involving persons other than one's partner, even incestuous and other forbidden activities, one wonders whether fantasy serves to increase sexual guilt for some or whether, once their illicit sexual feelings are acted out in fantasy, they are less likely to intrude into reality.

DECLINE IN SEXUAL ACTIVITY

We hear many voices deploring changes in society, from the cry that morality is an almost nonexistent force, to the complaint that Americans are now frightened about sex. Conventional wisdom has it that everyone is supposedly stopping, or at least considerably slowing down, former promiscuous sexual activity. The "newest" and latest findings, as reported in the popular press and mass media, often glibly make predictions about the sex lives of Americans to a sensation-thirsty readership. However, one cannot build a reliable fund of knowledge from the latest rumor, or from persons who report their own experiences as if they were the gospel truth about all Americans.

TABLE 8.25

COMPARED TO 3 YEARS AGO, MY SEX ACTIVITY IS:				
	Very Religious	Religious	Slightly Religious	Not Religious
N =	266	865	983	618
Much more	26%	23%	22%	19%
More	26	22	22	14
Same	24	29	26	34
Less	14	17	19	23
Much less	10	9	11	10
Much more + More	52%	45%	44%	33%
Less + Much less	24%	26%	30%	33%

We considered it an important task to ask all our respondents how, if at all, they had changed their sexual activity in the past 3 years. The data we received were sorted on several scales and appear in appropriate chapters. Table 8.25 shows the sorting on the scale of religiosity.

With the increasing concern about AIDS in recent years, one might have expected that a generalized fear would decrease sexual activity for everyone, as part of a diminished emphasis on the sort of gratuitous sex that was evidenced in the 1960s. However, we found that the more religious our respondents were, the less likely they were to have cut down on sex and the more likely to have increased their sexual activity. We believe that this is so because the more religious are not only more likely to be currently married but also because they are more likely to remain virgins if they are not yet married. This is supported by our findings (Table 8.26) that the unaffiliated are less likely to have increased their sexual activity compared with those affiliated with the major religions.

TABLE 8.26

COMPARED TO 3 YEARS AGO, MY SEX ACTIVITY IS:				
	Protestant	Catholic	Jewish	None
N =	973	684	296	298
Much more	20%	21%	20%	17%
More	21	23	19	13
Same	30	29	26	35
Less	20	17	23	26
Much less	9	10	12	9
Much more + More	41%	44%	39%	30%
Less + Much less	29%	27%	35%	35%

TABLE 8.27   Survey Item D.10.

I HAD SEXUAL EXPERIENCE BEFORE MARRIAGE:				
	Very Religious	Religious	Slightly Religious	Not Religious
N =	262	861	978	614
Very much	21%	23%	29%	37%
Much	23	27	30	29
Little	15	23	20	19
Very little	12	12	9	8
None	29	15	12	7
Very much + Much	44%	50%	59%	66%
Little + Very little	27%	35%	29%	27%

PREMARITAL SEX

Moving from more theoretical questions on whether it is important for a man or a woman to have premarital sex, we asked our sample to respond to the statement "I had sexual experience before marriage." Tables 8.27 and 8.28 show the responses, by religious affiliation and by gender, respectively.

As shown in Table 8.27, there is a negative relationship between religiosity and premarital sexual activity. The more religious a person is, the less likely that he or she has had much premarital sex. However, because the question did not refer to only coital sexual intercourse, the none category is not an accounting of those who remained virgins. Many of the others who said that they had had varying degrees of sexual experience may have been virgins who engaged in oral or anal sex or mutual masturbation; that is, they remained "technical virgins."

The negative relationship between religiosity and premarital sex held true for both the males and females surveyed, as shown in Table 8.28. In all levels of religiosity, females were less likely than males to have had extensive premarital sex.

ATTITUDES ABOUT SEX ACTS

We believed that we should examine the reactions of our respondents, and seek specific data about the panoply of sex acts in vogue. We did this by asking each of the respondents to rate the acceptability of a wide range of sex acts. What they generally desired or accepted is particularly significant; most of those interviewed worried about being "normal" and were anxious about whether their sex practices were "normal." Many

TABLE 8.28   Survey Item D.10.

| I HAD SEXUAL EXPERIENCE BEFORE MARRIAGE: | | | | | | | |
| | Very Religious | | Religious | | Slightly Religious | | Not Religious | |
	Men	Women	Men	Women	Men	Women	Men	Women
N =	124	138	412	449	475	503	314	300
Very much	30%	14%	32%	15%	36%	21%	35%	38%
Much	22	23	32	22	32	28	36	20
Little	14	15	20	27	19	22	16	22
Very little	5	19	6	17	4	14	9	8
None	29	29	10	19	9	15	4	12
Very much + Much	52%	37%	64%	37%	68%	49%	71%	58%
Little + Very little	19%	34%	26%	44%	23%	36%	25%	30%

expressed anxiety about functioning in the area of sex, where they have very little opportunity for social affirmation of their normalcy. The standard acceptable by almost every religious system—heterosexual intercourse, male superior—may be the only sex act that is approved by all religions; in some states, it is the only one specified as legal. The sexual position of female superior has been addressed by feminist groups, who believe that its unpopularity with men symbolizes their desire for male dominance. However, we found in our interviews that most of the men approve of this position. As women have become more able to request or to arrange orgasm for themselves during intercourse, this practice has become more widespread. Although many men we interviewed felt that, either way, man or woman on top, is acceptable, and that variety is nice, some men reported that they could not function in the female superior position.

ORAL SEX

Oral sex has become a popular and growing practice. For some religious people, this act presents a problem because it is a sexual practice that cannot result in pregnancy. Unless it is merely a means for arousal to allow coitus to proceed, leading to the possibility of pregnancy, it is not a sexual practice approved by many religions. Male superior heterosexual intercourse is favored because many believe that it is the easiest position for a woman to become pregnant, although this may be little more than a myth. What did our religious respondents think of oral sex?

Not unexpectedly, the more religious were less likely to approve of oral sex (Table 8.29). There was a progressive rise in acceptance among the less

TABLE 8.29   Survey Item D.12.

RATING SCALE: ORAL SEX:				
	Very Religious	Religious	Slightly Religious	Not Religious
N =	265	863	980	618
Very normal	45%	48%	59%	71%
All right	32	36	30	23
Unusual	7	5	4	3
Kinky	16	11	6	2
Never heard of it	0	0	1	1
Very normal + All right	77%	84%	89%	94%
Unusual + Kinky	23%	16%	10%	5%

religious groups. In our interviews, we found that some religious persons did not want to respond to this question because they knew that they should disapprove of the act, but they actually practiced it and did not want to lie about their response. The approval rate of 77%, by the very religious group, for oral sex—an act that, until very recently, was believed to be deviant—demonstrates that adherents of the mainstream religions, as a whole, have moved far along in the Second Sexual Revolution.

ROMANTIC SELF-IMAGE

Although romance before and during marriage has generally enjoyed broad acceptance, in examining our current popular music, dances, movies, and poetry, we might suspect that it has gone underground or

TABLE 8.30   Survey Item G.1.

ROMANTICALLY I AM:				
	Very Religious	Religious	Slightly Religious	Not Religious
N =	269	867	983	620
Very romantic	33%	33%	29%	23%
Romantic	50	48	50	46
Realistic	14	16	14	24
Cautious	3	2	6	6
Cynical	0	1	1	1
Very romantic + Romantic	83%	81%	79%	69%

even disappeared. We asked our respondents whether they believed that they are, indeed, romantic.

Table 8.30 shows a positive relationship between religiosity and perceiving oneself as being romantic; that is, the more religious are more likely to say that they are romantic or very romantic. At the other end of the scale, very few persons described themselves as cynical or cautious, with the concentration of such responses coming from the less religious. However, the less religious our respondents were, the more likely they were to describe themselves as "realistic." How did these groups, particularly those who were more religious, fare with the more intimate aspects of sex? The generalization that religious people find it easier to relate to a deity, and have trouble relating to humans as love objects, is simply not true, as indicated in Tables 8.31 and 8.32.

A bit more sexually tinged than romance is the area of sexuality, which we surveyed on a scale of 1 to 5, with possible responses ranging from deliciously sensuous to grossly distasteful.

There was no relationship between religiosity and the sensuousness of sex as perceived by our respondents. This is a quite important finding because it contradicts the popular stereotype of very religious people, who are supposedly aloof from sex except for procreation. Our finding was also important in light of the fact that a large number of respondents, including those who are very religious, were not married. What were their differences when examined by religious denomination? The results were intriguing, as shown in Table 8.32.

As in Table 8.31, we found that there were no clear religious differences in perceived sensuality. In general, the results showed that belonging to any of the major religions did not inhibit members' ability to experience their sexuality, in spite of caveats about particular beliefs and practices. Catholic and Jewish responses, the highest of all groups, were very close to each other. The contradictions of American sex practices

TABLE 8.31   **Survey Item G.2.**

SENSUALLY, I FEEL THAT SEX IS:			
	Very Religious	Religious	Slightly Religious	Not Religious
N =	269	864	982	619
1 Deliciously sensuous	57%	56%	57%	59%
2	32	30	32	33
3	10	12	10	6
4	0	2	1	1
5 Grossly distasteful	1	0	0	1
Line 1 + Line 2	89%	86%	89%	92%

TABLE 8.32 Survey Item G.2.

SENSUALLY, I FEEL THAT SEX IS:				
	Protestant	Catholic	Jewish	None
N =	976	686	297	301
1 Deliciously sensuous	51%	64%	62%	56%
2	36	26	31	32
3	11	9	5	10
4	1	1	2	2
5 Grossly distasteful	1	0	0	0
Line 1 + Line 2	87%	90%	93%	88%

can be clearly seen here. Because the sensuousness is universally favored but sexual activity may be looked on askance, these two groups can report the highest sensuality ratings and the lowest sex activity levels.

SEXUAL ACTIVITY

Our respondents' level of sexual activity was the best indicator of whether they practiced what they endorsed philosophically. The data relating to a statement on personal levels of sexual activity were sorted according to respondents' religiosity, as shown in Table 8.33.

When we combined below average and inactive, we found that there was a negative relationship—although not very strong—between religiosity and sexual activity. The more religious our respondents were, the

TABLE 8.33 Survey Item G.3.

I CONSIDER MYSELF TO BE SEXUALLY:				
	Very Religious	Religious	Slightly Religious	Not Religious
N =	265	862	984	618
Very active	19%	13%	17%	21%
Active	36	32	37	33
Average	20	33	30	31
Below average	12	12	11	11
Inactive	13	10	5	4
Very active + Active	55%	45%	54%	54%
Below average + Inactive	25%	22%	16%	15%

TABLE 8.34   **Survey Item G.4.**

ARE YOU FUNCTIONING AT YOUR BIOLOGICAL MAXIMUM SEXUALLY?			
	Very Religious	Religious	Slightly Religious	Not Religious
N =	258	859	981	616
Yes	59%	55%	47%	44%
No	41%	45%	53%	56%

more likely they were to perceive themselves as being sexually inactive. Many Americans regard religious individuals as the censors and critics of sexuality. However, in their personal lives, **most** religious people appear to be as sexually active as other Americans.

How can we know whether the level of sexual activity described is enough for an individual's personal needs? How much sex is enough? The only one who can answer that question is the individual. We probed our respondents on whether they felt they were functioning at their biological maximum sexually.

As presented in Table 8.34, we found that the more religious our respondents were, the more likely they were to believe that they were functioning at their biological maximum. We attributed these ratings to the beliefs, among many religious persons, that sex is "natural" and one merely carries out this biological imperative. The opposing view, usually held by less religious persons, is that sexual skills and performance are a functioning of attitudes and skills that must be learned and can always be improved on.

SEX EDUCATION

We next checked to see whether the sources of original sexual knowledge varied by religious group. We had asked respondents to identify the source of their sexual knowledge. Their replies, on the religiosity scale, are shown in Table 8.35.

The findings reflect an ongoing debate in this country: Where should youth receive their sex education? Some advocates of sex education in schools argue that too many children receive their sex knowledge, often erroneous, from their peers—sometimes called "the street." Others argue that the home and church are sufficient and preferred sources. In this case, both may be correct. The proponents of sex education in public schools are often more likely to be from the nonreligious segment of the community, and the opposing vocal groups are usually the very religious. Thus, 45% of the very religious would be home-and-church advocates, and the percentage of all other groups would be about 34%.

TABLE 8.35   **Survey Item G.11.**

I LEARNED ABOUT SEX FROM:				
	Very Religious	Religious	Slightly Religious	Not Religious
N =	266	863	984	619
Home	37%	31%	33%	34%
School	16	28	24	15
Church	8	2	1	1
Streets	39	39	42	50
Home + Church	45%	33%	34%	35%

FIRST SEXUAL EXPERIENCE

When we had discovered where our respondents learned about sex, our next question logically related to when they first practiced what they had learned. Table 8.36 gives details on their ages at their first full sexual experience.

An important issue in religious doctrine is abstention. We found, in our interviews, that abstention was only a minimal practice, but the age of sexual initiation revealed the extent to which respondents held out before having sex. If faith equals restraint, then women, by far, are the keepers of the faith. The religious women were the most restrained, with only 5% reporting having sex before age 15. Among the very religious

TABLE 8.36   **Survey Item H.15.**

SELF-IDENTIFICATION: AGE AT FIRST FULL SEXUAL RELATIONS:								
	Very Religious		Religious		Slightly Religious		Not Religious	
	Men	Women	Men	Women	Men	Women	Men	Women
N =	124	138	413	446	476	503	316	301
By age 10	0%	0%	2%	0%	2%	1%	2%	2%
11–14	19	8	16	5	21	7	11	11
15–18	41	40	57	53	54	55	60	54
19–25	28	49	24	40	19	35	26	31
26 +	12	3	1	2	4	2	1	2
By age 14	19%	8%	18%	5%	23%	8%	13%	13%
After age 18	40%	52%	25%	42%	23%	37%	27%	33%

women, the rate was 8%. However, of those who waited until they were age 19 or over, the very religious women reported the highest degree of restraint. Women reporting onset of sex experience by age 10 were similar for all groups. There seems to be cultural pressure that acts as an equalizer, modifying the religious restraints in children of all ages in America.

Were there differences in sex initiation age among the major religious groups? Table 8.37 reports our findings.

Men reported earlier sex initiation than women, in all religions. More Jewish men and women reported first experiences after age 18 than did the other groups. Catholic and Protestant men, and Catholic and Protestant women, showed much the same pattern of both early and late first sex experiences. Only the none group showed a significantly lower number of those beginning sex over the age of 18. As suggested earlier, the none group may have absorbed some traditional sex values as children. They followed the pattern of Protestant and Catholic men in having early sex experience, and they did not start as late as did the Jewish men. The none group is interestingly positioned in relation to the other groups. Were there many in this group, from various backgrounds, who were highly individualistic, rejected the authority of the various religions, and sought their own comfort level? Religions seem able to restrain children when they are very young, before puberty and up to about 12 or 13; but when they reach 14 or 15 and beyond, popular cultural pressures take over and parents become accustomed to hearing "But all my friends are doing it." The none group joins the adult sexual world largely between ages 15 and 18—earlier than all others—and probably less restrained by residual religious training.

TABLE 8.37   **Survey Item H.15.**

SELF-IDENTIFICATION: AGE AT FIRST FULL SEXUAL RELATIONS:							
	Protestant		Catholic		Jewish		None
	Men	Women	Men	Women	Men	Women	Men	Women
N =	477	493	330	351	144	150	144	156
By age 10	2%	0%	2%	1%	1%	2%	3%	1%
11–14	19	8	16	8	11	2	17	7
15–18	54	52	58	51	46	53	62	61
19–25	23	38	21	38	36	40	17	29
26 +	2	2	3	2	6	3	1	2
By age 14	21%	8%	18%	9%	12%	4%	20%	8%
After age 18	25%	40%	24%	40%	42%	43%	18%	31%

TABLE 8.38   **Survey Item H.28.**

I AM CONCERNED ABOUT SEXUALLY TRANSMITTED DISEASES:				
	Very Religious	Religious	Slightly Religious	Not Religious
N =	270	867	985	619
Very much	65%	62%	61%	51%
Much	16	20	23	29
Unsure	6	5	5	6
Slightly	10	7	6	9
Not at all	3	6	5	5
Very much + Much	81%	82%	84%	80%
Slightly + Not at all	13%	13%	11%	14%

SEXUALLY TRANSMITTED DISEASES

With continued and increased sexual involvement, whether casual or committed, at all levels of society, we felt we should query our respondent population as to how much anxiety they felt about the prospect of getting infected with sexually transmitted diseases (STDs). Table 8.38 summarizes their replies.

In keeping with the newly developed awareness of extensive sexual activity by the religious groups, it is not surprising that there is virtually no difference in concern about STDs between the religious and the nonreligious groups.

SUMMING UP

Compared to the general society, religious people share most of the same sexual activities that nonreligious people practice. In some areas, the religious actually outstrip the general population in sexual practices that may be considered unconventional (Table 8.18). To be certain that the population of each group was representative, in addition to their own rating on the religiosity scale, we tested the respondents on the issues key to religious groups today.

While primarily equally active on a broad range of sex practices, religious people have some difficulty enjoying their sex lives. There is a need to manifest a well-defined set of values for the public and for raising children, but many religious people live by another set of values privately. Hedonistic desire and active libidos are great equalizers. Recent trends in American society have reduced the amount of guilt feelings, allowing Americans of all religious persuasions to function sexually in strikingly similar ways, even as they support extremes of opinion regarding the most intensely debated issues of abortion, contraception, and sex education in the schools. Possible reasons for the decline in the sexual authority of the organized religions may be found in the loss of religion's spiritual and moral authority. Religious leaders have become increasingly controversial and several have become embroiled in sexual situations of questionable morality. Witness the recent scandals involving Jimmy Swaggart, Jim and Tammy Bakker, and others.

A case in Ireland, in the fall of 1991, aroused worldwide interest. A 14-year-old girl who had been raped by an older man, a friend of her father, was denied the right by an Irish court to go to England for an abortion. Ireland does not permit abortions, but many Irish women who desire an abortion travel to England for the procedure. Apparently, public feelings were so outraged that an appeal to the Irish Supreme Court succeeded in permitting her to go to England to have an abortion. The issue did not die there; in the aftermath of this case, groups in Ireland are now demanding that abortion be legalized nationally. As if this were not enough of a challenge to the Catholic Church in Ireland, an investigation of a popular and widely known bishop, Eamon Casey, followed reports that he had had an affair with an American woman, had fathered a child with her, and had given her a considerable sum of money over the years. The Casey case had some of the flavor of the televangelist scandals in America. The media reported that the bishop had claimed that it was well known that he was against abortion and followed the doctrine of the Church in matters sexual. However, on May 11, 1992, he publicly admitted that he had fathered the baby and had paid support for the now 17-year-old boy. He stepped down as bishop but remained in the Church. These two incidents reflect the dynamics of a conflict that some claim is imposed on people by impossible religious strictures.

From Freud on, many experts have postulated that religion is often misused by some as a cover for sexual guilt. We believe that the superstructure of religion is strong and is able to incorporate the joys of sex into the religious life-style. Few conflicts are evident in our data between the religious life and the erotic. One no longer has to make a choice between pleasure and faith.

CHAPTER NINE

Politics and Sex

SOME SIGNIFICANT FINDINGS ABOUT POLITICS AND SEX

✦ 16% of the ultraliberals and 23% of the ultraconservatives surveyed reported frequent or ongoing extramarital affairs.

✦ The ultraliberals were more interested in variety in sex than either independents or ultraconservatives were.

✦ 34% of the ultraconservative men and 46% of the ultraconservative women believed that abortion is murder, but 27% of the ultraconservative women reported having had an abortion.

✦ Ultraconservatives reported having had their first full sexual relations at an earlier age than either independents or ultraliberals.

✦ Three times as many ultraconservatives, compared to either independents or ultraliberals, rated sadomasochism as an acceptable practice.

✦ 15% of ultraliberals, 17% of independents, and 29% of ultraconservatives believed that simultaneous orgasm is a must for gratifying sex.

QUESTIONNAIRE SUBJECTS TABULATED IN THIS CHAPTER

	Table
The Family as a Social Institution: Current Views	9.1
Easy Divorce	9.2
Religious Values: Passing on to Children	9.3
Contraception	9.4
Abortion	9.5, 9.6
Abortion Frequency	9.7, 9.8
Women Who Have Had Abortions, by Ages	9.9
Women Who Have Had Abortions: Postabortion Reaction	9.10
Age at First Full Sexual Relations	9.11
Traditional Sex Roles in Modern Society	9.12, 9.13
The Importance of Love	9.14
Media Portrayal of Sexuality	9.15, 9.16
Sex Education	9.17, 9.18
Variety of Sex Techniques	9.19, 9.20
Sex for Money	9.21, 9.22
Simultaneous Orgasm	9.23, 9.24
Women's Sexual Aggressiveness	9.25, 9.26
Extramarital Affairs	9.27
Fantasizing	9.28
Comparative Sexual Activity, Three Years Ago Versus Now	9.29, 9.30
Oral Sex	9.31
Sadomasochism	9.32
Profane Speech During Sex	9.33
Self-Ratings of Sexual Activity	9.34

The American political system is distinguished by its stability. Rather than a range of small parties representing single issues, American voters are presented most often with a choice between the two major parties, whose platform "planks" cover a vast array of issues, some of them clearly political, such as defense, international relations, and economic strategies, and some clearly social. Attitudes toward what is taken to be appropriate sexual behavior, and their influence on public morality, are included in the social agenda of American politics.

The two-party system makes for great stability, but it does not, as is frequently pointed out, necessarily offer much choice. Voters who are deeply committed to single, often social, issues find themselves voting for candidates irrespective of party affiliation. As a result, party affiliation has lost much of its former appeal among American voters, who usually prefer to think of themselves as philosophically "independent" under any circumstances.

In our investigation of the connection between political identification and sexual attitudes and behavior, we chose to sidestep political party identifications. Instead, we asked people to identify themselves as ultraconservative, conservative, independent, liberal, or ultraliberal. The largest number (876) of people in our sample identified themselves as independent, in contrast to an almost equally weighted count of 213 ultraconservatives and 212 ultraliberals. To compare the most contrasting views and to avoid overlap among the groups investigated, we utilized the ends (ultraconservatives and ultraliberals) and the center (independents) of political identification, leaving out those who called themselves liberals (748) and conservatives (694). Many people may think they can predict what the responses from the political "ultras" will be on sexual issues. Our findings indicated that one cannot always predict accurately and reminded us constantly that politics and sex make strange bedfellows.

Issues and attitudes concerning the family have emerged as part of the political agenda. Is the traditional American family becoming obsolete? If so, is that good or bad? What social phenomena, such as divorce, women's liberation, gay liberation, or pornography, threaten the family? Should these influences, as some claim, then be limited, so as to protect the structure of the family and traditional values? Many recognize these questions as fundamental to the forces shaping contemporary American politics.

At the same time, we know that the role of the family is crucial in the formation of the sexual and moral attitudes of its members. Parental guidance and peer pressures constitute the basis on which an individual develops into an adult sexual being. Beliefs may change between childhood and adulthood, but new attitudes and behaviors that conflict with those learned within the family may result in problems of adult ambivalence and guilt. In turn, it is possible that ambivalence and guilt could lead to rejection of family values in general, in favor of a less encumbered sexual life. We were interested in how our politically self-identified sample felt about the importance of the family, and whether there would be significant differences among people identifying with different political ideologies. Table 9.1 indicates that the family has champions under all banners.

Predictably, the sanctity of the family was a core belief for ultraconservatives; less predictably, it was equally regarded, with only a minor difference, by independents. Even among the ultraliberals, 64% agreed that the family is the most important institution in society. A striking difference occurs in the levels of disagreement with the statement: the ultraconservatives and independents demonstrated a very low level of disagreement with the proposition and with each other, and 32% of the ultraliberals were ideologically opposed to the proposition. What does

TABLE 9.1   Survey Item A.1.

THE FAMILY IS THE MOST IMPORTANT INSTITUTION IN SOCIETY:			
	Ultraconservative	Independent	Ultraliberal
N =	211	874	211
Strongly agree	62%	55%	31%
Agree	32	38	33
No opinion	1	3	4
Disagree	5	3	19
Strongly disagree	0	1	13
Strongly agree + Agree	94%	93%	64%
Disagree + Strongly disagree	5%	4%	32%

Authors' note: The "Conservative" and "Liberal" groups indicated on the questionnaire (see survey item H.5, in Appendix B) are not included in the tables in this chapter, as explained on page 265.

this 32% disagreement signify—a rejection of the family itself, or, rather, rejection of the social constraint implications for a whole range of behavior, which ultraliberals know may be imbued in a defense of the family? Further research may define and clarify the intended rejection.

Does their judgment of the importance of the family reflect on how people feel about the sanctity of marriage, or on their determination to make a marriage work or to seek a divorce? Much has been said about the deterioration of marriage in contemporary society, and we know from factual statistics that one out of two American marriages ends in divorce. Insofar as a conservative agenda stresses the importance of the family, we wondered whether this emphasis would be reflected in negative attitudes toward divorce, and how attitudes toward divorce would correlate with the percentages of attitudes regarding the family. Table 9.2 shows how the responses sorted out.

The patterns of attitudes toward divorce paralleled those toward the institution of the family, but with a much lesser degree of commitment. As we might have expected, ultraconservatives demonstrated a much greater negativism toward divorce than did the other groups. They also demonstrated the lowest percentage of no opinion, suggesting that these are apt to be people who have fixed opinions about many social issues. There was much wider disagreement between ultraconservatives and independents on the issue of divorce (64% versus 53%, in contrast to 94% versus 93% on the question of the family), and a major difference between the two showed up in the no opinion category, which suggests that independents really are open to persuasion on social issues within the political process.

Fundamentalist religious groups actively entered the political arena with the Moral Majority movement, specifically directed toward

TABLE 9.2   **Survey Item A.3.**

DIVORCE IS TOO EASY NOW:			
	Ultraconservative	Independent	Ultraliberal
N =	209	870	210
Strongly agree	41%	21%	8%
Agree	23	32	22
No opinion	10	21	19
Disagree	19	22	38
Strongly disagree	7	4	13
Strongly agree + Agree	64%	53%	30%
Disagree + Strongly disagree	26%	26%	51%

furthering social objectives through the political process. We have come to associate ultraconservatives, therefore, with strong religious affiliations and beliefs, which have become central in their life-view. To explore this connection, we asked about respondents' commitment to pass on their religious values to their children. (See Table 9.3.)

Again, as in the question on the family, we found that the independents were more apt to resemble the ultraconservatives than the ultraliberals. When we combined very important and important, the independents produced a firm commitment (76%) to passing on religious values. Isolating very important from important, the ultraconservatives' responses of very important were fully ten percentage points higher than independents'. Once more, it appears to be not the fact of a commitment, but the strength of their commitment, that distinguishes

TABLE 9.3   **Survey Item B.2.**

PASSING ON RELIGIOUS VALUES TO MY CHILDREN IS:			
	Ultraconservative	Independent	Ultraliberal
N =	209	870	200
Very important	43%	33%	11%
Important	32	43	36
Not sure	15	13	17
Unimportant	9	9	15
Very unimportant	1	2	21
Very important + Important	75%	76%	47%
Unimportant + Very unimportant	10%	11%	36%

ultraconservatives from independents. The ultraliberals were less committed to passing on religious values: 15% said it was unimportant and 21% declared that it was very unimportant to them. From another perspective, however, 47% of the ultraliberals, or nearly half of those who responded to the survey item, were committed to passing on religious values.

Both questionnaire responses and our in-depth interviews confirmed that different political associations do authentically represent varying frames of mind and different attitudes, and that these attitudes are significantly contrastive across the political spectrum. However, values and attitudes cannot be assumed automatically to give insights into behavior. What people say is not always what they do, and we wanted to explore possible differences in behavior among the three groups.

One of the social issues associated with conservative political agendas has involved limiting the easy availability of contraceptives and opposing the teaching of contraception in the schools. The conservative reasoning is that easy contraception leads to ease of and implied approval of sexual relations outside of marriage, and such ease is strongly condemned as antithetical to family values. A certain religious involvement is strongly present on this issue. Insofar as the Bible instructs people to "be fruitful and multiply," any interference with following this instruction is regarded by some religious groups as immoral. If social agendas associated with organized religions inform the thinking of ultraconservatives, one should see a rejection of the use of contraception for themselves. However, as Table 9.4 suggests, the facts say otherwise.

Again, the independents appeared almost indistinguishable from the ultraconservatives, and both were strongly differentiated from the ultraliberals, but in a direction that it might have been difficult to predict. A sizable majority of our sample was using contraception, but, compared to the liberals, significantly larger shares of conservatives *and* of independents were doing so. Several explanations for these results may be suggested. It is possible that our ultraconservative sample was not as committed to social issues as we might have supposed, or that their social-issues agenda did not include prohibition of contraceptive use by married adults. Indeed, as suggested above, not all religions insist on a

TABLE 9.4   **Survey Item H.19.**

DO YOU USE CONTRACEPTION?			
	Ultraconservative	Independent	Ultraliberal
N =	205	872	207
Yes	66%	65%	55%
No	34%	35%	45%

rejection of contraception, and the rejection of contraception that is often heard may have more to do with sex outside of marriage than with birth control within marriage. Whatever the explanation, our data told us that our ultraconservative respondents were using contraception at a ratio of about two-thirds to one-third. They were avoiding risk and not leaving anything to chance.

Ultraliberals also used contraception more often than not, but their percentage trailed the other two groups. This seemed quite contrary to our image of an ultraliberal as one who insists on the right of people to live their own lives determined by their own perceptions and needs; one for whom family is not the primary focus and who, we might have expected, would want to control the size of his or her family. Perhaps, by contrast with the conservatives, the liberals were more willing to take chances. On the other hand, within this group there may have been an overrepresentation of people for whom contraception is not an issue, or people who follow alternative sexual behaviors.

Although statements about contraception frequently are strident in tone, nothing compares with the intensity of feeling and political action that surround the issue of abortion in the United States. Anti-abortion activists, strongly identified with conservative political agendas, seek every means to overturn the 1973 Supreme Court decision in the *Roe v. Wade* case, which legalized abortion. The pro-choice forces deplore the weakening of that law by the recent Supreme Court decision to delegate power over abortion to the states. As of 1992, there are several cases pending before the Court which could be used to further weaken or overturn *Roe v. Wade*. Within the next few years, the government's position regarding abortion could become modified. Depending on one's point of view, such a change would be either a disaster or a blessing.

Because we knew that both pro-life and pro-choice supporters hold their convictions deeply, we attempted to explore the depth of their feelings by posing a statement that equated abortion with murder. The responses we received are given in Table 9.5.

The ultraconservatives and the independents were somewhat different in the level of their agreement with the statement: the ultraconservatives' conviction was much stronger than that of the independents. Interestingly, a similar relationship applied to the two categories of disagreement: 26% of the ultraconservatives strongly disagreed with the statement and 19% of the independents strongly disagreed. In the intense category of disagreement, the percentages were even more dramatically contrastive in reverse. Whereas 24% of the ultraconservatives had no opinion, the remainder were only slightly more in agreement (40%) than in disagreement (36%) with the statement. This served to remind us that the term ultraconservative in American politics signifies a *range* of concerns. Although we expect a clustering of political, economic, and social attitudes, we cannot take for granted, in any individual case, what any of those attitudes may be.

TABLE 9.5   **Survey Item A.11.**

ABORTION IS MURDER:			
	Ultraconservative	Independent	Ultraliberal
N =	210	872	209
Strongly agree	32%	13%	5%
Agree	8	18	5
No opinion	24	18	10
Disagree	10	32	24
Strongly disagree	26	19	56
Strongly agree + Agree	40%	31%	10%
Disagree + Strongly disagree	36%	51%	80%

The results for the ultraliberals more nearly corresponded to what might have been expected. Only 10% agreed with the statement, and 80% disagreed.

Were these results skewed by sex? We explored that possibility by analyzing the differential responses of men and women. As Table 9.6 shows, the women, more than the men, tended to respond as would be expected in accordance with their political orientation.

The ways in which men and women looked at abortion produced some interesting results. Within the no opinion category, the highest percentages of both men and women were among the ultraconservatives, which suggests a sizable number of people for whom this issue is still unresolved. The lowest percentage of no opinion (6%) was found among ultraliberal women, who were most rejecting (89%) of the association of abortion

TABLE 9.6   **Survey Item A.11.**

ABORTION IS MURDER:						
	Ultraconservative		Independent		Ultraliberal	
	Men	Women	Men	Women	Men	Women
N =	103	107	434	438	99	110
Strongly agree	28%	35%	11%	15%	9%	2%
Agree	6	11	18	19	7	3
No opinion	26	22	20	15	14	6
Disagree	8	12	36	28	21	27
Strongly disagree	32	20	15	23	49	62
Strongly agree + Agree	34%	46%	29%	34%	16%	5%
Disagree + Strongly disagree	40%	32%	51%	51%	70%	89%

with murder. The greatest difference of opinion between the sexes was between the ultraliberal men, 70% of whom disagreed, and the ultraliberal women (89%). In all other categories, the highest range of difference was 12%. For example, between the ultraconservative men and women, 46% of the women agreed with the statement, in contrast to 34% of the men. The difference between the sexes, for the independents, followed the same pattern, but with considerably less difference between them and with lower percentage ratings (29% and 34%) than for the ultraconservatives. Among the liberals, the position was switched, with significantly more men than women (16% versus 5%) agreeing with the statement.

With such pronounced differences among the three groups on the issue of abortion as murder, we wondered whether practice would correspond with belief. What was their experience with abortion: who had had abortions, at what age, and how had they reacted? Although a number of men indicated on their questionnaires that they had been parties to abortions for wives or lovers and had felt the experience personally, we surveyed only women on these questions and explored further only with those women who had had an abortion. The women's responses are shown in Table 9.7.

A comparison of Tables 9.6 and 9.7 demonstrates a lack of congruity between belief and practice regarding abortion. We see from Table 9.7 that there was little difference in practice between the ultraconservative and ultraliberal women, both of whom had a higher incidence of abortions than did the independent women. Table 9.6 had shown a great disparity between the two "ultra" groups of women in their views on abortion. Thirty-two percent of the ultraconservative women had disagreed that abortion was murder; 27% (Table 9.7) had had abortions. Among the ultraliberals, 89% had disagreed that abortion is murder and 30% had had abortions. Americans are politically mobile, and some people in any group had at some time been affiliated with other groups. As an example, in our interviews, a number of women in the ultraconservative group indicated that they were conservative on this issue now because they personally had had abortions that traumatized them and changed their outlook. We also had occasion to note, in our interviews,

TABLE 9.7		Survey Item H.24.	
I HAVE HAD AN ABORTION:			
	Ultraconservative	Independent	Ultraliberal
N =	109	443	112
Yes	27%	22%	30%
No	67	75	65
No answer	6	3	5

that individuals who held philosophical views were fairly quick to change them when they had a personal crisis. In this vein, there were those in all groups who may have honestly claimed that they were against abortion, but then had an abortion when they found themselves in a position where they "had to" have one.

What about women who have had more than one abortion? Does the number of abortions bear any relationship to political posture? Our respondents' answers, as given in Tables 9.8, 9.9, and 9.10, were of special interest.

How are we to understand our findings of the actual experiences of women with abortion when we remember, on the one hand, our findings on the differences in attitudes between ultraconservative and ultraliberal women (Table 9.6), and, on the other, the moralistic rhetoric surrounding the issue of abortion? The responses we received can only make us wonder, when 62% of the ultraconservative women reported that they experienced a sense of relief after having had an abortion, in contrast to only 23% of the ultraliberal women. The mind-set of the individual experiencing the abortion can indeed be emotional, and, for the ultraconservative person, it can be traumatic because it offends the basic belief system. Thus, such women experience a greater sense of relief when the procedure is over. To others, who accept the legitimacy of abortion, there is little regret, only sadness that this was a necessity. On the two issues of sadness and regret, the contrast was striking; we leave the reader to speculate on the reasons. Of the ultraconservative women, 9% reported sadness and 14%, the largest percentage in all groups, reported regret. Of the ultraliberal women, 60% reported sadness and 3% reported regret. The ultraconservative women had relatively more abortions than the independents, although fewer than the ultraliberals (Table 9.8), and they had them through later ages (Table 9.9). Although our figures revealed interesting insights into the practices of women holding different political views, they could not give us a causal connection between those experiences and views.

Our personal interviews were much more useful for seeing causal connections. Our observations, through interviews with ultraconservative women, suggest that they look back on their abortion experiences with

TABLE 9.8   **Survey Item H.24.**

I HAVE HAD AN ABORTION: YES RESPONSES: NUMBER OF ABORTIONS:			
	Ultraconservative	Independent	Ultraliberal
N =	29	98	33
1 abortion	51%	72%	43%
2 abortions	40	17	19
3 or more	9	11	38

TABLE 9.9   **Survey Item H.24.**

I HAVE HAD AN ABORTION: YES RESPONSES: AT AGE:			
	Ultraconservative	Independent	Ultraliberal
N =	29	97	33
Under 15 years	0%	7%	6%
15–17 years	38	22	6
18–21 years	34	57	73
22–25 years	3	21	24
26–30 years	21	20	30
31 and over	48	14	12

Columns total more than 100% because of multiple responses.

more regret than do the others and that some of them report that their personal experiences galvanized them to prevent others from having abortions. Here again, we could not be sure that we were not dealing with a kind of fictionalizing of one's life and with self-deception. Can we say that, causally, having an abortion produced such a trauma that it caused a woman to try to further reject subsequent abortions? Anti-abortion forces frequently highlight women for whom that was the case, women who assert that the guilt and regret they experienced committed them to the abolition of abortion for all women. For the ultraconservative women as a group, that was apparently not the case: their number of second abortions was almost twice that of the other groups, and 14% went on to a third or fourth abortion.

Writers through the ages have been fascinated by the conflicts and problems of people who espouse a strict sexual morality which they desire to impose on others while they themselves succumb to sexual temptation.

TABLE 9.10   **Survey Item H.25.**

POSTABORTION REACTION WAS:			
	Ultraconservative	Independent	Ultraliberal
N =	29	98	33
Relief	62%	41%	23%
Pleasure	7	1	6
No reaction	7	11	8
Sadness	9	29	60
Guilt	1	9	0
Regret	14	8	3

The literary fictions seem very real to us, in light of the recent sex scandals of conservative televangelists Jim Bakker and Jimmy Swaggart. We must remember that an American political identification is made on the basis of many considerations, and that social issues constitute only a part of the reason people espouse a specific political position. The revelations in our data so far, that people behave in ways that would seem contrary to their political self-identification, may be an indication of the complexity of membership in any political identification. Specifically, ultraconservative women who have had abortions may not share the attitudes toward abortion that we tend to associate with an ultraconservative political posture. They may be ultraconservative on issues of the economy, affirmative action, and the military, but not on issues of personal morality. We may be justified in believing that they have a problem in terms of endorsing candidates and interacting with others on political issues.

With this proviso in mind, we can go on to examine other aspects of sexual attitudes and functioning with reference to political identification, to see whether the attitudes associated with a political posture are reflected in the behavior of the people who associate with that posture.

Ultraconservatives' political agenda has condemned what they see as an increasing sexual permissiveness in American society. Young people are encouraged to "just say no" to a whole range of behaviors; among them, in the first rank, is premarital sex. We were interested in comparing respondents' ages at first sexual experience, and we are making the assumption that, through age 18 at least, most of those sexual encounters were premarital. As Table 9.11 shows, most of our sample had had a full sexual encounter by the age of 18, with the ultraconservatives reporting the highest percentage (70%) and the ultraliberals the lowest (58%). If we are correct in assuming that this represents, on the whole, premarital sex, then ultraconservatives exhibit a conflict in advocacy and behavior.

TABLE 9.11   **Survey Item H.15.**

HAVE YOU HAD FULL SEXUAL RELATIONS? YES RESPONSES: AT AGE:			
	Ultraconservative	Independent	Ultraliberal
N =	204	855	206
By age 10	6%	0%	1%
11–14	13	12	13
15–18	51	55	44
19–25	29	30	41
26 +	1	3	1
By age 14	19%	12%	14%
By age 18	70%	67%	58%

When they overtly deny their sexuality, humans make life much more stressful for themselves, creating a need for a kind of double-entry sexual bookkeeping of belief and practice. A unique kind of pain may result from an attempt to reconcile belief and practice.

> I tell you, some people have cracked up with the sex lives they have been pursuing. It's just too much for them. I am fairly attractive, right? And except for a brief three years when I lived with a man, I have lived the life of a single woman.
>
> I have no trouble attracting almost any man I want, and most of them are successful, or I wouldn't bother with them altogether. Most of them are also sophisticated sexually, and on my level of function. But I have seen changes due to the pressures on people who have gone from being really religious to having casual sex. Some of it is even funny.
>
> There was this gorgeous guy I was dating. My girlfriends' eyes popped when they saw him. I thought, "Wow, this guy will make a good catch, but he is weird in bed." All I knew about his views was that he told me he was a conservative. Until he told me that he had been in a seminary and came within a year of becoming a priest, I thought he was nuts. He is very affectionate and considerate of me in bed, and obviously I am not the first woman he has made love to. But the strange part of this is how he feels so terrible about his gratification. It's almost as if he doesn't deserve pleasure. When he has an orgasm, which can take hours, he cries. He really cries tears. I've known some of my female friends who cry when they have orgasm, but not men. He tells me that he wasn't really meant to have unbridled pleasure, and that this balances it out for him. At first I thought, "Hey, did I do something wrong?" Anyway, it's too much of a downer for me.
>
> —A 31-year-old woman

WOMEN'S LIBERATION

The history of women's liberation movements is a very long one, and we are mistaken if we think that the 1960s produced the first significant attack on traditional sex roles and issues of women's rights. On the other hand, the contemporary movement has probably involved more people in more debate and has become part of the political agenda of more voters than ever before. In large measure, the current intensity may be directly related to the intense media exposure of the issues, made possible by the technology and widespread presence of television. We were interested in how our sample perceived an interconnected set of issues concerning the relations of men and women in contemporary society, and the political forces that influence those relations.

We specifically addressed the validity of traditional sex roles in modern society, knowing that the complexity of the considerations that people would take into account when responding to this question promised a wide range of answers.

✦ IN THEIR OWN WORDS

I believe that women should be women and let men be men. Men and women are not called the opposite sex for nothing. All of this talk about men and women being equal makes little sense to me. It is still the man who pays for a date and pays for the affairs he has by coin of the realm. I have no problems with a woman who may say that she can only have orgasm if she has oral sex performed on her, but I believe strongly that the inner identity of a man as a man, and a woman as a woman is paramount. People have tried to change this, but these are biological facts of life, not political fashion we are talking about.

—A 51-year-old bank executive

✦　✦　✦

How can anyone not be affected by the changes going on about us? I believe that it denies a person's humanity not to have the sensitivity and sympatico to be able to relate to the other sex. Nothing in life stands still, and I have found that, to the extent that men and women can get away from stereotypical sexual roles and demands on each other, it is replaced with mutual respect. You relate in ways that both are comfortable with. I would rather have my lover be my partner than a servant. I think that it is not just women who are being liberated. In the liberation process, men are being freed also. My experience is that the quality of sexual pleasure is much higher between free people.

—A 49-year-old professor of science

The results in Table 9.12 conform to our experience that an ultraconservative position favors "conserving" things as they were, while ultraliberals press for change. Independents, a much larger group, frequently agree with the conservatives, as we have seen earlier in this chapter. On the place of traditional sex roles today, the independents were in between the other groups (30%) in their agreement, but, in their disagreement, they were more aligned with the ultraconservatives than with the ultraliberals. In other words, well over half of our sample of both ultraconservatives and independents believed that traditional sex roles belong in contemporary society, in contrast to 29% of the ultraliberals who held that view.

TABLE 9.12

TRADITIONAL SEX ROLES HAVE NO PLACE IN MODERN SOCIETY:			
	Ultraconservative	Independent	Ultraliberal
N =	211	874	209
Strongly agree	1%	6%	23%
Agree	18	24	36
No opinion	20	14	12
Disagree	41	49	26
Strongly disagree	20	7	3
Strongly agree + Agree	19%	30%	59%
Disagree + Strongly disagree	61%	56%	29%

The responses did not, of course, tell us what people think these traditional sex roles are. Should women have careers? Should a married woman take the option of not having children? Should a single woman have a child without being married? Should a couple share home tasks? Must it be the man who always suggests sex, and pays for dates? Must a woman be locked in a passive and subordinate position in a relationship? We sorted the responses further, to see how our results might be affected by separating men and women. (See Table 9.13.)

Thirty percent of the ultraconservative women were unwilling or unable to express an opinion on this subject. In agreeing with the statement, they had the lowest percentage of any group (14%) in our breakdown, but they disagreed with it (56%) less than did ultraconservative men (63%). In

TABLE 9.13

TRADITIONAL SEX ROLES HAVE NO PLACE IN MODERN SOCIETY:						
	Ultraconservative		Independent		Ultraliberal	
	Men	Women	Men	Women	Men	Women
N =	103	108	434	440	99	110
Strongly agree	1%	1%	5%	6%	21%	25%
Agree	22	13	18	29	35	39
No opinion	14	30	14	14	18	3
Disagree	37	47	52	47	23	30
Strongly disagree	26	9	11	4	3	3
Strongly agree + Agree	23%	14%	23%	35%	56%	64%
Disagree + Strongly disagree	63%	56%	63%	51%	26%	33%

other words, the ultraconservative men, more than the ultraconservative women, believed in retaining traditional sex roles. Among the independents there was a 12% difference between the sexes: 35% of the women agreed, versus 23% of the men; 51% of the women disagreed versus 63% of the men. The ultraliberals showed a different breakdown. The women (64%) overwhelmingly saw change as necessary, but 7% more women than men took the opposite position. This apparent inconsistency stems from the lack of opinion among 18% of the ultraliberal men as against only 3% of the ultraliberal women.

How liberated were our women respondents from romantic love? One of the norms of our society is that romantic love is to be treasured above all else, that love underlies sexual desire—or, at least, should underlie it—and that love binds couples together. Sometimes, love causes pain, and some people are unwilling to risk the pain. We were curious about how respondents of particular political affiliations felt about that risk, and gathered their responses in Table 9.14.

Our respondents, across the political spectrum, agreed that love is worth the risk of pain, but there are slight, perhaps inexplicable differences. The ultraconservatives came out the least willing to take a risk, a result that would fit a stereotype of conservatives as being unwilling to admit the new because of a desire to maintain the proven verities. The ultraliberals followed the pattern of the ultraconservatives, and the independents were the most willing to take risks for love. Perhaps independents, because they are less committed to a particular stance, are also the most open and risk-accepting of the three groups.

Because the media, and particularly television, are recognized by all political persuasions as a powerful opinion-making force in our society, political strategies have included attempts to determine the content of media messages. The issue of portrayal of sexuality on television and in films, and the consequent effect on the position of women, has become

TABLE 9.14   **Survey Item A.2.**

IT IS BETTER TO LOVE AND BE HURT THAN NOT TO KNOW LOVE:			
	Ultraconservative	Independent	Ultraliberal
N =	211	871	207
Strongly agree	41%	36%	41%
Agree	35	52	40
No opinion	8	4	8
Disagree	13	7	5
Strongly disagree	3	1	6
Strongly agree + Agree	76%	88%	81%
Disagree + Strongly disagree	16%	8%	11%

of paramount concern. We dealt with this issue in our questionnaire, and Table 9.15 shows the responses we received, sorted according to the three political groups.

How differently, or similarly, men and women felt about this question is revealed in Table 9.16.

According to these results, although all groups agreed that media portrayal of sex should be less hostile to women, the differences in their degree of commitment to this proposition were striking. In Table 9.15, whereas ultraconservatives endorsed the proposition by only slightly more than half (52%), 90% of the ultraliberals concurred. The independents fell midway between, at 67%. Looking at the breakdown by sex in each political category (Table 9.16), we found that women invariably supported the proposition more than did men, and that, for ultraconservative and independent men, there was a high degree of uncertainty on the subject. Ultraconservative women had the highest degree of uncertainty, as shown in their relatively high rate of not sure responses. The media portrayal of sex, and its hostility to women, emerged as a strongly significant agenda item for ultraliberals.

The media have given a considerable amount of exposure to those people, largely representing a socially conservative agenda, who object to sex education in public schools. We might be led to believe that this voice represents the view of some large segment of the population whose children are being exposed to a subject to which the parents object. In order to determine whether there was a consensus on this subject among our respondents, we posed the issue with only three possible responses (as a form of forced choice): one each strongly positive and strongly negative, and one undecided. We then looked at the results, first by political preference alone (Table 9.17), and then separately for males and females within each political preference (Table 9.18).

TABLE 9.15 Survey Item B.5.

MEDIA PORTRAYAL OF SEXUALITY SHOULD BE LESS HOSTILE TO WOMEN:			
	Ultraconservative	Independent	Ultraliberal
N =	207	870	208
Very important	18%	31%	64%
Important	34	36	26
Not sure	33	27	5
Unimportant	9	5	4
Very unimportant	6	1	1
Very important + Important	52%	67%	90%
Unimportant + Very unimportant	15%	6%	5%

TABLE 9.16   Survey Item B.5.

MEDIA PORTRAYAL OF SEXUALITY SHOULD BE LESS HOSTILE TO WOMEN:						
	Ultraconservative		Independent		Ultraliberal	
	Men	Women	Men	Women	Men	Women
N =	101	106	433	437	98	110
Very important	14%	26%	23%	38%	50%	82%
Important	37	29	30	40	36	12
Not sure	29	38	36	19	7	3
Unimportant	10	7	9	2	7	0
Very unimportant	10	0	2	1	0	3
Very important + Important	51%	55%	53%	78%	86%	94%
Unimportant + Very unimportant	20%	7%	11%	3%	7%	3%

The level of agreement with this proposition was surprisingly high. Apparently, an overwhelming proportion of respondents, of all political leanings, wanted their children to receive sex education in school. Although our interviews revealed that there was some argument about how sex education should be taught—whether programs should include discussions of ethics, values, AIDS, condom distribution, and morality, or be value-free—the results were significant. In no other area concerning sex were our respondents of all political orientations in agreement as much as they were on the need for sex education in the schools.

Within this area of basic agreement, there were some interesting variations, particularly between men and women. For all three groups, the women felt most strongly about sex education, with ultraliberal women more committed than women in the other two groups. Ultraconservative men emerged as the most negative toward the proposition. Our interview results showed that women of all political groups seemed to be the home educators on sex as well as on all of life. Women have not been liberated from this traditional role. Even as men have become more

TABLE 9.17   Survey Item G.8.

SEX EDUCATION SHOULD BE TAUGHT IN THE SCHOOLS:			
	Ultraconservative	Independent	Ultraliberal
N =	209	871	210
Definitely yes	89%	91%	96%
Maybe	8	9	3
Not at all	3	0	1

TABLE 9.18   **Survey Item G.8.**

SEX EDUCATION SHOULD BE TAUGHT IN THE SCHOOLS:					
	Ultraconservative		Independent		Ultraliberal	
	Men	Women	Men	Women	Men	Women
N =	103	106	433	438	99	111
Definitely yes	88%	91%	90%	91%	95%	97%
Maybe	7	8	9	9	3	3
Not at all	5	1	1	0	2	0

involved with child rearing, it is still the mother who teaches the children whatever sex is taught at home. The role of the school in teaching sex education would then be to alleviate some of the pressure on the family for the responsibility of teaching sex education.

INDIVIDUAL SEXUAL PRACTICES

Having investigated a range of questions regarding sex and social issues, we turned to questions relating to attitudes toward individual sexual practice. Did political affiliation predict how a person was apt to feel or behave about sex and sex acts? Is sex for procreation or pleasure? Our questionnaire directly confronted the issue of sex for pleasure, and we explored the responses according to political affiliation alone (Table 9.19) and then in a breakdown of men's and women's answers (Table 9.20).

As shown in Table 9.19, among those in agreement, there was a significant (16%) difference between the lowest and highest ratings. The

TABLE 9.19   **Survey Item C.7.**

A LARGE VARIETY OF SEX TECHNIQUES IS A MUST FOR MAXIMUM PLEASURE:			
	Ultraconservative	Independent	Ultraliberal
N =	210	871	209
Strongly agree	8%	9%	11%
Agree	38	30	44
No opinion	22	17	10
Disagree	24	37	33
Strongly disagree	8	7	2
Strongly agree + Agree	46%	39%	55%
Disagree + Strongly disagree	32%	44%	35%

TABLE 9.20   Survey Item C.7.

A LARGE VARIETY OF SEX TECHNIQUES IS A MUST FOR MAXIMUM PLEASURE:					
	Ultraconservative		Independent		Ultraliberal	
	Men	Women	Men	Women	Men	Women
N =	103	107	433	438	99	110
Strongly agree	11%	6%	14%	5%	13%	9%
Agree	39	37	33	25	47	41
No opinion	23	20	16	18	12	10
Disagree	23	25	33	42	26	39
Strongly disagree	4	12	4	10	2	1
Strongly agree + Agree	50%	43%	47%	30%	60%	50%
Disagree + Strongly disagree	27%	37%	37%	52%	28%	40%

ultraconservatives were in the middle (46%), and the independents had the lowest response rating (39%) for agreement. Twenty-two percent of the ultraconservatives had no opinion, compared to 10% of the ultraliberals. Men rated sexual variety more highly than women in all three political groups, with the largest difference between the sexes occurring in the independent category. (See Table 9.20.) The strength of the endorsements, by a large number of people, of the statement that variety is a must for maximum pleasure suggests that a research for sexual satisfaction is regarded as a legitimate activity, regardless of one's political orientation.

One of the possible variations in sexual experimentation is that of sex for money. We wondered whether the frequency of people who had experienced sex for money would vary according to political affiliation. Although, as discussed in Chapter 11, professional prostitution is only one aspect of the larger issue of sex for money, we would expect that attitudes toward prostitution would be included in the social agendas of political orientations. We asked our respondents about their experiences with sex for money (Table 9.21), and then compared the positive responses of each political group (Table 9.22).

TABLE 9.21   Survey Item H.26.

HAVE YOU EVER HAD SEX FOR MONEY?			
	Ultraconservative	Independent	Ultraliberal
N =	203	864	204
Yes	19%	10%	18%
No	81%	90%	82%

TABLE 9.22   **Survey Item H.26.**

HAVE YOU EVER HAD SEX FOR MONEY? YES RESPONSES:			
	Ultraconservative	Independent	Ultraliberal
N =	39	86	37
Once	15%	27%	22%
Occasionally	67	53	62
Often	18	20	16

Here, too, the independents were different from both the ultraconservatives and the ultraliberals, whose experiences with paid sex were much alike. The ultraconservatives and the ultraliberals had been more frequently involved in sex for money.

All groups seemed to participate in the sex-for-pay practice. The First Sexual Revolution did not eliminate the need for paid sex, which was supposed to be one of its benefits. Sex for money has retained its popularity in our society. The ultraconservatives, generally identified with things traditional, tended to favor sex for money, a practice that is at once disposable and avoids entangling commitments.

A sexual issue that has been a source of interest and contention among professional investigators, such as sexologists, psychiatrists, and biologists, and between men and women in general, is the desirability of simultaneous orgasm. Men have so often made this a goal, and even a demand, that it has put pressure on women, who may go so far as to fake orgasm in order to comply with their partners' timetables. We phrased our questionnaire statement on this topic in the imperative, using the word *must*, to be certain that respondents understood and acknowledged the insistence in the need for this type of sexual gratification. Again, we categorized the responses first by political affiliation (Table 9.23) and then by sex, within each affiliation (Table 9.24).

There are a number of differences worth noting in these responses. The ultraconservatives' demand for simultaneous orgasm far exceeds the other two groups', and suggests a need for greater control in sexual matters by the ultraconservatives, supporting what we have seen in earlier tables. Particularly striking is the sizable disparity between the expectations of men and women, most pronounced among the ultraconservatives, but significant among the others as well. Ultraliberal women were the most rejecting of the proposition, and this suggests a greater degree of "liberation" among this group than among any of the others; however, ultraliberal men were revealed as less liberal on this issue than were ultraliberal women.

An unexpected finding was the large percentage of ultraconservative women who had no opinion—the choice over four times the average of

TABLE 9.23 Survey Item C.9.

SIMULTANEOUS ORGASM IS A MUST FOR GRATIFYING SEX:			
	Ultraconservative	Independent	Ultraliberal
N =	209	872	207
Strongly agree	9%	4%	9%
Agree	20	13	6
No opinion	20	12	4
Disagree	30	58	48
Strongly disagree	21	13	33
Strongly agree + Agree	29%	17%	15%
Disagree + Strongly disagree	51%	71%	81%

such responses in the other two women's groups. One may speculate on several possible explanations for this finding. Was it simply a reflection of a belief that nice ladies do not make sexual requests; they respond rather than demand? Or, did it indicate some conflict between the women's and their partners' attitudes on this issue? With four times as many ultraconservative women disagreeing as agreeing, these no opinion answers are likely weighted toward the disagree side, but may be conflicted in the women's ability to recognize and/or admit their preference.

Sex in America in the 1980s stressed technical proficiency for its own sake. Sex in the era of the Second Sexual Revolution seeks *mutual fulfillment*, implied in simultaneous orgasms. As the 20th century draws to a close, we heard from many respondents that sex is more art than

TABLE 9.24 Survey Item C.9.

SIMULTANEOUS ORGASM IS A MUST FOR GRATIFYING SEX:						
	Ultraconservative		Independent		Ultraliberal	
	Men	Women	Men	Women	Men	Women
N =	103	106	435	437	99	108
Strongly agree	14%	3%	6%	2%	14%	3%
Agree	27	11	14	12	11	2
No opinion	10	30	14	8	5	3
Disagree	30	33	57	58	43	54
Strongly disagree	19	23	9	20	27	38
Strongly agree + Agree	41%	14%	20%	14%	25%	5%
Disagree + Strongly disagree	49%	56%	66%	78%	70%	92%

biological function, more for pleasure than for procreation. These attitudes cross the political spectrum and, from ultraconservatives and ultraliberals alike, we received responses favoring sophisticated sex and variety in sexual practice.

There is general agreement that women's liberation has influenced the behavior of women, and it is often asserted that women have become more aggressive. We were interested in how our sample would respond to a statement about women's sexual aggressiveness. We used the word aggressive, and not assertive, to establish a stronger image of change from traditional passivity on the part of women. However, we did not insert any implications of value judgment into the questionnaire statement, although we assumed that the responses had a value judgment imbedded in them. Again, our analysis considered the political groups as a whole (Table 9.25), and then separated them by sex (Table 9.26).

Table 9.25 indicates that all of the groups, in declining percentages from the ultraconservatives through the ultraliberals, agreed that women have become more sexually aggressive. However, when the responses were separated by sex, we saw an interesting difference (Table 9.26). The women in the three groups showed only a small differential; not so the men. Among the ultraconservatives, the men, by 10% more than the women, believed that women have become more sexually aggressive. In the other two groups, also by a 10% difference, the women perceived this heightened sexual aggressiveness. Although we have no way of proving this, we may be tempted to believe that this aggressiveness is more approved by independents and ultraliberals, insofar as it is the women's judgment about themselves that brings the percentages up. Among the ultraconservatives, the men's perception elevates the result. Given that the ultraconservative men agree in significantly higher proportions than the men in the other two groups, one might speculate that these men find women's increased

TABLE 9.25   Survey Item D.2.

WOMEN HAVE BECOME MORE SEXUALLY AGGRESSIVE IN THE PAST 5 YEARS:		
	Ultraconservative	Independent	Ultraliberal
N =	210	872	208
Strongly agree	26%	18%	23%
Agree	62	61	51
No opinion	7	12	13
Disagree	5	8	13
Strongly disagree	0	1	0
Strongly agree + Agree	88%	79%	74%
Disagree + Strongly disagree	5%	9%	13%

TABLE 9.26   Survey Item D.2.

WOMEN HAVE BECOME MORE SEXUALLY AGGRESSIVE IN THE PAST 5 YEARS:					
	Ultraconservative		Independent		Ultraliberal	

	Men	Women	Men	Women	Men	Women
N =	103	107	434	438	98	110
Strongly agree	29%	21%	18%	17%	26%	18%
Agree	63	61	55	66	43	61
No opinion	6	9	14	10	12	15
Disagree	2	9	12	6	19	6
Strongly disagree	0	0	1	1	0	0
Strongly agree + Agree	92%	82%	73%	83%	69%	79%
Disagree + Strongly disagree	2%	9%	13%	7%	19%	6%

sexual aggressiveness (whether real or perceived) threatening to their conservative expectation of male dominance in sexual matters.

The sanctity of marriage has been one of the cornerstones of the conservative social agenda; fidelity, presumably, is intrinsic to preserving the sanctity of marriage. We were curious about how faithful our sample was to that institution. Responses to our survey item on extramarital sexual activity were considered our best source of data. (See Table 9.27.)

These findings can be interpreted from a "cup full" or a "cup empty" perspective. On the positive, "cup full" side, considerably more than 50% of our total sample had had no extramarital affairs. This statistic varied from a high of 69% of independents who had had no affairs, to a low of 49% of liberals. When we looked at the figures for those having often

TABLE 9.27   Survey Item D.5.

I'VE HAD EXTRAMARITAL AFFAIRS:			
	Ultraconservative	Independent	Ultraliberal
N =	142	600	151
Never	57%	69%	49%
Only once	15	10	5
Rarely	5	13	30
Often	22	6	15
Ongoing	1	2	1
Often + Ongoing	23%	8%	16%

and ongoing extramarital affairs, we found that the greatest number, almost one-fourth, were ultraconservatives, the people who identify with
social agendas that celebrate the sanctity of marriage.

▸ IN THEIR OWN WORDS

> I love doing conventions, particularly the Republicans. I mean the really
> conservative Republicans. The liberal Republicans aren't as exciting. Not
> only Republicans; almost any very conservative group, for example, reli-
> gious or economic, at business shows. Many of these come to these func-
> tions without their wives, but even if they have their wives, they sneak
> around and they serve up sex action like you wouldn't believe. They are
> intense about sex. Somehow being forbidden makes it more exciting. It is
> fun. They are excellent at wining and dining women as if we were dum-
> mies, but if that's the role they like, it's okay with me. They certainly make
> up for any lack of couth with their generosity. You know you are with a
> "real" man, and they have a great need to be the man, both in and out of
> bed. You don't find this around much, except in the old-time movies. That's
> life, right? Go with the flow.
>
> —A 31-year-old hostess/demonstrator

The heightened awareness of sexuality, of which the 1960s were the
harbinger, along with social changes that encouraged women to seek
personal fulfillment, have combined to change the way women perceive
themselves sexually. Some seek to engage in extramarital affairs for sexual satisfaction, but many others use fantasy to make their actual sexual
activity more exciting and gratifying. When we asked both men and
women how much fantasy played a part in their sexual functioning, the
responses were revealing. (See Table 9.28.)

TABLE 9.28   **Survey Item D.7.**

TO SUCCESSFULLY FUNCTION SEXUALLY I FANTASIZE:		
	Ultraconservative	Independent	Ultraliberal
N =	205	868	203
Not at all	37%	21%	21%
Slightly	47	59	46
Much	9	13	20
Very much	3	6	12
Totally	4	1	1
Much + Very much + Totally	16%	20%	33%

Some fantasy is considered almost universally acceptable, and even healthy, in that it offers an element of excitement that enhances and modifies the physical sexual activity. Too much fantasy, however, runs the danger of rendering the partner an object whose sole function is to gratify the fantasy. In Table 9.28, the figures indicate that the degree of fantasy indulged in intensely (much + very much + totally) varied from a low of 16% for ultraconservatives, through 20% for independents, and up to 33% for ultraliberals. Across the political spectrum, the degree of fantasy activity seems small in comparison to nonfantasizers, but it may indicate a problem in relating to sex partners who may resent the inner-directedness of the fantasizer's attention. We can probably expect some part of a population to indulge in such intense individual fantasy activity, and the percentages that we show may indicate a loss of communication between sex partners.

The liberation of sexuality associated with both changes in attitude toward sex and the development of efficient contraceptives has been severely challenged by a new and frightening set of concerns. No longer is the ultimate consequence of sex an unwanted pregnancy, although that problem has certainly not disappeared; now, the danger is a range of sexually transmitted diseases, including herpes and, particularly, AIDS. Some radical critics have suggested that the contagion is a punishment by a higher power for contemporary sexual excess; others have predicted that the presence of the STD dangers would dampen the previous enthusiasm for sexual freedom. Have these concerns diminished the American libido? We queried our respondents about whether their sexual activity had changed in the previous 3 years and sorted the data by political affiliation, as shown in Table 9.29.

The data indicated that, although a considerable number of the entire sample population reported an increase in sexual activity, the ultraconservatives reported the highest incidence of increase, a large

TABLE 9.29   **Survey Item D.9.**

COMPARED TO 3 YEARS AGO, MY SEX ACTIVITY IS:			
	Ultraconservative	Independent	Ultraliberal
N =	208	867	209
Much more	23%	24%	16%
More	33	20	9
Same	23	26	31
Less	17	20	24
Much less	4	10	20
Much more + More	56%	44%	25%
Less + Much less	21%	30%	44%

56%. Independents dropped substantially behind them with an increase of 44%, and the ultraliberals were represented by just one-fourth the number surveyed.

The percentage of people who had lessened their sexual activity followed the same pattern in reverse. Ultraliberals, perhaps responding to the current dangers and perhaps reflecting a previously less circumspect sexual life, had diminished their sexual activity by 44%. Independents were far behind, with 30%, and 21% of the ultraconservatives had responded to what we might have imagined were warnings coming from their own side of the political spectrum.

What are the implications of these findings? Have the ultraconservatives been liberated, or the liberals become conservative? Probably both and neither; we are looking at a situation in which multiple factors are at work. First, we cannot be certain, as we have stressed before, that all of our ultraconservative respondents politically shared an ultraconservative social agenda. It is important to recognize this, to avoid the stereotyping that so often leads to poor political analysis. The same is true of our ultraliberals: they may have believed in significant economic restructuring, but may have been very prudish about sexual issues. Even if our ultraconservatives espoused a restrictive social agenda, they often did so in relation to other people; their sexual needs and cravings made their own demands. Finally, society and social attitudes are changing. Ultraconservatives may think these are changing too fast and to the detriment of important older values, but even they cannot avoid being influenced by a general liberalization of social attitudes.

Liberals, on the other hand, may support a pro-choice platform and be in favor of the dissemination of contraceptive education, but they are not the sex maniacs or free-love advocates that their opposition prefers to portray. Further, whatever social agendas they, too, may advocate as a group, personal behavior is still an individual matter, and what people say and what they do are often far apart. Because a liberal posture is associated with educated elites in America, the degree of information about sexually transmitted diseases may be more widely disseminated among this population and may be influencing their behavior more significantly than that of other groups. From our personal interviews, we came to understand that, although sexual anxiety was high among some people, the majority seemed indifferent to the possibility of personal threat and were continuing, or even increasing, the level of their sexual activity.

Within each political camp, how did the men and women differ on this item? Table 9.30 has some indications.

The ultraconservative group, at 59% for men and 52% for women (combining much more and more responses), reported the greatest increase in sexual activity, a report that blurs the anticipated relationship between traditional political identification and sexual behavior. The independents and ultraliberals reported less of an increase, but the lowest rate of

TABLE 9.30   **Survey Item D.9.**

COMPARED TO 3 YEARS AGO, MY SEX ACTIVITY IS:

	Ultraconservative		Independent		Ultraliberal	
	Men	Women	Men	Women	Men	Women
N =	103	105	434	433	99	110
Much more	25%	21%	29%	19%	16%	15%
More	34	31	19	21	8	13
Same	27	17	25	28	36	24
Less	12	24	20	19	21	27
Much less	2	7	7	13	19	21
Much more + More	59%	52%	48%	40%	24%	28%
Less + Much less	14%	31%	27%	32%	40%	48%

increase reported in all groups (24%, for ultraliberal men) still indicates that one-fourth of the respondents in that group reported an increase.

The ultraliberals led in decreased activity. The ultraliberal women reported the greatest decrease in sex activity—48%, or one-and-one-half times the decrease reported by independent or ultraconservative women—and the ultraliberal men reported a 40% decrease. Sexual activity continues to be a strongly individual choice for Americans and is often contrary to religious doctrine, political persuasion, or any other restraint.

In interviews, we found that, whereas most individuals engaged in sex for pleasure, and some for procreation, there were different attitudes among political groups. The conservatives, and particularly the ultraconservatives, did few things casually, especially involving sex. They often had a need to feel right, or justified, in decisions and actions, unlike the independents and liberals, who were more casual and needed no justification other than the wish or opportunity to have sex. We came away with a feeling that the ultraconservatives were making a point of denial of anxiety and were determined not to let their sex activity be curtailed. It did appear that, by comparison with 3 years ago, many conservatives now felt freer to express themselves as they preferred, and this freedom had raised their sex activity level over these 3 years' time.

With no axe to grind and generally a casual sense of relatedness to sex, the independents and ultraliberals eased off their former sex activity. The threat of STDs and/or AIDS—especially among the ultraliberals—is likely to have influenced their recent, more restrained activity level. It is not really possible to hypothesize how these groups would be rated 2 or 3 years hence; these results only show what is happening now.

Overall, sexual activity has increased in America, but has this increase extended to a variety of types of sexual activity, and particularly sex acts that are not associated with procreation? There had always been a religious, and indeed a legal, onus on nonprocreative sex; we wondered whether this attitude still influenced contemporary behavior. We chose to focus on oral sex, a previously condemned practice.

As indicated in Table 9.31, almost all respondents had heard of oral sex; less than 1% claimed ignorance of the practice. Almost 4 out of 5 (77%) of the ultraliberals considered oral sex very normal, as did more than half of those in the other two groups. Very few people, and those mostly among the independents, considered this practice kinky, which is not necessarily a rejection of the practice.

An interest in oral sex, in a variety of sexual techniques, and in simultaneous orgasm represents personal sexual decisions that do not usually negatively impose on sexual partners. Sadomasochism, on the other hand, does impinge on others in several ways, from creating a slight nuisance, to exerting unwelcome control, to inflicting great pain and damage. Our questionnaire sought to discover to what degree sadomasochism was practiced among our sample, and we then gathered the data on this practice by political orientation. (See Table 9.32.)

In a revealing departure from their self-projected image of sexual moderation and restraint, 18% of ultraconservatives found sadomasochism acceptable, compared with 6% of independents and 6% of ultraliberals. Ultraconservatives also had the lowest percentages of respondents who evaluated it as kinky (51%) and unusual and kinky combined (61%). These ratings have implications about their need for rigid control, guilt, and sex linked with pain. Evidently, some people relieved their guilt about sex through physical pain. In interviews with individual respondents and with several publishers of magazines focused on sadomasochistic activities, we were told that sadomasochism allows the individual to abdicate responsibility and to follow orders. These orders take the form of a routinized sexual activity that leads to a special kind and amount of hurt, either inflicted

TABLE 9.31   **Survey Item D.12.**

RATING SCALE: ORAL SEX:			
	Ultraconservative	Independent	Ultraliberal
N =	200	860	201
Very normal	59%	54%	77%
All right	28	30	20
Unusual	6	6	2
Kinky	6	9	1
Never heard of it	1	1	0
Very normal + All right	87%	84%	97%
Unusual + Kinky	12%	15%	3%

TABLE 9.32   Survey Item D.12.

RATING SCALE: SADOMASOCHISM:			
	Ultraconservative	Independent	Ultraliberal
N =	181	849	200
Very normal	6%	1%	3%
All right	12	5	3
Unusual	10	17	14
Kinky	51	62	72
Never heard of it	21	15	8
Very normal + All right	18%	6%	6%
Unusual + Kinky	61%	79%	86%

externally by another or produced by the individual on his or her own person. Many sadomasochists report that, although they may have a preference for either receiving or inflicting pain, they can enjoy the reverse position as well. Others who are not so flexible are capable of sexual response as only the victim or only the victimizer. For most, sadomasochism is the way they cope with their deep underlying sexual conflicts.

"Talking dirty," another sexual variation, is practiced between consenting partners for sexual stimulation and enhancement. The contrastive responses to talking dirty (Table 9.33), which does not involve inflicting physical pain or punishment, may give some insight into what we have suggested as a real problem of sexual conflict for ultraconservatives.

Ultraconservatives found talking dirty a relatively unacceptable sexual outlet. By contrast, 65% of the ultraliberals endorsed the practice, as

TABLE 9.33   Survey Item D.12.

RATING SCALE: TALKING DIRTY:			
	Ultraconservative	Independent	Ultraliberal
N =	199	870	204
Very normal	15%	18%	33%
All right	27	42	32
Unusual	23	17	9
Kinky	27	22	26
Never heard of it	8	1	0
Very normal + All right	42%	60%	65%
Unusual + Kinky	50%	39%	35%

TABLE 9.34   **Survey Item G.3.**

I CONSIDER MYSELF TO BE SEXUALLY:			
	Ultraconservative	Independent	Ultraliberal
N =	211	873	210
Very active	11%	14%	27%
Active	45	36	30
Average	21	31	33
Below average	13	12	5
Inactive	10	7	5
Very active + Active	56%	50%	57%
Below average + Inactive	23%	19%	10%

did 60% of independents. These percentages seem to follow the espoused positions of these groups on the power of language to sexually arouse (an ultraconservative position) and the desirability of allowing freedom of expression, with sexual arousal as a possible consequence (an ultraliberal position).

Sexual activity is an expression of an internal image. How do people view themselves sexually? Do they think of themselves as prudish, loose, restrained, or sophisticated, based on their internal image? To reveal the internal image clearly, techniques that are not possible in the questionnaire procedure are required. However, we wanted to give people a chance to evaluate themselves, on the assumption that they would be making a comparison based on an internalized image of their sexuality. The self-evaluations are shown in Table 9.34.

Ultraconservatives may be conservative in philosophy or theory, but they are no different, as a group, from others in the society, in terms of sexual activity or practice. By some margin, ultraconservatives were more apt to see themselves as either more or less sexually active than the others. Do these ratings perhaps reflect some degree of judgment about the desirability of greater or lesser sexual activity? By 10 percentage points, compared to the next group, they were less inclined to see themselves as "average."

SUMMING UP

In this chapter, we have attempted to analyze the sexual activities and attitudes of a sample of Americans distinguished by a broad spectrum of ideologies with which they identify. We have called these "political" ideologies, but political groupings in America include social policy, as well as other political concerns. The groupings themselves are very broad and may include significantly different points of view about one or another aspect of a total ideological platform. We assume, however, that, if the differences become too pronounced, dissenters simply break away and align themselves in another configuration, and that we can, therefore, expect that there will be some attempt toward agreement on important issues by people who remain joined within political ideologies.

The positions of ultraliberals and ultraconservatives are understood to be contrastive in the social agenda areas of sexual behavior. To simplify, ultraliberals are presented as saying, "Sex is normal, sex is enjoyable. If you don't want to get pregnant, use contraceptives; if you get pregnant, and don't want to be, you can choose to have an abortion. We endorse a humanist perspective as it concerns human sexuality and believe that an individual human being can and should determine one's own fate and have control over one's own body."

Ultraconservatives, by contrast, in social agenda proposals, can be understood as saying, "We are individuals here to serve a higher will and morality. Sex may be beautiful, but it is not recreation or a game. It is permissible only in the context of marriage, and only for the purpose of procreation. If you find yourself pregnant and don't want to be, you cannot kill the fetus inside of you, but will have to carry it through birth. If you still don't want the baby, you can offer it up for adoption."

If the comparative positions of ultraliberals and ultraconservatives as stated are correct, our findings reveal that ultraconservatives show a distinct separation between theory and practice. In many areas of sexual practice, including the exotic, the ultraconservatives could not be distinguished from the ultraliberals, or, if different, were more involved in "forbidden" practices. While preferring stability, ultraconservatives have been modifying their behavior to accommodate to the contemporary world. There have been great changes in the permissibility of contraception, in the approval of sex education in the school (with some limitations around actual agendas), in the teaching of values, and in the specificity of the information disseminated. Abortion remains a major issue that allows little room for compromise. In practice, however, we have seen that ultraconservatives are not following what is understood to be the ultraconservative agenda. They are having abortions, including repeat abortions, just like everyone else.

We come away with a strong sense that, in the area of politics and sexuality, which is, after all, an attempt to acquire power to enforce ideology, people operate with a perspective that says, "You do what I say, and I'll do what I want." No matter how strongly people believe that social constraints should be enforced, they want freedom for themselves, and there is probably no place where this is more true than in the area of sexual freedom. If laws are enacted to constrain sexual expression, some people will break the laws, as they have always done.

CHAPTER TEN

Education and Sex

SOME SIGNIFICANT FINDINGS ABOUT EDUCATION AND SEX

✦ Women with the highest education report having the greatest number of sex partners—twice as many as any other group of women—and the most sexual experience before marriage.

✦ The acceptability of oral sex increases with education.

✦ For both men and women, the appeal of parenthood decreases as education increases.

✦ The number of women who masturbate increases with education. Those who have never masturbated were 41% of the high school group but only 7% of the postgraduate group.

✦ Becoming a parent is most highly rated by men and women who are at the lowest education level.

| QUESTIONNAIRE SUBJECTS TABULATED IN THIS CHAPTER |

	Table
Easy Divorce	10.1
The Family as a Social Institution: Current Views	10.2
Parenthood	10.3
Abortion	10.4
Delaying Careers for Child Rearing	10.5
Number of Sexual Partners	10.6
Comparative Sexual Activity, Three Years Ago Versus Now	10.7
Recently Increased Caution About Sex	10.8
A Double Sexual Standard	10.9
Personal Professional Fulfillment	10.10
Media Portrayal of Sexuality	10.11
Variety of Sex Techniques	10.12
Oral Sex	10.13
Profane Speech During Sex	10.14
Initiation of Sexual Activity	10.15, 10.16
Extramarital Affairs	10.17
Sexual Experience Before Marriage	10.18, 10.19
Sensuous Nature of Sex	10.20, 10.21
Self-Ratings of Sexual Activity	10.22
Masturbation	10.23

When people think "America," they think "freedom." Wars are fought to achieve and defend freedom, immigrants come to America seeking freedom, and the lives of Americans are permeated with the notion that freedom is the country's highest national achievement. This emphasis on national freedom is intrinsically linked with the idea of personal freedom, and Americans are quick to react negatively to any possible threat to their personal freedom. Today's American is an autonomous individual who is free to pursue any goal and to explore any mode, including the sexual, of personal expression. The American ideal is one of unconstrained possibility.

But this ideal is, in fact, constrained by a range of factors. The rights of others, national goals, and societal interests direct the establishment of laws that place limits on unrestrained personal freedom. Personal psychohistorical factors that shape ego development impose limitations on the range of individual adults' choices and decision making; personal circumstances, such as access to income and educational achievement, over which individuals have only limited control, will determine who they are and what they do. Because they exist in a situation of constrained freedom, and for their own well-being, it behooves Americans to understand the elements of that constraint.

Although individuals are not unprepared to admit that their distinctive attitude toward romantic love and personal sexuality is influenced by their personal histories, they may be overlooking the possibility that a regularity of attitude exists that is somewhat determined by social group factors such as educational level. The purpose of this chapter is to explore the regularities in sexual attitudes and reported behaviors in groups of Americans distinguished by levels of educational achievement.

Our attention here is focused on how the level of education attained influences personal sexual attitudes and behavior. We know that certain factors tend to cluster: high educational achievement frequently is associated with a family background that will influence the level of education to which an individual aspires. At the same time, America is a fluid society with a reality, not just an ideal, of personal social mobility. Being "self-made" is still a possible dream in America. Needless to say, being well-educated does not necessarily mean that one is wise in general, or wise in respect to sexual attitudes and decisions. In fact, the picture that emerges in this chapter is that income levels rise as educational levels rise, and that expanded parameters of sexual choices and options are associated with this rise.

We deal with sexual similarities and differences associated with income levels in Chapter 11. In this chapter, we will explore how both traditional and new sex roles are affected by education, as well as education's effect on sexual interaction and expectations.

When we reviewed the returned questionnaires, we discovered that we had to eliminate the small number of respondents who had indicated a junior high school education. The high school group contained graduates as well as individuals who had not completed high school. Those who indicated "some" high school were very similar to those who had had a junior high school education; many were of middle age, or older, and had not had the opportunity to go on to or to complete high school. A number of persons in this group completely misunderstood the questionnaire and were unable to provide usable responses. Those who were left were so few in number that they did not provide a critical mass that constituted a viable subsample. For this exploration then, our sample was separated into four groups: high school, some college, college graduate, and postgraduate.

THE FAMILY

Is the family an endangered institution? Has the Second Sexual Revolution diminished the importance of family creation and stability, as so many critics of contemporary society assert? Although attitudes varied among the designated groups, our findings revealed a consistent valuing of family bonds. Attitudes toward divorce, shown in Table 10.1. constituted one measure of how respondents valued family stability.

Interesting differences in attitudes toward divorce appear both among levels of education and between the sexes in each level. As the level of education rises, the attitude toward divorce becomes more permissive. Women are more committed (strongly agree and agree) to maintaining marriages than are men, but this commitment generally decreases as the level of education increases; among the most highly educated, the attitudes of men and women are virtually identical.

These results are easy to explain merely with reference to the options open to women who have higher levels of education and, by extension, to those whose career preparation leaves them less vulnerable in case of marital dissolution. We can suppose that women who have the capacity to support themselves adequately feel less need to maintain marital relationships that are less than totally satisfactory to them, and these women welcome the possibility of easy divorce. That a divorce is easy to obtain does not mean that people will necessarily choose it as an option. The responses to this question are not to be taken as indications of the frequency of divorce in these groups.

Our interviews indicated that many of the less well-educated women may have curtailed their education specifically to get married, and now define themselves primarily in a married status and a housewife role. As long as the marriage remains stable, the home orientation can be a highly satisfying life for many women who do not crave the pressures and problems of the external workplace. Insofar as marital instability threatens the life-style that they value, it is easy to see why they would look with disfavor on easy dissolution of marriage.

TABLE 10.1   **Survey Item A.3.**

DIVORCE IS TOO EASY NOW:								
	High School		Some College		College Grad		Postgrad	
	Men	Women	Men	Women	Men	Women	Men	Women
N =	641	691	322	338	200	203	149	150
Strongly agree	27%	38%	25%	18%	18%	10%	10%	3%
Agree	30	30	37	46	23	40	25	26
No opinion	22	13	16	13	23	14	13	14
Disagree	17	15	20	21	30	33	45	48
Strongly disagree	4	4	2	2	6	3	7	9
Strongly agree + Agree	57%	68%	62%	64%	41%	50%	35%	29%
Disagree + Strongly disagree	21%	19%	22%	23%	36%	36%	52%	57%

We might expect that, if people favor easy divorce, they undervalue the family as an institution, as the social critics assert. We tested this hypothesis by asking how people of different levels of educational achievement felt about the importance of the family.

As shown in Table 10.2, on the whole, among all groups and between the sexes, the family was highly valued; the evaluation declined somewhat among the two highest educational groups. We found indications of a greater commitment to the family among women. The generally higher rating for all women suggested that women remain more closely linked to home as caretakers of the home life than do men.

The level of disagreement between the sexes at the highest education level stood out rather sharply from all the others, and one might wonder what institution in society these respondents would rank as more important. It is possible that these figures indicate a greater commitment to careers and to upward mobility among this population, as well as a postponement in the scheduling of marriage and child raising, compared to those less well-educated. Further, based on our interviews, we did not believe that the most highly educated were antifamily; rather, in line with findings throughout this study, we noted that they were highly independent.

We must be careful, in examining these figures, to realize that a respondent might separate marriage and the family and not regard them as two parts of the same institution. This is what the social critics of family life in America deplore, when they face suggestions for alternative family structures outside of the traditional Western nuclear family structure.

We have seen that education clearly influenced attitudes toward ease of divorce (and, by implication, fluidity of marriage) and toward the institution of the family. Even when there were differences among groups

TABLE 10.2   **Survey Item A.1.**

THE FAMILY IS THE MOST IMPORTANT INSTITUTION IN SOCIETY:							
	High School		Some College		College Grad		Postgrad	
	Men	Women	Men	Women	Men	Women	Men	Women
N =	642	690	322	341	201	204	148	149
Strongly agree	60%	54%	50%	61%	37%	57%	42%	53%
Agree	30	39	43	33	52	34	39	33
No opinion	5	3	2	2	7	4	4	3
Disagree	3	3	4	3	4	4	14	9
Strongly disagree	2	1	1	1	0	1	1	2
Strongly agree + Agree	90%	93%	93%	94%	89%	91%	81%	86%
Disagree + Strongly disagree	5%	4%	5%	4%	4%	5%	15%	11%

and between the sexes on these issues, overwhelmingly, our respondents seemed committed to marriage and the family. How, then, did they prioritize their relationship to parenthood? Is becoming a parent the most important thing in life?

The responses to this question, shown in Table 10.3, were provocative. One might easily have predicted that valuing parenthood would increase with educational level; quite the opposite was found. In addition, the sharp differences between those who had postgraduate education and everyone else were dramatic. Not only did fewer of the most well-educated agree with the proposition, but they also had stronger opinions about their disagreement.

Equally or perhaps even more noticeable was the fact that, except in the college graduate group, men more than women believed (strongly agree and agree) that parenthood is the ultimate human attainment. We know there is a difference between procreation and nurturance and we have to wonder whether there is a separation between the sexes in how they interpret what parenthood means. Men may be achieving ego satisfaction from the production of children, but women may be less enthusiastic about the responsibilities of caretaking, which may be what parenthood means to them. Whatever the interpretation may be, the data revealed that fewer than half of all the respondents, regardless of sex or level of education, supported the proposition that human achievement is most represented by parenthood.

Which brings up the issue of abortion. Is it an acceptable response to unwanted pregnancy, or is it a heinous crime? Table 10.4 summarizes the respondents' views.

Not surprisingly, the high school group most strongly agreed with the thesis that abortion is murder, and the women in that group held that

TABLE 10.3   **Survey Item A.8.**

BECOMING A PARENT IS THE ULTIMATE HUMAN ATTAINMENT:							
	High School		Some College		College Grad		Postgrad
	Men	Women	Men	Women	Men	Women	Men	Women
N =	639	690	320	341	198	204	148	150
Strongly agree	11%	9%	8%	8%	7%	12%	9%	1%
Agree	31	27	28	27	24	19	10	14
No opinion	16	15	20	14	21	7	7	9
Disagree	35	38	34	42	36	44	51	49
Strongly disagree	7	11	10	9	12	18	23	27
Strongly agree + Agree	42%	36%	36%	35%	31%	31%	19%	15%
Disagree + Strongly disagree	42%	49%	44%	51%	48%	62%	74%	76%

TABLE 10.4   **Survey Item A.11.**

ABORTION IS MURDER:								

	High School		Some College		College Grad		Postgrad	
	Men	Women	Men	Women	Men	Women	Men	Women
N =	641	690	321	341	203	206	149	150
Strongly agree	20%	20%	13%	13%	5%	11%	7%	4%
Agree	16	19	18	11	15	12	12	9
No opinion	13	15	24	18	27	14	15	7
Disagree	27	24	32	26	40	33	36	28
Strongly disagree	24	22	13	32	13	30	30	52
Strongly agree + Agree	36%	39%	31%	24%	20%	23%	19%	13%
Disagree + Strongly disagree	51%	46%	45%	58%	53%	63%	66%	80%

view more strongly than the men did. By contrast, moving up the education scale, we found that each successive group reported less agreement. College men and women had the highest incidence of no opinion responses; their reason for reserving judgment on this issue was not clear. Having children and not permitting abortions seemed to be most favored by high school women, and one has to consider whether their views reflected a lack of mobility and choice in the high school group generally. The more highly educated groups—those with more income and satisfying careers, who prefer children when they are convenient—obviously differed from the high schoolers.

When they had a less-than-total commitment to parenthood as the greatest goal of human life, how did these people feel about the postponement of personal goals in favor of children? Specifically, we were interested in the issue of women's careers outside of the home, which comes into conflict with the nurturance of children. Table 10.5 provoked much thought.

The relationship between a mother and her child touches a universally responsive chord, a chord composed of biological, social, cultural, and historical notes. Its composition is further complicated by conflicting psychological studies that have attempted to determine whether young children are better (or worse) off when their mothers postpone their own ambitions to attend to the children's needs. Are several hours of "quality time" each day, spent between a career-oriented mother and her young child, as good as or even better than a continuous, nurturing interaction? Do children in day care make a better social adjustment than those in the continuous care of their mothers? Are mothers who are frustrated in their own lives able to provide the best environment for nurturing a child? Whatever one is inclined to believe, a psychological

TABLE 10.5   **Survey Item A.10.**

| MOTHERS SHOULD DELAY THEIR CAREERS DURING CHILDREN'S EARLY YEARS: |

	High School		Some College		College Grad		Postgrad	
	Men	Women	Men	Women	Men	Women	Men	Women
N =	640	690	323	340	200	204	147	149
Strongly agree	18%	21%	5%	8%	8%	7%	4%	2%
Agree	41	34	42	30	41	24	35	26
No opinion	7	6	17	10	5	11	14	9
Disagree	29	32	27	40	35	47	32	46
Strongly disagree	5	7	9	12	11	11	15	17
Strongly agree + Agree	59%	55%	47%	38%	49%	31%	39%	28%
Disagree + Strongly disagree	34%	39%	36%	52%	46%	58%	47%	63%

study to support that belief can be found; if a woman is uncertain, there is a wealth of conflicting data to make her even more uncertain.

The educational level our respondents achieved made a significant difference in what they were inclined to believe about the scheduling of career and motherhood. Fifty-five percent of the women in our high school sample believed that women should postpone their careers; this number declined as education was added, until the postgraduate level of 28% was reached. This is in no way surprising. Presumably people, particularly women, seek higher education in conjunction with their career orientations. Most women who finished postgraduate degrees did so because they had clear career goals in mind.

We should be sensitive, too, to the emphasis in this question. It does not explore the situation of working mothers; rather, it asks specifically about careers. We know that many women who are forced to work for strictly economic reasons would prefer to be home with their children if finances allowed. We also know that such working mothers face enormous problems in juggling work responsibilities with the adequate care of their children. Most of these women do not see their work as a career, the synonym for a fulfilling, absorbing, and, indeed, glamorous life-choice. Postponing a career suggests a real personal sacrifice in favor of child raising, and we saw that our sample of people who had most prepared for such a career-oriented life were least willing to make that sacrifice.

When we pursued the gender differences by educational levels, we found real differences of opinion on this subject between men and women: the men agreed more than the women did, at all educational levels. The least disagreement occurred among the high school educated who, we may presume, were the least career-oriented and, perhaps, the most home-committed. However, more than one-third (39%) of these women disagreed about career postponement, a proportion close to that of high school men (34%). The group that disagreed the most among themselves was the college graduates. The men favored career postponement 18% more than the women did. Interestingly, even among the postgraduate group, there was a substantial 10% difference of opinion between men and women. It would appear that career-oriented men do not necessarily feel that the same career commitment is pertinent for their wives and partners.

SEXUAL ATTITUDES AND BEHAVIOR

We have looked at the ways in which educational attainment influences attitudes toward the institution of the family, including the raising of children. However, human sexuality exists apart from its obvious biological function as the mechanism of procreation, and we were interested in how the full range of sexual expression was influenced by educational levels.

Along with the major social changes that have affected how men and women meet, interact, and express their sexuality, has come a growing awareness of the problem of sexually transmitted diseases. A more easy attitude toward sexual experimentation and experience, made possible by greater social acceptance and greater ease in controlling pregnancy, has been threatened by the real danger of acquiring life- and health-threatening diseases through those sexual encounters. Have the publicity and awareness of these diseases made people more cautious in their sex lives? (See Table 10.6.)

TABLE 10.6   **Survey Item G.7.**

HOW MANY DIFFERENT INDIVIDUALS (INCLUDING SPOUSES) HAVE YOU HAD SEXUAL RELATIONS WITH?							
	High School		Some College		College Grad		Postgrad	
	Men	Women	Men	Women	Men	Women	Men	Women
N =	641	681	321	332	204	203	150	149
None	2%	4%	1%	4%	1%	1%	0%	1%
1–10	23	46	36	46	25	37	32	25
11–30	33	34	34	37	30	52	31	47
31–60	19	10	20	7	27	6	22	12
61–100	9	2	4	3	9	3	9	7
101 +	14	4	5	3	8	1	6	8
1–30	56%	80%	70%	83%	55%	89%	63%	72%
61 and over	23%	6%	9%	6%	17%	4%	15%	15%

In the category of 1 to 30 partners, at all education levels, more women than men reported having sex partners within this range of numbers. In the higher-number categories, twice as many postgraduates had 61 to 101+ partners, compared to the other women. An important fact to be considered when researching pregnancy, health, and disease is the number of sex partners a person has had. Several famous basketball players reported in 1991 that they had had well over 1,000 sex partners each.

FREQUENCY OF SEX ACTIVITY

From the information on how many partners each group had had, we moved to what seemed the most closely connected data, the frequency of each group's sexual activity, shown in Table 10.7.

The table indicates that more people reported increases in their sex activity than decreases. Interestingly, the postgraduate group, previously the freest sexually, reported a decrease in sex activity. Women and men in each group were remarkably similar, with the exception of the college grads, where the men reported much more sex activity than the women. Those who predicted the demise of American sex were wrong. However, the sheer number of partners reported is far greater than the numbers reported in prior sex research literature. The high divorce rate, the large number of singles, and the trend to later marriages are possible explanations; however, in general, remaining virginal until marriage, and then having the spouse as the only sex partner, seems to be part of past history.

TABLE 10.7   **Survey Item D.9.**

COMPARED TO 3 YEARS AGO, MY SEX ACTIVITY IS:							
	High School		Some College		College Grad		Postgrad	

	Men	Women	Men	Women	Men	Women	Men	Women
N =	641	688	321	333	200	199	144	145
Much more	28%	19%	24%	26%	23%	16%	11%	14%
More	12	19	26	25	33	22	21	19
Same	27	26	31	27	29	29	33	31
Less	23	18	10	14	12	25	28	25
Much less	10	18	9	8	3	8	7	11
Much more + More	40%	38%	50%	51%	56%	38%	32%	33%
Less + Much less	33%	36%	19%	22%	15%	33%	35%	36%

SEXUAL CAUTION

Our questionnaire was supplemented by in-depth interviews in which we asked our respondents to compare their behavior in the 3 years prior to 1988 with their behavior in the years leading up to 1992, when information about AIDS and other sexually transmitted diseases was gaining more public attention. Many reported they had exercised some additional caution, but only about one-fifth of the total sample indicated that they were not only cautious but extremely careful, and, according to interview data, had significantly modified their behavior to alleviate their anxiety. A much smaller percentage, less than 25% for all groups surveyed, with the exception of postgraduate men, disagreed with the questionnaire statement. Most respondents fell between the extremes and seemed to continue to function sexually as before, but with a bit more caution.

Education plays a part, but a somewhat mysterious part, in enhanced caution in the face of danger from sexually transmitted diseases. As indicated in Table 10.8, the most cautious group in aggregate was the some college group, in which the men were more cautious than the women by 10%. Somewhat surprisingly, because one might expect that a "macho" image might override an inclination toward caution, men in most groups generally expressed themselves as having become more cautious than have women. This reversed itself in the postgraduate group, where more women than men had grown more cautious, with postgraduate women the most cautious of all the women surveyed, and, surprisingly, postgraduate men the least. Whereas one might be tempted to attribute this intensified caution to increased education and access to information, curiously, the postgraduate men were the most assertive about their lack of

TABLE 10.8 Survey Item A.14.

IN THE PAST FEW YEARS I HAVE BECOME MORE CAUTIOUS ABOUT SEX:

	High School		Some College		College Grad		Postgrad	
	Men	Women	Men	Women	Men	Women	Men	Women
N =	639	690	324	339	204	202	148	148
Strongly agree	22%	23%	29%	28%	19%	27%	16%	20%
Agree	53	39	51	42	57	38	48	54
No opinion	7	19	12	16	8	17	8	10
Disagree	12	16	7	12	13	16	25	13
Strongly disagree	6	3	1	2	3	2	3	3
Strongly agree + Agree	75%	62%	80%	70%	76%	65%	64%	74%
Disagree + Strongly disagree	18%	19%	8%	14%	16%	18%	28%	16%

caution, with 28% disagreeing or strongly disagreeing and saying, in effect, that they had not changed their attitude. The next lowest figure was 19%, expressed by high school women.

Everyone we interviewed on this issue had personal and compelling reasons why they behaved as they did. Those who were more cautious generally cited an article or research report that they had read or heard about, which detailed the dangers of promiscuous sex. Almost all respondents, no matter the level of education, reported themselves as interested and well-informed on the latest findings and forecasts about herpes, AIDS, and other widely publicized sexually transmitted diseases.

Because we know that sexual performance is partly a personal decision and partly determined by the accepted standards of the larger society, we were interested in how educational achievement would influence a perception of a double standard in the expression of sexuality. The double standard has held that men are expected to be dominant over women, more highly sexually charged, and possibly promiscuous, while women, by contrast, are supposed to be submissive, to show sexual restraint, and to behave monogamously. Sexual "liberation" was to have changed all that, and we were interested in exploring whether it had. Through our survey, we sought to determine the specific sense of sexual parity or equality perceived by our sample of educationally differentiated men and women. Table 10.9 summarizes our findings.

The men and women agreed that a double standard regarding sex still exists, but their perception of its existence varied considerably by educational attainment. The women, not surprisingly, produced a much higher affirmative response to this question on all educational levels compared to the men, and, from least to most educated, the percentages of those who recognized that a double standard exists climbed higher and higher.

TABLE 10.9   **Survey Item A.15.**

THERE IS STILL A DOUBLE STANDARD IN SEX REGARDING MEN AND WOMEN:							
	High School		Some College		College Grad		Postgrad	
	Men	Women	Men	Women	Men	Women	Men	Women
N =	639	689	321	340	201	202	147	149
Strongly agree	20%	33%	23%	40%	23%	40%	27%	44%
Agree	49	51	63	54	64	55	65	53
No opinion	23	11	9	2	7	1	2	0
Disagree	6	2	3	3	6	4	6	3
Strongly disagree	2	3	2	1	0	0	0	0
Strongly agree + Agree	69%	84%	86%	94%	87%	95%	92%	97%
Disagree + Strongly disagree	8%	5%	5%	4%	6%	4%	6%	3%

Fully 97% of the postgraduate women were sensitive to this double standard. We should be aware of the possibility that a recognition of a double standard does not automatically mean a deploring of it. It is quite conceivable that someone may recognize the existence of the double standard and conclude that it is appropriate. Those in the forefront of sexual liberation movements have said all along that the sexual double standard is not dead and, although it has gone out of vogue for men to openly proclaim their sexual superiority, underlying prejudices clearly still exist.

These underlying prejudices influence how people determine appropriate gender roles and evaluate their relative worth. Who works harder? Whose work is more important? Which work requires more skill and expertise? What is the basis of comparison? These questions have been debated between men and women for generations. It is part of female folk wisdom that "a man works from sun to sun, but a woman's work is never done," and comic plots have revolved around the smug male who finds himself totally incompetent and overwhelmed when confronted with running a household.

The entry of women into the work force has produced something of a revolution in social and sexual role changes for women, and in personal identity transformations. But it has introduced an area of conflict with those men who still believe that female career aspirations are less indulged than their own and should be less significant than what they see as an appropriate primary domestic orientation for women.

The bitter debate that began in late 1991 regarding the sexual harassment charges that Anita Hill brought against the Supreme Court nominee, and now Supreme Court Justice Clarence Thomas, continues as we write this, and there is a strong likelihood that it will go on for many years to come.

Women across America exploded in spontaneous rage at the way the all-male Senate Judiciary Committee regarded, doubted, and treated Anita Hill. The caustic manner of their questioning, their disbelief, and their readiness to dismiss her charges, seemed to many American women symbolic of the underdog position they themselves had been assigned socially, and even professionally. The greatest number of comments heard were centered on "her word against his," and, "if the issue came to whom would you believe, in the case of a man versus a woman, the man would win, hands down." Yet, as we shall see in Table 12.16, sexual harassment seems to be a widespread and even a universal problem.

We were interested in how people felt about the importance of their own professional commitment, and how their view would vary by degree of education as well as gender. The responses concerned only the individual answering, and not the respondents' evaluation of how others should feel about professional commitment.

Not surprisingly, Table 10.10 shows that, as the degree of educational investment in career preparation increases, the evaluation of the importance

TABLE 10.10   **Survey Item B.3.**

MY PERSONAL PROFESSIONAL FULFILLMENT IS:								

	High School		Some College		College Grad		Postgrad	
	Men	Women	Men	Women	Men	Women	Men	Women
N =	640	690	322	340	204	204	149	149
Very important	39%	46%	48%	47%	48%	48%	50%	61%
Important	51	44	48	50	48	51	49	39
Not sure	2	4	3	1	3	1	0	0
Unimportant	5	5	1	1	1	0	1	0
Very unimportant	3	1	0	1	0	0	0	0
Very important + Important	90%	90%	96%	97%	96%	99%	99%	100%
Unimportant + Very unimportant	8%	6%	1%	2%	1%	0%	1%	0%

of personal professional fulfillment increases. By a wide margin, most respondents understood their own professional satisfaction to be important; the differences were more pronounced between educational groups than they were between men and women within each group. Only among those with the least education did any see their professional fulfillment as unimportant, although even here the numbers were small.

The responses by men are not unexpected. Professional fulfillment fits the stereotype of the American male who is professionally ambitious and strives to succeed. For women, this focus is not stereotypic and, although there were always ambitious and successful professional women, the prioritizing of professional aspirations has not been understood as part of a female role. Our results, however, allow us to say with assurance that personal fulfillment, recognition as competent professional beings, and parity in sexual areas are of tremendous concern to women of all groups, and this concern increases with increased education.

Our understanding of appropriate roles and attitudes comes from learning, and much contemporary learning comes directly from the media. The media both shape attitudes and reflect attitudes, and women in particular are very sensitive to the potential influence of media images. A complaint is often heard that the portrayal of sex and violence, particularly with women as victims, has done great harm to the image of women in general and to their sexual liberation in particular. We asked our respondents (Table 10.11) to evaluate how they felt about one aspect of this issue.

Overall, the number of respondents of both sexes who felt that sexual portrayals of women by the media are hostile was substantial, and this perception increased by educational level. Considerably more men than women were unsure about how they felt on this issue. The greater the

TABLE 10.11   **Survey Item B.5.**

| MEDIA PORTRAYAL OF SEXUALITY SHOULD BE LESS HOSTILE TO WOMEN: |

	High School		Some College		College Grad		Postgrad	
	Men	Women	Men	Women	Men	Women	Men	Women
N =	639	688	320	339	202	204	147	151
Very important	21%	34%	23%	44%	29%	53%	41%	66%
Important	33	34	33	32	34	30	31	23
Not sure	33	25	32	20	23	15	19	8
Unimportant	5	6	11	3	11	2	8	3
Very unimportant	8	1	1	1	3	0	1	0
Very important + Important	54%	68%	56%	76%	63%	83%	72%	89%
Unimportant + Very unimportant	13%	7%	12%	4%	14%	2%	9%	3%

degree of education, the less unsure our respondents were, and women were less unsure than men in all categories. The evaluations of very important produced the widest differences between the sexes in all categories, again increasing by level of education; a rating of important showed much less difference between the sexes. The women were more intensely concerned with this issue and were apt to prefer the more definitive statement. The men, while believing change in the media is necessary, moderated the intensity of their responses.

It has been suggested that widespread response to the recently perceived dangers associated with promiscuous sex has been a retreat from the sexual enthusiasms of the pre-AIDS period to a condition of sexual restraint. We decided to investigate whether the challenge to sexuality had reduced people's interest in the pleasures of sexual experimentation. (See Table 10.12.)

Judging by the responses of strongly agree and agree, the men at the lower educational levels appeared to be the more ardent seekers of sexual variety. Between the men and women, the most noticeable difference occurred between the high school group and the others: the men in the high school group opted for more sexual variety, and the women for less, than any of the other groups. Contact with the larger world, implied by some experience with higher education, would appear to diminish a man's need for variety but increase female expectations. In general, in the new sexual milieu, women have been able to more freely experiment, both with techniques and with partners.

We have found that the interest expressed by men in sexual experimentation is often misunderstood and resented by their female partners, who frequently complain that it makes them feel inadequate. When we consider the difference in male and female responses, especially among

TABLE 10.12   Survey Item C.7.

A LARGE VARIETY OF SEX TECHNIQUES IS A MUST FOR MAXIMUM PLEASURE:								
	High School		Some College		College Grad		Postgrad	
	Men	Women	Men	Women	Men	Women	Men	Women
N =	641	681	322	330	200	204	148	148
Strongly agree	9%	7%	14%	8%	12%	5%	18%	4%
Agree	50	24	28	33	24	33	19	36
No opinion	15	10	17	22	24	17	18	14
Disagree	22	40	36	34	39	43	42	44
Strongly disagree	4	19	5	3	1	2	3	2
Strongly agree + Agree	59%	31%	42%	41%	36%	38%	37%	40%
Disagree + Strongly disagree	26%	59%	41%	37%	40%	45%	45%	46%

the least educated, it is apparent that a great deal of misunderstanding and conflict is possible. Our data do show that education seems to reduce gender differences.

Next, we looked at our respondents' reactions to two sexual practices that are believed by many to have achieved increased acceptance in recent years: oral sex (Table 10.13) and profane language during sex ("talking dirty") (Table 10.14).

Oral sex has, over the past several decades, become respectable in America, and is no longer seen as deviant. Across the educational groups in Table 10.13, there is a clear movement toward acceptance, going from lowest education level to highest. Many Americans call the acceptance

TABLE 10.13   Survey Item D.12.

RATING SCALE: ORAL SEX:								
	High School		Some College		College Grad		Postgrad	
	Men	Women	Men	Women	Men	Women	Men	Women
N =	641	688	321	338	203	203	149	148
Very normal	51%	47%	61%	56%	65%	62%	83%	76%
All right	34	33	29	35	25	32	15	22
Unusual	6	6	4	2	6	3	1	1
Kinky	9	14	4	6	3	3	1	1
Never heard of it	0	0	2	1	1	0	0	0
Very normal + All right	85%	80%	90%	91%	90%	94%	98%	98%
Unusual + Kinky	15%	20%	8%	8%	9%	6%	2%	2%

TABLE 10.14   **Survey Item D.12.**

RATING SCALE: TALKING DIRTY:							
	High School		Some College		College Grad		Postgrad
	Men	Women	Men	Women	Men	Women	Men	Women
N =	640	686	321	335	202	201	148	146
Very normal	16%	19%	16%	21%	21%	20%	20%	28%
All right	37	37	41	36	46	35	52	32
Unusual	25	21	22	16	21	18	11	10
Kinky	21	22	21	26	11	27	17	29
Never heard of it	1	1	0	1	1	0	0	1
Very normal + All right	53%	56%	57%	57%	67%	55%	72%	63%
Unusual + Kinky	46%	43%	43%	42%	32%	45%	28%	39%

and practice of varied sex techniques sophisticated; a few may call oral sex weird, but almost no one has not heard of it. The respectability of oral sex, and its equal acceptance by women, marks a dramatic change. It is no longer solely the man who determines, or teaches "the little woman," what is good and desired. The table shows that women who have higher education, in increasing numbers, felt oral sex was very normal or all right.

"Talking dirty" is reported as being a strong descriptive stimulus for sex, and seems to be rapidly growing in popularity. (See Table 10.14.) Women had for many years been "protected" from hearing obscenities, and men would be reminded by other men, "Watch what you say, there is a woman present." But women no longer swoon at obscenity. Men have always felt free to verbalize sexually, but women have not, at least not openly. It represents a great change for relationships that women can feel free to express intimate sexual feelings explicitly. Despite the fact that this practice does not refer to obscenities or hostility, but rather to descriptive and erotic language, responses to this item indicate that men's acceptance increases with education, but women's remains roughly the same for all groups (between 55% and 65%).

Much has been written about how to address disparate sexual desires between partners. One approach, endorsed by those who believe in open marriage, has been to urge experimenting with a range of partners. Masters and Johnson[1] offered sex therapy as an alternative approach, to enable partners to change their attitudes and practices within the marital relationship. Their approach recognizes that sexual gratification is achieved in very personal ways that develop both from deeply felt needs and from experience. With an increased openness of communication and a willingness to explore, men and women are brought from a condition of limited sexual experience and knowledge to a broader awareness of their own sexuality. In our interviews, we found that highly educated women were responsive to broadening their sexual horizons and were eager to participate as technically proficient sexual equals with their partners.

The double standard discussed earlier has held that men are sexually aggressive and women are passive, and that this difference is based not only on social custom but also on biological differences. The women's movement has changed much of that thinking by rejecting the idea of any biological basis for female passivity and by attacking the social expectations that denied women the possibility of acting out their sexual potential. We were interested in how our sample would respond to the possibility of assuming a passive role, and sorted the responses first by educational differentiation (Table 10.15) and then by sex (Table 10.16).

It may surprise some of our readers to discover that, at the two middle levels (some college and college grad), 27% of the men had a yearning for their partners to always initiate sexual activity, thus indicating a desire for passivity that has not been popularly associated with the male role. Although lower, the degree of agreement by high school educated men (17%) is most surprising. One might have assumed they would be the most committed to more traditional role playing. The responses by the most educated men may have been colored by the word always, and the strength of their disagreement may reflect a desire for greater flexibility in sexual role enactment. Of particular interest is the no opinion category, which, at all educational levels except college grad, drew at least twice as many responses from men as from women (almost 4 times as many in the high school group)—indicating women's indecision about their appropriate sexual role.

Some remnants of the old sexual attitudes remain. Among those with high school education, almost 30% of the women preferred that their

TABLE 10.15 Survey Item D.4.

I ALWAYS PREFER THAT MY SEX PARTNER INITIATE SEXUAL ACTIVITY:				
	High School	Some College	College Grad	Postgrad
N =	1,329	660	410	300
Strongly agree	1%	6%	3%	2%
Agree	21	19	20	12
No opinion	19	18	14	11
Disagree	54	51	57	67
Strongly disagree	5	6	6	8
Strongly agree + Agree	22%	25%	23%	14%
Disagree + Strongly disagree	59%	57%	63%	75%

TABLE 10.16   **Survey Item D.4.**

I ALWAYS PREFER THAT MY SEX PARTNER INITIATE SEXUAL ACTIVITY:								
	High School		Some College		College Grad		Postgrad	
	Men	Women	Men	Women	Men	Women	Men	Women
N =	640	689	321	339	204	206	150	150
Strongly agree	1%	2%	4%	9%	1%	4%	2%	2%
Agree	16	26	23	15	26	14	13	12
No opinion	30	8	25	11	16	12	15	6
Disagree	48	60	46	55	51	63	65	69
Strongly disagree	5	4	2	10	6	7	5	11
Strongly agree + Agree	17%	28%	27%	24%	27%	18%	15%	14%
Disagree + Strongly disagree	53%	64%	48%	65%	57%	70%	70%	80%

partners always initiate sex. On the other hand, close to two-thirds of them rejected this invariable sexual practice. However, a desire for sexual-role parity increases as education increases. We suggest that advanced education, personal status, and expanded knowledge of possibilities seem to enable men and women to speak the same sexual language and to communicate their personal sexual wishes, desires, and fantasies.

In Table 10.1, when we looked at how our sample felt about ease of divorce, we saw that, with a rising level of education, both men and women expressed the opinion that divorce seemed an accessible option to dissolve a marital relationship at will. We wondered whether this same latitude would be reflected in attitudes toward extramarital affairs, and whether new possibilities for sexual freedom and enhanced communication had impacted marital fidelity.

Table 10.17 shows that, on the whole, our sample reflected a high degree of marital fidelity—higher than one might have imagined in what is supposed to be a sexually permissive time. The men, on the whole, reported a higher incidence of marital infidelity than the women, and the more educated men had a higher incidence of often and ongoing affairs than did less educated men. This pattern did not hold for the women: high school graduates had the same incidence of often and ongoing extramarital experiences as did women with postgraduate degrees, and the two categories between had a much lower incidence. The most dramatic difference was between the men and women who were college graduates: the men reported the lowest incidence of never or only once and next-to-highest frequency of often and ongoing affairs. The women college grads had the highest incidence of abstention and the lowest incidence of participation in extramarital affairs.

TABLE 10.17   **Survey Item D.5.**

I'VE HAD EXTRAMARITAL AFFAIRS:								
	High School		Some College		College Grad		Postgrad	
	Men	Women	Men	Women	Men	Women	Men	Women
N =	432	453	217	221	136	133	101	99
Never	56%	64%	78%	77%	56%	81%	64%	59%
Only once	14	12	2	6	3	4	5	7
Rarely	15	13	10	12	22	11	11	23
Often	13	6	8	3	15	3	18	8
Ongoing	2	5	2	2	4	1	2	3
Often + Ongoing	15%	11%	10%	5%	19%	4%	20%	11%

We have suggested that advanced education often correlates with an increase in income. Because ongoing affairs can be expensive, and men generally pay the bills, less well-educated men may be less able to pay for the indulgence.

We found in our interviews that, regardless of their actual experience with extramarital affairs, interest in them runs high on the part of both men and women. Frequently, our respondents reported that the only impediment to an affair was the lack of an appropriate circumstance or a lack of time. Rarely do people seem to see these affairs as a real threat to marriage or the family, which reflects a willingness on the part of people to tailor marriage to meet their own personal needs. Old standards and demands for performance within marriage have changed; greater flexibility in life-style and more explicit expression of individual sexual values are now much more widely acceptable.

In spite of what appears to be a much greater openness to the idea of sexual flexibility within marriage, we should remember that an overwhelming number of our respondents reported a high degree of marital fidelity. We wondered whether an examination of their premarital sexual experience would reflect a similar dissonance between conservatism in behavior and what appeared to be liberal attitudes.

Traditional morality, as generally understood, insisted on premarital chastity for women as a nonnegotiable demand. This seems hopelessly old-fashioned today, and we assume that it is an anachronistic remnant of bygone days. Men and women freely discuss sex and negotiate their desires within a condition of apparent freedom. But does behavioral freedom correspond to verbal freedom, or are there still women who save their virginity as a gift for their husbands or for men who insist that this be done? In this chapter, we are concerned with sexuality and education, so we are here most interested in seeing whether educational attainment corresponded to premarital sexual behavior. (See Table 10.18.)

Again, the high school group comes out having the lowest experiential level of all. Possible reasons are that the high school group married younger, and that they are more restrained than the more educated groups.

By far, the group reporting the highest incidence of premarital sex overall was the male college graduates (Table 10.19). The female high school graduates reported the lowest incidence among the female groups—less than two-thirds of any of the others, and one-half that of the high school men. Percentages in the remaining categories of women were similar to each other; women who went on to postgraduate education reported the highest frequency of all. Here we must consider that going to college and then on to further study beyond college may postpone marriage and lengthen premarital adulthood, and during these years, these people may be sexually active. High school graduates, on the other hand, may be marrying younger, and their premarital sexual experiences might be occurring during their teen years.

Our interviews amplified the difference between the high school educated and those who had completed college education and beyond. College educated women reported that they regarded sex as a shared and egalitarian relationship in which the partners can talk about their preferences and make sexual requests of each other. These women added that they often initiated expressions of interest in sexual involvement with male friends and acquaintances.

The responses of the men showed no progressive pattern correlating with educational level. The college graduate men had a significantly higher incidence of premarital sex than did the other groups of men, but men who went on to postgraduate work had the lowest. Many of the men in this group reported that they were too busy in professional schools or

TABLE 10.18   **Survey Item D.10.**

I HAD SEXUAL EXPERIENCE BEFORE MARRIAGE:				
	High School	Some College	College Grad	Postgrad
N =	1,331	659	400	298
Very much	28%	29%	27%	26%
Much	21	29	43	33
Little	24	20	15	17
Very little	10	13	10	9
None	17	9	5	15
Very much + Much	49%	58%	70%	59%
Little + Very little	34%	33%	25%	26

TABLE 10.19   Survey Item D.10.

I HAD SEXUAL EXPERIENCE BEFORE MARRIAGE:								
	High School		Some College		College Grad		Postgrad	
	Men	Women	Men	Women	Men	Women	Men	Women
N =	641	690	319	340	201	199	149	149
Very much	38%	17%	29%	29%	31%	23%	27%	26%
Much	27	16	31	28	52	34	32	34
Little	15	32	24	15	15	15	20	14
Very little	8	12	8	18	1	18	6	12
None	12	23	8	10	1	10	15	14
Very much + Much	65%	33%	60%	57%	83%	57%	59%	60%
Little + Very little	23%	44%	32%	33%	16%	33%	26%	26%

other graduate programs to have time for much sexual experience. Another possibility was that the dominance needs of the men were satisfied by an alternate drive—success in career beginnings and other nonsexual experiences.

A preference for virginity at marriage is still endorsed by a limited group as a special gift. To some couples, the wife's virginity is regarded as a down payment on a lifetime of sexual exploration and pleasure; to others, it is regarded as payment in full. In this latter group, we found those who believed that a man should dominate the sexual interaction, controlling, teaching, leading, and, in general, asserting his masculinity. This seems to be the antithesis of sharing sex as a loving experience with mutual affection and respect.

The overvaluing of virginity at marriage has been criticized by some experts as "a big issue about a little piece of tissue." They feel that a concern with good sex is lost sight of, in the emphasis on that "little piece of tissue." On the other hand, a great deal of romantic fantasy is involved in the preservation and then the relinquishing of virginity, particularly that of women.

A very personal perception of sensuality is the primary basis for sex, but sensuality and sex are not exactly the same thing. Sensuality is the inner taste apparatus, that unconscious drive beyond the individual's control that communicates whether something feels wonderful, or good, or terrible. People can learn new sexual techniques and modify their attitudes, but basic perceptions such as sensuality are very difficult to change. We were interested in whether education seemed to correlate with perceptions of positive or negative sensuality, and we asked our respondents to rate their own sensual responses, not in terms of how they thought about sex, but how they "felt" about it.

My honeymoon was so wonderful that I get goose bumps even now when I think of it. Most of my friends had lots of boyfriends and I guess a great deal of sex when we were in school. I didn't indulge because I was convinced that the man I married would appreciate my waiting for him. I know it sounds like a romantic soap opera, but that is exactly what happened to me. I met him at college graduation, we looked at each other and we knew. It was right that I saved myself for him, and we are right together.

—A 47-year-old administrative assistant

Table 10.20 indicates that our total population revealed a positive attitude toward their sensuality, but an education effect did appear: high school graduates were the least inclined to associate sex with sensuality, and postgraduates were the most inclined. Sensuality is in vogue now, and many of our respondents were much more apt to feel sensual, or at least to say they felt sensual, even though they may have later described their actual sexual experiences, in interviews, as unimaginative and dull. People needed to see themselves as capable of sensuality, and we suspected that educated people, who consider themselves sexually sophisticated, were more aware of and in sympathy with current liberal attitudes than were those who were less well-educated.

On each educational level, the men emphasized sensuality more than the women did, but the spread between men with high school education and those with postgraduate education was 10%, whereas, among the women, the difference was 23%. Only 4% of the high school women sensually perceived sex as "distasteful" to some degree; no other group reported more than a 1% incidence for this judgment. (See Table 10.21.)

TABLE 10.20   **Survey Item G.2.**

SENSUALLY, I FEEL THAT SEX IS:			
	High School	Some College	College Grad	Postgrad
N =	1,331	654	408	297
1 Deliciously sensuous	54%	58%	54%	69%
2	27	37	39	29
3	17	4	6	2
4	2	1	1	0
5 Grossly distasteful	0	0	0	0
Line 1 + Line 2	81%	95%	93%	98%

TABLE 10.21   Survey Item G.2.

| SENSUALLY, I FEEL THAT SEX IS: | | | | | | | | |

	High School		Some College		College Grad		Postgrad	
	Men	Women	Men	Women	Men	Women	Men	Women
N =	641	690	320	334	203	205	147	150
1 Deliciously sensuous	64%	45%	63%	53%	53%	54%	72%	66%
2	24	29	32	42	41	38	26	31
3	11	22	4	4	4	7	1	3
4	1	3	1	1	2	1	1	0
5 Grossly distasteful	0	1	0	0	0	0	0	0
Line 1 + Line 2	88%	74%	95%	95%	94%	92%	98%	97%

Why would anyone, poorly educated or not, man or woman, find sex "distasteful"? Our interviews revealed that some less well-educated women found sex displeasing because of the lack of variety in their partners' perfunctory performances. Sex for them was not a shared experience by equal partners. Their partners' needs predominated, more often than not in the missionary position, and the mere repetition of the same act had gradually become boring.

For many people, sensuality and sexuality are closely connected. For others, sensuality and sexuality seem to be in a strange dynamic of trying to dissociate from one another. After exploring the issue of sensuality with our respondents, we tried to get from them an evaluation of their libido, their inner sexual drive, by asking them to rate themselves on their degree of sexuality. Their responses are shown in Table 10.22.

With the exception of the some college group, the men tended to rate themselves as very active or active more frequently than did the women. The largest differential was among the high school group. On the other hand, the women were willing to rate themselves as below average or inactive much more frequently than were the men. Being sexually aggressive, for men, and being sexually passive, for women, have been, traditionally, the approved stances, and we seemed to see here the expected male boasting about sexual prowess coupled with a "becoming" modesty on the part of the women. While men are permitted and encouraged to express themselves sexually, women have been taught that it is appropriate to restrain their sexual emotions and yearnings. In interviews, the women professed to be much more sexual and committed to the pursuit of personal sexual fulfillment than these numbers would suggest.

Numbers, we know, cannot tell the whole story. Many sexologists claim that relying on numbers to understand human sexuality is deceiving and

TABLE 10.22   Survey Item G.3.

I CONSIDER MYSELF TO BE SEXUALLY:								
	High School		Some College		College Grad		Postgrad	
	Men	Women	Men	Women	Men	Women	Men	Women
N =	640	686	320	336	203	203	149	151
Very active	18%	12%	20%	18%	25%	13%	20%	9%
Active	39	26	31	39	38	41	35	41
Average	30	34	35	21	31	26	34	27
Below average	6	15	10	17	5	15	8	18
Inactive	7	13	4	5	1	5	3	5
Very active + Active	57%	38%	51%	57%	63%	54%	55%	50%
Below average + Inactive	13%	28%	14%	22%	6%	20%	11%	23%

that the quality of the sexual experience and the sensuality factors associated with the sex act are crucial. Because our questionnaire responses were
supplemented by interview material, we have a greater sense of security in
relation to our analysis of what the response numbers reveal.

Education, particularly for women, made a real difference in perceptions of personal sexuality. Were the highly educated women who reported themselves as highly sensual and sexually active particularly
conditioned to enjoy sex because of their education? Probably not. But
what their education did do, and what the Second Sexual Revolution confirmed for them, was to encourage them to be aware of their sexuality
and permit them to develop their individual personae. Often, very different self-images emerged than had been encouraged by their families.
The liberating force of education can be seen at work in this process.

We had, so far, investigated individual self-ratings of sensuality and
sexuality in an abstract way. We next addressed a specific act of sexuality—masturbation—to see whether the incidence reported correlated in
any significant way with educational achievement. We chose to examine
masturbation because it is the most personal sex act, is usually the earliest performed, and is the most independent (of a partner). The criterion
we used to compare educational and gender differences was the person's
age at the first masturbatory experience.

Table 10.23 reveals the percentages of respondents in the two less educated groups who reported never having masturbated. A greater proportion occurred in these groups than in the two more educated groups.
Experimentation with masturbation, overall, tended to increase with increased education, so that, by the postgraduate level, only 1% of the men
and 2% of the women reported never having masturbated.

TABLE 10.23   **Survey Item H.16.**

AGE FIRST MASTURBATED:							

	High School		Some College		College Grad		Postgrad	
	Men	Women	Men	Women	Men	Women	Men	Women
N =	639	679	321	337	201	196	148	146
By age 10	20%	17%	20%	18%	20%	20%	14%	23%
Ages 11–13	64	31	37	22	51	24	51	15
Ages 14–16	7	20	27	19	19	15	23	13
Ages 17–21	2	9	8	17	6	23	7	25
Ages 22–30	1	5	1	8	0	8	2	17
Ages 31 and over	0	6	0	4	2	2	2	5
Never	6	12	7	12	2	8	1	2

By age 13, at least half the men in all groups had begun to masturbate; among the women, the highest percentage was among the high school group (48%) and the lowest, among the postgraduate group (38%). By age 16, most of the men had experimented with masturbation. This is not true of the women, of whom many more were added through age 21 and others continued to be added in significant numbers at older ages. This is particularly striking for postgraduate women, of whom 17% came to their first masturbatory experience between the ages of 22 and 30, and others reported not having masturbated until age 31 and beyond. Some experts feel that children who are being pressed to achieve academically defer biological gratification at a later age. This is not to suggest that they are not interested in sexual matters, but rather that they are distracted by other concerns and are less likely to experience peer pressure for precocious sex. On the other hand, we should note that the highest incidence of earliest onset of masturbation (23% by age 10) came from women in the postgraduate group. We found that it was not unusual for female respondents to list age 4 or 5 as their onset of masturbation—earlier than the males, who caught up and then surpassed the females in initial masturbatory activity by their early teens.

SUMMING UP

Educational achievement relates in many significant ways to sexual attitudes and behavior; grouped by education, our respondents reported very different sexual life-styles. The high school educated group, for instance, reported the earliest masturbatory experiences, and the females showed the least premarital contact. In addition, we learned from our interviews that, for many of the high school group, the male superior position for intercourse (the missionary position) was the single technique that was most employed, even though the high school educated males had expressed a need for sexual variety (see Table 10.12). The women in the high school group seemed, in our data, to be locked in a tiresome existence. One sees dramatic evidence in this chapter that the high school educated females consistently showed a greater lack of sexual development, of experience, and of sexual growth, compared to either the men in the high school group or the other women. Our image of the high school educated woman is that, compared to the other women, she feels the least sensual, is the least sexually active, has had the least premarital sexual experience, is the most passive, and has the least interest in professional attainment. She is also against (and fears) divorce, and she shows the least awareness of the sexual double standard.

Better educated groups seem to grow more slowly into their sexual roles, but they do this at a steady pace, with flexibility and a tendency toward more equality between men and women. These groups experiment with varied sex and, according to our interviews, they tend to continue sexual activity into an older age. Those with more education—most dramatically, the women in the postgraduate group—showed a greater ability to make choices and to enjoy a more varied diet of sexual experience. Because most of them have personal careers, they don't fear divorce; by putting their energies into their careers, they have less need of the family. They report much greater gratification in their sexuality, are aware of the sexual double standard, demand parity in initiating sex rather than playing the traditional passive female, have had the most premarital sexual experience, and report being the most sensual.

Numbers and frequency of sexual experiences tell only part of the story. Respondents in the college-educated groups stressed the emotional, sharing, and qualitative aspects of sexual fulfillment. Women in the more highly educated groups were more easily able to assert their sexual opinions and preferences and to maintain a greater sense of control over their sex lives.

Education tends to be a liberating force that enables people to evaluate the social and sexual values with which they were raised and to accept or reject them, as seems appropriate. Education provides the basis for making the choices that meet individual needs, avoiding mere conformance to social values. From many perspectives, the responses to the questions in our study demonstrated clear indications that an individual's sexuality was certainly influenced by the educational level he or she had achieved.

CHAPTER ELEVEN

Money, Power, and Sex

SOME SIGNIFICANT FINDINGS ABOUT MONEY, POWER, AND SEX

✦ 8% of mainstream, middle-income women reported having had sex for money, a higher percentage than either low- or upper-income women.

✦ Upper-income women reported having the most premarital sexual experience, compared to low- and middle-income women, but they also reported the lowest incidence of extramarital relations.

✦ Middle-income women had had less premarital sexual experience than either low- or high-income women.

✦ Middle-income men had had the highest incidence of extramarital affairs.

✦ 20% of all male respondents reported having had sex for money; the percentage was the same at the three income levels analyzed.

QUESTIONNAIRE SUBJECTS TABULATED IN THIS CHAPTER

	Table
The Importance of Love	11.1
Sexual Experience Before Marriage	11.2
Number of Sexual Partners	11.3
Marriage and Fulfillment	11.4
Extramarital Affairs	11.5, 11.6
One-Night Stands	11.7
Variety of Sex Techniques	11.8
Relationship with Spouse/Partner	11.9, 11.11
Initiation of Sexual Activity	11.10
Frequency of Sexual Activity	11.12
Self-Ratings of Sexual Activity	11.13
Sex Surrogates	11.14, 11.15
In-Vitro Fertilization	11.16
Abortion Frequency	11.17, 11.18
Sex for Money	11.19, 11.20

Power is fascinating and its expressions are intriguing. The public reads news stories and books and watches television productions and films about the rich and famous, vicariously experiencing some of their "good life." Later, most people put down the story or turn off their TV set feeling grateful that they do not have to suffer some of the penalties that power and money seem to carry with them. Most; not all. The rich and famous may be comparatively few in number, but those who wish to join their ranks represent a much larger population.

The question that is explored in this chapter is whether income level, that is, the availability of money, distinguishes attitudes toward sex and power. Our unexpected finding, for instance, that, in our sample of respondents, the proportion of middle-income women who had had sex for money was higher than in the other income groups, suggests a relationship between income level and standards of personal and social behavior.

Erik Erikson, the prominent psychologist, suggested that everyone lives with an internal image around which his or her conscious personality is organized. "Who am I? What am I? Where am I going?" The individual tests these questions against the internal image. They are the fundamental questions of ego-identity and they provide the sense of self that develops as all of us search for personal answers to who we are and what we are doing in this world. For most people, the self-image remains stable throughout life. Modifications occur as individuals go through the developmental stages from birth to death and undergo such transitions as marriage and parenthood, but, through it all, there remains a recognizable core of the "self." Part of the ego-identity is involved with expectations and experiences about financial status and is enhanced or suffers with the individual's success or failure to achieve and maintain a desired status.

PAYING THE POWER TAB

This chapter examines the varying experiences and views of the sexual world reported by our sample of respondents, differentiated by income and financial status. We believe that money is universally regarded as synonymous with power, and power may be a component of much sexual experience. A financial exchange is obviously involved in the buying and selling of sex in prostitution, but it is also present in the more subtle issues of the ability to attract sexual partners and to determine the type of frequency of sexual activity that will be performed. Our goal was to understand not only the observable sexual behavior associated with income level, but also the underlying inner views and moralities that may be associated with a differential access to money.

▶ *IN THEIR OWN WORDS* _____

> Let us not kid ourselves; it is an expensive deal to win and bed that gorgeous starlet type you happen to see in Maxim's. Fortunately, I have the money, and that becomes so attractive that they forget my age, and my potbelly. I often spend a lot of time and money flying with them first-class to Las Vegas. When we get there, I arrange a deluxe suite that sets me back up to $1,000 a night. Then she has to have money to lose on gambling, right? How about breakfast in bed and the largest bottle of Chanel #5 you have ever seen, just waiting to be unwrapped in the room? Flowers, forget it! The room looks like a florist shop. If it happens to be winter in New York, the poor thing needs a new fur coat. By this time she loves me and wants to marry me. But all I want is great sex and good companionship. I have had very few gorgeous young women ever turn me down, and they have to be gorgeous, or I'm not at all interested. You'd be surprised at how quickly they accept this, as long as the gifts keep coming.

Customarily, the man pays to finance a sexual affair. Although direct payment for sex may be absent, the gifts, dinners, furs, vacations, and other tangible signs of affection can add up to a lot of money. Men who want to be sexually successful without pretending to be establishing significant emotional relationships recognize the commercialization of their courtships.

People may dream of being rich and powerful, but the two may not always go together. Sexual power is something special and comes with its own strings attached. It is often used as a substitute power, to compensate for those situations in life over which people have no control. The practice of sex is costly, but, for those who have the money, it is an outlet for their frustration in other areas.

We were interested in exploring whether, in the sexual practices of Americans, there were variations related to income. Five income levels were listed in our questionnaire: $20,000, $30,000, $50,000, $70,000, and $100,000. We chose the first, third, and fifth—approximately $20,000, $50,000 and $100,000—to represent three distinct groups of people. We left out the two intervening levels, to avoid overlapping the groups. In this way, we knew that we had three groups that were totally independent. The numbers of our respondents in the original groups were as follows:

$20,000		$30,000		$50,000		$70,000		$100,000	
Men	Women	Men	Women	Men	Women	Men	Women	Men	Women
336	358	385	444	265	253	200	227	147	122

The incomes are not absolute, nor do they reveal the same facts in each case. For example, a single person earning $20,000 can live much more luxuriously than can a family of four on the same income. We must also remember that most Americans believe themselves to be "middle-class," regardless of what they earn, and that definitions of class involve many criteria other than income. However, access to money still makes a difference in how one lives and what one can buy in terms of sex as well as other commodities. This chapter will explore what those similarities and differences are; instead of middle-class, we prefer to use the term middle-income.

"Love makes the world go around," we have been told. We wanted to know whether that belief was shared by respondents in our three income levels. It is possible, after all, that money could compensate for love. How people evaluate their need for love can reveal valuable information about individuals and where they perceive they are in the world. We asked our respondents how important love was to them, and got the answers shown in Table 11.1.

Love's magic came through loud and clear in the respondents' remarkable agreement that love is important in life. In the lower- and middle-income levels, both the men and the women appeared nearly identical in their assessment of love as very important and important. The upper-income level revealed some interesting differences between the sexes. Of all the groups, more upper-income women (91%) and more upper-income men (76%) said love was very important. Still, one wonders about the quality of relationships among the affluent, when there is such a disparity between the proportions of men and women who rate love as very important in their lives.

TABLE 11.1   **Survey Item B.4.**

HOW IMPORTANT IS LOVE TO YOU?						
	$20,000		$50,000		$100,000	
	Men	Women	Men	Women	Men	Women
N =	335	357	261	251	145	120
Very important	70%	81%	74%	84%	76%	91%
Important	27	16	22	12	19	8
Not sure	2	2	3	2	2	1
Unimportant	0	1	1	1	2	0
Very unimportant	1	0	0	1	1	0
Very important + Important	97%	97%	96%	96%	95%	99%

Authors' note: The $30,000 and $70,000 income groups in our questionnaire (see Appendix B) are not included in the tables in this chapter.

SEX AND MARRIAGE

A comparison of our three income groups on the issues of premarital sex and chastity produced some interesting results. A qualification must be kept in mind, however: an individual's income level now might not reflect what his or her income level was during the period before marriage. Insofar as earnings increase, up to a point, with age, this statement may be generally valid for all respondents surveyed. The qualification might be even more pertinent to the women in our sample, whose financial status as married women depends to some degree on their husbands' earnings, and whose status might be significantly affected by divorce or widowhood.

As shown in Table 11.2, among our three groups, those in the middle-income ($50,000) category showed the lowest incidence of premarital sex, compared to those in either the higher or lower income group. This difference is particularly striking among the women in the $50,000 group, who reported the lowest incidence of premarital sex among any of the divisions, with one-fifth reporting no premarital sex. The conservatism that this number reflects corresponds to what we think of as "middle-class values," a term that connotes an adherence to traditional morality. This is the group that has the greatest investment in conformity and acceptability and is willing to suppress personal desire when it conflicts with social mores.

Affluence appears to make a difference in structuring an ethic that allows greater personal decision making in premarital sexual activity for both sexes. Among our respondents, the highest incidence of premarital sexual activity for all groups was among the most affluent men. The most affluent women reported an incidence of premarital

TABLE 11.2   **Survey Item D.10.**

I HAD SEXUAL EXPERIENCE BEFORE MARRIAGE:					
	$20,000		$50,000		$100,000	
	Men	Women	Men	Women	Men	Women
N =	335	354	262	249	145	119
Very much	36%	25%	34%	22%	35%	39%
Much	34	28	32	25	39	27
Little	15	20	16	24	19	11
Very little	6	10	6	9	3	11
None	9	17	12	20	4	12
Very much + Much	70%	53%	66%	47%	74%	66%
Little + Very little	21%	30%	22%	33%	22%	22%

sexual experience identical to that of middle-income men and just slightly less than the incidence among lower-income men. Our interviews confirmed the impression of greater freedom among the more affluent, and we observed a more free-flowing and less anxious attitude about sexual experience in this group than we did in either of the others.

The results of our investigation of premarital sexual experience suggested a great deal about changes in contemporary society. Traditional morality dictated female chastity as a nonnegotiable demand, and the middle-income people we surveyed observed this tradition slightly more than the other groups. The more laissez-faire morality of the wealthy often includes the ability to pay their way out of "mistakes." Lower-income people, for a variety of reasons, including less expectation of upward mobility and a recognition of the behavioral flexibility needed for survival, have frequently been more tolerant of "mistakes," even when the behavior is not condoned. Although the middle-income group remains the most conservative in premarital sex compared to the other groups, still, almost four-fifths of the middle-income women had had some premarital sexual experience—a far cry from earlier expectations of nonnegotiable chastity.

How much actual sexual experience had these respondents had? How much is very much, or very little? To complete the picture, we next researched the actual numbers of sex partners, as shown in Table 11.3.

The men outnumbered the women in every category, regarding having had many partners (61 and over); interestingly, they were least diverse in the $50,000 category. This seems to faintly echo the "middle-class values" that dictate restraint in sex. The men in the $20,000 and $100,000 groups far exceeded the "middle men." Women had a substantial representation in the 1-to-30-partners category and, as a sign of the times, roughly 10%

TABLE 11.3   Survey Item G.7.

HOW MANY DIFFERENT INDIVIDUALS (INCLUDING SPOUSES) HAVE YOU HAD SEXUAL RELATIONS WITH?						
	\$20,000		\$50,000		\$100,000	
	Men	Women	Men	Women	Men	Women
N =	333	352	263	247	143	112
None	0%	3%	1%	4%	0%	2%
1–10	22	34	33	49	25	44
11–30	36	46	31	30	26	38
31–60	21	10	24	10	26	9
61–100	7	4	7	4	12	1
101 +	14	3	4	3	11	6
1–30	58%	80%	64%	79%	51%	82%
61 and over	21%	7%	11%	7%	23%	7%

also reported 31 to 60 partners. Elsewhere in this chapter we note that the men in the \$20,000 category also have many sexual exploits they pay for, but these interactions are shorter lived than those of the \$100,000 group. Sex is expensive, and it is a fair assumption that some of the larger numbers reported by men are for prostitutes. Table 11.19 shows far greater activity in the often category by men in the two higher income groups.

Most people marry, and we can assume that they do so because they expect to find a fulfillment in their lives that is not offered outside of marriage. In the current popular stereotypes, the successful career woman, no matter how affluent, has sacrificed real happiness for unfulfilling success; and the bachelor living a free-wheeling life is harboring an unsatisfied desire to be immersed in domestic bliss. Putting aside these media-generated characterizations, we know that the factors that determine personal fulfillment in marriage vary greatly. They depend on the individuals involved and on the circumstances, including, in large measure, the financial circumstances of the marriage. With 76% of married women working outside of the home, the traditional notion of the husband as provider and the wife as dependent has lost a great deal of its power. Women have become increasingly able to imagine themselves self-supporting. We wondered whether our respondents' perceptions of marriage as necessary to personal fulfillment corresponded to differences in their access to wealth. Table 11.4 shows their replies.

Our respondents, in overwhelming numbers and across all income levels, strongly disagreed with the proposition that marriage is a necessary condition for personal fulfillment. The differences among groups and between men and women within groups are worth noting. There was

TABLE 11.4   **Survey Item A.6.**

TO BE TRULY FULFILLED, ONE MUST BE MARRIED:					
	$20,000		$50,000		$100,000	
	Men	Women	Men	Women	Men	Women
N =	331	353	261	249	144	119
Strongly agree	2%	2%	4%	4%	6%	6%
Agree	13	9	17	7	13	14
No opinion	10	6	10	5	17	13
Disagree	57	55	50	62	55	51
Strongly disagree	18	28	19	22	9	16
Strongly agree + Agree	15%	11%	21%	11%	19%	20%
Disagree + Strongly disagree	75%	83%	69%	84%	64%	67%

little difference between affluent men's and women's perceptions of personal fulfillment through marriage. Overall, a smaller proportion agreed that marriage was a necessary condition, but there was close agreement between the sexes. A much larger proportion perceived marriage as unnecessary for fulfillment, but, here again, the difference between the sexes was small. This group had the highest percentages, for both sexes, of no opinion responses. When we compared affluent women with lower- and middle-income women, we found that a much higher proportion of affluent women saw marriage as a positive condition of their lives. This difference would suggest that, for some of these women, marriage to a man with a larger income had contributed to a life-style that would not have been possible without that income.

The responses of men in the lower- and middle-income brackets varied significantly. The lower-income men viewed marriage as less fulfilling than those in the middle-income level did. Were some of them possibly reflecting the strain and frustration resulting from their efforts to be good providers? The responses of the women in these two categories were virtually identical; few of them saw marriage as essential to fulfillment. Marriage remains a social necessity, but it is obviously not unanimously viewed as satisfying personal needs. To many respondents, it seems, other paths to fulfillment were of equal value.

EXTRAMARITAL AFFAIRS

Because sex outside of marriage invariably carries some financial obligations, wouldn't the more affluent seem likely to have more extramarital affairs than those with lower incomes? Table 11.5 reveals the results of our examination of that assumption.

TABLE 11.5   **Survey Item D.5.**

I'VE HAD EXTRAMARITAL AFFAIRS:						
	$20,000		$50,000		$100,000	
	Men	Women	Men	Women	Men	Women
N =	223	228	183	173	110	99
Never	60%	67%	58%	72%	64%	84%
Only once	12	10	7	8	5	8
Rarely	20	15	12	12	16	5
Often	6	5	21	6	13	2
Ongoing	2	3	2	2	2	1
Often + Ongoing	8%	8%	23%	8%	15%	3%

With the exception of the lowest income group, the men surveyed reported considerably more often and ongoing extramarital affairs than did the women. Comparison of the middle- and upper-income groups revealed, however, that the men with middle income reported the higher frequency. Surprisingly, more of the highest income men, who can be assumed to have the ability to afford sex outside of marriage, reported never engaging in extramarital sex. Were they involved in a satisfying marriage in which financial pressures were relatively absent? What is the connection to our findings, in Table 11.2, that a much greater incidence of premarital sexual experience existed among the upper-income women than among other groups and, consequently, that these wives might be providing to their husbands the sexual satisfaction for which middle-income husbands looked elsewhere? Lower-income men reported a relatively high incidence of extensive premarital sex (70%), but they had the lowest incidence of often and ongoing affairs. Considering that extramarital affairs are frequently financially costly, we should not be surprised that economically marginal people might regard them as luxuries they cannot afford.

An interesting, and perhaps unexpected, picture of upper-income women had begun to emerge from our data. Of all the women in the three income groups, they came into marriage the most sexually experienced, having had the most reported premarital sex activities, but they had the highest commitment to romantic love and fidelity. Ninety-nine percent of them believed love in marriage to be important, and they registered the highest agreement and lowest disagreement that personal fulfillment could be found in marriage. In addition, they exhibited the lowest frequency of extramarital affairs. The emerging impression was that upper-income women were the most satisfied with married life and that their access to money and to the privileges that money confers may have been playing some significant part in their satisfaction.

By contrast, middle-income women, who reported the least premarital sexual experience, had a much higher rate of extramarital affairs than upper-income women did. Did these women who had had limited premarital sexual experience feel the need to expand their experience after marriage?

Women may not engage in extramarital affairs in overwhelming numbers, but our interviews revealed that women are quite open about their fantasies. "Well, if [fill in your personal choice] were interested, I certainly wouldn't turn him down." There was expressed interest in the possibility of a sexual involvement with male friends.

Even where no extramarital affair had been reported, intrigue and interest were widespread on the part of the men and women we interviewed. Both frequently attributed their nonengagement to factors such as lack of appropriate circumstances or availability of time. Their apparent need to apologize for not having an affair, as if recognizing that they were out of step with the times, reflected a real shift in attitudes toward marriage and toward the threat that extramarital affairs pose to that institution. This seemed a likely conclusion, but we decided to test it against our survey data. (See Table 11.6.)

Our survey demonstrated that, when our respondents, across all income ranges, were directly questioned about the effect of extramarital affairs, there was a high rate of agreement on the threat that such affairs pose to a marriage. The men saw a lesser threat than did the women, but men indulge in extramarital affairs more frequently than do women and are more likely to trivialize the experience than are the women who see their marriages threatened. Middle-income men, who, we found, had the greatest incidence of sex outside of marriage, reported the highest rate of agreement with the statement, but were

TABLE 11.6   **Survey Item C.2.**

EXTRAMARITAL AFFAIRS DO NOT SERIOUSLY AFFECT MARRIAGES:					
	$20,000		$50,000		$100,000	
	Men	Women	Men	Women	Men	Women
N =	330	352	261	250	144	119
Strongly agree	2%	3%	3%	4%	4%	2%
Agree	9	7	14	6	7	5
No opinion	9	3	4	2	13	6
Disagree	50	38	44	37	32	33
Strongly disagree	30	49	35	51	44	54
Strongly agree + Agree	11%	10%	17%	10%	11%	7%
Disagree + Strongly disagree	80%	87%	79%	88%	76%	87%

virtually indistinguishable from the other two groups on their rate of disagreement. Upper-income men revealed an interesting situation of uncertainty. They didn't agree with the statement but they exhibited the lowest rate of disagreement. In relatively large numbers, they didn't know how they felt about it. Upper-income women did have an opinion; of all the groups, they revealed themselves as most seriously alarmed by an extramarital affair. They had the highest incidence of strong disagreement with the statement.

Affairs suggest involvement that might distract from the primary commitment of the marriage. But what about more casual sex, the pick-up kind, the quick encounter at a convention or in a bar. We were curious about whether a one-night stand would be perceived in the same way as an affair. We injected the strongly connotative work degrading, to try to probe underlying moral attitudes among our respondents. (See Table 11.7.)

The results of this survey item revealed some sharp differences in response by sex and income level—differences that fit with responses to other questions. Middle-income men, who, we saw before, had the greatest incidence of extramarital sex, reported themselves significantly less offended by the one-night stand than did the other two groups. The middle-income women surveyed took quite the opposite stand, indicating the most strongly held opinions on the subject. By contrast, most upper-income men and women closely shared opinions on this subject. The differences among the men in the three income groups are striking; the upper-income men (59%) led those who felt the experience was degrading. Among the categories of women, the upper-income women saw the one-night stand as least degrading. The lower-income group voted between the other two, with less agreement on the subject than the upper-income group and more than the middle-income group. It is

TABLE 11.7   **Survey Item C.3.**

I FIND ONE-NIGHT STANDS TO BE DEGRADING:					
	\$20,000		\$50,000		\$100,000
	Men	Women	Men	Women	Men	Women
N =	333	355	262	248	144	118
Strongly agree	20%	36%	12%	42%	16%	30%
Agree	29	33	27	27	43	37
No opinion	20	14	28	12	15	17
Disagree	27	13	26	13	22	13
Strongly disagree	4	4	7	6	4	3
Strongly agree + Agree	49%	69%	39%	69%	59%	67%
Disagree + Strongly disagree	31%	17%	33%	19%	26%	16%

interesting to note, however, that the middle-income men were the most ambivalent on this question. They exhibited the smallest difference between agreement and disagreement and the largest percentage of undecided.

SEX PRACTICES

We wished to know what the level of interest in sexual practices was for our respondents on different income levels, and we posed several survey items that were relevant. This section presents the data gathered on sex practices, sorted for men and women in the three income groups we selected.

On the issue of variety in sex techniques, Table 11.8 shows pretty consistent division across the income levels by sex, with men preferring more variety in sexual techniques and women, less. Upper-income men again stood out as being the least concerned about techniques of sex, but their response was colored by the high number who reported having no opinion on the subject. Upper-income women, while not strikingly different from the other women, tended to disagree (49%) that variety in sexual techniques is necessary. In the middle-income group, the greatest disparity was between the opinions of men and women. We could only speculate on whether this disparity was related to middle-income women's comparatively limited premarital sexual experience, indicated in Table 11.2.

Where variety in sexual techniques was considered important, one would expect that these respondents would want a sex partner who is a good lover. Historically, this has been an area in which men have long

TABLE 11.8   **Survey Item C.7.**

A LARGE VARIETY OF SEX TECHNIQUES IS A MUST FOR MAXIMUM PLEASURE:					
	$20,000		$50,000		$100,000	
	Men	Women	Men	Women	Men	Women
N =	333	352	263	249	143	119
Strongly agree	17%	10%	11%	8%	15%	8%
Agree	36	29	41	27	33	30
No opinion	13	15	11	17	20	13
Disagree	30	39	33	35	27	42
Strongly disagree	4	7	4	13	5	7
Strongly agree + Agree	53%	39%	52%	35%	48%	38%
Disagree + Strongly disagree	34%	46%	37%	48%	32%	49%

felt they dominated. In the popular stereotype, men have been the experts in sex, the teachers of their inexperienced female partners. We were interested in how demanding our respondents were of their partners, male and female, so we asked them directly. Their responses, gathered by income level, are given in Table 11.9.

We had phrased this questionnaire statement with the imperative must, to suggest something more than a preference, which we assumed would have been expressed by most of the respondents. Only two majority percentages were tallied (51% and 57%, for the two lower-income groups of men, both in disagreement with the statement) and more respondents disagreed than agreed with the need to have an excellent lover as a partner.

Although the upper-income men were almost evenly divided in their opinion, as the men's incomes rose, so did their demand that their partners be excellent lovers. Alongside the indication in Table 11.5, that 64% of married men in the upper-income group had never had extramarital affairs, we wondered whether we had unearthed a description of the wives in these upper-income marriages.

The upper-income group is the only one of the three in which the men were more demanding than the women; the women in the three income brackets corresponded rather closely in their agreement and their disagreement. Lower-income men were significantly less invested in sexual excellence on the part of their partners; a lack of opinion was expressed by almost 20% of them. Middle-income men, who had the smallest proportion of no opinion responses, reported the greatest lack of concern with sexual excellence (57%).

That lower-income men agreed least that their partners must display sexual excellence may have been a reflection of the traditional male

TABLE 11.9   **Survey Item C.10.**

MY SEX PARTNER MUST BE AN EXCELLENT LOVER:						
	$20,000		$50,000		$100,000	
	Men	Women	Men	Women	Men	Women
N =	332	351	263	248	143	118
Strongly agree	6%	7%	10%	6%	10%	9%
Agree	25	29	25	34	33	29
No opinion	18	15	8	12	13	13
Disagree	46	46	54	40	42	46
Strongly disagree	5	3	3	8	2	3
Strongly agree + Agree	31%	36%	35%	40%	43%	38%
Disagree + Strongly disagree	51%	49%	57%	48%	44%	49%

macho attitude, which dictated that a man must perform while his woman was only a passive recipient who responded to his dominance.

We learned in our interviews that some high-income women, who had no husband or live-in partner, were not hesitant to pick up the tab for excellent sex. Generally, they formed an ongoing relationship with a man from a lower-income bracket, introduced him to social and cultural activities that he could not afford on his income, and gave him generous gifts. The man had to be attractive, younger, and, most important, a satisfying lover.

◆ *IN THEIR OWN WORDS* _____

It's not easy finding men with much life in them if I were to look for "appropriate" men. How many men in their late 50s and 60s still have the energy to party all night, come back and make passionate love the rest of the night? Well, I will tell you: too few. So I date younger men. Sometimes, even with a younger man, you pick a klunker and you feel so stupid about it. Why do men have such fragile egos?

I had been seeing this college professor. He was a great lover—tender, sensitive, and passionate. He was also younger than me. Brad was 34, and still looked boyish, which I love. We had been going together for about two years. The major problem was that of most professors—he didn't earn much money. Yet we both loved the theater. He was trying to make his money last, so I had to settle for the third balcony when we would go to the theater, and eating in greasy spoon restaurants after the theater or concert. He was always paying for things, and I could see that he didn't have much, and that it kind of hurt him to spend much. One day I said to myself, "You're liberated. Why can't you take him out? You make at least twice as much as Brad." Well, I thought this was a terrific idea. I don't at all mind spending my money for pleasure. So I bought three pairs of theater tickets for each of the next three months. Then I told him, and he exploded. Now, I believe in honesty, so I presented this great surprise to him as follows; I said, "Brad, I know how much you earn, and I know how much I earn, and I make a great deal more than you. You are a great lover, I enjoy you thoroughly and you're terrific in many ways. But I don't really like sitting in the third balcony when we go to the theater, and I would prefer to go to elegant restaurants rather than the greasy spoons we've eaten in. I have no problem about paying for things that I like, and I just bought tickets in the fifth row center for three shows over the next three months," and I ticked off the names of the shows. I thought he would be delighted, but you won't believe what this schmuck did. He called me a "castrating bitch" and said he didn't want to see me anymore and walked out. What did I do wrong?

—A 39-year-old corporate executive

This complainant went too far in flexing her fiscal muscle. Sensitivity in this area is still important when the woman is dominant.

Although greater numbers of both men and women reported themselves less rather than more concerned with their partner's sexual excellence, the percentages of those who were willing to express their demands seem to reflect an increasing openness and assertiveness. Gratification has come to be an end in itself, and sex is seen as an appropriate pleasurable experience.

With assertiveness surfacing in both men and women, we wondered how aggressive our respondents were prepared to be in initiating sexual activity. Table 11.10 gave some definitive answers.

Most men preferred that they, and not their sex partners, initiate sexual activity, but in the lower- and upper-income groups, the women were far more assertive about their wish to be initiators. The numbers of men who showed a more passive, possibly demanding role are revealing. Passivity among the men increased as their incomes rose, but women displayed almost the same proportion of agreement at all income levels. Some respondents we interviewed described a subtle demand: they were expected to know intuitively what their sex partners wanted, and when. The dominant male figure seems to be disappearing. About 20% of male respondents showed willingness, perhaps even eagerness, in requesting that their sex partners get things going.

Neither sex was prepared to be passive all the time, but middle-income men expressed more of a demand that their partner initiate than did the other groups. Many men wanted assertive sex partners, and the women wanted to be able to be assertive some of the time. The no opinion responses among the lower-income group were particularly interesting

TABLE 11.10   **Survey Item D.4.**

I ALWAYS PREFER THAT MY SEX PARTNER INITIATE SEXUAL ACTIVITY:						
	$20,000		$50,000		$100,000	
	Men	Women	Men	Women	Men	Women
N =	332	353	261	249	143	120
Strongly agree	2%	3%	3%	4%	3%	6%
Agree	15	23	16	24	22	21
No opinion	30	6	21	12	20	7
Disagree	49	61	54	52	49	62
Strongly disagree	4	7	6	8	6	4
Strongly agree + Agree	17%	26%	19%	28%	25%	27%
Disagree + Strongly disagree	53%	68%	60%	60%	55%	66%

because of the highest rate (30%) among the men and the lowest rate (6%) among the women. The lower-income women had a strong preference (68%) to be active in initiating sex. Similarly, for the middle- and upper-income groups, the men were more reluctant to express an opinion—or, perhaps, had no opinion—than were the women. Responses to this survey item showed the effect of liberated sex on women. They are no longer followers, locked into silence and passivity regarding their sexual preferences.

The obvious assertiveness and liberation that the women exhibited in their responses, as well as the congruent responses of men and women, revealed what appeared to be improved overall physical communication between the sexes. If that were so, we felt that another statement should be evaluated by those who were married or living with a partner—a statement about the emotional nature of their relationships. (See Table 11.11.)

Both sexes were in overwhelming agreement about friendship being intrinsic to their relationships. Their congruity in expression of caring for a spouse/partner told us a great deal about trust, caring, and gratification in their lives and in the sexual intimacy of their relationships.

The slight differences between men and women are interesting. The upper-class women overwhelmingly declared their mates to be their best friends, and this rating corresponded to our earlier observation that these women were the most invested in romantic love and fidelity (Tables 11.1 and 11.5). The lower-income women, on the other hand, were significantly less invested in their husbands as friends. This does not suggest that they were not invested in their husbands; rather, these women may have understood friendship as something one has with a mother, or sisters, or other women, and not a relationship between a husband and wife.

Let us now turn to the topic of the frequency of sexual relations. Stereotypically, men have been portrayed as always wanting more sex than their reluctant partners desire, and women, as warding off the sexual advances of men with excuses about headaches or the need to shampoo their hair. To test whether this stereotype currently applied, we asked our respondents about the frequency of all of their sexual activities. The responses according to income groups are shown in Table 11.12.

TABLE 11.11   **Survey Item E.1.**

MY SPOUSE/PARTNER IS ALSO MY BEST FRIEND:						
	$20,000		$50,000		$100,000	
	Men	Women	Men	Women	Men	Women
N =	192	205	151	144	85	70
Yes	86%	77%	84%	83%	88%	94%
No	14%	23%	16%	17%	12%	6%

TABLE 11.12   **Survey Item G.6.**

FREQUENCY OF ALL SEXUAL ACTIVITY IS:						
	$20,000		$50,000		$100,000	
	Men	Women	Men	Women	Men	Women
N =	334	351	261	248	142	120
Daily	20%	11%	12%	8%	7%	16%
Few times weekly	45	40	36	35	53	33
Weekly	18	20	30	30	18	29
Monthly	9	6	12	14	15	9
Rarely	8	23	10	13	7	13
Daily + Few times weekly	65%	51%	48%	43%	60%	49%

What was particularly striking in the table was the difference between men and women who reported daily activity. These people obviously could not be having sex with each other. The difference (9%) between men and women in the lower-income daily group matched the difference in the upper-income daily group, but the sexes were reversed: the lower-income men reported a 20% daily frequency and the upper-income women, 16%. By surprising contrast, the upper-income men reported the lowest daily frequency (7%), but had the highest rating, in all groups (53%), for a few times weekly. Did what seemed like a few times weekly to the men feel like daily to the women, or, because the survey item asked about ALL sexual activity, was masturbation a factor in the varying percentages?

The lowest income group, both men and women, reported the highest frequency. Was this because the lowest income group was likely to have a greater number of young people who had not yet reached their peak earning years? Were these respondents more prone to bragging (possibly compensatory bragging)? Or, as some sociologists suggest, because of this group's limited financial resources and fewer entertainment options, were they more frequently resorting to low-cost enjoyment—sex? Further research is needed to clarify the exact sources of the answers.

We had included an item in our questionnaire that asked our respondents to assess their own subjective sense of whether their sex practices were "normal." Many respondents indicated in their interviews that they were still anxious about the "normalcy" of their sex practices.

As indicated in Table 11.13, the responses of the men and women showed great congruity for all income groups; the vast majority of respondents rated themselves as normal. The standards used for these self-evaluations were not revealed, and we cannot know whether they included access to greater information or a sense of the self as a trend

TABLE 11.13   **Survey Item H.23.**

I REGARD MY SEX PRACTICES AS:						
	$20,000		$50,000		$100,000	
	Men	Women	Men	Women	Men	Women
N =	334	352	262	248	143	119
Completely normal	57%	56%	52%	59%	60%	70%
Normal	38	40	43	34	32	26
Slightly odd	4	3	3	6	4	3
Unusual	1	1	1	1	3	0
Kinky	0	0	1	0	1	1
Completely normal + Normal	95%	96%	95%	93%	92%	96%

setter. A subjective sense of normalcy is a rather intense feeling, and, much as individuals may feel that they are not truly normal, the denial process is so forbidding that it makes them take the best possible view of themselves. In this regard, responses to practicing kinky sex were elicited from only 1% of respondents in three categories. This incidence increased slightly for the rating of unusual, with a noteworthy 3% of upper-income men responding, and for slightly odd, with divergent responses. Surprisingly, 6% of the middle-income women saw themselves as slightly odd.

SEX SURROGATES

We were interested in gathering information on the general category of sex for money. Prostitution is the first thing that comes to mind, but there is another sexual service for money that is not regarded as prostitution. Masters and Johnson[1] had developed the concept of the sex surrogate as a therapeutic technique; it was initially very popular but subsequently generated controversy, litigations, and, supposedly, some divorces. Unlike the surrogate mother, who will, for a fee, bear a child for a family, the sex surrogate works with a couple to help them overcome their sexual performance difficulties. Because Masters and Johnson used only female surrogates, many felt that it was not fair to have someone to pleasure only the husband. Others complained that a surrogate who is having sex with the husband, even though it is for therapeutic purposes, is doing exactly what a prostitute does. In fact, several call girls whom we interviewed also worked as sex surrogates. The women we interviewed who were only sex surrogates, and not prostitutes, vehemently rejected the idea that what they did resembled

prostitution. These women all insisted that they were healers, therapists, and professionals.

Our survey revealed some interesting opinions on this subject. For example, Table 11.14 shows that there was more acceptance of sex surrogates (as being different from prostitutes) by those earning $100,000 than
by those in the lower two income groups. However, all groups and both
sexes agreed, to a remarkable degree, on the legitimacy of the sex surrogacy therapy. The fewest no opinion responses appeared in the upper-
income group. Had this group had greater personal experience with
therapies in general, reflecting their ability to better afford such therapies, or did they have a greater degree of education on the subject?

Surrogate motherhood aroused considerable controversy in the United
States in the 1980s. As a result of the legal problems and ethical issues
raised in recent court cases, 17 states have banned surrogacy, and several
others have indicated interest in either regulating surrogacy or making it
illegal. Millions of Americans with fertility problems have found hope
for childbearing in recently developed medical procedures, including
surrogacy. Following the signing of a contract that specifies fees and
obligations, the surrogate is inseminated with the sperm of the husband
of the infertile couple. At the birth of the baby, the surrogate mother,
according to contract, surrenders her rights to the infant, and the previously childless couple become parents. Because this procedure can entail
fees ranging from $10,000 to $40,000, or even more, including legal and
medical expenses, this is not an option for all income classes. Table 11.15
reflects the various views of our three economic groups to the place of
surrogacy in fertility planning.

It is not unexpected that the people who have the highest rate of acceptance of this expensive option are the people best able to afford it.

TABLE 11.14   **Survey Item A.9.**

SEX SURROGATES ARE THE SAME AS PROSTITUTES:						
	$20,000		$50,000		$100,000	
	Men	Women	Men	Women	Men	Women
N =	328	349	259	245	145	119
Strongly agree	4%	2%	7%	3%	3%	2%
Agree	10	6	5	8	5	11
No opinion	19	25	22	26	15	15
Disagree	45	40	31	37	53	46
Strongly disagree	22	27	35	26	24	26
Strongly agree + Agree	14%	8%	12%	11%	8%	13%
Disagree + Strongly disagree	67%	67%	66%	63%	77%	72%

TABLE 11.15   Survey Item A.4.

SURROGATE MOTHERS HAVE A DEFINITE ROLE IN AMERICAN FAMILY PLANNING:						

	$20,000		$50,000		$100,000	
	Men	Women	Men	Women	Men	Women
N =	328	349	258	246	145	118
Strongly agree	9%	5%	4%	5%	8%	4%
Agree	25	33	31	32	40	37
No opinion	32	24	38	30	25	28
Disagree	21	31	21	22	15	21
Strongly disagree	13	7	6	11	12	10
Strongly agree + Agree	34%	38%	35%	37%	48%	41%
Disagree + Strongly disagree	34%	38%	27%	33%	27%	31%

Between upper-income men and women, the higher acceptance by men may reflect the fact that the child that is produced will be biologically related to the father. In the lowest income group, both sexes rejected surrogacy, but they would be most unlikely to be able to consider it as an option. In these results, what may be most interesting is how many people were unwilling or unable to express an opinion on the subject. The publicity surrounding some of the litigation has undoubtedly left many people confused about how they stand on the issue.

Surrogacy is the most dramatic of the techniques currently addressing the painful problem of the inability to conceive and/or bear a child. Problems seem to be intensifying as women postpone childbearing until late into their 30s and as sexually transmitted diseases proliferate. One of the most successful of new techniques is that of in-vitro fertilization (IVF). In contrast to a natural pregnancy, in which the egg is fertilized by the sperm within the body of the mother (in-vivo fertilization), in-vitro fertilization takes place outside the body, in a test tube, where an egg removed from the woman is fertilized by the sperm donated by the man and then implanted in the mother's uterus. We were interested in whether the acceptance of this procedure as an option, in cases of infertility, would vary according to economic status. (See Table 11.16.)

With the exception of lower-income men, some of whom found the procedure problematic (21%) or even sinful (6%), there was widespread acceptance of IVF among all groups. Middle-income women were mildly enthusiastic; 70% of the men felt it was beneficial. The greatest acceptance was among the upper-income group, for both sexes. It is likely that the same financial and informational considerations suggested for surrogacy might be relevant here. Most respondents appeared to have accepted the legitimacy of this technique and were willing to let science

TABLE 11.16   **Survey Item G.9.**

IN-VITRO FERTILIZATION AND TECHNIQUES LIKE IT ARE:						
	$20,000		$50,000		$100,000	
	Men	Women	Men	Women	Men	Women
N =	319	341	257	244	140	117
Vital	11%	14%	12%	21%	23%	30%
Beneficial	62	68	70	57	63	54
Problematic	21	18	17	19	11	14
Sinful	6	0	1	3	3	2

help where nature had failed. Some men, particularly those whose egos are vulnerable because of a lack of financial achievement, may see IVF as an assault on their masculine power in the process of pregnancy.

ABORTION

Many couples and individuals struggle to have babies and go through extensive fertility workups; others are not ready for parenthood. The pregnancy may be at the wrong time, or with the wrong man, or a danger to the mother's health. Some of these people have abortions. Table 11.17 shows how many respondents in each income group had had abortions, and Table 11.18 indicates how many abortions they had had.

Abortions seemed to be an equal-opportunity option for all groups, although more upper-income women had had one abortion, compared to the other groups. One cannot help but wonder how the new restrictive laws on abortion, passed by some states in 1991 and 1992, will affect its availability to all income groups. Those in the upper-income brackets never had a problem finding a physician to perform an abortion, but those with low incomes are at the mercy of public clinics, which the

TABLE 11.17   **Survey Item H.24.**

I HAVE HAD AN ABORTION:			
	$20,000	$50,000	$100,000
N =	362	256	123
Yes	23%	27%	30%
No	73	69	64
No answer	4	4	6

TABLE 11.18   Survey Item H.24.

I HAVE HAD AN ABORTION: YES RESPONSES: NUMBER OF ABORTIONS:		
	$20,000	$50,000	$100,000
N =	82	69	37
1 abortion	68%	60%	70%
2 abortions	17	22	19
3 or more	15	18	11

federal government has increasingly restricted in the past several years. A demonstration, acknowledged to be the largest ever, with between 500,000 and 700,000 people, was held in Washington, DC, on April 5, 1992, in the hope of saving *Roe v. Wade* from reversal in some imminent decisions by the Supreme Court.

The women in the $50,000 income group reported the highest number of repeat abortions. Some observers will argue that effective contraception is readily available and that there should not be a need for abortions. However, unwanted pregnancies do occur, in large numbers, and the availability of abortion to terminate those pregnancies is a major issue today.

PROSTITUTION

In this chapter, in which we are considering the relation of income to sexual behavior, we have until this point not touched on the most obvious connection between money and sex—prostitution. Our working definition of prostitution comes from Samuel Janus's and Barbara Bess's contribution to *The Sexual Experience*.[2] "Prostitution," they wrote, "may be defined as the granting of nonmarital access established by mutual agreement of the woman and her client for remuneration that provides part or all of her livelihood." Prostitution is different from other trades in that it is not based on a product; it is a service industry in which the prostitute's body is rented for a fee.

To address the issue of whether our respondents had ever engaged in sex for money, we tried various approaches, in early pilot projects, that would phrase the question in the most productive manner. In interviews with respondents, including those who had completed questionnaires, we asked whether the respondent was a buyer or seller of sex. Based on the sex of the respondent, we tried "Have you purchased sex for money?" and "Have you been involved in the sale of sex for money?" and several variations of the wording of these questions. Because most respondents found these questions to be offensive and some saw them as sexist, we found we were not getting serious, considered responses. After further research and testing, we found that the simple question "Have you ever had sex for money?" produced the most serious responses. Our pilot interviews confirmed our assumptions, based on our earlier research, that men are, for the most part, the purchasers of sex and women are the sellers. Some very small percentage of this exchange is with male prostitutes who serve the homosexual community. We have never encountered any instances of lesbian prostitution. We know, too, that women engage in relationships with men (for instance, tennis and golf pros, and dance instructors) either casually or on a more extended basis in which the women are supporting the men. These affairs were not being addressed in this survey item of our questionnaire. Our question specifically addressed the "piece work" nature of prostitution, in which payment is made for each specific experience. With this distinction in mind, we proceeded to determine the extent of this practice on two levels: "Have you ever had sex for money?" (Table 11.19) and "How often?" (Table 11.20). We did not ask how much was charged or paid for the service. Experience has shown that the amount of payment is a highly variable factor, affected by location, day of the week, age and style of the prostitute, and perception of an ability to pay.

The responses we received were curious on several levels. Income did not affect the incidence of males having contact with prostitutes. The percentages were identical in the three categories, with four-fifths of all men reporting never having had sexual experience with a prostitute. It is interesting to compare these data with the middle-income males' higher extramarital affair response (Table 11.5). Their partners, it would seem, were not prostitutes.

Commercial sex can be costly, and we noted that the lowest income men who patronized prostitutes at all could not afford to do it often. Those who could most afford prostitutes, however, reported a lower frequency than did the men in the middle group, who, in general, seemed to engage in a higher frequency of sexual experience outside of marriage.

The responses by our sample of women produced dramatic results. We found a sizable group of women who acknowledged having been paid to

TABLE 11.19   **Survey Item H.26.**

HAVE YOU EVER HAD SEX FOR MONEY?						
	$20,000		$50,000		$100,000	
	Men	Women	Men	Women	Men	Women
N =	332	350	261	249	142	118
Yes	20%	5%	20%	8%	20%	3%
No	80%	95%	80%	92%	80%	97%

TABLE 11.20   **Survey Item H.26.**

HAVE YOU EVER HAD SEX FOR MONEY: YES RESPONSES:					
	$20,000		$50,000		$100,000	
	Men	Women	Men	Women	Men	Women
N =	332	350	261	249	142	118
Once	37%	31%	6%	32%	14%	50%
Occasionally	56	38	63	58	62	25
Often	7	31	31	10	24	25

have sex with men; in the middle-income group, 8% had had such experiences. In interviews, many of the women's responses indicated that they did not define what they were doing as prostitution, but, they said, they expected and received some form of compensation for their sexual favors, whether money, a promotion, or some desired goal. Many other women, however, acknowledged that money alone was their motivation for this kind of sex. The women who responded that they had had sex for money did so with alacrity and no hesitation; it was regarded simply as a job or as something they had to do to get what they wanted.

Prostitution, that "oldest profession" mentioned in the Old Testament, has received a great deal of attention from historians, sociologists, and, lately, feminists and sexologists who wonder why, when Americans see themselves as sexually liberated and free sex is readily available, prostitution is still flourishing. Is there something else besides money that draws apparently respectable women into occasional prostitution?

In our interviews, we observed that women involved in selling sex for money rarely spoke of the sex act under these circumstances as being personally gratifying. Rather, they explained how they were helping the men who were their clients, who might be having a variety of sex problems. Some of these women claimed that they were sex counselors and healers—indeed, some were sex surrogates. For many, however, there was no need for soul searching to justify what they did; it was simply a job and the only gratification they expected was from the payment they received.

The men we interviewed offered no other rationale for buying sex, apart from the pleasure it gave them. Many naively insisted that they were not selfish in the relationship, and that they made sure that their commercial sexual partner had also been sexually satisfied. In this consideration, they are most often deceived. Prostitutes learn very early how to fake enjoyment and simulate orgasm in very obvious and noticeable ways.

There is nothing new about prostitution in the United States. Even the name "hooker," the slang term for a prostitute, comes from the name of a famous American Civil War general, Joseph ("Fighting Joe") Hooker, who favored women who were the camp followers of his troops. The industrial revolution and the waves of migration from Europe brought many young women to large, overcrowded cities. Some of these immigrants found prostitution a lucrative possibility and established the first American brothels.

The continuing widespread practice of prostitution indicates to psychiatrists such as Dr. Bruce Lieberman[3] of New York City that "Americans may not be as liberated as they think themselves to be." If we consider the implications of our 8% of middle-income women indicating that they had had sex for money, we realize that, coupled with professional prostitutes, we have a sizable population of women selling sex for money. From our data, we estimate that over 4.2 million American women ages 18 to 64 have been engaged in various aspects of sex for pay. This number does not tell the whole story. The figures would be significantly augmented by inclusion of the "baby-pros," an age category that was not included in our study. These are the many preteen and early teenagers who frequent the downtown areas of most large cities in America. Besides the full-time baby-pros, there are the "weekend warriors," so named by the New York Police Department Vice Squad. These are the high school and college students who descend on New York City from upstate New York, Connecticut, and other surrounding hub states to earn extra money as weekend prostitutes. A similar situation exists in all urban areas. If we include these additional groups, then an estimate of 5 million American females engaged in prostitution seems reasonable.

How can we account for so many women's engaging in what is regarded as a fundamentally demeaning activity? The case is sometimes made that prostitution need not be demeaning and that women can control the situation. This may be true for some women, but the vast number of those who engage in prostitution do so because it offers a solution to their pressing problems, whether economic and/or psychological.

Prostitution has always been an answer to what unskilled women can do to answer pressing economic needs. Alongside this general economic situation now stands the growing problem of drug addiction, cultivated in young prostitutes by their pimps, which keeps the women attached to the only activity that can adequately finance their very expensive habit.

Mental health professionals have established that avowed prostitutes are largely drawn from a pool of precocious sexually molested children, and we suspect that our findings, although carefully researched from available data, still minimize the true extent of the problem. It is now accepted that approximately 25% of American women have been sexually molested before the age of 18, and most of those involved in incest were below the age of 10 at the first occurrence. Earlier research[4] revealed that 78% of prostitutes had been raped or otherwise sexually molested before the age of 12. These sexual aggressions often make it very difficult for the victims to develop a "normal" sense of appropriate adult interaction.

What about the customers of these women? Projecting our data to the general population, 20%, or about 18 million, of men in the United States have been involved in commercial sex with prostitutes. Our own research confirmed the findings of Dr. Harold Greenwald,[5] that married, middle-income, middle-aged Caucasian men constitute the greatest number of customers.

Are we then to conclude that sexual liberation is on sale; that the rights men and women have fought for are being auctioned off; that the women's movement has failed to ensure women dignity in their sexuality? Many Americans have struggled to achieve personal sexual gratification in manners of their own choosing, without loss of a sense of dignity, and they have fought to avoid the condemnation of old institutions. But where do we stand today? Has the First Sexual Revolution, which has passed, been bought and paid for? Is the Second Sexual Revolution in danger of substituting commerce for love? We think the answer is a resounding NO! The under- and above-ground sex industry was always there, but, just as Americans have preferred not to face the serious question of sex abuse, they have chosen not to know the full extent of prostitution—full-time, part-time, or by baby-pros.

The greatest number of Americans search for their personal sexual fulfillment in ways that make sense to them and do not degrade others. No matter how slick the package, prostitution is degrading. Our prediction is that, although there seems to be a universal need for prostitution, the numbers of those involved in commercial sex will diminish significantly as more Americans suffer less guilt and abuse, and find more dignity with their sexuality. We believe that the search for sexual answers will produce positive results for men and women.

SUMMING UP

There is no doubt that money does make a difference in the sex lives of Americans. America may be known as a country of equal opportunity, but those with more money seem to have more opportunity than others to express themselves sexually. As we have seen in this chapter, people take a variety of options in expressing their sexuality. Belief in the possibility of economic upward mobility in America is strong. Those with less money now can hope and plan for a time when they will be in a higher income category and will be able to afford sexual indulgences of which they can now only dream. In the meantime, they often mimic what they believe to be the sexual behavior of the rich and famous. Morality is shaped by social experience and then internalized to the personal level. Income level therefore plays a role in shaping personal morality. We found less difference in sexual attitudes and performance between income groups than we might have expected, but there was evidence that access to money, or the lack of it, influenced interpersonal relations of men and women by affecting behavior and attitudes.

Would our results have been significantly different if we had included the really wealthy? A number of our respondents earned over $500,000 annually, and we had several dozen legitimate millionaires, but we chose to focus on a more representative group of Americans who could easily exchange places, given a little different luck or perhaps a different amount of effort. We wanted to tap the broadest centers of each income group, in order to better reflect American society as a whole.

The major constraint on the expression of a free-wheeling sexual lifestyle is a lack of money. As we have seen, social restrictions on the expression of sexuality have been minimized. At the same time, an emphasis on the old values of the importance of marriage, of married love, and even of fidelity has been maintained for all groups. The wealthy have access to a variety of sex perks, such as commercial sex, extramarital sex, and even fertility aids; these are too expensive for the poor to readily afford, but even the lowest income group we surveyed did not feel left out of the sexual feast available today.

Increased buying power is an incentive for and a goal of economic achievement, and the ability to purchase expensive sexual experiences is one of the goals for which people may strive. The vision of that goal varies from person to person. One may look forward to personal sexual performance with the present partner, enhanced by more leisure; another, to a wider choice of sex partners; and still another, to luxurious environments in which to enjoy the sexual experience. Whatever the goal, sex is the fruit of their labor.

CHAPTER TWELVE

Region and Sex

SOME SIGNIFICANT FINDINGS ABOUT REGION AND SEX

✦ **The South has the earliest ages of sexual initiation and the most reported premarital sex.**

✦ **Marriage is most revered in the Midwest; parenthood is least attractive in the West.**

✦ **The South reports the largest increase in sexual activity in the past 3 years, and the West, the smallest.**

✦ **The Midwest consistently reports the least amount of sex activity of all four regions of the United States.**

✦ **Respondents from the Midwest saw themselves as less sexually active than those from any other region.**

✦ **Love is very highly ranked—90%+ in all regions.**

QUESTIONNAIRE SUBJECTS TABULATED IN THIS CHAPTER	
	Table
Marriage and Fulfillment	12.1
Parenthood	12.2
Abortion	12.3
Traditional Sex Roles in Modern Society	12.4
Family Planning	12.5
Abortion Frequency	12.6
The Importance of Love	12.7
Male Premarital Sexual Experience	12.8
Female Premarital Sexual Experience	12.9
Masturbation Frequency	12.10
One-Night Stands	12.11
Extramarital Affairs	12.12
Sexual Experience Before Marriage	12.13
Pornography	12.14
Sexual Experience at Work	12.15
Sexual Harassment	12.16
Self-Ratings of Sexual Activity	12.17
Number of Sexual Partners	12.18
Age at First Full Sexual Relations	12.19
Sexual Molestation	12.20
Comparative Sexual Activity, Three Years Ago Versus Now	12.21
Views on Personal Sex Practices	12.22
Sexually Transmitted Diseases	12.23

This chapter explores characteristic patterns of sexual behavior indicated by respondents to our questionnaire, grouped according to their locations in the four major regions of the country: the Northeast, the South, the Midwest, and the West. This separation by regions is the final sorting of the data that we performed. There are real differences in sexual attitudes and practices in the various regions of the country. Unfortunately, there are also strong popular stereotypes, more of the women than of the men. We do not endorse those stereotypes. A great diversity of cultures exists in each region, and their constant interaction continues to be influential in mutual effect and change.

Most Americans are primarily knowledgeable of the sexual interaction in their own communities. Television and the media serve as the great equalizers for sexual fashions nationally, but they do not totally dominate the personal and idiosyncratic regional sex truths. However, many people are not aware of some of the major sexual variations that are occurring, even in their own local areas. For example, although New York City is regarded by many in law enforcement as the prostitution capital of the United States, sophisticated Manhattan reacted with astonishment mixed with titillation when the commercial sex exploits of Xaveria Hollander ("the happy hooker") became public after her arrest.

When we grouped the responses to our research questionnaire by region, the particular sexual attitudes, variations, and awareness of the four regions of the country became distinct, and different sexual cultures became evident. The patterns that emerged raised intriguing questions: How is the regional pressure to have certain attitudes or behaviors communicated? To what extent are people encouraged, or constrained, to express their personal sexuality, by the morals or role models of their particular region? Is any specific region in the fast lane, and is any lagging behind, in terms of sexual sophistication and behavior? If so, which ones? To what extent does the prevalence of religion, or the lack of it, in a region affect sexual attitudes or practices? Some of our survey items went beyond these factors to identify the different life-styles, mores, and customs that exist in the various geographic areas and how they affect the sex lives of their inhabitants.

BASIC PERSONAL VALUES

Marriage, childbearing, and child rearing were once self-defining events in American adult life. In the ongoing Second Sexual Revolution, each is now immersed in choices and innovative possibilities. We begin our discussion of regional attitudes by examining responses on fulfillment in marriage (Table 12.1), parenthood (Table 12.2), and abortion (Table 12.3).

Responses from around the country were generally similar for all regions, with roughly three-fourths of the respondents disagreeing (to be fulfilled, one did *not* have to be married). This show of unanimity reflects widespread contemporary American values. The media exercise much influence in the acceptability of modes and life-styles among all Americans; the results in Table 12.1 imply that this image of self-gratification, coupled with the need for personal fulfillment, seems to run strong in all regions.

The Midwest did show a slightly stronger support of marriage; a trend toward traditional family values emerged repeatedly in our data from this region.

On the question of whether parenthood represents the greatest attainment in life (Table 12.2), it was interesting to observe the differences in regional values and responses. The lowest percentages of those agreeing with the concept of parenthood as the ultimate human attainment originated in the West and Northeast (27% and 32%, respectively). As

TABLE 12.1   Survey Item A.6.

TO BE TRULY FULFILLED, ONE MUST BE MARRIED:				
	Northeast	South	Midwest	West
N =	558	932	669	578
Strongly agree	4%	3%	4%	4%
Agree	11	12	17	13
No opinion	8	6	12	7
Disagree	52	53	53	56
Strongly disagree	25	26	14	20
Strongly agree + Agree	15%	15%	21%	17%
Disagree + Strongly disagree	77%	79%	67%	76%

indicated in several tables in this chapter, the sex roles in these two regions show more diversity and emphasis on personal gratification than those in the other two regions. The South (40%) and Midwest (37%) showed considerably more acceptance of traditional values. The issue of parenthood is very complex; it asks a person to subordinate his or her career or life-style plans for the sake of being a parent. Inevitably, complex and difficult questions were raised that touched on the most basic personal values.

We will increasingly see that much of the West, represented in the minds of most Americans by California, and the Northeast, similarly represented by New York, reflect differences beyond simple locale that make them distinct from the rest of the country. They have very different attitudes about life-style and what life should be. This diversity extends

TABLE 12.2   Survey Item A.8.

BECOMING A PARENT IS THE ULTIMATE HUMAN ATTAINMENT:				
	Northeast	South	Midwest	West
N =	558	930	666	573
Strongly agree	9%	9%	10%	7%
Agree	23	31	27	20
No opinion	16	20	14	12
Disagree	42	33	38	42
Strongly disagree	10	7	11	19
Strongly agree + Agree	32%	40%	37%	27%
Disagree + Strongly disagree	52%	40%	49%	61%

TABLE 12.3   **Survey Item A.11.**

ABORTION IS MURDER:				
	Northeast	South	Midwest	West
N =	559	936	668	579
Strongly agree	9%	17%	18%	13%
Agree	14	17	15	14
No opinion	14	21	15	13
Disagree	32	29	30	25
Strongly disagree	31	16	22	35
Strongly agree + Agree	23%	34%	33%	27%
Disagree + Strongly disagree	63%	45%	52%	60%

beyond urban versus rural values; each of the four sections of the country has both big cities and rural areas. Even the issue of abortion, which raises hackles in the rest of the country, is seen differently on the East and West coasts. We posed our question about abortion in very direct terms. (See Table 12.3.)

Only about one-fourth of those in the West and Northeast agreed with the concept that abortion is murder, but about one-third of those in the South and the Midwest (generally known as the Bible Belt) held that view. It is predicted by some experts that the early 1990s may see the reduction of abortion rights with the reversal of *Roe v. Wade,* the case in which the Supreme Court originally outlawed restrictions on abortion. Such a reversal would return abortion to the jurisdiction of the various states. Should this happen, it is entirely likely that there will again be a mass exodus of women seeking abortions from states that limit abortions; or government funding to enable poor women to have abortions would become available only in states that permit abortion. Regional differences and attitudes would then take on critical importance. Having found that there are regional differences in basic personal values, we wondered how much effect tradition might exercise in formulating these regional sex differences.

TRADITION—ITS DIMINISHING ROLE

How did people from each region feel about traditional sex roles, which dictated female passivity and ignorance, reinforced male superiority and arrogance, and declared a virtual "battle of the sexes"? Table 12.4 summarizes our respondents' feelings about this topic. Their answers were revealing.

TABLE 12.4   Survey Item A.13.

TRADITIONAL SEX ROLES HAVE NO PLACE IN MODERN SOCIETY:				
	Northeast	South	Midwest	West
N =	559	934	669	578
Strongly agree	9%	6%	5%	9%
Agree	24	24	26	27
No opinion	16	13	15	10
Disagree	45	47	47	45
Strongly disagree	6	10	7	9
Strongly agree + Agree	33%	30%	31%	36%
Disagree + Strongly disagree	51%	57%	54%	54%

In all four regions, approximately one-third of the respondents communicated agreement that traditional sex roles have no place in modern society. However, more than half of the respondents in all regions disagreed; they felt that there is a place for traditional sex roles. Despite greater sexual activity and/or promiscuity, sexual values regarding tradition have survived and were articulated in all four regions of the country.

Were the stereotypes of traditional sex roles reflected in the sexual practices of our respondents in their daily lives? As we saw so often in our findings, belief and behavior can be very different in the realm of sex. In order to better understand this pattern, we raised the controversial issue of contraception. We asked about family planning and provided a value scale for answer selections (Table 12.5).

Another divergence from the traditional family-oriented belief system was revealed. All four regions reported at least 94% agreement that

TABLE 12.5   Survey Item B.1.

FAMILY PLANNING IS:				
	Northeast	South	Midwest	West
N =	561	932	669	576
Very important	55%	63%	56%	60%
Important	41	34	40	34
Not sure	2	1	3	3
Unimportant	1	2	1	2
Very unimportant	1	0	0	1
Very important + Important	96%	97%	96%	94%

family planning is important. With an overwhelming majority of Americans in all sections of the country apparently in favor of family planning and, by implication, some form of contraceptive practice, it is surprising that contraception still remains a controversial issue. This raises the distinct possibility that the controversy is stirred by the activism of a very small group. Had an attitude of practicality entered the sexual, as well as the spiritual, lives of the majority of our respondents? During the late 1980s, the contraception issue became less controversial for the majority of Americans, in spite of what vocal minorities might claim.

By contrast, the issue of abortion became a renewed battleground. Against the backdrop of obvious awareness of and approval for family planning, how many of our women respondents in each region had had abortions?

As shown in Table 12.6, differing regional patterns emerged. Leading in the percentage who had had abortions were the Northeast (36%) and the West (33%), with the South (19%) and the Midwest (18%) both showing significantly lower incidences. This does not mean that there were greatly unequal amounts of sexual activity or numbers of pregnancies; the figures in the table reflect only the incidence of abortions. Many more women in the South and Midwest (77%) seem to have carried their pregnancies to term, regardless of whether they wanted or were able to. Our interviews indicated that local and/or religious pressure and traditional regional attitudes toward abortion exerted influence. So widespread is the knowledge of the regional differences in abortion that it is a common practice for childless couples in the Northeast to place ads in deep-South newspapers seeking out lawyers to arrange adoptions of "unwanted" babies. Compared to the South, there are far fewer babies available in the Northeast, where the availability and utilization of abortion is an easily employed option.

In the areas of sentiment, romance, and idealism, were attitudes toward love universal and equally distributed throughout the country? Much has been written about shifting cultural attitudes and the identification of what values in the 1990s might replace the "Me-decade" of the 1980s. If

TABLE 12.6   Survey Item H.24.

I HAVE HAD AN ABORTION:				
	Northeast	South	Midwest	West
N =	285	495	335	301
Yes	36%	19%	18%	33%
No	61	77	77	61
No answer	3	4	5	6

love is considered idealistically, that is, as the ability for one person to reach out and be welcomed as part of another person, then Table 12.7 indicates that the country may be shifting toward idealism in the 1990s.

All four regions responded almost identically: at rates of 96% and over, our respondents said love was important or very important to them. Love, as we have pointed out in comparing other groups in earlier chapters, is universally valued in America. This finding may indicate a major shift in basic cultural values and perhaps indicates strong support for placing a higher priority on relationships in the 1990s. Pledges of love, and other intimate feelings of sensuality, don't always come together in practice, but love, in theory, is here for all to enjoy.

Did our respondents believe that, to be able to enjoy love and the intimacy and sensuality that can accompany it, men and women should have equal sexual opportunities and experience? Both men and women in most regions of the country believed that men were permitted, and perhaps should even be encouraged, to be sexually experienced before they get married. This attitude has carried over from prior times, when men were supposed to teach their virgin wives about the wonders and mysteries of sex. As shown in Table 12.8, significantly more respondents chose the very important and important response options.

The South and Midwest showed relatively less emphasis, with 49% considering the premarital experience important and 18% not sure whether it was important or not. The emphasis on sex in the Northeast and West is consistent with other data in this chapter that show a greater sexual intensity in those regions.

When we knew that the majority of our respondents approved of men's having premarital sexual experience, we wondered whether they were any more ambivalent about women's premarital sexual experience. Table 12.9 indicates their opinions.

Their responses reflected some basic differences between concepts of liberation and equality versus established traditions. Regional differences

TABLE 12.7   **Survey Item B.4.**

HOW IMPORTANT IS LOVE TO YOU?				
	Northeast	South	Midwest	West
N =	557	934	665	578
Very important	82%	80%	77%	77%
Important	15	16	21	19
Not sure	2	3	1	2
Unimportant	1	0	0	1
Very unimportant	0	1	1	1
Very important + Important	97%	96%	98%	96%

TABLE 12.8   **Survey Item B.7.**

FOR THE MAN, SEXUAL EXPERIENCE BEFORE MARRIAGE IS:			
	Northeast	South	Midwest	West
N =	555	928	669	578
Very important	22%	14%	15%	19%
Important	40	35	34	38
Not sure	15	18	18	13
Unimportant	19	25	27	25
Very unimportant	4	8	6	5
Very important + Important	62%	49%	49%	57%
Unimportant + Very unimportant	23%	33%	33%	30%

were marked. The Northeast showed the most liberal values, with the highest frequency of respondents (57%) expressing their approval—5 percentage points lower than the approval for males (Table 12.8). The West showed a similar, but less intense pattern (51% or 6 percentage points less than for males), and matched the Midwest in considering this experience unimportant. The South—the most negative region on this issue—and the Midwest clearly showed different values, with less overall importance put on women's premarital sexual experience.

Like the men, the women in the Northeast and West have more freedom, but may face higher sexual expectations and performance pressures. To put the situation in perspective, for women in the South, premarital sexual experience is less valued, though most Southern responses revealed in this chapter's tables indicate that there is a great deal of precocious, premarital sex. These patterns raise substantial questions about the

TABLE 12.9   **Survey Item B.8.**

FOR THE WOMAN, SEXUAL EXPERIENCE BEFORE MARRIAGE IS:			
	Northeast	South	Midwest	West
N =	556	928	667	577
Very important	16%	8%	10%	13%
Important	41	30	32	38
Not sure	15	19	21	13
Unimportant	24	33	30	31
Very unimportant	4	10	7	5
Very important + Important	57%	38%	42%	51%
Unimportant + Very unimportant	28%	43%	37%	36%

nature of regional values and patterns and how they may affect the sexual liberation of women.

MASTURBATION

What about autoeroticism and masturbation? We know that people do masturbate, but does the prevalence of masturbation vary by region? Our findings are presented in Table 12.10, which shows a pattern of higher activity in the Northeast and West, with the South and Midwest trailing in this activity by large margins.

The results of our masturbation inquiries began to profile the South as a region quite different from the rest of the country. Not only did sizable numbers of young women from the South report never having masturbated (45%), but, contrary to previous researchers, we were getting responses from young men ages 18 to 26 who insisted *they* had never masturbated (see also Table 2.3). Inasmuch as masturbation may have moral overtones in certain places and at certain times, we considered that residents of this area of the country may refrain because of religious strictures. However, we found that respondents from this region did not eschew other forms of sexual activity; indeed, they reported having sexual intercourse more frequently (see Tables 12.13 and 12.21) and at a younger age (see Table 12.19) than in any other part of the country.

Our findings in the South were so dramatically different from those in the other regions that we sought explanation from our experts in that part of the country. The response we received was that it was not religious constraint that was suppressing masturbation in the South, but

TABLE 12.10   **Survey Item D.8.**

I MASTURBATE ON AVERAGE:								
	Northeast		South		Midwest		West	
	Men	Women	Men	Women	Men	Women	Men	Women
N =	274	278	435	486	330	325	277	294
Daily	12%	3%	4%	1%	5%	1%	8%	2%
Several times weekly	19	14	15	6	18	5	23	10
Weekly	26	15	19	6	24	12	23	19
Monthly	8	18	7	10	11	16	7	25
Rarely	25	32	25	32	24	40	25	33
Never	10	18	30	45	18	26	14	11
Daily + Several times weekly	31%	17%	19%	7%	23%	6%	31%	12%
At least weekly	57%	32%	38%	13%	47%	18%	54%	31%

something quite different. Professor Donald Schneller of Middle Tennessee State University explained that the boys and men in this region did not have to "condescend" to masturbation; rather, they had willing sex partners who were readily available to them.[1]

Paradoxically, our respondents from the South preferred traditional sex roles (see Table 12.4) but rated themselves on a par with the Northeast and West, in terms of being sexually active (see Table 12.17). This orientation to matters sexual, incongruous as it may seem, fashions these respondents to have dramatically lower masturbatory rates. However, we did detect a contradictory morality operating in the South, with its earliest age of sexual initiation and its extensive premarital experience.

Upon further research of individual questionnaires, we noted that the responses of older persons (27 and older) from the South tended to resemble the responses from the rest of the country and did not show this antimasturbatory attitude. The high percentage of women in the South who purportedly do not masturbate fits the traditional role of the passive sex participant who learns about sex from her partner, not from self-exploration.

Next, we considered the nature of premarital sexual experiences in the four regions of the United States, particularly casual, noncommittal, brief "passing-in-the-night" encounters.

DISPOSABLE SEX AND THE COMMUNITY

"What was your name again?" Those in the fast track—residents of Los Angeles and New York City, for example—often claim to have no time for and no interest in developing relationships of any depth. Sex is readily available; they indulge in it, say their goodbyes, and the partners disappear. How did our respondents feel about a practice that epitomizes this kind of sexual collision, the one-night stand? We deliberately phrased our survey item to have some emotional content. The responses are given in Table 12.11.

Most of the country expressed disapproval of one-night stands. Agreement that they were degrading ran over 50%, with the South (63%) apparently most espousing protection of the traditional honor of womankind. The Northeast and West were more tolerant: slightly over 25% of respondents in both regions rejected the statement.

The data from our respondents seemed to point to regional differences in attitude toward one-night stands, which may have translated into substantial regional influences affecting availability of one-night partners versus those desiring longer-term affairs. Much apparently depended on the values and attitudes of the participants, some of whom had surprising no opinion rates: 21% in the Northeast and Midwest (a seldom found pairing), and 18% and 16% in the South and West, respectively.

TABLE 12.11   Survey Item C.3.

I FIND ONE-NIGHT STANDS TO BE DEGRADING:			
	Northeast	South	Midwest	West
N =	556	932	665	576
Strongly agree	22%	29%	28%	26%
Agree	31	34	30	31
No opinion	21	18	21	16
Disagree	21	15	16	22
Strongly disagree	5	4	5	5
Strongly agree + Agree	53%	63%	58%	57%
Disagree + Strongly disagree	26%	19%	21%	27%

✦ IN THEIR OWN WORDS

Let me tell you, to me one-night stands are already a commitment. What is wrong if two people want to enjoy each other? They do it, maybe have a drink, and say good night, or good day, if it's still daylight. Everyone is so concerned with guilt and obligation. I don't force anyone to do anything. We both want to do great sex. What's wrong with that? I have great recall for faces, and most of the time, when I happen to meet some of the women again, let's say in a bar, they are thrilled that I remember them. Many, in fact, want to become my friend, and some do.

—A 39-year-old stockbroker

✦ ✦ ✦

During my earlier years, I admit it, I had some quick flings, and frequently I found myself picking up my underwear in the early morning hours to go home. I have now been around long enough to be able to know the difference between care, and I don't mean perpetual care or total love, I mean sensitivity and caring, to know the difference between it and the "wham, bam, thank you ma'am" kind of guys that are around. But I made a vow years ago, never again! It's too demeaning. Making love to someone you don't even know is like Sylvester Stallone punching a piece of meat in his movie *Rocky*. Another specific issue that many of these men exaggerate, and many even lie about, is their sexual expertise. Most of the creeps that specialize in one-night stands do so because they lack a great deal in bed. Many of these men are embarrassed to see the same woman again. It may seem cruel, but I once spotted one of these men that had left me high and dry in the same bar, and giving his same spiel to another young woman. I walked up to him, said a loud hello, turned to the young woman and said in an even louder voice, "He's a premature ejaculator!" Sweet revenge was mine.

—A 32-year-old single woman

Extramarital sex was our next topic. This activity is seen by some as immoral; others, perhaps more cynical, say it is simply based on availability: an additional sexual gratification occurs that happens to be outside of the marriage. Table 12.12 indicates how widespread this practice is in the different regions of the country.

Once again, regional differences emerged. Not totally unanticipated, the Northeast and West appeared to have, as one Minnesotan complained, "the most loose morals or liberal behavior in the country." These regions reported the highest percentages of extramarital affairs. The regional differences were more pronounced in the frequencies of those who had never had an extramarital affair, with the South and Midwest showing markedly fewer affairs overall.

Bearing in mind these responses concerning extramarital affairs, we thought it would be enlightening to find out how much sexual experience before marriage people from the four regions reported. (See Table 12.13.)

Reviewing the two highest frequency categories, we began to see regional contrasts between stated values and actual behavior. Somewhat surprisingly, the South, along with the West, experienced the most premarital sex. The Northeast was close behind, and the Midwest reported the lowest incidence of premarital sexual experience. In general, the pattern for the Midwest was that of a much more restrained and less sexually charged atmosphere. These emerging patterns raised questions about underlying attitudes. Was the Midwest inordinately staid, inhibited, uptight? Were the other regions excessively sensual, sexually free, or adventuresome? Or, was the Midwest showing a more healthy pragmatism, protecting itself from the possible disillusionment that can come with premarital sexual experience? Further research on guiding influences and personal motivations within each region would be of interest in answering these questions.

TABLE 12.12   **Survey Item D.5.**

I'VE HAD EXTRAMARITAL AFFAIRS:				
	Northeast	South	Midwest	West
N =	370	612	437	381
Never	55%	77%	70%	54%
Only once	11	7	9	11
Rarely	20	8	11	22
Often	11	7	9	10
Ongoing	3	1	1	3
Often + Ongoing	14%	8%	10%	13%

TABLE 12.13   Survey Item D.10.

I HAD SEXUAL EXPERIENCE BEFORE MARRIAGE:				
	Northeast	South	Midwest	West
N =	558	933	664	576
Very much	26%	34%	20%	30%
Much	30	27	28	30
Little	22	17	25	20
Very little	9	10	10	11
None	13	12	17	9
Very much + Much	56%	61%	48%	60%
Little + Very little	31%	27%	35%	31%

We found that individuals had fairly strong feelings about the moral tone of their neighborhoods. Wherever people lived, they expressed concern about their community and what happens in it. There had been much press coverage about the rise of pornographic material in neighborhood stores. We asked our respondents whether they viewed the available amount of pornography as a problem in their neighborhoods.

The results in Table 12.14 show that just over half of the population in each area of the country—except the South, which was slightly lower—agreed that there was too much pornographic material in neighborhood stores. The regional exception could be explained by the fact that, in the Bible Belt areas of the South, concerted campaigns by fundamentalist groups have succeeded in eliminating this material from neighborhood stores. What we were seeing, therefore, may not have been less concern

TABLE 12.14   Survey Item D.3.

THERE IS TOO MUCH PORNOGRAPHIC MATERIAL IN NEIGHBORHOOD STORES:				
	Northeast	South	Midwest	West
N =	558	933	668	575
Strongly agree	20%	17%	18%	22%
Agree	38	28	34	31
No opinion	19	24	22	20
Disagree	20	26	22	22
Strongly disagree	3	5	4	5
Strongly agree + Agree	58%	45%	52%	53%
Disagree + Strongly disagree	23%	31%	26%	27%

about pornography, but rather less availability locally and, hence, less of a perceived problem.

SEX IN THE WORKPLACE

Is sex in the workplace a widespread practice, accepted equally around the country? Millions of American women work outside of the home, and many spend more waking time with their coworkers and superiors than with their partners and families. This situation has created more opportunities and pressures, for both women and men, to have sexual relationships outside of the home. When we asked our respondents whether they had had sexual experience at work, the majority gave negative answers, as shown in Table 12.15.

Again, more sexual activity was indicated in the Northeast and West than in the South and Midwest. Was it because workplace sex is a practice that would seem to fit better in an urban setting, which allows for more anonymity? Or, were regional values once again reigning in sexual behavior in the South and Midwest? We concluded from our interviews that a combination of opportunity and values was the catalyst, and, for some, there were overtones of power and control that determined this behavior. Realizing that a man's sexual experience at work might very likely be a woman's experience of sexual harassment in the workplace, we cross-checked the replies of our female respondents to our survey item on sexual harassment at work. Table 12.16 presents the women's responses by region. Regarding harassment at work, respondents were asked, in the questionnaire and in interviews, to answer with a simple Yes or No.

From one-third to over one-half of women in different regions reported sexual harassment at work. These quite large numbers indicated that harassment is a problem for both sexes—for the women, as victims, and for

TABLE 12.15 Survey Item D.11.

I HAVE HAD SEXUAL EXPERIENCE AT WORK:				
	Northeast	South	Midwest	West
N =	557	932	665	576
Never	64%	76%	78%	62%
Once or twice	22	13	12	19
Occasionally	12	9	9	15
Often	2	2	1	4
Once or twice + Occasionally + Often	36%	24%	22%	38%

TABLE 12.16   **Survey Item G.10.**

I HAVE EXPERIENCED SEXUAL HARASSMENT ON MY JOB:				
	Northeast	South	Midwest	West
N =	283	486	332	295
Yes	50%	38%	44%	54%
No	50%	62%	56%	46%

the men, who may not be aware of the significance of their actions. Only recently has the problem of sexual harassment on the job become an open issue. Women we interviewed who reported sexual harassment felt a grievous lack of respect for themselves; the experience had been demeaning and even humiliating. It may take some time for male coworkers to see women as colleagues rather than proximally convenient sex objects.

SEXUAL SELF-IMAGE

Because discussion of harassment had raised the subject, it seemed useful to consider sexual self-image at this point. How did people in different regions who saw the same movies and watched the same television programs, but had different traditions and heritage, see their sexuality? Our statement for respondents' consideration pertained to how sexually active, or inactive, they regarded themselves.

The results in Table 12.17 showed that the Northeast, the South, and the West responded almost identically. The Midwest was the region that admitted to the least sexual activity. This was a significant difference. The South was displaying differences between its beliefs and behavior; its verbalized religious restraint was contrasted with behavioral promiscuity. The Midwest remained consistent, with results generally lower than the more sexually active regions of the country.

✦ *IN THEIR OWN WORDS* ─────────────────────────────

> I consider myself active, and if you caught me two years ago, I would have said very active. Since my wife died fifteen years ago, I have dated more than I did before I married. I truly believe that sex is the ultimate inspiration that keeps many of us seniors alive. Okay, so maybe we don't do all the fancy sex things they do in bigtown U.S.A., but I don't hear many of the people in Minnesota complaining.
>
> —A widower nearing age 70

TABLE 12.17   **Survey Item G.3.**

I CONSIDER MYSELF TO BE SEXUALLY:				
	Northeast	South	Midwest	West
N =	559	932	669	578
Very active	18%	18%	14%	16%
Active	36	36	30	37
Average	30	28	34	29
Below average	11	11	13	11
Inactive	5	7	9	7
Very active + Active	54%	54%	44%	53%
Below average + Inactive	16%	18%	22%	18%

Once again, our data raised questions. Was the South being hypocritical or just pragmatic? Was the Midwest inhibited or showing healthy emotional and sexual constraint? Were the Northeast and West more representative of the jet-age sex fantasies of most Americans? We could only speculate; our data did not provide the answers.

SEX PARTNERS: AGES AND NUMBERS

With all the implications of the data we had obtained, we had not yet fully explored the details of regional influence on sexual practice. To fill this gap, we turned to the information we had received on a very personal question—the total number of partners individuals had had sexual relations with—and sorted it by region.

The results (Table 12.18) showed great variety. One respondent, a female in the Northeast, added the comment, "I am a sex surrogate." In contrast was a 23-year-old Minnesota woman who complained that she felt there was too much social pressure to have sex, and, feeling that she had a forum through the medium of the questionnaire, she volunteered: "As a virgin, I felt myself discriminated against, but I am not alone, there are many other virgins, like myself, especially in the Midwest, but they are too embarrassed to come out and say it." A great many respondents, mostly from the apparently sexually charged Northeast and West, reported having sex with 100 or more different sex partners.

Among those who reported having sex with more than 60 individuals, the West (23%) and the Northeast (20%) again reported maximal contacts, the South (8%) was much lower, and the Midwest (3%) reported the fewest sex partners. At the other end of the spectrum, the philosophically more restrained South and traditional Midwest actually reported

TABLE 12.18   Survey Item G.7.

HOW MANY DIFFERENT INDIVIDUALS (INCLUDING SPOUSES) HAVE YOU HAD SEXUAL RELATIONS WITH?			
	Northeast	South	Midwest	West
N =	551	921	654	567
None	1%	2%	1%	1%
1–10	32	43	40	20
11–30	32	35	40	37
31–60	15	12	16	19
61–100	8	4	2	8
101 +	12	4	1	15
1–30	64%	78%	80%	57%
61 or more	20%	8%	3%	23%

behaviors that were reasonably similar to the West and Northeast in a range of more moderate numbers (11 to 30) of sex partners, even though those numbers still indicated that the South and Midwest were dabbling in sex outside traditional values.

Another substantive survey item, one that often colors what one enjoys sexually and how one enjoys it, is related to the age of sexual initiation. We asked all respondents to indicate the age at which they had had first full sexual relations. (See Table 12.19.)

The majority of respondents in all regions had already had their first full sexual experience by age 18. Of particular note are the data for the South, where more respondents had initiated sexual relations before 15 years of age. This raises a possibility of social pressures on young teens

TABLE 12.19   Survey Item H.15.

SELF-IDENTIFICATION: AGE AT FIRST FULL SEXUAL RELATIONS:			
	Northeast	South	Midwest	West
N =	558	928	661	573
By age 10	2%	1%	0%	3%
11–14	12	16	7	11
15–18	44	65	51	51
19–25	39	17	37	34
26 +	3	1	5	1
By age 14	14%	17%	7%	14%
Over age 18	42%	18%	42%	35%

to be intimate and sexual. What about those younger? The South is the region with the youngest sexual initiation, a fact that might initially seem at odds with its Bible Belt character, but leads into other data reflecting early and copious sex, in or out of marriage, reported by respondents from the region. The Northeast and West were slightly behind in precocious sex, and, again, the Midwest brought up the rear with the lowest response. The Midwest definitely projects a consistent morality and a sexual life-style of its own. It was the only region in which no respondents reported that they had had full sexual relations before age 10. We decided to assess the possibility that early sexual initiation might be connected with higher rates of child molestation. Table 12.20 shows the results when we asked our respondents whether they had ever been sexually molested as children.

The lowest incidence of child abuse was in the South. Our interview information, supported by findings of mental health experts in the South, indicated that the key question here revolved around defining voluntary and involuntary early sexual activity. Table 12.19 showed early initiation into full sexual relations in the South, but those children involved in sex relations very early (before age 14) did not consider this to be molestation. They were sexually active earlier than children in other regions of the country, which would imply at least some sexual exploitation, but they did not consider such activity abusive because the group mores permitted sexual activity at an early age as an accepted cultural phenomenon.

The true dimensions of child sex abuse, and the evidence of it, in spite of all the headlines, are barely beginning to surface. Our data support other studies that indicate that child sex abuse is far more widespread than has been previously revealed. Only now is the general public becoming aware of this menace. Most authorities report that, by age 19, one-fourth of all American women have been molested (see Table 3.18), most in childhood and many in early childhood. The numbers for boys are somewhat lower.[2] Some experts propose that these numbers may stay low because little boys "don't squeal"; they keep sex abuse secret more than girls do. In addition to the growing awareness of the frequency of sex abuse, we are becoming increasingly conscious of its devastating and enduring consequences. Any data about the age of sexual initiation must

TABLE 12.20   **Survey Item H.20.**

I WAS SEXUALLY MOLESTED AS A CHILD:			
	Northeast	South	Midwest	West
N =	558	935	665	578
Yes	19%	13%	17%	22%
No	81%	87%	83%	78%

be analyzed carefully; precocious sex, in which the child was sexually abused and traumatized, may be revealed.

TRENDS IN SEX ACTIVITY

What were the regional trends in sexual activity level over the past 3 years, as indicated by our respondents' replies? Table 12.21 was given some close attention in the context of the data unearthed in the earlier tables.

In its own contrary way, the South reported the highest increase of activity in the past 3 years. Given certain differences between the South and the rest of the country, the need to express and experience sex, perhaps in different ways, was universal. Even the Midwest, which had generally presented a placid, comfortable, and easy-going sex style, was second only to the South in reporting greatly increased sexual activity. Has the country gone topsy-turvy? We don't think so; we believe instead that, considering the more restrained sexual life-style of the Midwest all along, the past 3 years, in spite of cautions, may seem to show more sexual activity. Midwesterners have become comfortable with their limited activities, and by not expanding their experience beyond those limitations, they continue to feel more secure. It is important to remember, in this context, that increased sexual activity does not necessarily mean more sex partners; it could mean increased frequency with the same partner(s). The South's swell of sexual activity, also contrary to the usual lead of the Northeast and West, fits into the region's own stylistic self-limitations, exhibited in attitudes toward masturbation, for example; yet it is a confirmed sex life-style that begins very early and stays very active.

TABLE 12.21   **Survey Item D.9.**

COMPARED TO 3 YEARS AGO, MY SEX ACTIVITY IS:								
	Northeast		South		Midwest		West	
	Men	Women	Men	Women	Men	Women	Men	Women
N =	274	283	437	489	332	330	277	299
Much more	19%	16%	29%	33%	25%	13%	19%	12%
More	14	18	26	26	24	22	13	16
Same	37	32	29	20	24	30	29	29
Less	20	17	11	12	18	24	30	26
Much less	10	17	5	9	9	11	9	17
Much more + More	33%	34%	55%	59%	49%	35%	32%	28%
Less + Much less	30%	34%	16%	21%	27%	35%	39%	43%

SEXUAL VARIETY

To round out the picture of regional differences, we selected four specific varieties of sexual practice that are regarded as representing a high level of sexual experimentation: group sex, threesomes, sex slave, and open marriage.

Group sex involves individuals and couples who have sexual experiences in groups, often with a variety of partners. Threesomes, also known as *ménage-à-trois*, involves sex with two individuals of one sex and one of the other sex. Sex slave is a form of dominance and bondage: an individual submits to total dominance by another person in the sexual experience. In open marriage, married couples have sex with other couples, either jointly or separately. People in open marriages claim that their openness and honesty in sharing within the marriage what each has done actually enriches the marriage.

As shown in Table 12.22, the results were fairly consistent with the other regional data. The Northeast and West were the more sexually active regions of the country, regarding these four practices. Open marriage was chosen far less frequently, for several reasons. Most notably, the option applies only to married couples, so the number of possible respondents was significantly lowered; with fewer possible respondents, we would expect a smaller percentage of the entire sample to choose this option. Further, what seemed to be a stunning and daring idea during the 1970s and early 1980s began to fade into unpopularity as divorces mounted and STDs became epidemic. The increase in numbers of partners made participants realize that their chances of contracting some disease was much greater. Fairly widely accepted is the general caveat that, if one member of a pair has a sexual disease, the other is at least at high risk if not already infected.

Among those who responded positively to any of the options in Table 12.22, group sex participation was reported by almost one-fifth of those in the West, a surprisingly high figure. Threesomes were the most frequent activity, with the Northeast and the West each claiming over 20%

TABLE 12.22 — Survey Item H.27.

SELF-IDENTIFICATION: PARTICIPATION:				
	Northeast	South	Midwest	West
N =	545	917	657	564
Group sex	14%	8%	7%	19%
Threesomes	21	12	11	22
Sex slave	3	1	0	4
Open marriage	6	2	2	4

participation in this activity. The sex slave practice was understandably the least frequent in all regions; even sexually experienced persons consider it deviant. Some questionnaire respondents indicated experience with more than one practice. In any case, a sizable part of our population seems to find these sex games acceptable or even appealing.

If so many people practice so many diverse sexual games with so many partners, are any of them worried about sexually transmitted diseases? If so, how many are worried and how worried are they? In the past decade, the media have reported sexual hysteria on a grand scale, and this subject was particularly important to explore, in light of recent developments in the spread of AIDS and the resistance of STDs to treatment. We posed a survey item about respondents' level of concern regarding STDs, and got the answers shown in Table 12.23.

Most people expressed concern—between 75% and 88% in the various regions. Perhaps not too surprisingly, considering its lower level of sex activity, the Midwest reflected the lowest level of concern. That region has had less intense exposure to the ravages of sexually transmitted diseases and to potential contagion from unknown partners or a variety of partners.

As shown by our data, concern does not stop people from engaging in sexual activity. For some, the Russian roulette type of danger is experienced as an additional attraction. In each region, there were some respondents who were only slightly or not at all concerned about STDs. The highest percentage of the fearless was in the Midwest (18%); the Northeast followed with 13%, the West, with 11%, and the South, with 8%. Either the Midwest respondents suffered from naiveté, or a whole region is tragically denying this very real sexual health danger. By limiting their sexual adventurism, Midwesterners may feel confident that they are not exposed to the risks of STDs, even outside a monogamous relationship. To those living in the Northeast and West, this posture is

TABLE 12.23   **Survey Item H.28.**

I AM CONCERNED ABOUT SEXUALLY TRANSMITTED DISEASES:				
	Northeast	South	Midwest	West
N =	560	934	667	576
Very much	61%	66%	49%	62%
Much	21	22	26	22
Unsure	5	4	7	5
Slightly	8	4	11	7
Not at all	5	4	7	4
Very much + Much	82%	88%	75%	84%
Slightly + Not at all	13%	8%	18%	11%

remarkably reminiscent of the ostrich who buried his head in the sand to escape notice.

SUMMING UP

Sexual activity in the United States has not been stopped or even curtailed by the fear of sexually transmitted diseases, according to the evidence in this chapter and in our total study. The admissions of fear of STDs are not reflected in the rich and varied sexual activity of Americans in every region of the country.

Most Americans, as our study shows, learn about sex initially on the streets. The distinctions of each region then influence the nature of their sexual expectations and interaction. The major source of these regional distinctions is the family; as they grow into adulthood, children are directly affected by the kind of sex instruction they receive from their family and by the mores they absorb from their peers, which differ in each region.

Differences among the four major regions of the country are apparent in many aspects of sexuality. The West and the Northeast are by far the pacesetters of sexual America. These two are still the melting pot regions; the difference now is that Americans and others come there to become a part of what they perceive to be a dynamic, fast-paced life. As a result, there is less family tradition in both regions, and rather than having two, three, or four generations living in the same city or state, many in the West and the Northeast are first-generation residents or immigrants. Such a milieu does not lend itself to the consistency of long-term values.

Even the apparently conventional Midwest has its own variations. For a brief time, the Midwest seemed to be making a perverse contribution to big-time American prostitution, when a section of New York City's Eighth Avenue was nicknamed "The Minnesota Strip." It was so named because of the many young, blue-eyed, blonde-haired, red-cheeked, robust-looking farm girls, incongruously out of place in Manhattan, who were sent to New York contacts by their pimps in the Minneapolis–St. Paul area, the Midwest's prostitution hub, and began to overrun New York's tawdry hooker hangouts in the Times Square area.

The New South, as many Southerners like to call it, has gone through tremendous changes, yet has still managed to retain its charm and warmth as well as many of the values that made the South such a popular region in past decades. Much of the South is bound by the Bible Belt of religious fundamentalism, but its sex life in many ways reflects the serious contradictions of the televangelists who were caught practicing the opposite of what they were preaching. The South is at the same time frantic and denying; its passion is directed as much at the body as at the spirit, which may very well confuse its residents and lead to what appear to be contradictions between their stated beliefs and their actual behavior.

On the Midwest, Dr. Richard Sethre,[3] a prominent psychologist in Minneapolis, who was one of our original research associates and helped us to gather data, commented:

> Relationships in the Midwest tend to be squeaky clean as the result of two major interrelated factors: a lack of cultural/ethnic diversity and a cultural ethos that discourages individualism. In fact, anything that causes one to stand out in a crowd is suspect and this is a major influence on dating and sexual relationship patterns.
>
> Dating in small towns is a very public event, and tends to be limited to a narrow set of traditional options. Most of the action occurs at hangouts, even in the suburbs of the major cities. Deviating from established routine leaves the couple at risk of terminal ostracism.
>
> The rural culture also is remarkably homogeneous. While the rest of the country was charmed by *A Prairie Home Companion*, it left Midwesterners baffled with incredulity. Garrison Keillor caught the essence of rural life, especially its relationships, but those of us in the Midwest are puzzled by the rest of the country's romance with Norwegian bachelor farmers. Romance in the Midwest can be so excruciating that one sometimes wonders how the populace manages to procreate. The other culture, which is urban, has a higher tolerance of individuality, but it suffers from a different terminal condition, a deadly inferiority complex.
>
> Midwestern urbanites, painfully aware of how long it takes trends to arrive from either coast, are chronically trying to catch up. The result is an obsessive concern about hipness that rivals the rural concern about conformity as a major drain on their social energy.
>
> In contrast to the East Coast, which values verbal skills, Midwesterners of both cultures prefer a studious blandness. On the other hand, comparing Midwesterners with those from the West Coast can also be informative. Of course, the latter's drive to individuality is legendary, but they also enjoy sensuality that makes Midwesterners appear as stern and ascetic as their Amish neighbors. A typical conversation between two Californians would leave the Midwesterner baffled by what would seem to him to be intrusive intimacy. Those who visit Southern California seem hypnotized by how intensely the others can enjoy their bodies, clothes, music and of course, the weather. So why hasn't the Midwest been depleted by a major exodus? And how has the populace managed not only to survive, but even to date, relate and procreate? Probably because the qualities that strike the rest of the country as boring, bland and stifling permit them to develop stable, predictable and enduring relationships.

All of the variations illustrated by our data can raise additional questions about the desirability, and even the wholesomeness, of some of the patterns. Our results show clear regional differences. The Northeast and the West are preponderant in greater sexual activity; the South has contradictory, sharp ups and downs; and the Midwest stolidly follows several paces back, seeming to be the most content with itself.

CHAPTER THIRTEEN

Looking Forward from the Past

✦ Compared to Phase One of our study, 1983 to 1985, 12% fewer men and women remained virgins until age 18 in Phase Two, 1988 to 1992.

✦ Abortion has become more acceptable in the intervening years between Phase One and Phase Two—from 36% to 30% agreement that abortion is murder, and from 29% to 53% disagreement.

✦ Religion has become more important as a factor in marriage: the proportion of respondents agreeing has grown from 50% to 61%.

✦ The family has achieved a new prominence, with 13% more respondents agreeing that the family is the most important institution in society.

✦ For both men and women, premarital sex experience has increased, from 48% to 55% for men, and from 37% to 47% for women.

QUESTIONNAIRE SUBJECTS TABULATED IN THIS CHAPTER

	Table
Male Premarital Sexual Experience	13.1
Female Premarital Sexual Experience	13.2
Simultaneous Orgasm	13.3
Masturbation	13.4
Age at First Full Sexual Relations	13.5
The Importance of Love	13.6, 13.7
The Family as a Social Institution: Current Views	13.8
Religion and Marriage	13.9
Religion and Sex Practices	13.10
Abortion	13.11
Sex and Intimacy	13.12
Extramarital Affairs	13.13
Relationship with Spouse/Partner	13.14
Unequal Spousal Earnings Levels	13.15
Sexual Morality	13.16

When social historians look back to the period from 1983 to 1992, they will be examining a particularly dramatic time in the history of sexuality in America. These years will be seen as significant not only socially, politically, and medically, but also emotionally, as a new-found euphoria about sexual freedom was suddenly assaulted by a new medical reality. We can probably say with some confidence that no one in America has been untouched by that new reality, whether in terms of the blood supply, health technologies and precautions, immigration regulations, social and sexual relationships, or a need for caregiving. In our study, we took a close look at the difference these eight years made in the sociosexual life of Americans.

There is widespread agreement that the mid-1980s marked the end of the sexually unfettered development of the 1960s and 1970s. During the earlier period, new methods of contraception combined with new social attitudes to make for free-flowing, guilt-reduced sexual experimentation. The priorities, practices, and attitudes that characterized those years seem to have run their course. Or have they? We have found that the burgeoning sense of freedom, the choices of love or lust, the spirit of personal autonomy that marked the sexuality of those earlier years is still part of the American spirit. The emphasis is still on fun and social growth, but in new "safe" forms and with some changes. Americans have refused to allow careers, money, passion, and a spirit of liberation to be consigned to the dustbin of history because of the failure of medicine to conquer sexually transmitted diseases. There has been no sexual retrenchment. A new, more mature liberation is "in."

Although few have been left sexually unaffected during the turbulence of the past decade, women demonstrate the greatest degree of increasing liberation, even surpassing, as a group, the young of both sexes who were most affected by the changes of the 1970s. Anyone who believes that there has been a diminution of and/or a retreat from an intense demand for sex is wrong. There have been major changes in all areas of society, but a close look at practices and life-styles during this period reveals that there has been no reduction in sexual activity.

The fear of AIDS has produced some changes in behavior, but Americans, having tasted sexual freedom, refuse to turn back the sexual calendar. Health sources in the gay community claim that "safe sex" is now a preferred strategy, that condoms are more frequently used, and that other techniques are being substituted for anal intercourse. Heterosexual couples are now using condoms and vaginal creams, some with supposed anti-AIDS ingredients, but the incidence of sexual activity has not apparently diminished. How sex is performed has changed, but the omnipresence of sexual activity has not. While many now pay heed to the call for "safe sex," involving lotions, potions, and avoidance of some sexual practices and partners, Americans' sex lives are likely as active as, or more active than, in any other period of American history.

To determine the changes that have taken place in American sociosexual attitudes and behavior, this chapter compares two phases of our study. Phase One was conducted during 1983 to 1985. Phase Two, encompassing 1988 to 1992 and reflecting a broader frame of reference, surveyed the same key areas of American sexuality across a decade and provided a basis for comparison and contrast.

The years between the two studies were sexually critical and, indeed, at times, almost hysterical. Rarely has a week passed without the Centers for Disease Control in Atlanta issuing a new bulletin on AIDS statistics or research. The mass media, initially instrumental in publicizing the menace of AIDS, continue to provide constant hope for new cures, followed by renewed disappointment.

This period has also produced social changes in employment patterns and in family structures. As more women continue to enter the work force, the two-income family has now become the norm; over two out of three married women are working outside of the home. Dr. Michael Yapko, one of our original "gang of 200" and now a California psychologist and director of the Milton Erickson Foundation in San Diego, commented on these changes and expanded on some of the interpersonal adjustment problems that have emerged:[1]

> There has been much written on the changes in roles that have expanded the range of choices for both men and women. Much of the literature focuses on the choice many women made to put career ahead of family

as the main reason that older, better educated women are statistically more likely to end up alone. The discovery that delaying marriage and family may mean forgoing marriage and family is still having a negative effect in women's consciousness. The recent change in social roles based on gender is no doubt a leading basis for the difficulty people seem to have in establishing meaningful and satisfying relationships. As of this writing, more Americans now live alone than ever before—somewhere between 20 and 30 million. Many like it that way, but many more do not. The barriers that keep others out and one's self within are created and maintained by the lack of exposure to and tolerance for others. I see couples who break up because "She's put on ten pounds," and "He leaves his underwear on the floor." Does that sound like tolerance to you? I am often startled by the lack of insight people have regarding other people. Was it the self-indulgent focus on one's own needs evident in the Seventies that precluded the development of the ability to understand others?

Our comparative analysis, based on our Phase One and Phase Two, will focus on a number of topics relevant to sexuality. Often, several survey items explored a particular topic. We present the comparative data side-by-side, for clarity of examination. The large categories of concern are: sexual equality and sexual practice; age of sexual initiation; romantic love; the family; religion; abortion; sex and intimacy; marriage; and the state of the sexual world. Where our tables do not indicate separate responses for men and women, they are to be understood as the combined responses of both men and women.

SEXUAL EQUALITY AND SEXUAL PRACTICE

Does an endorsement of sexual equality in general mean an endorsement of a position that says men and women should behave with the same degree of freedom or restraint in sexual matters? We know that, in the past, men were permitted a degree of sexual freedom that was discouraged for women. Little boys, allowed to learn about their world with less constraint than little girls, were in a position to sexually explore themselves and their peers with some freedom, although suffering some adult disapproval when discovered. In adolescence, they were expected by their peers to try to gain sexual access to young women, and frequently achieved peer prestige if they were successful.

Little girls had less freedom to explore their own bodies and those of their friends. More closely supervised by adults, they were discouraged from self-exploration and frequently learned about their own bodies later, in sexual encounters with men. Whereas young boys were expected to seek sexual encounters, young women were not, and those who did suffered stigmas associated with the loss of one's "reputation." The possibility of pregnancy was omnipresent in the consciousness of young women contemplating sex.

Our interest was in whether and to what degree these attitudes had changed during the years under study. We examined our total sample's attitude toward premarital sexual experience for men. (See Table 13.1.)

Some significant changes in attitudes had occurred. Where 48% had advocated premarital sexual experience for men in the earlier period, 55% advocated it in the later period. Almost half the earlier sample believed that premarital sex for men was unimportant, but this minority diminished to just over one-fourth in the later period. Perhaps the most significant shift may be seen in the area of uncertainty: two-and-a-half times as many respondents were not sure in Phase Two.

The results of our interviews added detail to the numbers. Both sexes frequently expressed an expectation that a man would be in charge of sexual activities because he "knows" much more about sex and that this knowledge was necessary because the contemporary sexual world had become complex and one needed experience to cope with and enjoy sex today. Many interviewees expressed the attitude that women, too, needed premarital sexual experience. We explored this attitude in Table 13.2.

The need felt for female premarital sexual experience rose significantly from Phase One (37%) to Phase Two (47%) of the study, and the perception of a lack of importance declined even more dramatically (from 57% to 36%). Again, almost three times as many people at the later period were uncertain about how they felt on the issue. On the whole, there was an increasing acceptance, by and for both sexes, of the legitimacy of sexual experience preceding marriage.

Experts have argued for years about the relative contributions of nature (biology) and nurture (socialization) in the creation of a sexual being with specific appetites and capacities. It was long thought that women, or at least "decent" women, should not be expected to achieve orgasm. That myth was laid to rest with the women's movement, and the "right" of women to achieve an orgasm is now widely espoused. At the same time,

TABLE 13.1   **Survey Item B.7.**

FOR THE MAN, SEXUAL EXPERIENCE BEFORE MARRIAGE IS:		
	1983–1985	1988–1992
N =	4,480	2,728
Very important	15%	18%
Important	33	37
Not sure	6	16
Unimportant	35	24
Very unimportant	11	5
Very important + Important	48%	55%
Unimportant + Very unimportant	46%	29%

TABLE 13.2   **Survey Item B.8.**

FOR THE WOMAN, SEXUAL EXPERIENCE BEFORE MARRIAGE IS:		
	1983–1985	1988–1992
N =	4,474	2,738
Very important	9%	12%
Important	28	35
Not sure	6	17
Unimportant	41	30
Very unimportant	16	6
Very important + Important	37%	47%
Unimportant + Very unimportant	57%	36%

the expectation that a couple should achieve orgasm simultaneously has been ascribed largely to men, and is seen by some women as an expression of undesirable male domination. For some men, it is said, the ability to bring about simultaneous orgasm is an expression of their power, insofar as they can make a woman have an orgasm at just "the right time," and that time is generally determined by the man.

✦ IN THEIR OWN WORDS

When it comes to sex, many men are like little boys, with dominance or grandeur complexes that are just a pain. To me, the most obnoxious demand, and I do mean demand, is this childlike thing some guys have about coming together, and that unless you have simultaneous orgasm the sex experience is worthless. Orgasm is such a personal, intimate experience. This is a very sneaky thing, because, while it seems that the guy is concerned about your pleasure, he is really demanding that you orgasm when he wants you to for his needs. Some of these guys think they are symphony conductors orchestrating you in bed. When one of my girl friends pointed this out to me, it made instant sense; the light went on. I knew I was uncomfortable with this kind of demanding sex, but I couldn't put my finger on it. Of course, I said, that's it!

I had this guy, in fact, now that I think of it, two of them, who actually could not complete the sex act, they actually could not ejaculate, until the very moment that their partner had her orgasm. We, actually he, failed to see how insidious it is. I almost started thinking as they do—he cried loudly. I mean, real tears. He was moaning that he is a failure, that I will hate him, and he kept apologizing for his failure to make me come. Boy, did that surprise me. I'm not accustomed to men crying when they come to bed with me.

—A 36-year-old divorced former model, now in advertising

Table 13.3 gives a picture of how our respondents felt about the need for simultaneous orgasm.

A large majority of our sample of both men and women rejected the premise that simultaneous orgasm is a necessary aspect of satisfactory sex. This was true in both Phase One and Phase Two. Some interesting differences did emerge, however, between men and women and between the time periods. In both instances, and in some considerable degree (by up to 10%), men more than women agreed with the proposition. This would have been predicted by our interviews, although one might have expected larger differences between the sexes. What is surprising is that men in Phase Two agreed with the statement by 5% more than the men did 8 years before, and disagreed with it by 13% less than at the preceding time. We can only speculate on what these differences mean. On the one hand, men may not be listening to women's complaints about being forced to follow a male-set schedule for orgasm. On the other hand, recognizing that women are entitled to experience orgasm fully, men may now be attempting to satisfy the female need by accommodating their own scheduling to the female pace. These results may indicate a certain lack of communication between sexual partners, and the greater expression of no opinion in the later survey (three times as much for men) would seem to support a conclusion that confusion has intensified around this issue.

Related to the issue of orgasm is that of masturbation, and it is appropriate to examine here how Americans view autoeroticism in adults. Masturbation is generally associated with adolescence and is little spoken of as practiced by adults, but we know that it is a function of adult sexuality through marriage and into old age. Although mental health professionals have stressed the normalcy and appropriateness of

TABLE 13.3   **Survey Item C.9.**

SIMULTANEOUS ORGASM IS A MUST FOR GRATIFYING SEX:				
	1983–1985		1988–1992	
	Men	Women	Men	Women
N =	2,151	2,270	1,338	1,398
Strongly agree	4%	3%	7%	3%
Agree	15	10	17	11
No opinion	4	4	12	10
Disagree	48	54	52	52
Strongly disagree	29	29	12	24
Strongly agree + Agree	19%	13%	24%	14%
Disagree + Strongly disagree	77%	83%	64%	76%

masturbation, it can produce negative reaction from spouses who feel it is a form of cheating on them or who resent it because it involves sexual fantasies of which they are not a part. Still others have claimed that masturbation reduced the libidinal energy of their partners, thereby cheating them of full sexual participation. We were interested in how our sample felt about the issue and how their feelings might have changed in the course of our study. (See Table 13.4.)

From Phase One to Phase Two, there was some slight increase in an acknowledgment of masturbation into adulthood, but, on the whole, both men and women, by a sizable majority at both times, recognized the normalcy of the practice. A greater change was found in those people who rejected the idea. In Phase One, 28% of men and 31% of women denied masturbation as a normal adult activity; 8 years later, these figures had dropped to 12% among both men and women. The change in attitude was quite dramatic for women, perhaps as a function of women's learning that masturbation is a societally acceptable activity for themselves as well as for men. Of equal interest is the significant increase in the number of people who, 8 years later, held no opinion on the subject. Indeed, the remainder between those who disagreed in Phase One and those who disagreed in Phase Two seems to have moved into the no opinion category. This is not, of course, to suggest that these are the same people; numbers can never translate into the complexity of real people. The no opinion respondents suggest some contemporary ambivalence about a sexual behavior that was much less prevalent earlier.

TABLE 13.4   **Survey Item C.5.**

MASTURBATION IS A NATURAL PART OF LIFE AND CONTINUES ON IN MARRIAGE:				
	1983–1985		1988–1992	
	Men	Women	Men	Women
N =	2,160	2,331	1,340	1,396
Strongly agree	12%	10%	17%	20%
Agree	51	49	49	47
No opinion	9	10	22	21
Disagree	21	27	10	9
Strongly disagree	7	4	2	3
Strongly agree + Agree	63%	59%	66%	67%
Disagree + Strongly disagree	28%	31%	12%	12%

Not only do the majority of adults recognize the normality of masturbation, some of them use it imaginatively as an additional technique to enhance their lovemaking.

IN THEIR OWN WORDS

There are times she has woman trouble, you know, gynecological problems, urinary infections, or a heavy menstrual flow and all. So I'm not a rigid person. If I feel horny, and want her, we do other things. One of the other things we do a lot is masturbation. We have it developed to a fine art. We rent a porno movie, take a bath, rub each other down with baby oil, and it's kind of like playing teenagers again. You would be surprised at how varied and exciting masturbation can be. My goodness, it sounds like I am doing a commercial for it. Hey, gone are the days when you would touch yourself impurely under the covers; it's all different now. Of course, it's never happened to me, but I know guys who have difficulty maintaining an erection and masturbation is just the ticket for them. My wife and I not only masturbate each other at the same time, but we get pleasure watching each other masturbate individually as well. It is a terrifically exciting thing, and has tremendous possibilities, though I think we've tried them all.

At first I was just a bit hesitant to tell her about my affair with lady palm and her five daughters, you know what I mean? Much to my surprise, she told me that she, like many other women, had difficulty having orgasm from penetration, and had been a masturbator for a long while. Together, we put our two good minds to work and, *voilà!* love and joy with a whole extra dimension.

—A 49-year-old CEO of a garment firm,
divorced and remarried, and a father

This personal account confirms and dramatizes the views of mental health practitioners, urologists, and gynecologists whom we interviewed. They assert that masturbation is a natural function and that not only does it not interfere with marriage, it can enhance it by providing a personal outlet that is important for both men and women.

AGE OF SEXUAL INITIATION

There is a widespread perception among the American people that parents are currently losing control over the behavior of their children, more so than at any time in the past. In no area is that so much perceived as in sexual matters, where, we frequently note, greater numbers of children, at earlier ages than before, are engaging in full sexual experiences. As the importance of parental approval and effective control has declined, the influence and pressure from peer groups has shown a concomitant increase, and it is difficult for a young person to avoid an early sexual experience when everyone else is "doing it."

It has been argued that demands that adolescents postpone sexual experience until social maturity are contrary to biological imperatives because social maturity is very late in arriving in contemporary society. Social and sexual maturity have been associated in all societies, but, in simpler times, social maturity was achieved when sexual maturity was reached and the appropriate religious and cultural "coming of age" rituals were performed. For young women, the first menstruation was the significant marker of sociosexual maturity. For young men, cultural acknowledgments and initiations substituted for the biological ones, and these were performed when a man was ready to fulfill the duties of an adult. From this point of view, contemporary society seems to be fighting a losing battle with biological sexual urges and, coupled with a decline in the force of social sanctions and in parental influence, we should not be surprised that there is an increase in sexual activity among the young.

Because this issue has received great attention and is regarded by many in contemporary American society as a symptom of moral degeneration, we were particularly interested in the experiences of our sample and any changes that might have taken place over the decade of our research.

Table 13.5 shows that the figures for the sexual initiation of children below age 10 remained unchanged from Phase One to Phase Two, for both men and women. We have reason to suspect the figures for the very young, particularly those under 10 years of age, are underestimated. From data on molestation and from our clinical experience, we

TABLE 13.5   Survey Item H.15.

SELF-IDENTIFICATION: AGE AT FIRST FULL SEXUAL RELATIONS:				
	1983–1985		1988–1992	
	Men	Women	Men	Women
N =	2,154	2,325	1,337	1,391
By age 10	2%	1%	2%	1%
11–14	16	6	17	7
15–18	44	42	55	53
19–25	36	48	23	37
26+	2	3	3	2
By age 14	18%	7%	19%	8%
After age 18	38%	51%	26%	39%

have discovered a frequency of sexual abuse involving this age level, which our interviews and additional data confirm.

Between Phase One and Phase Two, the incidence of full sexual relations for children below age 15 barely increased. Within this early age group, boys had significantly more sexual experience, by a full 10%, than did girls.

It is in the 15- to 18-year-old group that a radical change in sexual activity occurred over the time spread. In this age group, that of full-blown adolescence, both men and women showed an overwhelming increase into full sexual activity. Forty-four percent of the men in Phase One reported first full sexual activity between ages 15 to 18; the proportion rose to 55% 8 years later. The women's responses paralleled those of the men, going from 42% in Phase One to 53% in Phase Two. The fact that such numbers occur in this age group now, when prevailing wisdom would suggest that most people should have retreated from unconstrained sexual activity, indicates just how nonthreatening AIDS appears to a very large number of young Americans at this time.

Our questionnaire did not ask whether the first sexual experience was before or within the context of marriage, but we did ask this in our interviews, and our results showed that few of those who became sexually experienced before age 18 were married, even if they were pregnant or became parents by age 18. This was particularly true in Phase Two, when many more people were marrying later, and therefore more of them were having their initial sex as singles. If we assume that our younger sample was not married before age 18, then, in Phase One, 62% of the men and 49% of the women had premarital full sexual relations by that age and these numbers increased in Phase Two to 74% of the men and 61% of the women. When we reversed these numbers, to dramatize the point of the growing unimportance of premarital virginity, we saw that the number of those who were virgins after age 18 dropped drastically during this decade. The percentage of virginal men decreased from 38% to 26%; that of women, from 51% to 39%. The percentage of virgins after the age of 26 remained constant over the time period at around 2%.

ROMANTIC LOVE

The search for love, for some people, is a way of life. They may never find true love, by their definitions, but they may search forever for that elusive romantic condition. The inability to find "love" may be a problem of definition. Romantic love as Western fiction has portrayed it may not correspond to real-life possibilities. On the other hand, experts suggest that those who never find love may be too cautious or too fearful of the commitments a love relationship involves. How much are people prepared to risk for love? Has the idealization of love changed during the past decade?

By a noticeable but by no means overwhelming degree, the romance with romance declined in America during our study's time frame. (See Table 13.6.) The desirability of finding a true love relationship, and the willingness to expose oneself to suffering in the process, is still highly valued by a vast majority of Americans.

Because there is a tendency to believe that women are more inclined toward romantic love than are men, we examined responses differentially by sex, as seen in Table 13.7.

We found some slight, and perhaps significant, differences between men and women. Respondents in agreement showed remarkably high percentages in both time periods, in spite of a significant shift downward. Women tended to respond with more strength of feeling about the desirability of love at any cost (3% over men in Phase One and 5% over men in Phase Two). Again, the no opinion category increased at the later period, an indication that some people have become more uncertain about a whole array of sexual interactions. Apparently, the mood since the late 1980s has become somewhat less accepting of love at any cost.

But romantic love exists and is thriving in America. Ours is still a romantic country, and most Americans are hooked on love. We found in our interviews, however, that the relationships between partners have undergone some changes. Although it is rare for partners in love relationships to be totally equal, fewer women accept the role of supplicant or inferior partner. Being "head over heels in love," a condition that speaks of loss of control, is not as desirable as it once was. Mature decisions about relationships based on respect as well as on love are becoming more prevalent. Our respondents revealed an increasing care in their selection of partners in love relationships, in order to reduce the

TABLE 13.6   **Survey Item A.2.**

IT IS BETTER TO LOVE AND BE HURT THAN NOT TO KNOW LOVE:		
	1983–1985	1988–1992
N =	4,501	2,754
Strongly agree	47%	37%
Agree	44	48
No opinion	2	5
Disagree	6	8
Strongly disagree	1	2
Strongly agree + Agree	91%	85%
Disagree + Strongly disagree	7%	10%

TABLE 13.7   **Survey Item A.2.**

IT IS BETTER TO LOVE AND BE HURT THAN NOT TO KNOW LOVE:				
	1983–1985		1988–1992	
	Men	Women	Men	Women
N =	2,161	2,340	1,341	1,413
Strongly agree	46%	49%	34%	39%
Agree	45	41	50	46
No opinion	1	3	6	5
Disagree	7	6	8	8
Strongly disagree	1	1	2	2
Strongly agree + Agree	91%	90%	84%	85%
Disagree + Strongly disagree	8%	7%	10%	10%

possibility of being hurt, but they retained a commitment to "taking a chance on love," as the old song advises.

THE FAMILY

While we are on the subject of old songs, we quote another one that says "Love and marriage go together like a horse and carriage." Few horses and carriages are around today, but there is still a strong commitment to the association of love with marriage, and, through marriage, with family building. The American family remains a valued institution, as we have seen in previous chapters; most of the marriage-and-the-family jokes aren't heard much anymore. Quips such as "What are the three rings of marriage? The engagement ring, the wedding ring, and the suffering" have disappeared along with the classic, "Marriage is an institution, but who wants to live in an institution?" Henny Youngman's oft-quoted phrase, "Take my wife, please," gets fewer laughs and is regarded as in poor taste by many, because it is becoming more irrelevant. Table 13.8 reveals that the commitment to the family has actually increased through the decade.

A remarkable increase of agreement regarding the importance of the family occurred from Phase One to Phase Two. In Phase One, 78% agreed, but 18% disagreed; by Phase Two, 91% agreed and only 5% disagreed. The rate of uncertainty remained the same.

How can we understand these figures? Have people rediscovered within the family a sense of security not provided otherwise in society? The family is a complex institution providing a range of supports that address social, financial, and emotional needs. In times of stress, the

TABLE 13.8   Survey Item A.1.

THE FAMILY IS THE MOST IMPORTANT INSTITUTION IN SOCIETY:		
	1983–1985	1988–1992
N =	4,500	2,760
Strongly agree	34%	54%
Agree	44	37
No opinion	4	4
Disagree	14	4
Strongly disagree	4	1
Strongly agree + Agree	78%	91%
Disagree + Strongly disagree	18%	5%

family is often the most reliable shelter. The time period of Phase Two has been a more stressful time, notably in economic terms, than was that of Phase One. The socioeconomic future of many young professionals has collapsed and they have found themselves turning to their families for emotional as well as financial support. The image of America in the late 1980s and early 1990s is that of a much more dangerous place than it was before, and the family as a secure retreat takes on greater significance.

RELIGION

We have been told by organized religion that "The family that prays together, stays together," and we were interested in how our study population responded to the connection between religion and marriage and whether the perception of the connection had changed over time. Does religion add some special virtue or merit to marriage?

The responses in Table 13.9 show some dramatic changes in religious commitment within marriage, in the short time span that we are considering here. The level of agreement with the premise that there is a positive connection between religion and marriage grew from 50% in Phase One to 61% in Phase Two, and the level of disagreement dropped even more significantly, from 42% in Phase One to 24% in Phase Two. The higher number of people uncertain about the connection, from 8% to 15%, is provocative as well, and suggests that people are being more thoughtful in their examination of the interconnections of aspects of their social world.

Do these figures mean that Americans are looking to organized religion to structure their lives and that they are willing to allow pastoral directives to dictate personal decisions, particularly in sexual practices?

TABLE 13.9   **Survey Item A.5.**

RELIGION IS AN IMPORTANT FACTOR IN MARRIAGE:		
	1983–1985	1988–1992
N =	4,491	2,749
Strongly agree	16%	21%
Agree	34	40
No opinion	8	15
Disagree	29	19
Strongly disagree	13	5
Strongly agree + Agree	50%	61%
Disagree + Strongly disagree	42%	24%

Our observation is that Americans fit religion into their lives, rather than fitting their lives into the framework created by religion. To see whether this was true and whether it had changed over time, we turned again to our two samples. (See Table 13.10.)

Organized religions have traditionally had a dominant stake in the sexual lives of their adherents. Not only is sex an important area of behavior in its own right, it is the channel through which new members of the religious group are produced, and organized religions are interested in expanding their numbers. Our respondents, while increasing a commitment to the importance of religion in marriage (see Table 13.9), increasingly rejected religious control over personal sexual expression. By Phase Two, only 35% of the men felt it appropriate to have their sexual behavior in

TABLE 13.10   **Survey Item B.6.**

THAT MY SEX PRACTICES ARE IN HARMONY WITH MY RELIGION IS:				
	1983–1985		1988–1992	
	Men	Women	Men	Women
N =	2,140	2,318	1,330	1,393
Very important	13%	11%	9%	12%
Important	37	39	26	26
Not sure	18	13	22	21
Unimportant	22	28	27	30
Very unimportant	10	9	16	11
Very important + Important	50%	50%	35%	38%
Unimportant + Very unimportant	32%	37%	43%	41%

harmony with their religion, compared with half of the men in Phase One. (See Table 13.10.) For women, the decline was also sharp, from half in the earlier period to 38% in the later. The degree of active rejection rose as well, but somewhat less dramatically because it was offset by an increase in the number of people who were not sure about the need to adjust their sexual needs to religious dictates. Although there was a downward trend in the interconnection between religion and sexual practice, more than one-third of our sample still felt it necessary to reconcile the two.

ABORTION

The diminished authority of religion over personal decision making is seen even more dramatically around the issue of abortion, which has become perhaps the most controversial and divisive issue in American society. Emotional appeals and mass demonstrations have been mounted by groups on both sides of the issue, but our findings show that anti-choice groups speak for a smaller minority of Americans in Phase Two than they did in the earlier time period of Phase One. (See Table 13.11.)

The data on this issue confirm our research indicating that support for an anti-abortion position dropped considerably from Phase One to Phase Two. Many Americans no longer refer to this issue as "pro-abortion" or "anti-abortion," but prefer the terms "pro-choice" or "pro-life," reflecting the fact that much of American society sees the issue as one of individual decision making. Not sure responses were higher in the earlier period, offering evidence that more people have resolved their own position. In

TABLE 13.11   **Survey Item A.11.**

ABORTION IS MURDER:				
	1983–1985		1988–1992	
	Men	Women	Men	Women
N =	2,160	2,336	1,343	1,411
Strongly agree	23%	16%	14%	15%
Agree	16	17	16	15
Not sure	35	35	18	15
Disagree	20	23	32	26
Strongly disagree	6	9	20	29
Strongly agree + Agree	39%	33%	30%	30%
Disagree + Strongly disagree	26%	32%	52%	55%

spite of increasing openness to religion by many Americans, there is less acceptance of religious intrusion into decisions that are understood to be specifically personal, such as sexual practices and abortion.

SEX AND INTIMACY

An aspect of the image of romantic love is that sex and intimacy are intrinsically combined: one has sex only in the context of love, and love is fully realized through sex. At the other extreme is the idealization of the platonic relationship that is uncompromised by sexual desire. Some women say that their most intimate relationships are with gay men with whom they know they will not have sex, and men are reputed to lose respect, and the associated emotional affinity needed for intimacy, for women who are sexually accessible. This complicated question has potentially many layers of meaning, depending on one's definition of intimacy. We were interested in the perception of our comparative samples in considering this question. Their replies are indicated in Table 13.12.

In both Phase One and Phase Two of our study, and among both men and women, there was overwhelming separation between sex and intimacy. Not surprisingly, but only by a small margin, women were more consistent in separating sex and intimacy, suggesting that they may find, more than men do, that sex interferes with, or detracts from, intimacy. The gap between the sexes widened somewhat from Phase One to Phase Two. Attitudes have not changed much on this subject over the period of our research, even though this was a time of great sexual activity and disquiet in American society.

TABLE 13.12 Survey Item C.12.

SEX AND INTIMACY ARE TWO DIFFERENT THINGS:

	1983–1985		1988–1992	
	Men	Women	Men	Women
N =	2,155	2,292	1,339	1,413
Strongly agree	25%	29%	21%	32%
Agree	46	45	48	43
No opinion	2	1	10	4
Disagree	18	18	16	16
Strongly disagree	9	7	5	5
Strongly agree + Agree	71%	74%	69%	75%
Disagree + Strongly disagree	27%	25%	21%	21%

Our survey item did not ask whether people thought that sex and intimacy *should* be two different things; our responses might have been different if it had. We know, for example, that many men who frequent prostitutes say that they do so for sexual outlets unencumbered by emotional ties.

MARRIAGE

There is good reason to believe that, in spite of a commitment to romantic love, the institution of marriage in America, which seemingly had fallen on hard times, has made a dramatic comeback. It is possible that marriage is in trouble because of the idealization of romantic love. With a statistic of one out of two marriages in America ending in divorce, we can suppose only that marriage is somehow not satisfying the expectations of those who enter into it. It seems reasonable to assume that people who enter into marriage expect that their marriages will be successful and are negatively emotionally affected when they fail. As easy as it is to get a divorce today, and as common as it is to do so, each divorce takes its toll on the people involved. There seems a fragility of will or an absence of skill to make marriage into a permanent structure for many in modern society. Yet marriage remains important; most people marry, and many do it several times.

We were interested in the factors that might enhance a relationship, such as friendship in addition to love, and the factors that might debilitate a relationship, such as extramarital affairs, and issues involving money. This section contains the results of several questionnaire items that were related to the success of a marriage.

Extramarital Affairs

Adultery in those distant "old days" was often the only accepted grounds for divorce, and 1930s comedies were filled with scenes, complete with detectives and photographers, of illicit meetings staged in hotel rooms for the purpose of eliciting divorce-court evidence.

Times changed, however. By the 1970s, open marriage was being espoused by some experts as conducive to a happy marriage; many couples were exchanging spouses and seeking, with their spouses' approval, other sexual connections. But extramarital affairs remained a reason for divorce, and many people remained unconvinced that sexual infidelity would strengthen their marriage. We wanted our sample to consider the question and enable us to see whether these attitudes had changed from our earlier to our later phase.

By a vast majority, our sample, in both Phase One and Phase Two, remained convinced that extramarital affairs negatively impact the

TABLE 13.13   Survey Item C.2.

EXTRAMARITAL AFFAIRS DO NOT SERIOUSLY AFFECT MARRIAGES:		
	1983–1985	1988–1992
N =	4,502	2,759
Strongly agree	4%	4%
Agree	19	8
No opinion	3	5
Disagree	36	39
Strongly disagree	38	44
Strongly agree + Agree	23%	12%
Disagree + Strongly disagree	74%	83%

marriage relationship. (See Table 13.13.) This conviction increased from 74% at the earlier period to 83% currently, and the percentage of people who thought marriage was not seriously affected by adultery decreased significantly by 11%, from 23% earlier to 12% later. These results correspond to our earlier findings (Table 13.8) of increased evaluations of family as an important institution.

A decade after our first study, we found that fidelity was more highly valued in marriage, in what seems a significant shift for Americans. It is less that fidelity is now stylish, or even that it is a reasoned response to dangers much more virulent than the "crabs" mentioned above, but more that marriage as an institution and a commitment to a spouse is now more highly valued. Because we were interested in examining the quality of the emotional commitment, we asked our respondents to consider how they felt about their spouses as friends. Most people assume that a feeling of friendship, accompanying love, affection, and mutual responsibility, enhances the total relationship and makes it more durable. We wanted our respondents to give a definite evaluation, so we did not present them with a gradation of choices. (See Table 13.14.)

TABLE 13.14   Survey Item E.1.

MY SPOUSE/PARTNER IS ALSO MY BEST FRIEND:				
	1983–1985		1988–1992	
	Men	Women	Men	Women
N =	1,236	1,335	770	802
Yes	83%	83%	85%	82%
No	17%	17%	15%	18%

Are you kidding? Ask a man who knows about extramarital affairs—like me. I've had it from both ends. Of course, they make a difference; they can be, and often are, devastating. I know that many people who think they are so free are sleeping around like crazy. My industry is certainly noted for that. What it does, or, at least, what it did in my case, was to destroy trust; you lose your sense of trust in your partner. Once you've lost trust, what do you have left to keep the two of you together?

I used to be able to kid myself that it was a fling, that it didn't hurt my wife. You know the old cliché, "What she doesn't know won't hurt her." But it did. I brought home crabs and gonorrhea. Try to explain that to your wife as some kind of strange accident you know nothing about. Maybe it was the toilet seat. That was bad enough, but the look in her eyes when she realized . . . and she was no dope. You get sexually transmitted diseases only one way—by having sex with somebody. Several times I promised myself I would try to stop. Notice what I said—"try to stop." With that tenuous beginning it was really a go, not a stop. Now you know why I've been married three times. But fate dealt me some funny cards too, when I discovered my second wife having an affair with my closest friend. That's life, isn't it? I was hurt plenty by it. Of course the marriage split up, but that didn't stop my wanderlust.

Maturity comes slowly, and maybe age affects it, too. At my age I am still sexually active, but my hormones aren't raging like they used to. I'm involved pretty heavily with a wonderful woman now; I'm not sure it's going to end in marriage. We seem to have something terribly wonderful, like I couldn't believe existed, even right now. But, you know, I haven't cheated at all, and it's been a good two years now. I play it like the alcoholics in Alcoholics Anonymous do. I play it a day at a time. So far, so good.

—A divorced 53-year-old man who has been married three times

In both periods, the results were virtually the same for both sexes, and the differences were trivial. The vast majority of Americans appeared to highly value their spouses. The commitment of friendship with spouses demonstrated here directly counters the findings claimed in *The Hite Report of 1976*[2] that a majority of women disliked, or even hated, their husbands.

The Male Ego

The television image of the "typical" American family in the 1950s included a working husband, a couple or trio of school-age children, and a wife/mother who stayed at home ministering to everyone else's needs. A few years before, during the Second World War, she might have been employed, contributing her best to the war effort in a factory, or an office, or in activities that men, who were away fighting, were not available to fill. When the war ended and the men returned, women were persuaded that their place was in the home, preferably the suburban home, being comfortably supported by a husband who was doing well financially in the prosperous postwar years. A "good provider" was a successful husband and a successful man; having a working wife—by implication, because money was needed—was regarded as a slur on a husband's ability to provide.

This has all changed; we know that 74+% of married women now work outside of the home. Often, this is precisely because they need the money. Sometimes, however, it is motivated by an interest in the work activity itself, and many women who are now prepared for careers that are well paying and prestigious prefer to work at these careers rather than to be supported by their husbands. Things have changed so much that now, rather than explaining why they are working, women often find themselves having to explain or justify why they *don't* work.

There is ambivalence about women working, however. Are other responsibilities, to husband, children, and home, being neglected? Are women under too much pressure, and will the successful woman threaten her husband's ego? Most women do not earn as much as men do for the same work, an issue that "equal pay for equal work" seeks to address. But some women do earn as much as their husbands, and some earn more. Many men, during these economically lean times, are having trouble finding or keeping jobs, and others have found their previously well paying jobs have disappeared because of technological change or corporate cutbacks. The result is often a reduction of income or a total loss of income. Would having a wife earning more than the husband prove devastating to their egos, or, alternatively, a relief because some of the pressure is being taken off them? We were curious about these issues and the possible changes in attitude that may have resulted from several more years of intensified female employment.

The results of this survey item were dramatic and revealing, in several ways. (See Table 13.15.) The stereotype of the husband whose fragile ego is damaged by a wife's earning more than he does was not borne out by our sample of men in either Phase One or Phase Two, although, by Phase Two, there was a sizable increase (by 10%) of men who disagreed with the possibility of a problem. The 21% in Phase One who felt that their wives' earning more than they did would create a problem dropped to 8% in Phase Two. We had not anticipated that women would agree with the possibility of a problem if their husband's earnings exceeded theirs, but, in Phase One, 6% of women agreed that a serious problem might be created. This percentage dropped by 2% by Phase Two. A shift in the later data is in the percentage of men who had no opinion on the subject—8% in Phase Two, in contrast to 5% in Phase One. We have seen this pattern appear repeatedly in the responses in this chapter, leading us to surmise that, as the world changes around them, some people are left

TABLE 13.15 Survey Item A.7.

IF MY SPOUSE EARNED MORE THAN I, IT WOULD BE A SERIOUS PROBLEM:				
	1983–1985		1988–1992	
	Men	Women	Men	Women
N =	2,158	2,333	1,342	1,413
Strongly agree	5%	3%	2%	1%
Agree	16	3	6	1
No opinion	5	5	8	4
Disagree	46	48	46	47
Strongly disagree	28	41	38	47
Strongly agree + Agree	21%	6%	8%	2%
Disagree + Strongly disagree	74%	89%	84%	94%

with uncertainty about how they feel about things. It appears, on the whole, that married partners are not particularly threatened by the superior earning power of a spouse (indeed, they might conceivably be delighted by it), and whatever ego assaults may have existed in the past have significantly diminished in the fiscally tight present.

THE STATE OF THE SEXUAL WORLD

In 1969, the famous anthropologist, Margaret Mead, delivered a series of lectures that were published one year later as *Culture and Commitment*.[3] In these lectures, she proposed a model of three types of societies, which she believed described the history of the human experience.

"Postfigurative" societies are those in which children learn all they need to know from the adults around them, and continue to believe and live as their forebears had done. This is the condition of pretechnological simple societies where change occurs, but slowly and sometimes imperceptibly.

With the expansion of human groups, in terms of size, geography, and technology, a new arrangement, defined as "configurative," is introduced. Here, individuals learn much of what they need to know from their peers, because the experience of older generations has not included an adjustment to these new developments. Mead suggested that great civilizations included both postfigurative and configurative adjustments.

The last arrangement that Mead identified was, she believed, totally new and a function only of contemporary society. She called this "prefigurative" and described it as a condition of society where the elders learn from the children. We have only to think of our current experience with computer technology to see an example of how the inventions and enthusiasms of the young are changing the world of their parents. Mead was careful to point out that none of these configurations exists alone, that a society doesn't change entirely from one model to the next, and that, even in the contemporary world, children still learn from their elders as well as their peers, and adults learn only some things from the young.

We introduce Mead's formulation here as something to think about as we consider how people feel about the current state of sex and sexual morality. A simple platitude would propose that adults always deplored the behavior of the young, that they always felt things were better and more moral when they were young. In a postfigurative society, the platitude probably would not apply. The adults would have seen themselves reflected in the young and would have recognized a continuation, through the generations, of approved social conduct.

We live, however, in a world of change. The influence of peers is at least as important as the influence of parents, and parents are often changing their behavior to accommodate the experiments of the young, but are just as often not very confident that what they are doing is right. We were interested in how people felt about the contemporary moral climate, and asked questions of our samples in both phases of our study, to try to ascertain their feelings. In 1983 to 1985, we asked people to describe their feelings about changes in the preceding 20 years; in 1988 to 1992, we asked how they felt about the preceding 3 years.

The responses (Table 13.16) indicated that well over a majority of Americans during Phase One felt that behavior and sexual morality had disintegrated. However, during Phase Two, far fewer respondents reported feelings of sexual disintegration in society. What makes this of particular

TABLE 13.16   **Survey Item C.1.**

COMPARATIVE WORDING:		
	Phase One:	Phase Two:
	In the last 2 decades sexual morality has disintegrated	In the last 3 years sexual morality has disintegrated
N =	4,495	2,759
Strongly agree	24%	14%
Agree	39	30
No opinion	25	14
Disagree	8	36
Strongly disagree	4	6
Strongly agree + Agree	63%	44%
Disagree + Strongly disagree	12%	42%

interest is that the late 1980s were a time of great tension about sexual matters regarding AIDS and other sexually transmitted diseases.

The 25 years before 1983, starting in 1958, witnessed dramatic changes in American society. At the end of the conservative 1950s, new voices emerged advocating freedom of personal expression in every area of life. Experimentation in sexual behavior, family structure, social configurations (such as communes), and drug use, to name just a few, were advanced and applauded. Significant new voices emerged demanding "liberation" for women, for gays, and for other minority groups. Abortion was legalized and "the pill" gave women greater control over pregnancy and the determination of their own sexual activity. The "melting pot" image of America was scorned; people were urged to be proud of their differences and to assert them. The young rejected the past, applauded the present, and looked forward to a transformed and unrecognizable future. In our Phase One sample, 63% looked back on these years as a time when sexual morality had significantly disintegrated, and only 12% disagreed with this premise.

By Phase Two, many of the changes of the earlier period were either entrenched in America or had been rejected. Drug use has emerged more as a problem than a source of pleasure for most Americans, and Timothy Leary, the Harvard professor who had advised young people to "turn on and drop out," is almost a quaint figure of a bygone era. The sexual arena has been significantly changed by the problem of sexually transmitted diseases, first with the wave of concern over genital herpes, which affects more than 25 million Americans, and then with the much more ominous specter of AIDS, whose victims increase every day. People are being encouraged to be more circumspect about their sexual activities and partners, and the mood of the times is not in the direction of sexual abandon. In spite of these developments, or perhaps because of them, fewer of our Phase Two sample (44%), looking back over the past several years, saw decline in sexual morality than did the earlier group (63%).

SUMMING UP

Our inspection of the comparative data derived from Phase One (1983–1985) and Phase Two (1988–1992) leads us to several conclusions.

The earlier period's inclination toward sexual experimentation and promiscuity has given way, to some extent, to a preference for somewhat more selective sexual interaction, possibly responsive to the need for "safer sex." The family, an institution under attack in the earlier period, has regained some of its esteem, and more Americans are looking within the traditional family structure to satisfy a range of needs that includes the sexual. More people now reject extramarital experimentation, not necessarily on a moral basis but as a threat to personal safety and to marriage and family. An interest in including religion in life experience has increased, but Americans reserve the right to make their own personal decisions about sexual matters, regardless of the directives of organized religions.

In spite of the warnings about sexually transmitted diseases, the young appear to be dissociated from the apparently new-found moderation of adults. Sexual encounters are occurring at increasingly younger ages, and premarital virginity has usually been shed before the 18th birthday; it appears that, for both males and females, virginity is little valued.

We studied our population for many variables, including age, gender, education, marital status, religion, politics, income, and region, and discovered that there were differences related to every one of them. It is instructive how many factors are a part of sexual attitudes and chosen practices. It is this fact that makes Americans both resilient and, at times, confused. The idea that individuals are totally free agents sexually is, with the exception of a very few, simply not true. Contributing to our national bewilderment are our intensely conflicting attitudes toward sex: we are alternately irresistibly drawn toward sex and then suffer intense guilt for the pleasure we obtain from it. One example of this is seen in the national controversy on pornography and its contribution to rape, violence, and, in general, the denigration of women. At the same time, if we consider just the big-name, very popular sex magazines, an estimated 35 million copies are bought by Americans every month. One item in our questionnaire inquired whether the respondent felt that there was too much pornographic material in neighborhood stores. Of the four regions of the country, just over half of the people in three areas responded that there was too much. In the religious South, where fundamentalists have been aggressively active against pornography, the Bible Belt's response was the lowest, with less than half agreeing that there was too much pornography in their neighborhood stores.

Perhaps the most telling finding from our comparison of the responses in the two time periods is the unrest and indecision displayed by our Phase Two respondents. For most items—with the exception of questions relating to abortion, the disintegration of sexual morality, and the importance of the family—the no opinion responses in Phase Two were two to three times what they had been in Phase One. We observed significantly less firm opinion and more irresolution in the second phase sample than in the first.

Are people more confused now? Is this a transitional period in which opinions and attitudes are fluid? Or are more people less decisive than they had been? We know that the old verities don't apply much any more! Are people suspicious of the future? Is their uncertainty, in general, a measure of the times, when caution and apprehension cloud the ability to make definite judgments? Has all of the current politicking about abortion and morality made people doubt their own opinions about such important social issues? We wonder! It is then no surprise that, in a time of such confusion, the family should be more highly valued. In an unpredictable world, the family represents a safe, dependable haven from the chaos surrounding it.

Nonetheless, this indecision has not seriously curtailed sexual activity, although it has altered sociosexual practices. Many Americans may now look before they take a sexual leap, but leap they do. Definite sexual changes are visible in American society. Of great interest to all Americans is the enormous change in life-styles and sex roles of the postmature population. Thanks to modern medicine and their own desire for active sex lives, society now sees these men and women as credible sexual beings. They are increasingly free of *shame* for acting as people who, for too long, had been regarded as absurd "dirty old men" and women. Some respondents in the 65+ age group even reported having daily sex. Active, healthy sex continues well into their 80s for increasingly greater numbers of both men and women.

An egalitarian attitude toward the sexual behavior of both men and women is becoming more pervasive, and there is a growing acceptance of the right of women to pursue their own sexual inclinations. The differences between the attitudes of men and women on a wide range of sexual topics have decreased over time. While we find less of the "battle of the sexes," and a greater sense of sex partnership, this difference is most remarkable in the group of women who have full-time careers outside of the home. On a number of sexual issues, they are more in agreement with men than with women who are homemakers. Instead of searches for why each group is different sexually, we found that there is, in general, a greater acceptance of each other as they are, by both men and women. In general, we find a greater sense of maturity of sexuality. We detect less of what the *New York Times* described so well, in outlining a difference between French and American culture: "Americans treated sex as something between a secret ritual and an embarrassing necessity."[4]

Comparison of Janus Report Sample with National Census Data

I n any study, the significance of the findings is directly related to the characteristics of the research sample from which the results are derived. If the sample is representative of a larger population, then it may be possible to generalize the findings to that larger population.

Because our study was performed in the absence of any governmental or private agency funding, we did not have the capacity to adhere to the rigorous requirements of stratified sampling, so the descriptors for our panel of respondents will not be fully concordant with those of the national population. Nevertheless, we were able, within the capabilities of our limited resources, to maintain a fair amount of control over the characteristics of our research sample.

How representative of the nation's population, then, is our sample? Can we conclude that our bank of respondents resembles a typical cross-section of the country? In this appendix, we compare the demographic characteristics of the Janus Report sample with those of the U.S. population 18 years and older, as stated in the Bureau of the Census publications cited.

The U.S. Government does not, of course, maintain or publish data on the numbers of citizen with particular political predilections, nor with varying levels of religious devotion, so we have no national statistics on these characteristics against which to compare our sample of respondents.

But, with regard to the other demographic details, we note a striking concordance between our sample and the population of the country as a whole, on the most important descriptors of gender and age, and also on geographic region represented. As for those remaining, we do find some divergence on education, marital status, income, and religious preference.

Although our sample is not an exact representation of the national population, we believe it is sufficiently congruent to suggest that our findings are, by and large, a valid reflection of the behavior and attitudes of the society as a whole.

One final note: The reader will no doubt observe that we have not included data comparing response patterns of different ethnic or racial subgroups. This omission was not an oversight; it was our intentional choice. Our sample includes respondents from most sizable minority groups—African Americans, Hispanic Americans, Asian Americans, and others. However, we had chosen not to identify them as such on our questionnaire and thus not to segregate them into homogeneous subgroups, but rather to include them unidentified in our general sample and thereby reflect as much as possible the heterogeneity of the American public.

THE JANUS REPORT SAMPLE   **U.S. POPULATION**

			Gender			
	49%		Males		48%	
	51%		Females		52%	

Source for U.S. population data: Note 1.

M	W	Total		M	W	Total
			Age			
19%	19%	19%	18–26	19%	18%	19%
27	27	27	27–38	29	27	28
21	21	21	39–50	21	20	20
17	17	17	51–64	17	17	17
16	16	16	65+	14	18	16

Source for U.S. population data: Note 1.

M	W	Total		M	W	Total
			Education			
2%	2%	2%	Less than high school	10%	10%	10%
48	49	48	High school	48	53	52
24	24	24	Some college	19	19	19
15	14	15	College graduate	13	11	11
11	11	11	Postgraduate	10	7	8

Source for U.S. population data: Note 2.

THE JANUS REPORT SAMPLE				U.S. POPULATION		
M	W	Total		M	W	Total
			Marital Status			
28%	31%	30%	Single	26%	19%	22%
58	57	57	Married	64	60	62
9	9	9	Divorced	7	9	8
4	3	4	Widowed	3	12	8
1	—	—	Unidentified	—	—	—

Source for U.S. population data: Note 1.

		Region		
	20%	Northeast	20%	
	21	West	21	
	24	Midwest	25	
	34	South	34	
	1	Unidentified	—	

Source for U.S. population data: Note 3.

		Income		
	25%	About $20,000 or less	42%	
	30	About $30,000	22	
	19	About $50,000	17	
	16	About $70,000	11	
	10	About $100,000 or more	8	

Source for U.S. population data: Note 3.

		Religious Preference		
	36%	Protestant	56%	
	25	Catholic	28	
	11	Jewish	2	
	17	Other	4	
	11	None	10	

Source for U.S. population data: Note 4.

The Janus Report Questionnaire

A. The Family and Society in America
B. Family Opinions
C. Sex and Society
D. Personal Views
E. For Marrieds and Partners
F. For Singles Only
G. Views and Experiences
H. Demographics

A. The Family and Society in America

Using the scale below, please rate your agreement or disagreement to each of the following items:

	Strongly Agree	Agree	No Opinion	Disagree	Strongly Disagree
1. The family is the most important institution in society	___	___	___	___	___
2. It is better to love and be hurt than not to know love	___	___	___	___	___
3. Divorce is too easy now	___	___	___	___	___
4. Surrogate mothers have a definite role in American family planning	___	___	___	___	___
5. Religion is an important factor in marriage	___	___	___	___	___
6. To be truly fulfilled, one must be married	___	___	___	___	___
7. If my spouse earned more than I, it would be a serious problem	___	___	___	___	___
8. Becoming a parent is the ultimate human attainment	___	___	___	___	___
9. Sex surrogates are the same as prostitutes	___	___	___	___	___
10. Mothers should delay their careers during children's early years	___	___	___	___	___
11. Abortion is murder	___	___	___	___	___
12. Both sexes can take care of babies equally well	___	___	___	___	___
13. Traditional sex roles have no place in modern society	___	___	___	___	___
14. In the past few years I have become more cautious about sex	___	___	___	___	___
15. There is still a double standard in sex regarding men and women	___	___	___	___	___

B. Family Opinions

Using the scale below, please rank the importance of each of the following items to you:

	Very Important	Important	Not Sure	Unimportant	Very Unimportant
1. Family planning is	___	___	___	___	___
2. Passing on religious values to my children is	___	___	___	___	___
3. My personal professional fulfillment is	___	___	___	___	___
4. How important is love to you	___	___	___	___	___
5. Media portrayal of sexuality should be less hostile to women	___	___	___	___	___
6. That my sex practices are in harmony with my religion is	___	___	___	___	___
7. For the man, sexual experience before marriage is	___	___	___	___	___
8. For the woman, sexual experience before marriage is	___	___	___	___	___
9. There is too much sex and violence in the media	___	___	___	___	___

10. My parents' marriage was: Always intact ___ They separated ___ They divorced ___ Never married ___

C. Sex and Society

Using the scale below, please indicate how much you agree or disagree with the following items:

	Strongly Agree	Agree	No Opinion	Disagree	Strongly Disagree
1. In the last 3 years sexual morality has disintegrated	___	___	___	___	___
2. Extramarital affairs do not seriously affect marriages	___	___	___	___	___
3. I find one-night stands to be degrading	___	___	___	___	___
4. Incest is a major problem in American society now	___	___	___	___	___
5. Masturbation is a natural part of life and continues on in marriage	___	___	___	___	___
6. I find that alcoholic beverages make sex more pleasurable for me	___	___	___	___	___
7. A large variety of sex techniques is a must for maximum pleasure	___	___	___	___	___
8. Making love is the best way to make up after an argument	___	___	___	___	___
9. Simultaneous orgasm is a must for gratifying sex	___	___	___	___	___
10. My sex partner must be an excellent lover	___	___	___	___	___
11. Pain and pleasure really go together in sex	___	___	___	___	___
12. Sex and intimacy are two different things	___	___	___	___	___
13. I find that the battle of the sexes still exists today	___	___	___	___	___

D. Personal Views

Please use the scale below to indicate your agreement or disagreement and respond to the questions below:

	Strongly Agree	Agree	No Opinion	Disagree	Strongly Disagree
1. My sex partner's pleasure is more important than my own	___	___	___	___	___
2. Women have become more sexually aggressive in the past 5 years	___	___	___	___	___
3. There is too much pornographic material in neighborhood stores	___	___	___	___	___
4. I always prefer that my sex partner initiate sexual activity	___	___	___	___	___

5. I've had extramarital affairs: Never ___ Only once ___ Rarely ___ Often ___ Ongoing ___

6. I have orgasm during lovemaking: Always ___ Often ___ Sometimes ___ Rarely ___ Never ___

7. To successfully function sexually I fantasize: Not at all ___ Slightly ___ Much ___ Very much ___ Totally ___

8. I masturbate on average: Daily ___ Several times weekly ___ Weekly ___ Monthly ___ Rarely ___ Never ___

9. Compared to 3 years ago, my sex activity is: Much more ___ More ___ Same ___ Less ___ Much less ___

10. I had sexual experience before marriage: Very much ___ Much ___ Little ___ Very little ___ None ___

11. I have had sexual experience at work: Never ___ Once or twice ___ Occasionally ___ Often ___

12. Your assistance in rating the following sexual practices on the scale below is very important.
Based on your opinion, place a letter from the Rating Scale next to EACH of the sex practices listed below.

Rating Scale   A. Very normal   B. All right   C. Unusual   D. Kinky   E. Never heard of it

Oral sex ___	Masturbation ___	Dominance/Bondage ___
Cross dressing ___	Fetishes ___	Verbal humiliation ___	Sadomasochism ___	Golden showers ___	Brown showers ___
Necrophilia ___	Group sex ___	Talking dirty ___	Adult sex with children ___

13. Please list the practices you have experienced: _____

_____   _____

409

E. For Marrieds and Partners

Please check off the answer or choice that is right for you.

1. My spouse/partner is also my best friend: Yes _____ No _____

2. Sex is more gratifying since marrying: Much better _____ Better _____ Same _____ Worse _____ Much worse _____

3. I rate my marriage as: Great _____ Good _____ Fair _____ Poor _____ Terrible _____

4. Did you live with your spouse before marrying? Yes _____ No _____ If Yes, how many years? _____

5. Is it important to me that my partner be open to sexual experimentation: Yes _____ Slightly _____ No _____

6. Sexually, I consider myself to be: Very proper _____ Proper _____ Moderate _____ Liberal _____ Very liberal _____

7. Sexually, I consider my partner to be: Very proper _____ Proper _____ Moderate _____ Liberal _____ Very liberal _____

8. I was initially attracted to my spouse/partner by his/her: (Please select and check off only one below)
   Looks _____ Personality _____ Sexiness _____ Wealth _____ Warmth _____ Power _____ Humor _____

9. My honeymoon was: (please check only one): Thrilling _____ Boring _____ Traumatic _____ Very sexual _____ Asexual _____

10. My spouse/partner is sexually sophisticated: Yes _____ No _____

F. For Singles Only

Indicate your agreement or disagreement to each statement below.

	Strongly Agree	Agree	No Opinion	Disagree	Strongly Disagree
1. The singles' life is the most gratifying life-style					
2. If I could live it over again, I would definitely be married					
3. I am still intimidated about approaching the other sex for sex					
4. I would like to become a parent even if I remain single					
5. Fear of divorce and its money problems keeps me single					

6. What is your major problem, if any, in being single? (Select only one): Loneliness _____ Family pressures _____ Finances _____

Social pressures _____ Finding a spouse _____ None at all _____

G. Views and Experiences

Please list or check off the choice most accurate for you. Please answer all questions.

1. Romantically I am: Very romantic _____ Romantic _____ Realistic _____ Cautious _____ Cynical _____

2. Sensually, I feel that sex is: Deliciously sensuous 1 _____ 2 _____ 3 _____ 4 _____ 5 _____ Grossly distasteful

3. I consider myself to be sexually: Very active _____ Active _____ Average _____ Below average _____ Inactive _____

4. Are you functioning at your biological maximum sexually? Yes _____ No _____

5. If No, how much below maximum sexual potential are you? 10% _____ 25% _____ 50% _____ 100% _____

6. Frequency of ALL sexual activity is: Daily _____ A few times weekly _____ Weekly _____ Monthly _____ Rarely _____

7. How many different individuals (including spouses) have you had sexual relations with? _____

8. Sex education should be taught in the schools: Definitely yes _____ Maybe _____ Not at all _____

9. In-vitro fertilization and techniques like it are: Vital _____ Beneficial _____ Problematic _____ Sinful _____

10. I have experienced sexual harassment on my job: Yes _____ No _____

11. I learned about sex from: Home _____ School _____ Church _____ Streets _____

411

H. Demographics

Please list or check off the response that is correct for you. Please *answer all* questions.

1. Male ——— Female ———

2. Age ———

3. Heterosexual ——— Homosexual ——— Bisexual ———

4. Religion: Protestant ——— Catholic ——— Jewish ——— Other ——— None ———

5. Politically, I am: Ultraconservative ——— Conservative ——— Independent ——— Liberal ——— Ultraliberal ———

6. Now: Married ——— Single ——— Divorced ——— Widowed ———

7. Length of present marriage ———

8. Present marriage is # ———

9. Number of children total ———

10. Education: Jr.H.S. ——— H.S. ——— Some college ——— College grad ——— Postgrad ———

11. Age I moved out of my parents' home ———

12. Annual family income, approximately: $20M ——— $30M ——— $50M ——— $70M ——— $100M+ ———

13. Religious observance: Very religious ——— Religious ——— Slightly religious ——— Not religious at all ———

14. Do you have a career outside of the home? Yes ——— No ——— If Yes, is it: Full-time ——— Part-time ———

15. Have you had full sexual relations? Yes, at age ——— Never had full sex ———

16. Age first masturbated: ——— Never masturbated ———

412

17. Have you had homosexual experiences? Yes ——— No ———

If yes, then please check: Once ——— Occasionally ——— Frequently ——— Ongoing ———

18. If divorced, the one primary reason was: Sex ——— Money ——— Rejection ——— Children ——— Emotional problems ———

Extramarital affairs ——— Open marriage ——— Other ———

19. Do you use contraception? Yes ——— No ——— If Yes, which? Condom ——— Pill ——— Tubal ligation ———

Rhythm ——— Abortion ——— Vasectomy ——— I.U.D. ——— Diaphragm ——— Cream/Jelly ———

20. I was sexually molested as a child: Yes ——— No ——— If Yes, at age ——— Once ——— Often ——— Ongoing ———

If Yes, who was the molester? Adult stranger ——— Relative ——— Person in authority position ———

21. Was the incident(s) reported to authorities? Yes ——— No ——— Any arrests? Yes ——— No ———

Convictions? Yes ——— No ———

22. My preferred way to achieve orgasm is: (select only one) Intercourse ——— Masturbation ——— Oral sex ———

Sadomasochism ——— Anal sex ——— Fantasy ——— Fetish ——— Other ———

23. I regard my sex practices as: Completely normal ——— Normal ——— Slightly odd ——— Unusual ——— Kinky ———

24. I have had an abortion: Yes ——— No ——— If Yes, how many? ——— What ages(s) were you? ———

25. Postabortion reaction was: Relief ——— Pleasure ——— No reaction ——— Sadness ——— Guilt ——— Regret ———

26. Have you ever had sex for money? Yes ——— No ——— If Yes: Once ——— Occasionally ——— Often ———

27. Please check if you have participated in: Group sex ——— Threesomes ——— Sex slave ——— Open marriage ———

28. I am concerned about sexually transmitted diseases: Very much ——— Much ——— Unsure ——— Slightly ——— Not at all ———

413

INDEX OF TABULATED RESULTS
BY QUESTIONNAIRE ITEM

Note: The numbers below refer to the pages on which tables appear incorporating results from responses to the corresponding questionnaire items (**A.1** . . .) Key phrases in italics help identify the survey item listed in full on the previous pages, 406–413.

A. The Family and Society in America

A.1 *family is most important,* 44, 56, 266, 299, 388
A.2 *better to love,* 161, 278, 386, 387
A.3 *Divorce is,* 58, 267, 298
A.4 *Surrogate mothers,* 223, 342
A.5 *Religion is important,* 389
A.6 *fulfilled . . . must be married,* 57, 330, 354
A.7 *spouse earned more,* 46, 396
A.8 *Becoming a parent,* 209, 300, 354
A.9 *Sex surrogates,* 341
A.10 *Mothers should delay careers,* 59, 212, 302
A.11 *Abortion is,* 61, 230, 231, 270, 301, 355, 390
A.12 *Both . . . take care of babies,* 60
A.13 *Traditional sex roles,* 38, 63, 153, 235, 236, 237, 277, 356
A.14 *become more cautious,* 33, 305
A.15 *still a double standard,* 40, 64, 306

B. Family Opinions

B.1 *Family planning,* 215, 356
B.2 *Passing on religious values,* 267
B.3 *personal professional fulfillment,* 66, 308
B.4 *How important is love,* 65, 327, 358
B.5 *Media portrayal of sexuality,* 279, 280, 309
B.6 *practices in harmony with religion,* 238, 239, 240, 389
B.7 *man, sexual experience before marriage,* 41, 68, 359, 379
B.8 *woman, sexual experience before marriage,* 42, 68, 241, 242, 359, 380
B.10 *parents' marriage was,* 165

C. Sex and Society

C.1 *last 3 years sexual morality,* 397
C.2 *Extramarital affairs,* 332, 393
C.3 *one night stands,* 75, 333, 362
C.4 *Incest is major problem,* 71
C.5 *Masturbation is,* 76, 243, 382
C.7 *variety of sex,* 79, 244, 281, 282, 310, 334
C.8 *after an argument,* 117
C.9 *Simultaneous orgasm,* 80, 284, 381
C.10 *partner must be an excellent lover,* 335
C.11 *Pain and pleasure,* 117, 245

C.12 *Sex and intimacy,* 82, 141, 391

C.13 *battle of the sexes,* 64

D. **Personal Views**

D.1 *partner's pleasure more important,* 83

D.2 *Women . . . more sexually aggressive,* 285, 286

D.3 *too much pornographic . . . in stores,* 364

D.4 *partner initiate sexual,* 85, 247, 248, 312, 313, 337

D.5 *extramarital affairs,* 196, 249, 286, 314, 331, 363

D.6 *orgasm during lovemaking,* 27, 86

D.7 *I fantasize,* 250, 287

D.8 *I masturbate,* 31, 77, 159, 186, 360

D.9 *Compared to 3 years ago,* 34, 88, 164, 251, 288, 290, 304, 370

D.10 *experience before marriage,* 87, 176, 252, 253, 315, 316, 328, 364

D.11 *sexual experience at work,* 365

D.12 *Rating Scale . . . of the sex practices,* 89, 90, 91, 114, 119, 120, 122, 125, 126, 127, 128, 254, 291, 292, 310, 311

E. **For Marrieds and Partners**

E.1 *spouse . . . my best friend,* 91, 181, 338, 393

E.2 *Sex more gratifying,* 181

E.3 *rate my marriage,* 190

E.4 *live with your spouse before marrying,* 177

E.5 *sexual experimentation,* 182

E.6 *Sexually, consider myself,* 187

E.7 *Sexually, consider my partner,* 188

E.8 *initially attracted to . . . by his/her,* 174, 175

E.9 *honeymoon was,* 178

E.10 *sexually sophisticated,* 189

F. **For Singles Only**

F.1 *most gratifying life-style,* 145, 146

F.2 *definitely be married,* 147

F.3 *intimidated about approaching,* 148

F.4 *like to become a parent,* 151

F.5 *Fear of divorce,* 151

F.6 *major problem . . . being single,* 152

G. **Views and Experiences**

G.1 *Romantically I am,* 154, 254

G.2 *Sensually,* 92, 155, 255, 256, 317, 318

G.3 *I consider myself,* 93, 156, 256, 293, 319, 367

G.4 *biological maximum,* 93, 157, 257

G.5 *below maximum,* 94, 158

G.6 *Frequency of ALL Sexual,* 25, 159, 339

G.7 *How many different individuals,* 95, 163, 303, 329, 368

G.8 *Sex education . . . in schools,* 97, 237, 280, 281

G.9 *In-vitro fertilization,* 224, 343

G.10 *sexual harassment on my job,* 102, 366
G.11 *learned about sex,* 97, 258

H. Demographics

H.1 *Male, Female,* most tables, especially Chapter 3, *53 ff.*
H.2 *Age,* most tables, especially Chapter 2, *19 ff.*
H.3 *. . . Homosexual . . . ,* 70
H.4 *Religion,* Chapter 8, *227 ff.*
H.5 *Politically,* Chapter 9, *263 ff.*
H.6 *Now: Married . . . Single . . . ,* Chapter 6, *169 ff.*
H.7 *Length of present marriage,* 199
H.8 *Present marriage is #,* 183, 199
H.9 *children total,* 210, 211, 219
H.10 *Education,* Chapter 10, *295 ff.*
H,11 *Moved out of my parents' home,* 220
H.12 *Annual family income,* Chapter 11, *323 ff.*
H.13 *Religious observance,* Chapter 8, *227 ff.*
H.14 *career outside of the home?,* 221
H.15 *full sexual relations,* 36, 221, 258, 259, 274, 368, 384
H.16 *first masturbated,* 78, 320
H.17 *homosexual experiences,* 69, 70
H.18 *If divorced,* 195
H.19 *use contraception,* 217, 233, 268
H.20 *sexually molested,* 73, 369
H.22 *achieve orgasm,* 98, 185
H.23 *I regard my sex practices,* 99, 340
H.24 *had an abortion,* 198, 219, 220, 221, 231, 232, 271, 272, 273, 343, 344, 357
H.25 *Post abortion reaction,* 222, 273
H.26 *sex for money,* 184, 282, 283, 345, 346
H.27 *participated in: Group sex . . . ,* 184, 371
H.28 *sexually transmitted diseases,* 100, 260, 372

Notes

Preface

1. "Who's Having Sex? Data Are Obsolete, Experts Say." *New York Times*, February 28, 1989, p. C1.
2. "Sex Survey Hits a Snag." APA (American Psychological Association) *Monitor*, July 1989, p. 34.
3. See, for example, "Stalled Sex Surveys Elicit APA Protest." APA *Monitor*, August 1990, p. 22. Also, "Sexual Behavior Studies Could Be Revived by Law." APA *Monitor*, April 1992, p. 8.

Chapter 1: Sex in the Twentieth Century

Authors' note: Some parts of Chapter 1 are based on information appearing in C. Degler, *At Odds: Women and the Family in America—From the Revolution to the Present*. Oxford, England: Oxford University Press, 1980.

1. A. C. Kinsey, W. B. Pomeroy, and C. E. Martin. *Sexual Behavior in the Human Male*. Philadelphia: W.B. Saunders, 1948.
2. ———. *Sexual Behavior in the Human Female*. Philadelphia: W.B. Saunders, 1953.
3. K. B. Davis. *Factors in the Sex Life of Twenty-Two Hundred Women*. New York: Harper and Bros., 1929.
4. W. H. Masters and V. E. Johnson. *Human Sexual Response*. Boston: Little, Brown & Co., 1966.
5. ———. *Human Sexual Inadequacy*. Boston: Little, Brown & Co., 1970.
6. N. O'Neill and G. O'Neill. *Open Marriage: A New Life Style for Couples*. New York: M. Evans & Co., 1972.
7. B. Friedan. *The Feminine Mystique*. New York: Dell, 1963.
8. S. Janus. *The Death of Innocence*. New York: William Morrow & Co., 1981.
9. Gay Men's Health Crisis—Information Center, New York. Data as of March 1992. Personal correspondence.

Chapter 2: Sexual Passages: From Late Adolescence to Postmaturity

1. Mark Sullivan, M.D. Personal communication.
2. J. Weinberg. "Sexual Expression in Late Life." *American Journal of Psychiatry* (November 1969), Vol. 126, pp. 713–716.

3. E. Pfeiffer and G. C. Davis. "Determinants of Sexual Behavior in Middle and Old Age." *Journal of the American Geriatric Society* (April 1972), Vol. 212, pp. 308–414.

4. D. Rubin. *Everything You Always Wanted To Know About Sex, But Were Afraid To Ask*. New York: Macmillan, 1976.

5. W. H. James. "Marital Coital Rates, Spouses' Ages, Family Size and Social Class." *Journal of Sex Research* (August 1974), Vol. 10, pp. 205–218.

6. Interesting geographic differences can be found in Chapter 12.

7. We also found that many people who deny masturbating may actually do so without consciously realizing it. The most common version of this nonacknowl-edged masturbation for men is to lie on one's stomach and rub the pelvic area against a crumpled sheet or pillow to reach orgasm. For women, many favor lying in the bath with a stream of water directed at the clitoris to achieve orgasm. Not actually having "touched" themselves with their hands, they feel that they have not really masturbated. (We are not including here nocturnal emissions that virtually every boy experiences.)

Chapter 3: Men and Women: A Study in Contrasts

1. A. C. Kinsey, W. B. Pomeroy, and C. E. Martin. *Sexual Behavior in the Human Male*. Philadelphia: W.B. Saunders, 1948.

———. *Sexual Behavior in the Human Female*. Philadelphia: W.B. Saunders, 1953.

2. S. Janus and C. L. Janus. "Child Sex Abuse: The Question of Conviction." Paper presented at the national convention of the American Psychological Association, Washington, DC, August 24, 1983.

3. P. Steinfels. "New Panel in Chicago to Study Sexual Abuse of Children by Priests." *New York Times*, June 16, 1992, p. A17.

4. E. Jong. *Fear of Flying*. New York: Henry Holt, 1973.

5. M. Klein. *Your Sexual Secrets: When to Keep Them, When & How to Tell*. New York: E. P. Dutton, 1988.

Chapter 4: Sexual Deviance

1. American Psychiatric Association. *Diagnostic and Statistical Manual of Mental Disorders*, 3rd Ed. Rev. (DSM-III-R). Washington, DC: Author, 1987. See also 2nd Ed. (DSM-II), 1968, and 3rd Ed. (DSM-III), 1980.

2. S. Janus. *The Death of Innocence*. New York: William Morrow & Co, 1981, p. 17.

3. S. Janus and C. L. Janus. "Child Sex Abuse: The Question of Conviction." Paper presented at the national convention of the American Psychological Association, Washington, DC, August 24, 1982.

4. S. Janus and B. Bess. "Prostitution: Option or Addiction?" Paper presented at the national convention of the American Psychiatric Association, Toronto, Canada, May 5, 1977.

5. Lt. William McCarthy, New York (City) Police Department, retired. Personal communication.

Chapter 5: The Singles' Scene

1. J. Barry. "Forever Single." *AdWeek's Marketing Week*, October 15, 1990, p. 20 ff.
2. Current Population Reports, P-20, No. 450. *Marital Status and Living Arrangements: March 1990*. Washington, DC: U.S. Department of Commerce, Bureau of the Census, May, 1991, p. 13.
3. "The Marriage Crunch." *Newsweek*, June 2, 1986, p. 54 ff.
4. Current Population Reports, P-20, No. 450, p. 5.
5. J. Scanzoni. "Social Exchange and Behavioral Interdependence." In R. L. Burgess and T. L. Huston (Eds.), *Social Exchange in Developing Relationships*. New York: Academic Press, 1979.
6. H. Hendrix. *Getting the Love You Want: A Guide for Couples* (pp. 122–125). New York: Harper & Row, 1988.

Chapter 6: Marriage and Divorce

1. J. H. Wallis. *Marriage Observed*. London: Routledge and Kegan Paul, 1970.
2. H. J. Carman and H. C. Syrett. *A History of the American People*. New York: Alfred A. Knopf, 1952.
3. Quoted in Carman and Syrett, *A History of the American People*.
4. W. M. Kephart and D. Jedlicka. *The Family, Society, and the Individual* (6th ed.). New York: Harper & Row, 1988.
5. F. P. Rice. *Human Sexuality*. Dubuque, IA: Wm. C. Brown, 1989.
6. A. DeMaris and G. R. Leslie. "Cohabitation with the Future Spouse." *Journal of Marriage and the Family* (February 1984), pp. 77–84.

   R. E. L. Watson. "Premarital Cohabitation vs. Traditional Courtship." *Family Relations* (January 1983), Vol. 32, pp. 139–147.
7. R. R. Clayton and H. L. Voss. "Shacking Up: Cohabitation in the 1970s." *Journal of Marriage and the Family* (May 1977), Vol. 39 (2), pp. 273–283.
8. J. Lauer and R. Lauer. "Marriages Made to Last." *Psychology Today* (June 1985), p. 22 ff.
9. M. Hunt. *Sexual Behavior in the 1970s*. Chicago: Playboy Press, 1974.
10. P. Blumstein and P. Schwartz. *American Couples: Money, Work, Sex*. New York: William Morrow & Co., 1983.
11. M. Hunt. *Sexual Behavior in the 1970s*.
12. W. H. Masters and V. E. Johnson. *Human Sexual Response*. Boston: Little, Brown & Co., 1966.
13. M. Hunt. *Sexual Behavior in the 1970s*.
14. "Divorce." In *Encyclopedia Americana*, Vol. 9. Danbury, CT: Grolier, Inc., 1922.

    Monthly Vital Statistics Report. *Advance Report of Final Divorce Statistics*. Vol. 35 (6) (Suppl.), September 25, 1986. Washington, DC: National Center for Health Statistics, 1986.

    ———. Vol. 39 (12) (Suppl. 2), May 21, 1991. Washington, DC: National Center for Health Statistics, 1991.

———. *Annual Summary of Births, Marriages, Divorces and Deaths: U.S. 1989.* Vol. 38 (13), August 30, 1990. Washington, DC: National Center for Health Statistics, 1990.

———. Vol. 39 (13), August 28, 1991. Washington, DC: National Center for Health Statistics, 1991.

15. C. Rubenstein. "The Modern Art of Courtly Love." *Psychology Today* (July 1983), Vol. 17, p. 40 ff.

16. M. Hunt. *Sexual Behavior in the 1970s.*

17. A. C. Kinsey, W. B. Pomeroy, and C. E. Martin. *Sexual Behavior in the Human Female.* Philadelphia: W.B. Saunders, 1953.

18. N. O'Neill and G. O'Neill. *Open Marriage: A New Life Style for Couples.* New York: M. Evans & Co., 1972.

19. U.S. Department of Commerce, Bureau of the Census. *Statistical Abstract of the United States, 1985.* Washington, DC: U.S. Government Printing Office, 1985.

20. N. F. Cott. "Eighteenth-Century Family and Social Life Revealed in Massachusetts Divorce Records." In N. F. Cott and E. H. Pleck (Eds.), *A Heritage of Her Own: Families, Work and Feminism in America* (pp. 107–135). New York: Simon & Schuster/Touchstone Press, 1980.

21. W. Waller and R. Hill. *The Family* (rev. ed.). New York: Dryden Press, 1951.

Chapter 7: Children: To Have or Have Not

1. Current Population Reports, P-20, No. 447. *Household and Family Characteristics: March 1990 and 1989.* Washington, DC: U.S. Department of Commerce, Bureau of the Census, December 1990, p. 3.

2. "Only One U.S. Family in Four Is 'Traditional.'" *New York Times,* January 30, 1991, p. 19.

3. *New York Times,* January 30, 1991.

4. "Households Still Shrinking, But Rate Is Slower." *New York Times,* December 10, 1989, p. 47.

5. C. Carmody. "Threats to Mass Circulation on Demographic Landscape." *New York Times,* January 7, 1991, p. D6.

6. "Households Still Shrinking . . . ," *New York Times.*

7. J. Smolowe. "Last Call for Motherhood," *Time,* Fall 1990, p. 76.

8. L. Lieberman. Personal communication, July 1990.

9. S. Fleck. "The Family." In A. Freedman, H. Kaplan, and B. Sadock (Eds.), *The Sexual Experience* (pp. 155–180). Baltimore: Williams & Wilkins, 1976.

10. L. Kutner. "Choosing to Forgo the Pleasures of Parenthood." *New York Times,* February 14, 1991, p. C8.

11. Monthly Vital Statistics Report. *Advance Report of Final Divorce Statistics,* Vol. 35 (6) (Suppl.), September 25, 1986. Washington DC: National Center for Health Statistics, 1986.

12. Yankelovich–Clancy–Shulman poll of 505 Americans aged 18 to 24, taken in September 1990. Cited in "The Road to Equality," *Time,* Fall 1990, p. 14.

13. C. Knowlton. *The Fruits of Philosophy*, Chicago: International Publishing Co., 1891 (1832).

14. S. Ditzion. *Marriage, Morals, and Sex in America: A History of Ideas.* New York: Bookman Publishing Co., 1953.

15. S. Smolowe. "Last Call for Motherhood."

16. Kevin Sack. "New York Is Urged to Outlaw Surrogate Parenting for Pay." *New York Times,* May 13, 1992, p. B5.

Chapter 8: Religion and Sex

1. R. Westheimer and L. Lieberman. *Sex and Morality: Who Is Teaching Our Sex Standards?* New York: Harcourt Brace Jovanovich, 1988.

2. A. C. Kinsey, W. B. Pomeroy, and C. E. Martin. *Sexual Behavior in the Human Male.* Philadelphia: W.B. Saunders, Co., 1948.

———. *Sexual Behavior in the Human Female.* Philadelphia: W.B. Saunders Co., 1953.

Chapter 10: Education and Sex

1. W. H. Masters and V. E. Johnson. *Human Sexual Response.* Boston: Little, Brown & Co., 1966.

Chapter 11: Money, Power, and Sex

1. W. H. Masters and V. E. Johnson. *Human Sexual Response.* Boston: Little, Brown & Co., 1966.

2. S. Janus and B. Bess. "Prostitution." In A. Freedman, H. Kaplan, and B. Sadock (Eds.), *The Sexual Experience* (pp. 594–610). Baltimore: William & Wilkins, 1976.

3. Bruce Lieberman, M.D. Personal communication, May 1990.

4. Janus and Bess. "Prostitution."

5. Harold Greenwald, M.D. Personal communication, March 1988.

Chapter 12: Region and Sex

1. D. Schneller. Personal communication, 1991.

2. S. Janus. *The Death of Innocence.* New York: William Morrow & Co., 1981.

3. R. Sethre. Personal communication, 1990.

Chapter 13: Looking Forward from the Past

1. Michael Yapko, Ph.D. Personal communication.

2. S. Hite. *The Hite Report: A Nationwide Study of Female Sexuality.* New York: Macmillan, 1976.

3. M. Mead. *Culture and Commitment: The New Relationships Between the Generations in the 1970s* (rev. ed.). New York: Columbia University Press, 1978.

4. A. Riding. "France Rethinks Its Wink At Sex Harassment." *New York Times* May 3, 1992, p. A9.

Appendix A: Comparison of Janus Report Sample with National Census Data

1. Current Population Reports, P-20, No. 450. *Marital Status and Living Arrangements: March 1990.* Washington, DC: U.S. Department of Commerce, Bureau of the Census, May 1991.

2. Current Population Reports, P-20, No. 451. *Educational Attainment in the United States: March 1989 and 1988.* Washington, DC: U.S. Department of Commerce, Bureau of the Census, August 1991.

3. Current Population Reports, P-60, No. 174. *Consumer Income, 1990.* Washington, DC: U.S. Department of Commerce, Bureau of the Census, March 1991.

4. *Statistical Abstract of the United States 1991.* Washington, DC: U.S. Department of Commerce, Bureau of the Census, 1991.

Index

Abortion:
  and deviance, 105
  in Ireland, 261
  and law, 14, 398
  and political leaning, 263, 269–274, 294
  and religion, 203, 215, 229, 230–234
Abortions (admitted):
  age at, 203, 220, 273
  age first sex, 221
  age left home, 220
  by career/no career, 221
  by income level, 343–344
  by marital status, 169, 198
  by number of children, 218–222
  by political leaning, 271, 272, 273
  reaction to, 222, 273
  by region, 357
  by religion, 203, 231, 232
Abortion (opinion on):
  by education, 300–301
  by gender, 61–62, 231
  phase comparison, 375, 390–391
  by political leaning, 270
  by region, 355
  by religion, 230, 231
Abuse, sexual, see Child molestation; Harassment
Adolescence and sex, 19–51
Adultery, see Extramarital sex
Age, 19–51
  list of subjects tabulated by, 20
  sample population breakdown by, 4, 402
AIDS:
  and anal sex, 90
  and condom usage, 132, 217
  impact of, 1, 16, 17–18, 32, 288, 305, 306, 372, 398
  and media, 377
  nonthreatening to youngsters, 385
  number of deaths (1992), 17
  and sex education, 96, 280
American Journal of Psychiatry, 20–21
American Psychiatric Association (APA), 105, 106
Anal sex, 90–91, 98, 185, 377
Appliances, sexual, 98
Argument, making up after, 103, 116
Artificial insemination, 222–223
Asphyxiation, 104, 111
Attraction, partner's, 174–175

Baby Boomers, 11, 12, 13, 138 139, 206–207
Baby-pros, 347–348
Bakker, Jim and Tammy, 261, 274
Battle of the sexes, 64–65
Bernardin, Cardinal (Chicago), 73
Bess, Barbara, 130, 344
Bestiality, 12
Bible:
  homosexuality in, 106
  masturbation in, 242
Biological clock, 23, 146, 150
Biological sexual maximum, 53, 93–95, 157–158, 257
Bisexuals, 70–71
Blumstein, P., 186
Bondage, 108, 109, 110, 119–120, 371
Brenner, David, 37
Brown shower, 108, 109, 112, 126
Burns, George, 51

California Magazine, 137
Call girls, *see* Prostitution
Careers, 23, 46–48, 211–212. *See also*
    Homemakers *vs.* career women
    postponement of (for children),
        59–60, 211–212, 301–302
Casey, Eamon, 261
Caution, sexual, 16, 19, 32–35, 100, 305
Celibacy, 171, 172
Centers for Disease Control, 377
Child molestation, 53, 72–74, 104, 113,
        347, 384–385
    and prostitutes, 131
    by region, 369–370
Childless marriage, 209–210
Childrearing, *see* Parenthood
Children:
    adult sex with, 103, 108, 109, 113,
        128–129
    and AIDS, 17–18
    desire for, 150, 203–225, 295
    and divorce, 213–214
    number of (sample population
        breakdown by), 210
City University of New York, 5
Clayton, R. R., 178
Clitoris, 28
Clockwork Orange, 81
Cohabitation, 169, 176–178
Coitus reservatus, 173
College sex, 43
Commercialized sex, *see* Money, sex
    for; Prostitution
Commitment, 13, 16, 141, 143
Complex marriage, 173
Conception technologies, 222–224
Conditional empathy, 59
Condoms:
    and anal sex, 90
    distribution of, 96, 280
    and prostitutes, 132
    sample population use of, 76
    and women, 43, 84, 89, 100–101, 217
Connecticut, 176
Contraceptives, 11, 14, 43
Contraceptives, use of:
    by marital status, 203, 216–217
    by political leaning, 268–269

by religion, 7, 227, 232–234
    specific types, 217
Coprolagnia, 112
Coprolalia, 90
Cott, Nancy F., 200
Courant Institute of Mathematical
    Sciences, 5
Cross dressing, 103, 108, 109, 110–111,
    120–121
Culture and Commitment, 396–397
Cunnilingus, 82, 89

Data gathering, 3–5
Date rape, 119
Dating services, 160–162
Davis, Glenn C., 22
Defecation, *see* Brown shower
Deviance, 103–134
    good, 105–106
    and novelty (thin line between), 133
    rating scale used, 108
    two categories, 108
Dial-a-porn 900 numbers, 90
Diaphragm, 43, 100, 215
DINKS, 139
Divorce, 169–202
    laws, 142
    Mormon, 172
    rates (1900–1990), 192
    reasons for, 169, 194–195
    whether it's too easy, 58–59,
        266–267, 298–299
Dominance/bondage, 108, 109, 110,
    119–120, 371
Double standard, 39–40, 51, 63–65, 306
Douche, 85, 215
DSM, 105
Durkheim, Emil, 104

Earnings of spouse, 46–48, 394–396
Education, 207–209, 211, 295–321
    list of subjects tabulated by, 296
    sample population breakdown by,
        4, 402
Ego, male, 394
Ejaculation, 28
Equal Rights Amendment, 15
Equality, sexual, 378–380

Erection, 28
Erikson, Erik, 324
Eroticization of America, 133
Everything You Always Wanted To Know About Sex, But Were Afraid To Ask, 22
Excellence required, 335–337
Exhibitionism, 107, 113–114
Experimentation, importance of, 182
Extramarital sex:
  and divorce, 195–198
  in Kinsey Report, 12
Extramarital sex (admitted):
  by education, 313–314
  by gender, 169
  by income level, 323, 330–331
  by married/divorced, 196
  by political leaning, 263, 286–287
  by region, 363
  by religion, 227, 249
Extramarital sex (opinion on), 332, 392–393

Family model and singles, 144–145
Family planning, 203, 214–217, 356–357
Family resurgence, 147–148
Family *vs.* household, 205–207
Family, importance of:
  by age, 44–46, 50, 207–209
  by education, 207–209, 297–303
  by gender, 56, 207–209
  phase comparison, 387–388
  by political leaning, 207–209, 265–266
Family, traditional functions of, 207–208
Fantasy, 98, 185, 250, 287–288
Fear of Flying, 74
Feigin, Simeon, M.D., 116
Fellatio, 89
The Feminine Mystique, 14
Feminist movement, 89
Fertility, 23, 223. *See also* In-vitro fertilization
Fetish, 98, 108, 109, 111, 122–124, 185
Fidelity, *see* Extramarital sex
Financial status, *see* Income level

First sex, age at:
  by current age, 19, 21–22, 35–37
  by gender, 258–259
  phase comparison, 383–385
  by political leaning, 263, 274
  by region, 21–22, 351, 368–369
  by religion, 227, 258–259
Flagellation, 109
Fleck, Stephen, 208
Foot fetish, 111, 123–124
Fourteenth Amendment, 14
Free love, 173
Freud, Sigmund, 9–11, 84, 104, 261
Friedan, Betty, 14
Friendship and sex, 91, 179–181, 338, 393–394
Frotteurism, 107
The Fruits of Philosophy, 215
Fulfillment:
  importance of professional, 66–67, 308
  marriage essential to, 57, 330

Gang of 200, 2, 377
Gay community, 90, 205, 345, 377
Gender, 54–102
  list of subjects tabulated by, 54
  sample population breakdown by, 402
Gender *vs.* sex, 9
Germany, 55
Golden shower, 108, 109, 112, 125–126
Government regulating sex, 106
Greenwald, Harold, 348
Group sex, 103, 108, 109, 113, 127, 184, 371
Guilt and religion, 229

Hanging, death, 111
Harassment, 101–102, 365–366
Hendrix, H., 161
Herpes, 16, 288, 306
Hickeys, 110
Hill, Anita, 101–102, 307
Hill, R., 200
Hollander, Xaviera, 353
Hollywood and sex, 11

Homemakers *vs.* career women, 55–56, 94
  and masturbation, 77
  and oral sex, 88–89, 98
  and orgasm, 85–86
Homosexual(s), *see* Gay community
  in the *Bible*, 106
  experience reported, 53, 69–71
  in Kinsey Report, 12
Honeymoon, 178–179, 317
Hooker (origin of term), 346
Hormone therapy, 49
Household *vs.* family, 205–207
Household, single-person, 206
Hunt, Morton, 186, 190, 196
Hustler, 113

In-vitro fertilization (IVF), 224, 341–343
Incest, 71–72, 113, 128
  institutionalized, 129–130
Income level, 323–349
  list of subjects tabulated by, 324
  sample population breakdown by, 326, 403
Infertility, 23. *See also* Fertility; In-vitro fertilization
Initial sexual experience, *see* First sex, age at
Initiate sex, prefer partner to:
  by education, 312–313
  by gender, 85
  by income level, 337–338
  by religion, 227, 246–249
Instruction, sex (source of), 23, 40. *See also* Sex education
Intercourse (preferred way to orgasm), 98, 185
Intimacy, 82–83, 141, 391–392
Ireland, 261
IUD accident during sex, 37

James, W. H., 26
Janus, Samuel, 130, 344
Jedlicka, Davor, 176
John Jay College of Criminal Justice, 5
Johnson, Virginia, 10, 14, 186, 340
Johnstone, John, 130
Jong, Erica, 74
Journal of Sex Research, 26

Keillor, Garrison, 374
Kephart, William, 176
Kinsey, Alfred C., 10, 11, 12, 196, 243
Klein, Marty, 76
Knowlton, Charles, 215

Lauer, Jeanette and Robert, 179, 180
Leary, Timothy, 33, 398
Levinson, Sam, 157
Lieberman, Bruce, 347
Lieberman, L., 207–208, 240
Living Single, 137
Loneliness, 140, 151–152
Los Angeles, prostitution in, 131, 361
Love, 13, 143
  whether worth risk of pain, 161, 278, 386–387
Love (importance of):
  by gender, 65–66
  by income level, 326–327
  by marital status, 161
  by phase comparison, 385
  by region, 351, 358
Love bites, 110
Lovers' knot, 43–44

Male sexual function, 28
Marital status, 135–167, 169–202
  list of subjects tabulated by, 136, 170
  sample population breakdown by, 4, 183, 403
Marriage, 169–202
  age differences in, 199–201
  changing popularity of, 143
  nature of, 174–175, 200
  phase comparison, 392
  singles' attitude toward, 143, 147
Marriage (importance of):
  by gender, 57
  by income level, 329–330
  by region, 351, 353–354
Marriage experiments, 171–173
Marriage Observed, 171
Marriages in sample population:
  length, 199
  self-ratings, 189–190
Martin, Lloyd, 129

Masochism, see Sadomasochism
Masters, William, 10, 14, 85, 186, 340
Masturbation:
  and age, 30–32, 51
  age at first time, 78, 319–320
  in the Bible, 242
  and education, 295, 319–320
  and gender, 75–79, 86, 169
  in Kinsey Report, 12
  and marital status, 169, 186
  mutual interpersonal, 32
  now normal, 105, 106
  parental condemnation, 118
  phase comparison, 381–383
  preferred for orgasm, 98, 185
  and religion, 242–244
Masturbation (attitude toward):
  by gender, 76
  by religion, 242–244
Masturbation (frequency of):
  by age, 31
  by gender, 77
  by marital status, 159–160, 186
  by region, 30, 360–361
Masturbation ("never" responses):
  by education, 295
  by marital status, 186
McCarthy, William, 132–133
Mead, Margaret, 396
Media portrayal of sexuality, 279–280,
    308–309
Menopause, 50
Menstruation, 23, 40, 97
"Midnight Blue," 13
Milton Erickson Foundation, 377
Minneapolis/St. Paul, 373
Minnesota Strip, 373
Missionary position, 108, 321
MOMS (Mothers Opposed to
    Mandatory Sex), 96
Money, see Income level
Money, sex for, see Prostitution
  by income level, 323, 344–346
  by marital status, 184
  by political leaning, 282–283
Mormons, 172–173
Ms. magazine, 14
Muppies, 139
Myths/fears about sex, 36–37

National Organization for Women
    (NOW), 14, 39
Nazi doctrine, 55
Necrophilia, 108, 109, 113, 126–127
Networks, singles, 145, 152, 167
New man, 143
New woman, 55
New York City, 373
  prostitution in, 131, 132, 347, 353, 361
New York Magazine, 137
New York Times, 73, 206, 400
New York University, 5
Newsweek, 142
Nocturnal emissions, 37
Normal, 98–99, 252–254, 339–340
Noyes, John Humphrey, 173
Number of partners:
  by education, 295, 303–304
  by gender, 95–96
  by income level, 328–329
  by marital status, 163
  by region, 367–368

Onanism, 106
One-night stand, 13, 74–75, 83, 333,
    361–362
Oneida Community, 171, 173
O'Neill, George and Nena, 13, 14
Open marriage, 12, 13, 14, 146, 184,
    195, 197, 371
Oral sex, 89, 105
  preferred way to orgasm, 53, 98,
    185, 186
Oral sex (attitude about):
  by education, 295, 309–311
  gender, 88–89
  by political leaning, 291
  by religion, 253–254
Orgasm:
  and age, 19, 21, 27–28
  and asphyxiation, 111
  and bondage, 110
  and career women/homemakers,
    85–86
  during lovemaking, 19, 21, 27, 86
  faking, 81, 84, 141
  and gender, 85–86
  and masturbation, 12, 31, 77, 99

Orgasm *(Continued)*
    and oral sex, 89
    preferred way to achieve, 53, 98, 185
    simultaneous, 53, 80–81, 263,
        283–284, 380–381
    vaginal *vs.* clitoral, 84
    women's right to, 85–86, 379–381
Orgasm clinics/workshops, 76, 85
Orgasmic response system, 77

Pain/pleasure, 117, 245–246
Paraphilia, 104
Parenthood:
    attitude toward, 209, 295, 300, 351,
        354
    and gays, 205
    sharing, 60–61, 212
    single, 15, 135, 150–151, 205
Parents' marital status, 135, 165
Partners, number of, *see* Number of
    partners
Passages, sexual, 19–51
Pedophiliacs Information Society, 129
Penile implants, 49
Penis captivus, 36
Penthouse, 113
Performance anxiety, 12, 15
Personal ads, 136–137
Pfeiffer, Dr. Eric, 22
Phases of study, 1–6
    comparisons, 375–400
    list of subjects tabulated by, 376
Pilot studies, 1–3
Playboy, 113
Playing doctor, 101
Pleasure, importance of partner's, 83
PMS, 55
Political leaning, 207–209, 263–294
    list of subjects tabulated by, 264
    sample population breakdown by, 265
Polygamy, 172–173
Polygyny, 171
Pornography, 13, 79, 113, 116, 133, 364,
    399
Postmaturity and sex, 20–21, 23–27,
    28–29. *See also* Age
Power, 323–349
Prairie Home Companion, 374
Pregnancy, unwanted, *see* Abortion

Premarital sex:
    and divorce, 175–176
    and gender, 176
    and income level, 331–332
    in Kinsey Report, 12
    and marital status, 176
    and phase comparison, 375
    and region, 351
    and religion, 227, 252–253
Premarital sex (admitted):
    by education/gender, 314–316
    by gender, 87–88
    by income level, 323, 327–328
    by region, 363–364
Premarital sex (opinion on):
    by age, 40–43
    by gender, 67–69
    phase comparison, 379–380
    by region, 358–360
    by religion, 241–242
Profanity, *see* Talking dirty
Professional fulfillment, 66–67, 308
Prostate surgery, 28
Prostitution, 26, 89, 99, 111, 130–133,
    340–341, 344–348, 373
    origin of term "hooker," 346
Psychology Today, 179

Questionnaire (Appendix B), 1–6,
    405–414

Rape, 74, 104, 108, 119
Region, 351–374
    list of subjects tabulated by, 352
    sample population breakdown by,
        4, 403
Relationship, 91, 140
Religion, 227–261
    and abortion, 203, 215
    and children, 267
    and deviance, 105, 106
    importance in marriage, 375,
        388–390
    list of subjects tabulated by, 228
    sample population breakdown by, 403
    sex practices in harmony with,
        238–240, 388–390
Religiosity, 229
Remarriage, 199

René Guyon Society, 129
Research, sex, 9–11
Rice, F. Philip, 177
Roe v. Wade, 14, 218, 232, 269, 344, 355
Romance, 154–156, 254–255, 385–386
Rubber fetish, 111, 122
Rubenstein, C., 196
Rubin, David, 22
Rudd, Mark, 33

Sadomasochism, 83, 103, 108, 109–110,
      114–118
   and political leaning, 263, 291–292
   preferred way to orgasm, 98, 185
   and religion, 245–246
Safe sex, 90, 96, 164, 377
St. Paul, Minnesota, 373
Sample population (breakdown):
   by age, 4, 402
   by education, 4, 402
   by gender, 402
   by income level, 326, 403
   by marital status, 4, 183, 403
   by number of children, 210
   by political leaning, 265
   by region, 4, 403
   by religious preference, 403
   by sexual orientation, 70
Sample population (Census Data
      comparison), 401–403
Sample population (design), 3–5
Scanzoni, J., 160
Schneller, Donald, 130, 361
Schwartz, P., 186
Searching for mate, 160–162
Self-image sexually, *see* Sexual activity
      (relative, self-rating)
Sensuality, 92, 155, 255–256, 317–318
Sethre, Dr. Richard, 374
Sex (definitions of), 9
Sex education (attitude toward):
   by gender, 96–98, 280–281
   by political leaning, 280–281
   by religion, 237–238
Sex education (own experience):
   by gender, 97
   by religion, 257–258
Sex roles (attitude toward):
   by age, 37–40

by gender, 53, 62–63, 276–278
by marital status, 153
by political leaning, 276–278
by region, 355–356, 361
by religion, 227, 234–237
Sexual activity (frequency of):
   by age, 19, 24–27
   by education, 304
   by income level, 338–339
   by marital status, 25, 159
   by region, 351
Sexual activity (relative, self-rating):
   by education, 319
   by gender, 92–93
   by marital status, 156
   by political leaning, 293
   by region, 366–367
   by religion, 256–257
Sexual activity (trend in):
   by age, 34
   by education, 304
   by gender, 87–88
   by political leaning, 288–290
   by region, 370
   by religion, 250–251
   and singles, 53, 135, 164
Sexual orientation (sample population
      breakdown by), 70
Sexuality, perception of self/partner,
      187, 188 189
Sexually transmitted diseases, *see* STDs
Shakers, 171–172
Showers, *see* Brown shower; Golden
      shower
Silk fetish, 111, 122
Single(s), 135–167
   attitude toward marriage, 143, 147
   and family models, 144–145
   households, 206
   list of subjects tabulated, 136
   major problem, 151–152
   networks, 145, 152, 167
   parenthood, *see* Parenthood, single
   reasons why, 150–152
   searching for mate, 160–162
Sissies/tomboys, 120
Slave, sex, 184, 371
Smith, Joseph, 172
SNAG (single new-age guy or girl), 139

Snuff films, 113
Social security benefits/marriage, 15
Sophistication of partner, 189
Spanking, 118
Stallone, Sylvester, 362
STDs, appearance of term, 1
STDs, concern about:
  by education, 305
  by gender, 100–101, 164
  by political leaning, 288, 290
  by region, 372
  by religion, 260
  and singles, 142
Steinem, Gloria, 14, 150
Sterling Mental Health Clinic, New
  York, 116
Submissives, 110, 111
Suicides, autoerotic, 111
Sullivan, Mark, M.D., 20
Supreme Court, 14, 218, 232, 307
Surrogate motherhood, 223–224,
  341–342
Surrogate(s), sex, 12, 96, 340–343, 367
Swaggart, Jimmy, 261, 274
Swinging, 7, 12

Talking dirty, 89–90, 292–293, 311
Teenage pregnancy, 16–17, 51
Thomas, Clarence, 101–102, 307
Threesomes, 184, 371
Tomboys/sissies, 120
Transvestism, see Cross dressing
Trend, 3-year, see Sexual activity
  (trend in)
Tubal ligation, 217, 233–234
Twentieth century, sex in, 7–18
Tyler, Robin, 76

Urination, see Golden shower
Urolagnia, 112

Vaginal cream, 43, 377
Vaginal lubrication, dysfunctional, 32
Vaginal orgasm, 84

Vaginal tent, 215
Vaginum dentatum, 36
Variety, sexual:
  and education, 309–312
  and gender, 79
  and income level, 334
  and marital status, 182, 183–189
  and political leaning, 263, 281–282
  and region, 371
  and religion, 244–245
Vasectomy, 216–217, 233
Verbal humiliation, 108, 109, 111–112,
  124–125
Vibrators, 76–77, 79, 82, 85, 115
Victoria, Queen (on sex), 10
Virginia, University of, 5
Virginity, 37, 40, 43–44, 96, 252, 316, 385
  loss of, see First sex, age at
  virgin wives, 95–96
von Sacher-Masoch, Leopold, 109
Voss, H. L., 178
Voyeurism, 107, 113–114

Waller, Willard, 200
Wallis, J. H., 171
Weekend warriors, 347
Weinberg, Dr. Jack, 20
Westheimer, R., 240
What's next syndrome, 143
Wishes/realism, 156
Women and aggression, 285–286
Women's movement, 11, 14, 142, 201,
  275, 312
Workplace, sex in, 365–366

Yapko, Michael, 377
Young, Brigham, 172
Youngman, Henny, 387
Your Sexual Secrets: When to Keep Them,
  When and How to Tell, 76
Youth and sex, 21–23
Yumpies, 139
Yuppies, 139–140